T0091288

PRAISE FOR *CHEFS, DRUGS AND ROCK & ROLL*

"I loved reading *Chefs, Drugs and Rock & Roll*. It was fast, furious and fun, falling neatly into the canon of pop histories along with *Please Kill Me: The Uncensored Oral History of Punk* and Patti Smith's memoir *Just Kids*.... As irresistible as a bowl of house-made chips."
—*Wall Street Journal*

"Friedman insists on being described as a chef writer, and that might be his intention, but what he has achieved is the most complete and approachable history of America's awakening to and conquest (if momentary) of fine dining and the incidental rediscovery and reintroduction of fresh, or real, food into the American diet."
—*Salon*

"Using interviews with more than 200 figures, [Friedman] captures the beginnings of a remarkable transition.... For those who didn't experience the 1970s and 80s, this book is an excellent way to learn about the pre-Food Network, non-televised revolution that gave us the American restaurant scene we have today."
—Kitchen Arts & Letters

"If you want a little spicy dish without the need for utensils, dive into Andrew Friedman's *Chefs, Drugs, and Rock & Roll*, a comprehensive look at how the superstar American chef of today evolved from the rebels—and even acid-dropping hippies—who took cooking seriously at a time when no one else did."
—*LA Weekly*

"Friedman brings each chef to life.... [His] passion for the subject infuses every anecdote, detail, and interview, making this culinary narrative an engrossing experience."
—*Publishers Weekly*

"One couldn't ask for a better guide through the complex social world of some of the major figures in the American restaurant scene of the past several decades."   —Spectrum Culture

"A tasty venture in a culinary wonderland. . . . Friedman is at his best when exploring the intricacies of the relationships among restaurant owners and chefs. . . . An intriguing perspective on a profession that very quickly captivated our attention."   —*Kirkus Reviews*

"Behind the scenes with just the right amount of gossip, Friedman paints an exciting and detailed picture of a distinct time and place. . . . One of the best 'fly on the wall' books I've read."   —The Fold

"The depth of research is quite astonishing. I haven't read anything like it."   —Ruth Reichl

"Andrew Friedman's genuine curiosity and deep admiration for chefs and the American restaurant industry have enabled him to capture some of the greatest history of our times. I encourage you to accept his invitation to join in the most fascinating tableside storytelling as heard from the colorful characters who shaped our contemporary restaurant culture."

—Michael Anthony, Executive Chef, Gramercy Tavern

"As the editor in chief of *Food & Wine* magazine for over twenty years, I had the privilege of eating in many of the best restaurants in America. After reading *Chefs, Drugs and Rock & Roll*, I possess a whole new understanding of what was happening behind those kitchen doors: the creativity, the chaos, the bad deals, the golden relationships and the broken ones. On every page, there's a snippet of information or a revelation from a juicy interview that provides color and context for some of the most important, formative moments in American culinary history."

—Dana Cowin, author of *Mastering My Mistakes in the Kitchen*

"In *Chefs, Drugs and Rock & Roll*, Andrew Friedman tells the tale of the misfits, creative outliers, and occasional Harvard scholars who found their surrogate homes, unexpectedly, in kitchens across the United States and became the unlikely heroes of modern American cuisine. Now turn away from your favorite chef's Instagram feed and turn the pages of this wonderfully written chronicle of the birth of a nation of foodies."

—Rocco DiSpirito, chef and healthy lifestyle crusader

"A wonderfully interesting and absorbing read. Not just another account of the American food revolution, but a whole new assessment that relates developments in food to the culture of the 1970s and 1980s generally. Like the older generation of postwar Francophiles, the chefs in Friedman's book changed by going abroad, but instead of the cute auberges their inspiration was more varied, psychedelic, and radical."

—Paul Freedman, author of *Ten Restaurants That Changed America*

"We spend so much time talking about what's new in our industry that sometimes we forget to talk about its past. Andrew Friedman has taken on the responsibility of helping to make sure that this generation of chefs and restaurateurs, as well as our guests, understands what came before us. And thank goodness for that, because it's important that we look back before we move forward. This book rocks." —Will Guidara, restaurateur, Eleven Madison Park, The NoMad, Made Nice

"In the 1950s, a bunch of creative kids reinvented the rules of the music business and created rock and roll. In the 1970s, a similar bunch took on the restaurant business and started a revolution that is still building today. In his deeply researched *Chefs, Drugs and Rock & Roll*, Andrew Friedman brings vividly to life the pioneers who made this happen." —Russ Parsons, author of *How to Pick a Peach*

ALSO BY ANDREW FRIEDMAN

Knives at Dawn:
America's Quest for Culinary Glory at the
Legendary Bocuse d'Or Competition

CHEFS, DRUGS AND ROCK & ROLL

HOW FOOD LOVERS, FREE SPIRITS,
MISFITS AND WANDERERS CREATED
A NEW AMERICAN PROFESSION

ANDREW FRIEDMAN

An Imprint of HarperCollinsPublishers

Judy Rodgers interview used by permission from Joyce Goldstein. Chefs from Hell invitation and rules used by permission from Gerry Dawes.

CHEFS, DRUGS AND ROCK & ROLL. Copyright © 2018 by Table 12 Productions, Inc. All rights reserved. Printed in the United States of America. No part of this book may be used or reproduced in any manner whatsoever without written permission except in the case of brief quotations embodied in critical articles and reviews. For information address HarperCollins Publishers, 195 Broadway, New York, NY 10007.

HarperCollins books may be purchased for educational, business, or sales promotional use. For information please e-mail the Special Markets Department at SPsales@harpercollins.com.

A hardcover edition of this book was published in 2018 by Ecco, an imprint of HarperCollins Publishers.

FIRST ECCO PAPERBACK EDITION PUBLISHED 2019.

Designed by Suet Yee Chong

Library of Congress Cataloging-in-Publication Data has been applied for.

ISBN 978-0-06-222586-3

19 20 21 22 23   LSC   10 9 8 7 6 5 4 3 2 1

*In loving memory of Therese Friedman and
Joan Bredin-Price, who encouraged me in all things,
great and small.*

*And for Josh Ozersky, who loved chefs,
and whose last meal came much too soon.*

Gastronomy and cooking for me have always been about being a link in a chain, taking from the past, making my contribution, working hard on creating a legacy. I've had a lot of people show me a lot of different things, to make me who I am. And I try to do that to my younger cooks. They're going to be much better cooks than I am; that's just how it works. You get better and better, just being a link in the chain. In a culinary endeavor, where the traditions are so rich, it benefits you to know what happened before you; to study it and learn about it, to read about it and be fascinated by it. You have to understand who these people are, so you can move forward.

—David Kinch

CONTENTS

STAFF MEETING

Okay, gather 'round, everybody. Just a few things before we open the doors.

This first note is for the kitchen: What follows is intended as a narrative, impressionistic summary of the transformation of professional cooking in the United States during the 1970s, '80s, and early '90s. While many prominent chefs from the era are profiled, this book by no means constitutes a comprehensive survey of everybody who contributed to the industry over the twenty-plus years it covers.

In our interview, Patrick O'Connell, chef-proprietor since 1978 of the landmark hotel and restaurant The Inn at Little Washington in Washington, Virginia, made a helpful point: "We all have so many parallels. We had a party at Per Se for [the great French chef] Paul Bocuse; it was about thirty American chefs that Thomas Keller had invited and everybody was asked to stand for a moment and tell their story, and it usually involved some inspirational intersection with Bocuse and the great Michelin-starred restaurants of that era when we had nothing comparable yet in America. You would listen to their stories, and except for your own idiosyncrasy and personality, it was *Oh my God*. You had no idea we were all on the same trip and didn't even know each other."

With those parallels in mind, I have focused primarily on the broad historical strokes and on the central hubs where the most chefs were concentrated—the Bay Area, Los Angeles, and New York City—and on game changers rather than those generally acknowledged to have been cooking the best or most influential food, although they are often the same. The example of La Côte Basque says a lot: Readers who were around in the 1970s and '80s will be surprised, if not scandalized, that Jean-Jacques Rachou casts a longer shadow here than André Soltner, but New York City cooks who were there will understand, and that decision should make sense to one and all by the time the dust clears.

With all of this in mind, many godlike talents, including some who took precious time to treat me to deeply revealing interviews, are scarcely mentioned, if at all, and related developments, such as the contemporaneous expansion of the American wine industry, have been necessarily relegated to the sidelines and footnotes.

Logic aside, please know that making these decisions caused me great personal anguish and was responsible for at least one lapsed deadline. And *please* accept my sincere apology if I failed to find the right spot to pay respect to you or your mentor.

For the dining room: In the interest of full disclosure, you should know that I have collaborated on books with many of the chefs in this story—though I have avoided it while working on this project—and count many more as friends and acquaintances. And so while I was fortunate to gain access to the breadth of people interviewed, I'm also inclined toward discretion. All of which is to say that this book, despite its title, isn't by any means a "tell-all," and that certain people known industry-wide for a range of illicit behaviors and weaknesses don't show any powder on their noses here, either because they wouldn't cop to it themselves or denied it on the record.

My wish was to write a strictly oral history, with the story told exclusively in the voices of the participants. But too many memories proved incomplete or flawed. So I consulted a mountain of books and periodicals and did more writing than originally planned, although the story is still largely carried by the words captured in a few hundred interviews. Quotations from those interviews (listed at the back of the book) are cast in the present tense ("he says"), whether the subject is living or deceased, while those from third-party sources are in the past tense ("she said"). Additional sources are listed by chapter at the back of the book as well. With everybody's best interest at heart, and with the consent of the participants, I have performed some minor editing on some quotations from my interviews to eliminate false starts, confusing colloquialisms, and the like; for elegance, I have avoided the use of ellipses to indicate omitted portions of quotations except where considerable text has been deleted. In no cases have my adjustments altered the speaker's meaning.

Okay, thank you. Let's have a good service . . .

Andrew Friedman

PREP WORK

We all had the same acid flashback at the same time.
—Jonathan Waxman

Y ou could begin this story in any number of places, so why not in the back of a dinged-up VW van parked on a Moroccan camping beach, a commune of tents and makeshift domiciles? It's Christmas 1972. Inside the van is Bruce Marder, an American college dropout. He's a Los Angelino, a hippy, and he looks the part: Vagabonding for six months has left him scrawny and dead broke. His jeans are stitched together, hanging on for dear life. Oh, and this being Christmas, somebody has gifted him some LSD, and he's tripping.

The van belongs to a couple—French woman, Dutch man—who have taken him in. It boasts a curious feature: a built-in kitchen. It's not much, just a set of burners and a drawer stocked with mustard and cornichons. But they make magic there. The couple has adventured as far as India, amassing recipes instead of Polaroids, sharing memories with new friends through food. To Marder, raised in the

Eisenhower era on processed, industrialized grub, each dish is a revelation. When the lid comes off a tagine, he inhales the steam redolent of an exotic and unfamiliar herb: cilantro. The same with curry, also unknown to him before the van.

Like a lot of his contemporaries, Marder fled the United States. "People wanted to get away," he says. Away from the Vietnam War. Away from home and the divorce epidemic. The greater world beckoned, the kaleidoscopic, tambourine-backed utopia promised by invading British rockers and spiritual sideshows like the Maharishi. The price of admission was cheap: For a few hundred bucks on a no-frills carrier such as Icelandic Airlines—nicknamed "the Hippie Airline" and "Hippie Express"—you could be strolling Piccadilly Circus or the Champs-Élysées, your life stuffed into a backpack, your Eurail Pass a ticket to ride.

Marder flew to London alone, with $800 and a leather jacket to his name, and improvised, crashing in parks and on any friendly sofa and—if he couldn't score any of that—splurging on a hostel. He let himself go, smoking ungodly amounts of pot, growing his hair out to shoulder length. In crowds, he sensed kindred spirits, young creatures of the road, mostly from Spain and Finland. Few Americans.

Food, unexpectedly, dominated life overseas. Delicious, simple food that awakened his senses and imagination. Amsterdam brought him his first french fries with mayonnaise: an epiphany. The souks (markets) of Marrakech, with their food stalls and communal seating, haunt him. Within five months, he landed on that camping beach, in Agadir, still a wasteland after an earthquake twelve years prior. He lived on his wits: Back home, he'd become fluent in hippy cuisine; now he spent his last pennies on brown rice and vegetables, cooking them for strangers who shuttled him around. Just in time, people started feeding him, like the couple in whose van he was nesting. Food was as much a part of life on the beach as volleyball and marijuana. People cooked for each other, spinning the yarns behind the meals—where they'd picked them up and what they meant in their native habitats. Some campers developed specializations, like the tent that baked cakes over an open burner. Often meals were improvised: You'd go to town, buy a pail, fill it with a chicken, maybe some yogurt, or some vegetables and spices, and figure out what to do with it when you got back.

Marder might as well have been on another planet. "This was so un-American at that time," he says.

He was supposed to become a dentist, but his heart was never in it; it was just one of those non-dreams foisted on him and his friends by tradition-bound elders. Back in L.A., he'd been a stoner, but a motivated one, laying the groundwork for independence— caddying, pumping gas, anything for a buck. And so he was primed for a course correction when he dropped acid that Christmas and a new, previously unimaginable path materialized: "I'm sitting in the back of the van and I'm whacked out," Marder says. "I'm always thinking about my life. *What am I going to do?* Obviously I'm not going to be a dentist. I can't go back to school and take organic chemistry. I just sit up and go, 'God! I know what I want to do. *This* is what I want to do. I want to learn. I want to be a *chef*.'"

I met Bruce Marder as I met many of the chefs and industry veterans interviewed for this book: in their sixties, seventies, and eighties. So it's hard to fathom how young they were—scarcely in their twenties—when they began shaping the professional cooking trade in the United States. Now they are gray, their edges sanded, their stories perfected through years of retelling. But once upon a time, even the most iconic of the lot were impulsive, sometimes irresponsible, occasionally self-destructive—just living their lives.

Marder isn't famous, but he's been successfully operating as a chef-owner for four decades. His clubby Santa Monica Italian charmer, Capo, commands one of the highest check averages in the greater Los Angeles area. He's also a partner and guiding culinary light in a handful of other restaurants and Red Rooster Bakery, where he honors a late-career fascination with breadmaking. At his West Beach Cafe, which he opened in 1978 in a barren bunker of a space a half block from the sands and surf of Venice Beach, Marder was churning out template-shattering food before many of his contemporaries who have attained legend status, yet he remains relatively anonymous. His improvisational eclecticism, juxtaposing American, French, and Italian influences in dishes such as oysters topped with California caviar, porcini risotto with fresh thyme, basil linguine with morels and walnut oil, duck breast tacos, and stuffed calamari and steak with fries, made stodgy French restaurants— the only serious game in town in those days—look instantly stale. Wolfgang Puck protégé Kazuto Matsusaka says that many chefs used to eat at West Beach Cafe for the express purpose of pilfering Marder's ideas; Jeremiah Tower, one of the titans of his generation of chefs and no slouch in the influence department himself, considers Marder an underappreciated visionary and frequently cites the restaurant as transformative. In his youth, Marder was attractive and confident enough for celebrity: Two female contemporaries confess they had crushes on him once upon a time, and former *New West* magazine and *Los Angeles Times* writer Ruth Reichl described him in print as possibly the most handsome chef in Tinseltown.

And yet, Marder has never been especially well known, or even popular among his peers, many of whom just plain don't like him. Why is not a mystery: He's antisocial, even to customers. He doesn't cavort with fellow chefs, doesn't make the charity rounds, doesn't play the PR game, doesn't give a hang what anybody thinks. For all his influence, he's never been nominated for chefdom's Oscar, a James Beard Foundation Award.

"I just think he's not a self-promoter," says Reichl. "He just isn't. He's missing that ego piece. If I were him, it would drive me crazy. He kick-started this before anyone. West Beach Cafe was a game changer in L.A. You want to talk about California cuisine? Nobody was serving it before him. *Nobody.* That casual, grilled, pared-down, unadorned, looking-to-California-as-opposed-to-France-or-Italy food. And that laid-back space. Look at what he did."

Marder shrugs. "The image I have in my mind is of the guy who was the owner of [Paris's] Taillevent, [the late Jean-Claude] Vrinat. I met him in Burgundy at a winery. He wanted to be in his restaurant and he wanted to take care of his customers. That's who I am. All these stars, you go to their restaurant and they're not in their restaurant. I don't feel that anybody's as passionate about what I do as I am."

Marder is given to frank pronouncements, and not just about his colleagues. He met the woman who would become his first wife at the wedding of a mutual friend. When he asked her out, she protested that she was married. He didn't mince words: "You're not happily married and you know it."

My first meeting with this notorious figure was at the bar at Capo in October 2013. Based on reputation, I feared a hostile witness. I needn't have worried: When I thanked him for making time, he disarmed and amused me by deadpanning, "Well, I just thought this might be more fun than less." After the interview, we spent hours sipping wines, sampling pastas, splitting a sublimely charred steak from a wood-burning fireplace behind the far end of the bar. To my surprise, I liked Marder, in part because his professed passion was manifest: He forensically detailed the selections in Capo's bread basket, and recounted how he'd picked up his method of saucing pasta at Dal Pescatore in northern Italy. I also admired his attention to front-of-house matters: Late in the evening he pointed to the paintings around the dining room, explaining how a master decorator once taught him the trick to illuminating artwork, letting the light itself show without too much, if any, emphasis on its source.

We were joined for that interview by his girlfriend (now wife),

Shelly Kellogg, a resolutely sunny soul. She was also with him in New York City more than a year later, to attend Marder's daughter Olivia's New York University graduation. We conducted a follow-up interview over breakfast at the West Village restaurant Buvette that week, during which I broached the subject of his personality, or lack thereof.

"If I can be blunt, you're not known as the most gregarious person," I said.

"Well, that's true," he rumbled. He likes the portrait of him Colman Andrews, prolific author and onetime editor of *New West* magazine, offers in his memoir, *My Usual Table:* "What I was like at West Beach Cafe: 'First, you thought he was a jerk, and then when you get to know him, he's really quite funny.' I think that's pretty accurate." When I interview Andrews, who considers Marder a friend, he tells me that *jerk* was actually, if such a thing is possible, a euphemism. For *asshole*.

Chef history, like any history, is told by the victors. And so this book begins with Marder to keep us—author and reader—honest, to add a grain of salt, a reminder of the role of promotion and politics in the allocation of credit. Marder has a seat at this table, but others who mattered are surely absent, swallowed up by the sea of time, whether through modesty, mortality, geography, or quirks of personality.

I also begin with Marder because—let's face it—you can't beat that van story, and also for a passing moment that occurred between us at Capo. He was deep into recounting the West Beach Cafe, the two of us leaning close over a votive, a little buzzed on red wine. Restaurants at some level are homes, imbued with life by their occupants, and spiritually transformed by those who succeed them. West Beach Cafe shuttered in 1996, but the space, just two miles down the coastline from Capo, now houses another restaurant, James' Beach. That seems somehow impossible as Marder evokes another time and place—another world, really—of the canvases by Venice painters that hung on the walls, the art world clientele, the notorious after-service cocaine parties. (At some point around midnight every evening, he told me, it was "Katie, bar the door.") Both of Marder's adult sons, dressed in preppy ensembles, were working the dining room at Capo that night, and they periodically stopped by the bar to listen and chuckle along with the bartender at their old man's sex-and-drug-laced recollections. Some might find this appalling; to me, it was touching.

"West Beach was the bomb," Marder growled, sotto voce, at the climax of the tale, lost in a reverie, a little disbelieving of his own success. "It was the bomb. It was the bomb. It was the bomb. I walked in there every night and it was the bomb."

I can still hear Marder's world-weary voice, see his wonder-struck eyes and craggy, bestubbled face, flecked with candlelight, as he repeated that phrase. It reminded me of the last moments of Ridley Scott's *Blade Runner*, released in 1982, smack-dab in the midst of West Beach's heyday. "I've seen things you people wouldn't believe," says replicant ringleader Roy Batty as he sits dying before Rick Deckard, recounting the cosmic astonishments he's witnessed. "All those moments will be lost in time," he muses. "Like tears in rain."

Marder and his contemporaries, the chefs in this book, saw things we people wouldn't believe. They took a centuries-old profession with no real American strain and made it their own. There's a timeworn argument over whether cooking should be considered an art or a craft. Lost in the crossfire is that it's more ephemeral than either. Many of these chefs fret that they and their contemporaries have been forgotten, when an eyeblink ago they were household names. I share their disappointment, but impermanence comes with the territory: Any chef will tell you that they have to prove themselves, from scratch, every day. By the same token, the dishes they cook don't hang in a museum, can't be ordered from Amazon, won't pleasantly surprise you when you happen upon them on

HBO. Meals pass through us. Restaurants close. Chefs, like General MacArthur's old soldiers, just fade away. Save for menus, cookbooks, and—more recently—documentaries, there's no element of cooking that won't inevitably be lost to the ages, including those who savored it. Gone forever. Like tears in rain.

You only have to go back to the early sixties, into basically the generation that sought to overthrow the government, in a sense, the antiwar movement, that bunch of us who objected to the way our parents' generation was thinking. It has to do with art, it has to do with revolution, the Andy Warhol revolution, if you will. It has to do with the novel, with perhaps In Cold Blood, *the first novel to create the genre of the nonfiction novel. It probably has to do with the overthrow of music by the Beatles and Elvis. There's no creative effort, I would think, that was not questioned by my generation. I'm a post–World War II baby. That generation that stood up against the Vietnam War, that welcomed the Beatles and Elvis, that even sanctioned nonrepresentative painting. All of those aesthetics were questioned over a period of a decade, perhaps. And not just questioned, but they were kind of overthrown. So why not food, too? Because food suffered in a sense by not being thought of as an aesthetic endeavor, a creative endeavor, or a personal endeavor, as movies were not. All of these things were thought to be the bailiwick of the privileged few who laid down the rules and said how things were to taste, look, sound, and read. And that all kind of happened at that time. And food was just maybe the caboose of that train.*

—Tony Bill, filmmaker and restaurateur

This is the story of the dawn and rise of the American chef, which for our purposes commenced when Americans, from coast to coast, and in large numbers, began voluntarily, enthusiastically cooking in restaurants for a living—a once forbidden and unrespected professional course—screw the consequences. Many started like Marder, spontaneously, rebelliously, often in isolation, with no idea there were others like them Out There. A few stuck their toes in the water in the 1960s, a few more in the 1970s, and then hordes jumped into the pool in the 1980s and '90s, after which there was no looking back.

These weren't the first American chefs, or even the first prominent ones. There had always been exceptions, like the astounding Edna Lewis, who for five years ending in 1954 had been the chef and a business partner at Café Nicholson in Midtown Manhattan— that she did this as both an African American and a woman in the 1950s is nothing short of miraculous. But those stories were few and far between, not part of an overarching national phenomenon. And the lower kitchen ranks were more often than not populated with lost souls who lacked ambition or the aptitude for a traditional career, weren't pursuing a love of food and/or craft, or acting on Marder-like epiphanies, a version of which became a rite of passage for an entire generation. Professional cooking was viewed as menial, unskilled labor performed, often in unsavory conditions, by anonymous worker bees. The United States Department of Labor categorized chefs as domestics through 1976 when—after lobbying by the American Culinary Federation, who themselves required nudging by Louis Szathmary, the Hungarian American Chicago chef, writer, and television personality—it recognized them as professionals. *Domestics* suggests chauffeurs and housekeepers; most Americans regarded cooks as something grittier. "I came from a nice family," says Mary Sue Milliken, who today co-owns Border Grill and other restaurants with business partner

Susan Feniger. "My dad had a PhD and my mom went to college and my sisters both went to college. I think they looked at me like I had said, 'I'm going to go be an auto mechanic.' They thought, *Oh, God.*"

"Cooking was not really considered a career," remembers Mario Batali, one of the most visible chefs in the United States today, who double-majored in Spanish theater and business management at Rutgers University before falling in love with the pro kitchen at Stuff Yer Face restaurant in New Brunswick, New Jersey, in 1978. "It was the first thing you did after you got out of the army, and the last thing before you went to jail. And that was because anybody could get a job and put on a white apron and go peel potatoes and make soup and do the grunt work, because it was the lowest common denominator in the city. Not necessarily in the country, where you would have been forced into construction or farming. But if you lived in an urban area you just got hired as a cook. You didn't have to train."

"One of the comparisons I make today that illustrates the difference between then and now is back in the day you never would put your uniform on or anything that made you look like a cook on the way to work," says San Francisco–based chef Jan Birnbaum, who started his career in New Orleans and New York. "Because it wasn't a proud thing to be. You're that guy behind the door who has no skill. He's certainly not intellectual, and he probably is either a criminal or he's amongst them. There's just a whole lot of undesirable stuff. Today the streets of San Francisco, man, they proudly walk down the street all the time in full uniforms." Even in France, historically the Western capital of fine dining, this stigma attached to the profession through the 1960s. Chefs were not renowned or celebrated; at best, they were regarded as craftsmen. Alain Sailhac, who grew up in the mountain village of Millau, France, and would go on to become the chef of Le Cygne and Le Cirque in New York City, remembers the moment he first became enticed by the kitchen, in the mid-twentieth century: At age fourteen, at his brother's wedding, he struck up a conversation with the chef, which sparked an interest he couldn't shake.

"Why do you want to be a cook?" demanded his father, who wanted his son to take up the family's glove-manufacturing business. Sailhac persisted until his dad relented, walked him into the town's only one-star restaurant, where the chef was a World War I buddy. "Do you want to take my son?" asked the senior Sailhac. "He wants to be like you, a stupid chef." (Even after he became a cook, Sailhac hid his profession from women; if they learned he worked in a restaurant, he told them he was a *chef de rang* [dining room captain], which was more prestigious.)

Consider, too, Auguste Escoffier, whose crowning achievement, *Le guide culinaire*, first published in 1903, was the kitchen bible of its day. The book codified basic recipes and techniques, set forth a system for organizing the kitchen *brigade*, and recommended a front-of-house structure. Yet Nathan Myhrvold, author of a defining tome on modernist cuisine, unsentimentally dubs Escoffier "the Henry Ford of the conventional kitchen. . . . His masterwork was fundamentally motivated by gastronomy as a manufacturing process rather than as an art. . . . He was an artisan striving to run a factory rather than be an artist."

So what happened? To impose biblical simplicity on the narrative would be dishonest; there was no Garden of Eden, no aproned Adam and Eve from whom all future American chefs descended, no single moment that lit the fuse. The movement was scattershot but not coincidental, produced (Big Bang–style) by a confluence of events and phenomena: the Vietnam War and the resistance at home; the counterculture; easy access to travel; the music, movies, and literature of the day; drugs, including "the pill"; and a new approach to restaurant cooking, to name the factors most often cited by those who were there as the ones that propelled them into the kitchen.

"It's a universal mind," says Thomas Keller, chef-owner of a restaurant empire founded on Yountville, California's The French Laundry, of the national reach of those influences. "We all talk about universal minds and how people come up with the same idea relatively around the same period of time without having had conversations about it personally. They're just doing the same thing."

Jonathan Waxman, a California chef who has toggled back and forth between the coasts throughout his career, puts it slightly differently: "We all had the same acid flashback at the same time," he says. "But each of us did it differently."

I was against the Vietnam War. I saw hypocrisy everywhere, racism everywhere. In New Jersey, there were race riots going on in Asbury Park. It was the next town over from where I grew up. Our high school was closed for racial tension when Martin Luther King got shot. I saw hypocrisy in justice. And I didn't want to be a part of that world. I wanted an alternative existence. I was in the draft; it was something that you had to think about. You couldn't say, "I'm against the war because war sucks." It was, "I might have to go to the war." I had friends whose older brothers were killed in Vietnam. It wasn't the elephant in the room; it was the room that we grew up in.

—Jasper White, chef and restaurateur

Shots rang out over Kent State. Sixty-seven rounds over thirteen seconds. The date was May 4, 1970. Within weeks, Crosby, Stills, Nash & Young were eulogizing the victims—student protestors slain by National Guardsmen—in song: "Four dead in Oh-hi-oh."

Violence had erupted periodically, traumatically, throughout the prior decade—thunderclaps in a slow-moving storm that felt like it might never end: Lee Harvey Oswald shot and killed President John F. Kennedy in Dallas, Texas, on November 22, 1963, terminating the Camelot era; James Earl Ray assassinated Reverend Martin Luther King Jr. at the Lorraine Motel in Memphis, Tennessee, on April 4, 1968; Jordanian Sirhan Sirhan claimed Bobby Kennedy two months later, on June 6, 1968 in the kitchen of Los Angeles's Ambassador Hotel. No leader was safe, least of all those who preached nonviolence and progressivism. Nor were casualties confined to the political class. In August 1969, followers of Charles Manson, known as his "family," murdered actress Sharon Tate and four others in the hills of Benedict Canyon, thickening the air of mayhem. Other losses were self-generated but no less searing: Jimi Hendrix, discovered unresponsive in a London apartment on September 18, 1970, and pronounced dead in a hospital later that day; less than a month later, on October 4, Janis Joplin succumbed to an accidental heroin overdose at the Landmark Motor Hotel in Hollywood, California. Both were twenty-seven years old, just kids.

The struggle for civil rights threaded through the decade: In 1961, the Freedom Riders, a student activist group comprising both African American and white members, protested segregation on buses and in waiting rooms throughout the South, requiring protection from law enforcement. On August 4, 1964, three civil rights workers who had been missing since June were found murdered in Philadelphia, Mississippi; later that month Dr. Martin Luther King Jr. delivered his rousing "I Have a Dream" speech at the March on Washington. Malcolm X, leader of the black nationalist movement, was shot and killed in New York City's Washington Heights neighborhood in February 1965. There were historic gains—President Lyndon Johnson signed the Civil Rights Act in July 1964, and followed it with the Voting Rights Act of 1965 and the appointment of the first African American to the Supreme Court, Thurgood Marshall, in June 1967—but they came at a high cost in an undeclared second civil war.

At the University of California, Berkeley, a ban on on-campus politics of any kind triggered the Free Speech Movement, which grew directly out of the civil rights movement—students had protested racial discrimination in hiring practices throughout San Francisco, prompting complaints to the university, and a Berkeley professor was prevented from promoting CORE (the Congress of Racial Equality) on campus. The movement peaked on December 2, 1964; more than one thousand students occupied the university's student union building, Sproul Hall, and the movement's leader, Mario Savio, delivered what became known as his "An End to History" speech on the steps of the building. "The time has come for us to put our bodies on the machine and stop it," he declared. Two days later, close to eight hundred were arrested, the largest mass incarceration of students in U.S. history.

In 1965, the United States began deploying troops to Vietnam, a conflict opposed by much of the nation. The resistance redoubled in 1969, when the draft was instituted, taking the form of two lotteries.* The nightly news, at a time when it was confined to thirty minutes each evening, delivered reports of carnage to American homes. For young men, the existential dread of being called up washed over life itself, causing many to reflect on the conservative preordained career paths laid out for them by their parents.

"There was a disturbance in 'the Force' about the Vietnam War and the uncertainty of *Hey, you might be shipped out and you can't count on tomorrow*," says chef Jimmy Schmidt, who came of age in Detroit, Michigan. "I think that led to being more adventurous, a kind of anti-the-status-quo-type situation. Let's go live it while you can live it. I was still around when they had the mandatory draft and I had to go get my draft card. You didn't know whether you were

---

* The lotteries were surreally televised, as birthdates were drawn at random and posted on a board, indicating the sequence in which registered participants would be called up.

going to get shipped out or not. I remember getting it, going, *I don't want to go into engineering; I want to do something with my life.* That also, I think, led to people traveling and going to Chicago and watching some band, like the Grateful Dead, Eric Clapton, all that kind of stuff. The Doors were out; the Rolling Stones played at the Illini Assembly Hall; that kind of was big stuff going on that was pretty massive for a kid in a small town. That was the days of *Easy Rider** and that type of thing going on in the movie front."

Music, which in the pre-Internet age could be disseminated most quickly and democratically via the radio, left the deepest crater, from the songs of folk singers such as Joan Baez to the transformation of the Beatles from besuited, mop-topped lads from Liverpool to full-fledged renegades, along with a shift from "I Want to Hold Your Hand" in 1963 to "Helter Skelter" in 1968. (Of course, there was also the Woodstock Music & Art Fair in 1969.) Perhaps most influential was Bob Dylan, who turned folk music on its ear throughout the 1960s, channeling the very forces that crisscrossed the republic. "He probably single-handedly changed the world," says San Francisco chef Mark Franz, formerly of Stars, and today of Farallon and Waterbar. "The way he wrote music. The way he wrote his songs. They dragged us forward and made us look at what was going on and made us conscious. And then drugs and all of the things that came around because of that. It was, I think, a natural progression. Art, writing, cooking—it was a renaissance."

---

* *Easy Rider*—Dennis Hopper's trippy 1969 independent film about two young men motorcycling from California to New Orleans—was the tip of the cultural iceberg. There were also Ken Kesey's psychedelic novel *One Flew Over the Cuckoo's Nest*, published in 1962, and—at the other end of the decade—author Tom Wolfe's *The Electric Kool-Aid Acid Test*, which profiled Kesey and his Merry Pranksters as they traveled cross-country in a brightly painted school bus. Even the razzmatazz of Broadway was supplanted: The musical *Hair*, about hippies confronting the draft, which debuted in 1968, included the Great White Way's first nude scene.

I'll tell you another thing that played into it: a certain idea of women's lib. I know that's an old-fashioned term. It was a moment where there was the pill. So we were free. We were free from worrying about pregnancy. There was just a hunger to be independent, to be our own bosses, to just strike out in our own world. I thought that that was a huge part of it. I wanted to be free. It was the exact right moment that coincided with that. . . . There was a huge counterculture movement going on. Berkeley, when I went there, was a battle zone. Students were completely up in arms over Cambodia. The culture changed. There was a huge liberalizing of culture so that all the old forms were just blasted and turned upside down and everyone was kind of reinventing themselves as a hippy or they were going through those whole counterculture movements. And I think that in some way this thing became possible, of just laying out, starting from scratch, not knowing a thing, fulfilling yourself. I think all of that was part of it. The women's movement, the counterculture movement, the antiwar thing. The whole society changed.

—Patricia Unterman, chef and writer

As the seventies settled in, mistrust of authority and the government swelled. At about two o'clock in the morning on Saturday, June 17, 1972, police in Washington, D.C., discovered five men rummaging around the Democratic National Committee offices on the sixth floor of a building in the Watergate complex. They turned out to have intelligence backgrounds and ties to the Nixon administration and were attempting to bug the DNC mothership and photograph party files while they were at it. So began the slow drip that would claim the Nixon presidency in 1974.

Other forms shattered their conventions, including comedy: Lenny Bruce was arrested repeatedly for testing obscenity laws. Norman Lear revolutionized the TV sitcom, thitherto populated by the domestic and the silly, with shows that reflected the current reality, such as *All in the Family*, which premiered in 1971, featuring sociopolitical duels between bigoted Archie Bunker (Carroll O'Connor) and son-in-law Mike Stivic (Rob Reiner). *Saturday Night Live*, which debuted in October 1975, began life as a truly subversive show that exploded the lie of television with commercial parodies that poked at the supposedly contented facade of American life (the fake ads often ended with the actors mocking the exaggerated laughter on which real commercials ended), and *Weekend Update*, a satirical newscast.

A newfound interest in food and cooking was of a piece with these shifts. The frozen dinners (unironically known as TV dinners) and industrialized food meant to nourish young Americans was no longer adequate. Just as they sought authenticity from their leaders and the arts, they craved something real to please their palates and sustain their bodies.

Ever since watching the Vietnam War on television in '69 and seeing the riot in Chicago's Grant Park and the Democratic Convention and then Watergate and the continuation of the war and the continuation of things like the Kent State disaster, those things made me feel that our country had taken an absolutely wrong turn. And I believe very much in the world that I grew up being taught about in terms of America being a country about freedom and the ideals of democracy. And I felt like we were making serious criminal errors, and I was really disappointed by it. It was fractious: Many people in our community thought we should bomb the hell out of Vietnam and get it over with, and then there were people that thought, Why are we over there? What are the real reasons that we're over there?

I was on some of the campuses where there were very big demonstrations. I was in Carbondale, Illinois, shortly after Kent State. There was actually going to be a Woodstock-like celebration in May, one year after Woodstock. May 4 was Kent State, and the celebration was planned for, like, May 15. We already had our tickets. So when Kent State happened, the government was getting very nervous. Bunch of us still went down to Carbondale for this festival. They issued the National Guard in. Fifteen hundred National Guard were ensconced on that campus. I was never militant at all. I was sitting in a trailer drinking some soft drink when suddenly storm troopers burst through the door and arrested all of us in the trailer for trespassing. They had declared a curfew on the town for sundown. It was still dusk and I wasn't outside. Anyway, they mistook me for another guy that had been seen demolishing a phone booth. I knew the guy, and I did look a little like him. But there were moments like that that were personal. There were things like watching it on the news. There were things like hearing your next-door neighbor was dead from Vietnam. And then there were things like, fucking arrest me, and throw me in a jail that hasn't been used since the Civil War, and I want the fuck out of here. I've had it with this. I've just got to go someplace that there isn't this.

Around April 1971, I hitchhiked to Champaign-Urbana, where some friends were having a party. I was just not in a good place in my head. I was just disturbed by the darkness of the political climate, the few opportunities I was having with anything. And suddenly the party was sort of breaking up and I said, "Where's Steve?" That was the older brother to my best friend. They said, "He went down to

Key West." I'm like, "Isn't that the last island down there?" And they're like, "Yeah, he's all the way down there." I said, "Jesus, that's incredible. I bet it's warm."

There were two brothers that were at the party and I said, "Anybody want to go to Key West?" And these two brothers said, "Yeah, we'll go." We left about an hour later. Drove thirty-six hours, Champaign-Urbana down the little rickety highway to Key West. It was a few months before Jimmy Buffett got there and a few months before Key West was beginning to become the party town that it became soon after.

When we pulled into town, it was like two in the morning. We woke up our friend and he said, "Sure, camp out. You guys get the couch and you can have a sleeping bag and sleep on the porch." And we camped out. And it was the next day I was falling in love, head over heels, with Key West. The smell of it. Flowers, the wooden homes, the rickety little streets, the little tiny cafes to go and get food I had never even seen before—Cuban sandwiches and cafe con leche* and maduros plantains† and picadillo.‡ The same things that are the hallmarks of Cuban food now.

We were saturated in music but it was mostly still playing LPs on turntables. The Allman Brothers, Derek and the Dominoes, Dave Mason. All that kind of music. We were [Dead] Heads. We loved music. We would have been musicians of some sort if we had the talent to have been them. We knew everybody that played in the bands. We studied the backs of album covers like they were religious texts. We just were all into it. We'd go fishing. We'd try and eat for

---

* Coffee with steamed milk.
† A banana-like fruit, sautéed.
‡ Seasoned ground beef.

free. And finally, we'd get jobs. Some were house painters. Some were carpenters.

I lived there for a month. And quite frankly, we just got wrecked every day, and zoned out, flowered out, and then realized that it suddenly ended with a thud and I had to go back to work, figure something out. Nobody was hiring me in Key West. It was still a pretty financially depressed town, I guess.

So I went back to Illinois, got a job doing different things. Met a girl,* got into a relationship, decided to take her to Key West. Seventy-two, we went down, stayed at a campground. She liked Key West but not as much as me. We broke up, went back home. Seventy-three rolls along. Got a job in a diner. Saved up money for nine months this time. We [Van Aken, childhood friend Wade Harris, and Rick Taylor, a friend from Hainesville, Illinois] got a drive-away car from Chicago to Miami. Dealerships need cars moved from one city to another and a cheap way to do it is to get somebody to just drive it there. We had a Lincoln Continental Mark IV. Here we are with hair down the middle of our back pulling into gas stations in Tennessee and people looking at us like we were moving scads of marijuana or something to have a car like that, not realizing we didn't own the damn thing.

I was down there a couple days and one of the guys that I had lived with in Illinois that had come down two years before with me in that first trip, he had made it. He financially was doing okay. He got a job as a carpenter. Had his own place he was renting. And he told me about the possibility of this barbecue place to go get a job at. So I found this guy, this big gentleman named Bud, asked him if he

---

* The "girl" is now Norman Van Aken's wife of many decades, Janet.

was hiring, and he said yeah. And he hired me on the spot. I
said I don't have any experience with barbecue; all I've done
is flipped eggs. He said, "That's okay, man. You're working
the midnight shift. Everybody's going to be so fucked up by
the time you get to them that they won't know what you're
cooking." Okay. Fine. Worked the midnight shift. Did that
for about three weeks, and then I got enough money to send
[Janet] a bus ticket to Key West.

And when I got to Key West, I was in America but I
was also, like, in another country with another set of values
that seemed so far removed. And it was peaceful. And it
didn't matter that I had long hair. Even old people would
say good morning to me. And it was welcoming and it was
a Pacific mentally-spiritually kind of a place that I just felt
like, okay, this makes sense again. I'm back in an America
that I can relate to even though it's so far away from my
home. And it was like being welcomed to the bosom of some-
thing again, and I loved it. I was so happy. And my disap-
pointment with the politics and the situation was softened
because I was somewhere else and I didn't have to contend.
And it was not long after that Nixon was bounced out of
office and things kind of got a little bit back on their feet.

—Norman Van Aken, chef

For those who could afford it, international travel beckoned. Some needed a break from the turmoil; some craved new experiences and perspective, on the United States and themselves. An accidental by-product was that exposure to European attitudes toward food proved transformative to many.

"We're the generation that traveled with backpacks," says Los Angeles chef Evan Kleiman, who today hosts the current-events radio program *Good Food*. "When you travel, you eat, and you're eating preindustrialized food. In Europe during the seventies, there was no such thing as frozen food. There was no such thing as industrialized products. There weren't even supermarkets. So you were eating food that is akin to what people who grew up in America were eating pre–World War II. So you go there and you have this unbelievably pristine experience for very little money. There's so much that's evocative about it. And we're all young so we're all either finding people to go out with—I'm using the words *go out* loosely; everybody's hooking up, right? You're out there, you're either traveling with a boyfriend or girlfriend or you're single and you're meeting kids that are traveling from all over the world, and you're having this sort of seminal experience that's filled with sensuality. So you're experiencing your own sexuality. You're drinking wine. You're eating food that's two steps from the field, in a totally joyous, non-Puritanical, nonjudgmental way. For a lot of us it's the first time that we've ever experienced food in this context. When we came back, I went to my mother: 'I want to make the broccoli different but I need fresh garlic.' And she's like, 'Fresh garlic? I have this garlic *powder*.' And then what happens is slowly we start doing it."

Overseas culinary epiphanies could be more or less divided into two categories. The first was everyday food as it was woven into daily life in France, Italy, and other popular European destinations of the time, the market culture that drove home cooking and unfussy, soulful bistro staples, all of which dovetailed perfectly with the hippy movement toward pure, "real" food in the United States. Much of the historical blood flows to Berkeley, because of the confluence of factors there, but similar strains were present elsewhere: "Among our friends who had nothing to do with the restaurant world, people were interested in cooking," says New York City chef Michael Lomonaco. "And it wasn't just that they were going to recipe swaps. I think a lot of this dates back to the hippies of the sixties, communal living, and the back-to-the-land movement, the back-to-the-farm movement. This purity of the late sixties, the early seventies. You have to look at it through this prism. People were weaving. People were making things with their hands. Texture. Ceramics was huge. Pottery classes. We were living in Brooklyn at the time. Park Slope had a kind of a Greenwich Village vibe to it. It had ceramic shops, and small bakeries were making breads and cakes and brownies and things that were more natural, with natural ingredients. There was a lot of talk of naturalness in food. I think that rippled through the culture. And everybody was kind of interested in food."

"I think that the hippies had a lot to do with it," says former Stanford Court pastry chef Jim Dodge, who grew up in a family resort and hotel business in New Hamsphire. "They weren't the best cooks but they were looking for pure, pure ingredients, organic ingredients, good quality. They wanted to know how things were grown. I remember going to the organic farm with my father every day to pick up select produce, and the pride that this young hippy family had. They had long beards and dressed extremely casual. They lived in a very modest house. There was a lot of focus on organic. I think the biggest thing was that they were making their own breads, which nobody did at that time. Just for themselves, although some of them would sell breads. In New Hampshire and especially Vermont, I think there were a lot of organic restaurants and cafes. They were opening organic food stores at that time so they were bringing awareness to it."

Bronx-born Barbara Lazaroff, who would go on to cocreate Spago and other restaurants with future husband and business partner chef Wolfgang Puck, attended New York University, starting in 1970. On Friday nights, she participated in informal dinner parties with friends. She describes one frequent host, a well-funded Saudi student named Nassar, who had the biggest apartment, mostly unfurnished, with pillows scattered about. "We would put newspaper all over the floor and every Friday it would be a different cuisine. That's the first time I tasted sashimi and sushi. One person was from Abu Dhabi, another was from Saudi Arabia, another from Japan,

Argentina, Peru. One person was Bolivian. A number of Africans from countries I don't think exist anymore because I can't keep track of how many times they've changed. So it was absolutely everything I aspired to immerse myself in but couldn't afford to: *travel*. I was traveling through the stories and the cuisine and the lives of these other people."

Wonderful as it sounds, writer L. John Harris cautions against idealizing the era: "I was in the art department at UC Berkeley," he remembers. "That's when food became almost like theatrical performance art. There's that whole side in the seventies of cooking with friends and making it visually beautiful. It was food experienced as a kind of ritual for artists to be interested in, but ingredients were kind of irrelevant. There was a side of food at the time that was performance—theatrical and visual—in addition to taste. We were living in communes. We were cooking for each other. There was a gourmet club we went to that cooked out of Julia Child and all of that. This is in the late sixties, early seventies. . . .

"It was a mission. I felt like we were discovering something. It was certainly important to us. This is very California and it can sound very pretentious and very hippy dippy, but our generation was about changing things, whether it was antiwar or whatever. Some people discovered that you can change things through food. You can create pleasure. You can create community through food. Food *is* community. This was the beginning of the breakdown of the American family. We were re-creating the family. We were living in communes. We were disgusted with the American system. I marched against the war, of course. But I didn't think of food in that way at that time and I don't think most people did. I think we ignore the fact sometimes that this discovery of good food was about pleasure. It wasn't about changing the system at that point. I think that came a little bit later. I think we had discovered a great source of delight and pleasure and sensual gratification in a very sterile, corporate world. So we weren't on a political mission at that time, I don't think. History tends to compress reality into very simple sound bites. It was a vast period in the seventies where we were about food as pleasure, sensual awareness, and community."

The new interest in food wasn't limited to the counterculture. A proliferation of hobbyist cooking schools and classes materialized to meet the moment; a 1971 *New York Times* article listed no fewer than twenty-four Gotham-based businesses proffering cooking classes—everything from fantasy-camp instruction by the likes of writer James Beard and Mexican cooking priestess Diana Kennedy to crash courses in Chinese food, kosher buffet catering, and macrobiotic practices.

In their newfound fascination with food and cooking, many Americans were guided by a small group of writers and television personalities: James Beard, a failed thespian and opera singer of Hitchcockian stature who had lived for a short time in Paris, turned his attention to food full-time by 1940 and became a prolific author, television personality, commercial pitchman, and networker. He loomed large, as did Julia Child, whose first book, *Mastering the Art of French Cooking*, published in 1961, helped demystify the intimidating European cuisine to generations of home cooks. Child's first television show, *The French Chef*, debuted in 1963, amping up the effort. There was also Englishman Graham Kerr, less well remembered than the others, but notable for the humor and bonhomie on display on his show *The Galloping Gourmet* (1969 to 1971), on which he took a thematic approach to cooking, combining travelogue footage, history, and instruction; sipped wine on camera, often running into a frame with his drink nearly splashing out of the glass;

---

* The show's title also forever confused the use of the word *chef*. If you've ever wondered why casual observers have mistakenly referred to home cooks as "chefs," the problem began there. Sara Moulton, who worked for Child for several years, says that the icon never liked the title because she'd never been a true chef, which would have entailed working in a restaurant.

appeared in a variety of costumes (from a tuxedo to a knight's armor); and charmed a live studio audience.

Richard Olney, an American expat living in France, also developed a cult following for his books *The French Menu Cookbook* (1970) and *Simple French Food* (1974), notable for their masterfully written recipes, chock-full of information, opinion, and evocative detail. A similar fandom sprung up around Brit Elizabeth David for her books such as *French Provincial Cooking* (1960). Craig Claiborne ushered in a golden age of newspaper food writing when he became the *New York Times* food editor in 1957; in the role, he introduced the paper's standard-setting restaurant review system. And food magazines such as *Gourmet* and *Food & Wine* were beginning to make their marks, although they wouldn't begin covering chefs until years later.

I view the American food revolution as having started in France. One of the markers is August 1975. Paul Bocuse appears on the cover of Newsweek *magazine. That was one month before I came to The Culinary Institute of America to be a student. And to have a chef be on the cover of* Newsweek *magazine back in the day when* Newsweek *and* Time *actually meant something, that was a big thing. I remember buying as many as I could buy—I could only afford probably four of them—and bringing them home because I wanted to have them and show my parents what it was to be a chef. Things were starting to change then, and young people like myself were saying, "Wow, this isn't just a job." The French created an aspiration for us.*

—Tim Ryan, president, Culinary Institute of America

The other dominant genre of culinary experience available to Americans overseas during these years was restaurant food on a level beyond imagining, thanks primarily to the rise of a new style of cooking commonly referred to as *nouvelle cuisine*. The movement was first trumpeted as such in *Le nouveau guide*, the brainchild of food critics Henri Gault and Christian Millau, who founded the *Guide* with André Gayot. The *Guide* debuted in 1969, in part as a response to what the authors saw as the staid *Guide Michelin*, which had been evaluating restaurants according to its three-star scale since 1931. Gault and Millau contended that Michelin had failed to praise an emerging new guard of French chefs who broke away from the time-worn canon of haute cuisine recipes first codified by Escoffier in *Le guide culinaire* in 1903.

"Michelin: Don't forget these 48 stars!" screamed the first issue's hand-scrawled headline accompanying an image of chefs including Paul Bocuse, Michel Guérard, and Louis Outhier, who were changing the construct of French cuisine, abandoning the Escoffier playbook in favor of a freer, more personal style. The best-known edition of the *Guide* was the 1973 issue featuring an article revolutionarily titled "*Vive la nouvelle cuisine.*" In it, the authors put forth not only the name of the movement itself, but also distilled it down, with religious undertones, into the "*Dix* [Ten] Commandments." The list seems quaint, but at a time when food was tiptoeing away from plat-ter service and table-side carving to the style of dishes plated by the chef in the kitchen that has endured and evolved through today, it was transformative. The ten commandments included such rules as simplifying where possible, reducing cooking times, cooking season-ally, employing lighter sauces, rediscovering regional dishes, availing oneself of modern equipment such as nonstick pans, cooking with diet and health in mind, and being inventive.

There's just one problem: Like most culinary catchalls, *nouvelle cuisine* oversimplifies, emphasizing certain aspects of the trend while omitting the nuance and individuality that distinguishes any chef. Created by journalists to corral electrifying but disorient-ing change into a manageable construct, the term *nouvelle cuisine* was promotable but confusing. (Mimi Sheraton, restaurant critic for the *New York Times* from 1975 to 1983, suggests discarding the delineated elements in favor of the less specific, literal translation of *nouvelle cuisine*: "new cuisine.") In the case of Gault and Millau, the name they assigned their movement conveniently echoed the name of their publication: In today's parlance, *nouvelle cuisine* might have been considered a brand extension of *Le guide nouveau*. (The movement was also commonly—and unhelpfully—confused in the United States with *cuisine minceur* or "slimming food," the specialty of chef Michel Guérard, also one of the chieftains of nouvelle cuisine.)

Despite these shortcomings, the name *nouvelle cuisine* stuck. One of its defining underpinnings was the visibility of the practitioners of this bold, new style, the chefs whose personal marks showed in their dishes. The inaugural cover of the *Guide* depicted close to fifty toques at a time when you'd have been hard-pressed to name more than a handful. Just as each commandment includes some version of the words *nouveau*, *découvrir*, and *invention* (often multiple times), many of them also illustrate their principles with preparations associated with specific chefs.

"Nouvelle cuisine carved out some independence for the chef," writes Nathan Myhrvold. "Escoffier (and [Marie-Antoine] Carême before him) had explicitly sought to establish rules and conventions. Nouvelle cuisine gave more leeway to the individual chef."

The simplified historical storyline is that the nouvelle cuisine chefs began the shift to a more personalized cuisine, but Fernand Point deserves much credit, not only for shifting to a new style before the nouvelle cuisine era, but also for mentoring many of the chefs who would congregate under its umbrella. Bocuse, Guérard, and brothers Jean and Pierre Troisgros all apprenticed for him in the late 1940s and early 1950s. Point devised a new menu each day—rendered in dramatic script by his wife, Marie-Louise "Mado" Point—a new approach for the time.

"If I take a little step back, I think Fernand Point is the beginning of the story," says San Francisco chef Roland Passot, a native of Villefranche-sur-Saône in eastern France. "He was that figure, that man who was drinking Champagne at eight in the morning; by noon he'd already have had two or three bottles. People were flying in from all over the world. He had presidents of France and other countries coming to his restaurant." (Point's morning Champagne ritual has been romanticized by many. Less frequently cited is his short life span: He died at age fifty-eight in 1955.)

But there's no doubt that Paul Bocuse was the visionary of his generation and understood the value of moving chefs into the public eye: "Bocuse was very street smart," says Passot. "It came to him naturally. He was like the godfather of those chefs. He was the one who was leading the pack. I think he was the driving machine of getting chefs out of their kitchens. I don't want to call them rebels, but they were my idols. And he got together in force with that group of chefs, Michel Guérard, Roger Vergé, even Gaston Lenôtre, to really expose themselves and to show chefs not just cooking behind the stove, but being businesspeople and celebrities. That was a turn."

Bocuse, in addition to being an innate and master marketer, traveled the world, maintained relationships with chefs in many countries, employed Japanese cooks in his restaurant before others in France were doing it. He also went where no French chef of his stature had gone before, visiting the United States to perform cooking demonstrations and participate in special dinners that garnered press coverage and furthered the cause.

Americans were seduced by nouvelle cuisine both for the personality in the food itself and the attention paid to the chefs, which altered their perception of the profession and put faces to the movement. And some of those Americans could imagine themselves in kitchen whites. David Liederman, a New York City college student, was so dazzled by his meal at La Maison Troisgros that he made a bet with Jean Troisgros that if he could beat him in tennis, he could return and work in the kitchen. Jonathan Waxman remembers being in France in his twenties and seeing four nouvelle cuisine leaders on the cover of *Paris Match* magazine. "I said, 'That looks pretty cool,'" he says. "Being a chef. Being on the cover of a magazine."

A useful counterpoint is the experience of the late Judy Rodgers, best known as the chef of San Francisco's Zuni Café, who spent a year living with the Troisgros family in Roanne, France, from 1973 to 1974. Though she never officially worked in their restaurant kitchen, she did occasionally help with rudimentary prep work there, tasted their full repertoire, received culinary wisdom directly from the brothers, and recorded every recipe in her notebooks. Despite such extraordinary access, she responded more to the food she ate *outside* the restaurant's dining room: "About three weeks into my stay at Troisgros, I know that I preferred staff meal to dining in the dining room. I loved the experience of dining in the dining room, and it came off beautifully, and the food was frankly a lot simpler and more sort of easy and enjoyable to eat than a three-star meal in Paris or a three-star at Bocuse, but still, I knew that for me, the dining experience, the conviviality of the food that I was eating at staff meal or at Jean's sister's, where she was doing traditional Burgundian food for the most part, I just liked that better. My body liked it better, and I was a strapping sixteen-year-old. I could eat anything, but I knew I liked that better. Plus, it just struck me at that point in my life that my God, I was already sixteen, and there was no way I was going into food and the stuff that they did after seven o'clock in the kitchen was something that you had to begin training for at age fourteen, and I was over the hill."

It was almost like an underground.

—Alice Waters

Most accountings of this subject, in this era, begin, compul- sorily, with Alice Waters's Chez Panisse. Mention the modern American restaurant movement—or even contemporary American cuisine—to the casual observer, and it's the first restaurant most will toss out. But Chez Panisse wasn't the first establishment of its kind in America. It wasn't even the first in Berkeley, where it was predated by The Pot Luck, purchased by Hank Rubin in 1962, and by Narsai's, a restaurant by Rubin's onetime kitchen manager, Narsai David. "Pot Luck was doing regional French menus on Monday nights way before Jeremiah Tower or Alice Waters did," said chef Mark Miller.

For more of-the-moment cuisine, there was Bruce LeFavour's The Paragon, in Aspen, Colorado. A native of Amsterdam, New York, LeFavour had dropped out of Dartmouth College to join the army, did a tour of duty in counterintelligence in eastern France, tak- ing in the sights and food of Burgundy, Alsace, and Paris in his off hours. He fell in love with Europe, backpacked around, then stayed in France for three years. Returning stateside for a friend's wedding, he was so taken with Colorado that he decided to stay and write a novel, but couldn't secure a publisher. In the meantime, he had mar- ried, had a child, and was confronted with bills to pay. He and his wife, Patricia, opened a restaurant with him as the chef, modeling his food on the (not yet named) nouvelle cuisine he'd sampled in his travels. The restaurant was intimate, comprising private rooms; the year was 1965.

On the East Coast, a fondness for both Italy and France guided John Novi, an Italian American artist, preservationist, and self- proclaimed hippy who purchased the Depuy Canal House, an eighteenth-century structure in High Falls, New York, and spent five years renovating it with plans to convert it into a restaurant. He refinished the interior with the help of volunteer teens from a local civic association. A radio blasted music while they worked; Simon and Garfunkel's "Mrs. Robinson" in particular takes him back.

"It was a free-for-all," he says of those days, when he hosted all-night jam sessions and parties in the unfinished space. "Everybody loved everybody. I was living instinctively and following what my mother used to call my destiny. And I look back on my life now and I realize that's exactly what I did: I was very natural and I wanted to work as naturally as possible with food."

In 1968, he visited Europe, taking a circuitous route to his family's native country. "I just wanted to live in Italy with my relatives. I drove south, went into Austria, Brussels, and then I went to France, stayed in hostels and worked my way down to the family."

Novi only spoke broken Italian but after a month found work in a kitchen at an Italian restaurant with an American name: The Picnic. He assimilated the European service style. "I learned, number one, courses. I couldn't compare it to anything, to my parents. And when I came back, I opened up with a seven-course meal. I learned to serve the salad after the entree, not before. I loved the whole idea. I would splurge and go into a fine-dining restaurant on my way down to Italy. And I found these carts come to the table loaded with cheese and I just loved that idea. I had to do that here." (He was able to get cheese from Robert Schneller in Kingston, New York, where he also bought his meat.)

Novi recalls an epiphany when he found himself in possession of a sea bass. "A twenty-pound fish, the objective being to fillet it properly, needed study. And I had to do it right. I'm a perfectionist." And so, just like that, he decided to become a chef. Eight months after the restaurant opened in 1969, it received four stars from Craig Claiborne in the *New York Times*, which puzzles Novi to this day: "We were busy. And it was a Sunday night. They had dinner and then they went into the bar and they ordered drinks. It was just a strange happening because, number one, Craig Claiborne ordered a margarita at the table and it went out to Susan, who was our barmaid at the time. Susan Hines. And Susan went up to him. She said, 'I'm really sorry, but I don't know how to make a margarita.' So she said, 'Do you mind coming into the bar and making it?' So Craig Claiborne went into the bar, went behind the bar, and made his own margarita and taught her how to make a margarita. And he ends up in the article calling her the demure barmaid. So how we ended up with four stars . . . ?"

Those restaurants are long gone and largely forgotten, as is LeFavour's later effort, the well-regarded Rose et LeFavour in St. Helena, California. But Chez Panisse abides, to put it mildly. The restaurant has risen to legend status and many people reading this are no doubt familiar with much of its lore; as Manresa's David Kinch said to me in an interview, "People know who Willy Bishop is," referring to the bearded, beatnik painter who cooked at Chez Panisse in the early 1970s. It has launched countless careers, and working there became a rite of passage for several generations of mostly California-based cooks and chefs. It's also widely credited with at least one evolution in American restaurant practice: "What Chez Panisse did . . . not when they first, first opened, but as they found their own identity, was revolutionary because it was a restaurant that wrote menus based on what was *available*," says Colman Andrews. "Every other restaurant wrote menus and then found ways to make it available. And if you couldn't get it fresh or you couldn't get a top thing, you got the second best, or if you couldn't get fresh you got it frozen or canned or whatever, or you say, 'Oh, tonight we're out of this.' But that was, even before the idea of sourcing organic produce from the small farmers, the idea that what you found, even if it was what you found at the wholesale market, determines what you're going to cook. Gee, really? Okay. And it certainly wasn't the first place to do this but it was also kind of revolutionary in that there was no *fonds de cuisine*. There were no stocks made up. There were no sauces. Everything was à la minute or pan sauce or sauceless or something. And those things had a tremendous influence."

Waters herself has used her platform to advocate for food-related issues worldwide, and in the process taken on an almost messianic

air. Over the near half century since Chez Panisse's debut, founder
and restaurant have become inseparable.

I didn't know what to expect when I met Alice Waters, for whom
I made a trip cross-country for a three-hour audience. I arrived at
the restaurant in the early afternoon of a mid-August weekday. My
sense of her was deeply developed enough from afar that I didn't
scroll through the usual options when I walked upstairs and asked
the hostess at the casual Chez Panisse Café to announce me to her
office. I didn't ask for "Chef Waters," as some houses expect, or "Ms.
Waters." "Alice is expecting me" seemed, and was, appropriate.

I was led to a table in the window of the dining room facing out
onto Shattuck Avenue. There was, set out for me, a glass teapot,
loose herbs suspended in the water within, tingeing it. Waters appeared and we shook hands, sat across from each other. I confess
that where I usually ask subjects to recount their entire story for me,
this was one case where I didn't, because her time was limited, but
also because there's no single figure in the restaurant community in
the United States whose biography has been more well documented,
whose formative moments have taken on more an air of folktale. It
also must be said, as others who have been down this road before
me too have noted, that for every Chez Panisse loyalist, there's a
detractor who will privately, sometimes bitterly, grouse that for all
of its influence on the industry and on the eating habits and food
knowledge of Americans, both restaurant and founder have been
inflated historically, but won't go on the record with their grievances.
Happily, our focus here is not the American restaurant, or American
food, but the evolution of the American *chef*, and where that arc is
concerned, Chez Panisse's early days offer a useful and unambiguous
case study in how, and how quickly, things changed.

Waters's story traces—*personifies*—all of the aforementioned
influences: Born in Chatham, New Jersey, on April 28, 1944, she
grew up with only the most tangential interest in food. "I didn't think
about it very much because I grew up in New Jersey, and my family

rarely went out to dinner," she says. "We were six of us and we just didn't have the money to go out to dinner. So I can't say that I had much of an idea, except we always wanted to go and eat ice cream at Howard Johnson's. And I liked to go to New York for my birthday every year. I wanted to go to the Museum of Natural History and to eat at the Automat because I wanted to be able to choose what I wanted to eat and then have it right away. And I just loved the lemon meringue pie being cut and put on the tray, and opening the door. It was a big thing for me. But I really didn't know much about the restaurant business at all."

The family had a garden "but I was a picky eater. I had to come to the dinner table but they kept wanting me to eat food that didn't taste good, in my mind. I mean, when I think back, my mother wasn't a cook and she had a hard time taking care of her kids. I loved corn on the cob and tomatoes right out of the garden, and when my father grilled steaks. But I had parfait pie and mince pie at Thanksgiving because my mother knew how to make a piecrust really well."

Her father worked for the Prudential Life Insurance Company, which required relocations to Indiana and then to Van Nuys in Southern California. She matriculated at the University of California, Santa Barbara, then transferred with friends to UC Berkeley in 1964. "We arrived sort of front and center of the Free Speech Movement," she says. "I just felt like I was in over my head, that I was in a really big city that I didn't know about and I was sort of holding on to my friends, pretty much." She recalls "a lot of drugs, a lot of parties going on simultaneously. . . . I was a little bit into Ferlinghetti and that sort of beatnik side."

In 1965, she and a friend traveled to Paris for a semester at the Sorbonne, setting up camp in the Second Arrondissement. She was immediately overtaken by the sensuality of France, especially the food, from her morning *café au lait*, pastries, and yogurt, to the oysters, onion soups, and bistro fare. "I would call it my awakening. It was just unlike anything I'd ever experienced," she says. That summer, she traveled through the South of France and discovered its distinct culinary pleasures—the traditional variety—founded on olive oil, herbs, garlic, and vegetables.

Back in the States, she began cooking, turning for guidance to Julia Child's television show and to the books of Elizabeth David, especially *French Provincial Cooking*, which she cooked through from cover to cover. She fell in love with graphic designer David Goines, a Free Speech Movement leader, and moved in with him. Food became a part of their lives. They were close with Charles Shere, a musicologist, and his wife, Lindsey Shere, a passionate baker. They'd have roaming dinner parties—savory courses prepared by Waters at her and David's, then a stroll over to the Sheres' for dessert. But cooking was just a passion; it would never, she says, have occurred to her to go into the restaurant business.

"I got very involved with Vietnam," she says. "I was kind of an assistant to Bob Scheer* and I traveled around with him, took him every place he spoke. I was very, very influenced by his thinking, and very, very disappointed when he lost when he ran for Congress."

Waters graduated Berkeley in January 1967 and wasn't sure what to do with herself. At another time, she says, she would have followed a conventional path. "I probably would have said, 'I'm going to be a housewife like my older sister.' I didn't even have an ambition to work. I figured I'd be a mother."

She tried a job in a restaurant, The Quest, but it had none of the magic of those Paris bistros and she didn't last long. "So I taught school and then I went and took Montessori training. But I really felt that public education was incredibly valuable and we had to support it. We had to participate in it. And even though I was learning Montessori and it was a private school and a special way of seeing the world, it just fit perfectly with my whole edible education that I had

---

* A budding journalist and cofounder of the New Left journal *Root and Branch*, who took on the war-supporting local congressman in the Democratic primary.

in France, that I was touching and tasting and smelling and seeing all of this around me. I only stopped teaching because I left that job."

As they did for so many in Berkeley, art and food began to intertwine for Waters, like a double helix. She started a recipe column in the *San Francisco Express Times*, "Alice's Restaurant," named for the Arlo Guthrie song—each column was a recipe, written in prose by Waters and graphically designed by Goines in a style that would help define the visual identity of Chez Panisse. "There was a lot in print happening both in terms of posters and communications that was sort of binding us as a group of young people trying to stop the war in Vietnam and caring about civil rights," she says. "It was almost like an underground. I mean, I always thought I was part of a counterculture. And I still feel like I'm part of a counterculture, truly, deeply."

I asked Waters how she connects the larger shifts of the 1960s with an elevated sense of food and its possibilities.

"I think a big part of it is just in our genes," she says. "There's certain things that are universal, and eating is one of those. I think the impulse to come to the table and communicate with other people is as old as civilization. I think the idea of cooking locally is certainly no new idea. That's been here always. So these values, once they're awakened, you can't go back, you just go forward. You want to be hospitable, and cooking and the table are a big part of that. And you're experimenting. I'm sure a lot of people came to it the same way I did, which was through an experience like going to France. I know that Elizabeth David did that. Julia Child did that. Many, many people. They traveled and/or they had parents that had traveled or were influential, and they came back and they just said, 'You know, I want to do this. I want to have a table like this. I want to cook for my friends.'"

After breaking up with Goines, Waters dated Tom Luddy, a film producer and director of the Pacific Film Archive, and they'd stage get-togethers with friends. Waters would cook; Luddy would screen a movie. He introduced her to the film adaptations of playwright Marcel Pagnol's 1930s "Marseille Trilogy"—*Marius* (1931), *Fanny* (1932), and *César* (1936).

I asked Waters about two phrases regarding food and Berkeley that were repeated in multiple interviews for this book: "At the time, there was a culture of food," and "Food could change the world." Many attribute the latter to Waters.

"Well, it's very interesting," she said. "I didn't realize that Mario Savio, head of the Free Speech Movement, was Sicilian. I didn't hear about his life until he died in his fifties [in 1996]. And I just loved hearing at his memorial that he was drinking a bottle of wine every night with dinner with his friends. And surely he had Italian food on the table. And he brought a very big vision of this idealistic world, made it real for all of us who were listening to him. But there was a movement in Berkeley, from back in the sixties, that was probably connected to growing grass, but it was more than that. It was, like, *grow your own*. You don't have to be dependent on these big fast-food industries. It was the weaving of politics and food that's sort of the commune that we can eat vegetables, you can be vegetarian. That was a big part of it. But back before Chez Panisse began, The Cheese Board and Peet's Coffee, Tea & Spices were already places [in Berkeley], so I knew I wanted to be in this neighborhood. I lived not far away. I think there were a lot of people eating with intention. Whether it was well or not, it was with intention. So as people became more educated and traveled, they became more sophisticated."

"There was also this other thing called The Swallow Cafe," says L. John Harris. "The Swallow Cafe gave birth to writers, not chefs, interestingly. So [S. Irene] Virbila of the *L.A. Times*, Ruth Reichl, myself, Maggie Klein, all were at The Swallow Cafe. And many others who didn't go on. The Swallow was almost like a pre–Chez Panisse in the sense that it was people who loved working with food but wanted to do it in a way that was real and authentic. It was started by a Cheese Board person. . . . By then The Cheese Board had become a collective business, which was the influence of the owners having lived in Israel and spending time on a kibbutz. The idea was that collectivization was the way to save humanity . . . so you limit profit but you spread authority. Everybody gets an equal share of everything and you work it out through consensus. There was no hierarchy of authority. So The Swallow was like a step toward Chez Panisse in a funny way. And it was connected to the film archives physically. So there was this whole Tom Luddy connection and then that spread itself through Chez Panisse," named for the widower Panisse in the Pagnol films.

In 1971, Waters decided to take the leap and open the restaurant that had been gestating in her mind, one that would re-create the pleasures of food and the table she'd come to appreciate in France.

"It's funny. It didn't seem a big leap at all," she says today. Maybe this was, in part, because as it had for Marder, LSD gave Waters a nudge: "I only did LSD once," she says. "It was mind-altering, and all of a sudden, I understood what Bob Dylan was saying. It was a kind of blowing your mind, if you will. Just not seeing the world in that same way.

"I just thought my friends are coming over and I'm cooking for them and they aren't paying and I can't teach anymore. And it's what I had a passion for. I cooked every night. I thought, *Well, I can just open a restaurant*. I was empowered, really empowered, by the counterculture. I felt like I could open it up and people would come."

But for all of the influence Chez Panisse would exert on the restaurant and food industries, the role of a *chef* was largely incidental at the restaurant's first iteration. Chez Panisse's first chef was not the icon Waters (less a chef than, in the words of Bay Area chef and California food historian Joyce Goldstein, "a restaurateur and a spiritual leader and an activist"), but the virtually unknown Victoria Kroyer (now Wise), a graduate student at UC Berkeley, who had burned out and decided to throw in the academic towel. By chance, she had much in common with Waters: She'd been caught up in the Free

Speech Movement, been to France, loved to cook. An ex-boyfriend happened by the space while it was being renovated, told her to hightail it over there and apply for a job. Wise landed the gig without so much as an audition menu. "I really was the first one, and nobody had the presence of mind to suggest that," says Wise, who was hired after an interview with Waters's friend and restaurant investor Paul Aratow and his friend Bobby Weinstein. "We were running around trying to get silverware for the table. There was a leak in the refrigerators, and we tried to have at least one counter in the kitchen free so that we could set something down. It was chaotic and hilarious. Isn't that crazy?" (Lindsey Shere was appointed pastry chef at a time when even many more formal establishments didn't enlist a dedicated dessert specialist.)

"If you're the head of the stoves in a restaurant, well, you're the chef," says Wise. "That's all. But it was exactly the informality of its manifestation that it just was so different. It was freer. If people assumed that being a chef was like coming out of a hotel school or hospitality school—it was not like that. It was much more freewheeling, frankly. And now of course there are culinary schools all over the place and they're active and they're full, but there weren't such things then. I think there was The Culinary Institute of America at Hyde Park. That was it. And that was the formal training. We were a bunch of people, you know, kind of smart-ass college kids saying, 'Well of course we can cook. We've been to France. We know what it tastes like.' And off we went."

For a sense of the bicoastal nature of the zeitgeist, consider another restaurant, one that opened in New York City, among the industrial lofts below Houston Street—many of them occupied, illegally, by artists—just four months after Chez Panisse, in December 1971. The restaurant was, appropriately enough, called FOOD, and it was created by artist Gordon Matta-Clark and his girlfriend, photographer and dancer Carol Goodden, as a sort of edible installation. Matta-Clark wasn't a chef, not in the way we understand the role today; he was an artist, one who personified the burgeoning SoHo art scene. Among his claims to fame was Anarchitecture, which was, according to his friend, sculptor Ned Smyth, "a dramatically physical, deconstructivist architecture, rather ahead of its time." A sort of inner-city Christo, Matta-Clark created conceptual pieces such as "Cuts," for which he and Smyth cut pieces out of walls of abandoned buildings in the South Bronx, then photographed the altered space, ideally with a window at the far end; if the cityscape in the cutout featured an elevated subway car, all the better. He and Smyth lugged saws, power tools, and a generator into the buildings, sometimes encountering fully furnished dwellings that "looked as if the occupants had simply walked out." That was spooky, but it was nothing compared to the threat of encountering "junkies who would steal copper wire and pipe to sell as scrap to get money for drugs." (Though he usually got away with his missions, his cutting of a Hudson River pier necessitated him leaving the country for a spell.)

Matta-Clark also shared of himself via food. The story of the restaurant began on the afternoon he sliced meat from a slow-roasted pig, slapped it between slices of bread, and handed out pork sandwiches to hundreds of people participating in "Under the Brooklyn Bridge," an alternative-space art show. The day prior to the show, Goodden procured a suckling pig from the Jones Street meat market. They injected it with pepper water, jury-rigged a grill, lit a fire with branches from the swamps of New Jersey, hung a hammock, and spent eighteen hours under the bridge, tending to the pig. The next day, as a saxophone player provided the living soundtrack, Mabou Mines performed a Beckett play, and Tina Girouard fashioned a house from dirt, Matta-Clark sliced the pork and served approximately five hundred people sandwiches.

FOOD was the love child of food and art that was part and parcel of the downtown art scene. There was also the dinner party circuit to which Matta-Clark and Goodden belonged—one memorable party Goodden hosted in her loft was a spring flower party (a theme guests freely interpreted by bringing flowers, bringing *edible* flowers, or coming *dressed as* flowers). Matta-Clark made the semi-joking suggestion that Goodden should open a restaurant. She liked the idea of not giving food away, so she said that she'd do it if he did. Within a week, she'd negotiated to take over the space at 127 Prince Street, at the corner of Wooster Street, that housed Comidas Criollas, a failing eatery. The couple, with fellow artists, opened FOOD, which blended art, cooking, utopian philosophy, and counterculture in a restaurant unlike any the city had seen.

At the time, SoHo was an undeveloped frontier of named streets beneath upper Manhattan's numbered system, and there were scant few restaurants—mainly just Fanelli Café. Says Bill Katz, who would go on to design Chanterelle restaurant at the tail end of the decade, "It wasn't SoHo then. It wasn't called SoHo. SoHo came later; that's a real estate term. This was before that."

"FOOD was on the northwest corner of Prince and Wooster," says Katz. "And it's mythic because he had artists who would cook, and they would cook the most far-out things you ever could imagine. That was the first restaurant in our neighborhood."

As at Chez Panisse, the concept of a chef was more necessity than focus at FOOD, which served a vegetarian menu two nights a week and welcomed guest chefs including artists such as Robert Rauschenberg. And the training that would in time become de rigueur for New York City whisks was far from a prerequisite. In August 1971, Smyth, freshly arrived in New York City having hitchhiked from Colorado, answered a notice in FOOD's window and spoke with Goodden.

"You can be a waiter or busboy," said Goodden. "But what I really need is an assistant chef."

"What do I have to do?" asked Smyth.

"Can you chop and boil vegetables?"

"Yes."

He was hired.

When FOOD opened, there was no telephone, the windows were still soaped, and the dining room—all white walls, high ceilings, and square oak tables under which forty to fifty mismatched chairs were tucked—was still a construction site. Soups and stews were served from a cauldron in the center of the room. The menu changed nightly and ran the gamut: soup accompanied by housemade breads and fresh (notably) unsalted butter; chicken stew over rice; and shrimp gumbo.

There were conceptual dinners that would have been right at home in the 2010s: Matta-Clark's "Bone Dinner" remains legendary: a meal of oxtail soup, roasted marrow bones, and other dishes; at the end of the meal, the bones were scrubbed clean and strung together to be worn home by guests. At another, he served live shrimp swimming in egg whites. The dish was titled "Alive." Eat your heart out, René Redzepi.

Graphic designer Milton Glaser and his cocolumnist Jerome Snyder, writing in their "Underground Gourmet" column in *New York* magazine, rhapsodized about FOOD, which they described as a "restaurant commune." The last line of the review, quoting a woman at FOOD who recognized Glaser, spoke to the noncommercial idealism of the day: "Please don't write about this place," she pleaded.

FOOD, at least in its first incarnation, had a short life, just three years. Goodden sold the space and the new owners kept the name (Goodden couldn't stop them because it was so generic). Matta-Clark died of pancreatic cancer at age thirty-five, in 1978.

Despite the similarities between Chez Panisse and FOOD, Goodden said that Waters's restaurant had no influence on FOOD, although she thinks she may have used some recipes from the *Moosewood Cookbook* (from the vegetarian restaurant that opened in Ithaca, New York, in 1973) during FOOD's life span. Years later she said she "still [didn't] know much about [Chez Panisse]." Goodden, a native of England, said that she and Matta-Clark were more influenced by "European food/cooking/shopping/presentation" and the social place of food in European life.

There were, at the time, comparable restaurants elsewhere downtown. In particular, Goodden cited a like-minded delicatessen on Second Avenue and a restaurant called either The Back Porch or The Front Porch, which "oddly . . . kind of had the same ideas as we did—fresh food, homemade food, soups and sandwiches, stews, inexpensive, casual. But they didn't influence us nor we them."

Just as Waters found opening a restaurant to be the most natural thing in the world, Wise thought little of morphing into a chef. "It didn't seem a big deal to me either, to assume the role of a chef. I mean, I was cooking. That's what I was doing."

Chez Panisse, as restaurants do, came together: There were red-and-white-checkered tablecloths, mismatched silver, flea market chairs, and fresh flowers. And the opening, as openings are, was chaos: "Just before opening night, Alice walked into The Cheese Board and said, 'I need help,'" remembers L. John Harris, who pitched in as a waiter. When the night arrived, Waters, in a polkadot dress from the Bizarre Bazaar, was still nailing a runner to the stairs as customers were queued up outside. Nobody had thought to make a sign, so Goines wrote *Chez Panisse* with chalk in angular block letters on the wooden fence outside. The opening menu was *pâté en croûte, canard aux olives,* and a plum tart.

Waters, Wise, and company didn't even know there was such a thing as restaurant purveyors. "There were a lot of ethnic markets in San Francisco, and at the beginning of the restaurant, we felt that was the place to shop because the ducks were hanging," says Waters. They also purchased food from a Japanese produce concession at the U-Save on Grove Street and from the Berkeley co-op. The restaurant was sincere but rough around the edges, to put it mildly, without the air of institution or the high-mindedness that attaches to it today.

"Alice, I think, would probably be the first person to tell you that Chez Panisse today is not the Chez Panisse that Alice built, not the Chez Panisse that Alice expected, not the Chez Panisse that Alice wanted," says Narsai David. "I mean, it has evolved into something far beyond anything that she had ever dreamt of. She started out doing a very, very casual, very simple, straightforward place where the kitchen had the freedom to come up with new ideas and play with different things, and she just made an enormous contribution. But it at the same time was—well, in a funny way it was almost a little too touchy-feely, you know? The silverware was bought used at flea markets and such. I don't mind the fact that the silverware didn't match, but when the silver plating had worn off and you had the brass [or] copper base metal on your tongue, it just didn't feel right. It certainly was not a heavy enough reaction that it interfered with her success. I mean, from day one she was successful."

Waters's main role in those first days was technically as a waitress, selling the set menu to customers. The restaurant was initially open from breakfast until late night, but quickly became a dinner-only affair.

One customer in those early days was Mark Miller, a UC Berkeley graduate student studying art history and Japanese anthropology. Born and raised in Massachusetts, Miller had come to Berkeley in 1967. As a break from the rigors of academia, he began cooking out of the *New York Times Cookbook* and a paperback of one of James Beard's books. Miller, a friend of Wise's, would become a part of the fabric of Chez Panisse, often hanging around the kitchen after hours, kibitzing with the staff. He would also go on to start a sophisticated and strikingly designed newsletter, *Market Basket*, which reviewed food products such as soy sauce and chocolate, long before it was fashionable.

Early reviews for the restaurant were positive. Wise left Chez Panisse, temporarily to follow a boyfriend to Montreal, then after a brief return, for good. In a melding of food and cinema, she became Francis Ford Coppola's private chef, then opened Pig-by-the-Tail, a charcuterie shop, on the same block as Chez Panisse in what became known as Berkeley's "Gourmet Ghetto."

The restaurant placed an ad, interviewed four candidates to replace Wise. Then a fifth emerged: Jeremiah Tower. It's a sign of how fraught his relationship with the restaurant would become that even the story of his audition is disputed: As he tells it, he showed up at Chez Panisse and was asked to taste a soup. He found that it only needed salt, but dolled it up with wine and cream to show off. Waters took one slurp and hired him. Others who were there insist he went through a more lengthy process including writing several proposed menus. However he got the gig, Waters and Tower produced an alchemy that rocketed the restaurant to new heights. Tower, a Harvard grad and food obsessive who had dined all over the world, read menus like novels—studied them like texts—and had regularly thrown extravagant dinner parties in Cambridge, came to the task with a fervor, creating ambitious menus and working with Waters to procure the necessary ingredients to prepare them. The two also began a dalliance, indulging in Champagne and caviar after hours, and sleeping together, which got people's attention because Tower, though not yet out, was gay.

"The reason Jeremiah became prominent, or was able to, is that he was in a highly liberal, political construct in Berkeley because Alice thought she could make him straight," says Clark Wolf, a restaurant consultant who was around the Berkeley food scene. "It was a real simple situation. He was willing to trade that part of it for opportunity. And by that I mean he was willing to flirt, which is a very minor term for a much more complex situation, right? Alice, I think she believes that it's just a phase, with anybody. And I love Alice very much and I respect her but that can only be self-involvement. If you don't understand somebody else's actual reality, it's only because you can't go beyond your own."

Tower transformed the kitchen immediately, ordered that the rock and roll on the stereo be replaced by opera. He began crafting menus the likes of which hadn't been seen anywhere, marrying his academic cleverness with his depth of culinary knowledge. Within days, he was offering obscure French preparations and before long the menu, written in French in Waters's calligraphy, was paired with a typewritten sheet featuring English translations, something that hadn't been necessary in Chez Panisse's more culinarily conservative early days.

In service of the food, the odd couple scoured the Bay Area for ingredients, sourcing from Italian delis, meat markets, fish shops, and also welcoming an early generation of foragers who would bring them mushrooms, fruits, eggs, and other ingredients.

"The two of them really were the two scientists or the mother and father of what we are really talking about now," says Jonathan Waxman. "I think that Alice had always had a vision about what she wanted. *Auberge of the Flowering Hearth*[*] is a very strong influence on her. She has lots of influences. The idea of cooking food in one's home that was really of the earth. It has always been Alice's vision. Whether it was pure French food or regional food of France, that is how the whole thing started and it evolved from there. Jeremiah came with a much more cosmopolitan attitude. He had been around the world, he had been on the SS *France*. He knew clubs in London. He had eaten in Germany. He really had a sophisticated palate. Much more sophisticated than most people at Chez Panisse at that point.

"The two of them coming from different backgrounds were able to create this amazing food. It wasn't about anything specific, there

---

[*] Roy Andries de Groot's fabled 1973 book-length tribute to a country French restaurant.

was no agenda, there was no light at the end of the tunnel—like, why we are doing this?—they were just passionate about it. . . . I think, honestly, it is probably the most important thing that happened. Chez Panisse in the early seventies, Alice, Jeremiah, that collaboration. I think it is everything."*

Chez Panisse's reputation grew, garnering national attention and drawing a more and more fashionable crowd, to the horror of many of its founders and early customers.

October 7, 1976, brought a seminal event in the life of the restaurant, and of American chefdom and cuisine: Tower conceived and prepared a Northern California Regional Dinner, treating American ingredients and preparations with the same reverence usually reserved for French food. The eight-course menu featured Spenger's Tomales Bay bluepoint oysters; cream of fresh corn soup with crayfish butter; Big Sur Garrapata Creek smoked trout steamed over California bay leaves; Monterey Bay prawns sautéed with garlic, parsley, and butter; preserved California-grown geese from Sebastopol; Monterey Jack cheese; caramelized figs; and nuts and pears from the San Francisco Farmers' Market. It was a smash success.

"Jeremiah was able to be creative with menus," says Waxman. "Alice was much more of a scholar in terms of cookbooks, not that Jeremiah wasn't a scholar, he actually was, but he would take liberties with that and push the envelope. You know, injecting tangerine juice in a leg of lamb, that is pretty far out there for 1973 or '74 in California. But the two of them in that collaboration—I remember the menu had to change every day, five days a week. It was so amazingly provocative that it was incendiary, it was explosive."

---

* That's the kind of statement that rankles East Coasters, and even some native Californians. Says Wolf: "In [Waxman's] life I'm sure it was. It's just not that important. Do you know what I mean? The entire world does not exist in Berkeley. It just doesn't. And what you have to understand is some of those people really want to maintain that bubble because it maintains their sense of themselves and the world. But there are nettles in New Hampshire."

Tower, in a revelation that would repeat throughout the 1970s and '80s around the country, realized, "We didn't know what you're not supposed to do. *This is how you open a restaurant. This is how you run a restaurant.* None of us knew. So we did the best we could, what we wanted to do. And as it turned out, it wasn't that bad. Let me tell you a story about Jean Troisgros: He came into Chez Panisse in '74 or 5 or something like that. And he came and ate in the dining room and came into the kitchen and said, you know, 'I really want to meet you.' . . . And he walked in and I nearly fell through the floor into a dead faint. My one hero who was not American. And he said to me, 'Boy, I really envy you.' And I think my heart nearly stopped. I said to him, 'You envy *me*? I mean, Jean, for God's sake. It's so much the other way around.' He said, 'Oh, no, no, no. You have the freedom to do whatever you want, and I have a three-star restaurant. I can't do anything I want.' And he said, 'Would you please let me send my nephew Michel to come and do a *stage** here?' I said, 'Well, Jean, that's going to make bloody history.' No one's ever come from France, let alone from a three-star restaurant to do a *stage* in America, let alone in Berkeley. And he did. . . . When Michel Troisgros arrived, he was just going to do beurre blanc sauces. That's it. And I'd say, 'No, we're not.' He would make the beurre blanc anyway, and 'We're going to put it on'—'No, Michel, we're not.' He couldn't believe it. So there was a strength in not knowing what you're supposed to do."

It was a lesson that was repeated more than once. Says Tower: "Jean-Pierre Moullé—French-trained from France—came to California, and he was my sous chef with Willy Bishop. There were three of us. And for the first whatever period, Jean-Pierre will tell you, he would just look at me like, 'Mmm, that's not done.' I'd say, 'Well, this is a menu we're going to do.' And he was looking for what he thought

---

*   A short-term cooking job, often for no pay, undertaken in exchange for knowledge, contacts, and references. The term is an Americanization of the French word *stagiaire*, which refers to the person working in the position.

everybody in France at the time thought: If you had a great restaurant, you had to have a great menu, meaning great ingredients—foie gras, duck breast. Certain marks you had to hit. So he was polite but very resistant for a few months before he finally . . . Then whatever food we were cooking, people would be always piling into the kitchen. And when they started to say—in those days they had been to France and come back—once a week at least somebody would come in and say, 'We just ate at blah, blah, blah in Paris, and this is much better.' And Jean-Pierre heard that a few times and started to come around."

Says Waters, "Well, at the beginning it was the greatest collaboration. I mean, really, really wonderful. Because I think in some ways it put Jeremiah in a position of having to think about one menu, and to do it in a certain, if you will, Berkeley way, which was not his inclination, really, at all. But it helped us. It lifted us up to—or me particularly—into just worlds of food that I hadn't thought about. And it was great. It was really, really great. It was a period. Who knows whether it could have endured?

"What was great about it is that we were both—I think of ourselves as being intellectual cooks, and that we just went into every cookbook. He would say, 'Oh, well, should we do *pâté en croûte?*' I'd say, 'Oh, yeah, do that!' And I'd bring it out to the dining room and just sell it to the people who ate it. . . . And we did all of those dinners for winemakers. We were in a real adventure of experimentation. You know, I'm kind of an olive oil person but I sure made a lot of beurre blancs. It was an edible education for Chez Panisse."

Tower left Chez Panisse in January 1977, returning briefly in 1978 to help out Waters when she left for vacation. Many who were there from the restaurant's inception were delighted to see him go, allowing the restaurant to reclaim its original path. "There are two camps," said Tower. "There's someone like Darrell Corti [the Sacramento wine expert and gourmet-foods-shop owner] who sent a Sicilian Mafia funeral wreath when I did the week of Escoffier menus, saying, 'This is the end, Chez Panisse can never be greater than this.' And the other camp is I destroyed the little Pagnol-movie neighborhood thing. And the truth is, you know, both."

The Tower years at Chez Panisse foretold, though didn't necessarily influence, similar narratives throughout the United States: An American chef had found his way to center stage, and more would soon follow. Often drowned out by the opera of the Tower-Waters relationship—which would soon turn as sour as past-date milk—is that for all the interpersonal layers, at one level, it was a conflict between owner-founder and chef, another theme that would play out not just at Chez Panisse, but across the industry and the country.

1

NEW WORLD ORDER

*No, it might happen pretty easily—but the dream isn't big
enough.*
—Norman Maine (James Mason), *A Star Is Born* (1954)

HOW WOLFGANG PUCK LED THE RESTAURANT REFORMATION,
CREATING A NEW INDUSTRY TEMPLATE BY PUTTING THE CHEF
FRONT AND CENTER, WHILE A DISPARATE GROUP OF EXPRES-
SIVE YOUNG LOS ANGELES COOKS WENT THEIR OWN WAY AND
INTO BUSINESS FOR THEMSELVES

In 1975, not long after he moved to Los Angeles and took over
the kitchen at the flagging French restaurant Ma Maison, a
young, unknown chef named Wolfgang Puck hit a nightclub
with Formula One racecar superstar and fellow Austrian Niki
Lauda. Puck found himself slow dancing with a stranger. Who
knows what the song was: maybe Peter Frampton's "Baby, I Love

Your Way," or another recent chart topper, Johnny Mathis's "Feelings." Whispering small talk, he told the woman what he did for a living, which so failed to impress her that the moment the song ended, she bolted without a word, leaving him alone on the floor.

"I said, *I'm not going to say I'm a cook anymore; I'm going to say I'm a racecar driver*," remembers Puck, whose voice, four decades later, retains its Austrian severity.

Patrick Terrail, Ma Maison's aristocratic playboy proprietor, wasn't burdened by such insecurities, not anymore. With Puck in the kitchen, his restaurant found its footing and his stock was ascending. Studio executives, agents, producers, and other members of the sunglass set were discovering Ma Maison in droves, making it their new canteen, a shabby-chic alternative to The Bistro, Chasen's, Musso and Frank, and Scandia, one of which had been around since the silent film era.

The diametrically opposed existences that Terrail and Puck experienced under the same professional roof weren't unusual: Owner-impresarios had always been the face of their restaurants, the ones who'd put their money on the line, and to whom fame and fortune accrued; chefs were the anonymous workhorses who toiled behind the swinging doors, rarely ventured into the dining room, and who, it was generally believed, were replaceable. But winds of change were blowing through the industry in 1970s Los Angeles. Thanks in part to the influence of nouvelle cuisine, food was shedding its uniformity, chefs were attaining prominence, and a growing population of what would in time become known as "foodies" knew who was in the kitchen, and wanted to be known *by* them. Eventually the old model toppled, most spectacularly at Ma Maison, but also in a handful of restaurants where the traditional power structure was turned on its head, leaving owners stunned and chefs on top of the world.

"I DON'T CARE WHO YOU ARE, BECAUSE MY FATHER'S VERY RICH."

Patrick Terrail was born into a world where restaurant proprietors were king. His family was industry nobility: Uncle Claude owned the venerable La Tour d'Argent in Paris. His great-grandfather Claudius Burdel had owned and operated Café Anglais, where he hosted Czar Alexander II and Kaiser Wilhelm in the fabled Great Sixteen, an opulent private dining room. His grandfather André, a pal of Henri Soulé who would go on to open New York City's Le Pavilion, bridged the generations, relocating the wines of Café Anglais to La Tour d'Argent, of which he became the proprietor in 1910. In 1960, young Patrick, freighted with the great expectations of his lineage, came to the United States to matriculate at the Cornell University School of Hotel Administration in Ithaca, New York. Hospitality coursed through his veins, but the restaurateur within was first awakened at thirty thousand feet when he spent a summer globetrotting as a Pan Am steward: The airline's caterer of record was Paris's Art Nouveau gastronomic temple Maxim's, and Terrail prepared everything from caviar and Champagne to filet mignon and duck à l'orange. "It's not like today," he says of in-flight service. "It was very, very elegant." He went to work for Joe Baum's Restaurant Associates as assistant food and beverage manager at the landmark Four Seasons restaurant* in New York City, where he

---

* Opened in 1959 in Midtown Manhattan's Seagram Building, The Four Seasons was a four-hundred-seat restaurant of breathtaking ambition. Built at a cost of $4.5 million, designed by Philip Johnson, with a marble pool and the likes of Picasso and Miró hung on the walls, its extensive menu was created by James Beard, future *New York Times* critic Mimi Sheraton, and Swiss-born, French-trained chef Albert Stockli. It was ahead of its time in proffering a seasonal menu that also indicated the provenance of many ingredients, and in putting forth a

absorbed Baum's vision and ambition. He was especially impressed that "people ate there every damn day." And not just any people, but captains of industry and a who's who of the entertainment trade. James Beard, whose consultation had helped define the restaurant, regularly threw dinners at The Four Seasons; President Kennedy celebrated his birthday there, just before speeding off to Madison Square Garden, where Marilyn Monroe serenaded him with history's most famous rendition of "Happy Birthday."

A few professional dalliances followed: Terrail owned an events business in New York, then managed a fifty-room hotel in Tahiti, dividing his time between the South Pacific and Los Angeles. In 1970, he settled in L.A.: The weather recalled Greece, where he'd spent his high school years, shopping the open-air markets with his mother and developing his intuition for fresh fish, meats, and vegetables. L.A., the scent of reefer everywhere, felt open, free, and Terrail made friends at a time when intimacy came easy: At a future studio chief's party, amyl nitrate and 'ludes were set out in bowls like chips and salsa. He arrived at another gathering, off Mulholland Drive, to find "everybody half-naked in the pool." Much of this shocked him, but he was no innocent; for fun, he'd go to the farmers' market at the corner of West 3rd Street and Fairfax and pick up women by milking his French accent, convincing them he was a fashion photographer.

Terrail started down the restaurant rabbit hole following a perceived opportunity: There was no patio dining to exploit Los Angeles's year-round sunshine, as there was in the South of France. He acquired and converted a carpet warehouse on Melrose Avenue in West Hollywood. For the menu, he planned to rip off an Upper East Side New York City restaurant, Martell's, which served a va-

---

style of food that was, according to author Paul Freedman, "not exactly American but rather modern, eclectic, and cosmopolitan—revolutionary for its time and thereby offering a challenge to French preeminence in high-end dining."

riety of brochettes.* Terrail christened the restaurant Ma Maison, meaning "My House," wanting it to have the feeling of a home. It was as casual as a restaurant could be, largely owing to his limited budget, with Astroturf flooring outside, Ricard umbrellas shading the tables, cheap plates, and plastic ducks and geese that lit up at night scattered about. The restaurant opened in October 1973 with no chef, just a menu devised by Terrail, then twenty-six, to be executed by a team of cooks.

He made an accidental splash after arranging lunch with the *Los Angeles Times* food writer Lois Dwan at the venerable Scandia on Sunset Boulevard. His sales pitch for the new spot was so convincing that she surprised him the next day with an article expressing her excitement for a restaurant she believed would be unique in a city dominated at the time by those showbiz dowagers.

Terrail was unprepared for his close-up. Not having a proper chef, he says, revealed his stupidity and ignorance, and the inaugural months were a disaster, exacerbated by arrogance: If a customer felt his standing entitled him to a better table, a common Hollywood sentiment, Terrail was apt to reply, "I don't care who you are, because my father's very rich." Though he had begun to attract some industry clientele, with smash-cut suddenness Ma Maison was failing so badly that he'd lie awake in the dead of night sobbing, thinking about killing himself.

Los Angeles magazine's George Christy saved him the trouble, figuratively speaking, penning a review so brutal that Terrail retreated to France, seeking a chef. He consulted with Yanou Collart, famed publicist to nouvelle cuisine's superstars and to his old Pan Am connections at Maxim's. The trail led him to Louis Outhier's Restaurant L'Oasis in La Napoule, near Cannes, where he spent three days licking his wounds, soaking up inspiration: The elegant experience, the seamless blend of haute and contemporary,

---

* Skewers of marinated beef.

the commitment to the guest's pleasure, and Outhier's personal passion—the visit was an extended epiphany that altered Terrail's understanding of the possibilities of a modern restaurant. (Freudians might be amused to know that the self-made Outhier was one of very few Michelin three-starred chefs who didn't hail from a restaurant family.)

Today, Terrail lives in Hogansville, Georgia, a small city (population 3,000) fifty miles outside Atlanta, where he publishes the lifestyle magazine *85 South Out and About,* named for the nearby interstate. He's married to Jackie Lloyd, an American woman decades his junior, and the two have a young son. I meet him on an Easter Sunday, but because my flight is late he directs me to rendezvous at a barbecue at a friend's house. There, in Southern suburbia, I first encounter the man I've seen in photographs cozying up to, and yukking it up with, everybody from Jack Lemmon to Kelly LeBrock to Joan Collins to Michael Caine at the epicenter of 1970s Hollywood. There's a whiff of witness protection about this second act, this still-elegant Frenchman a sore thumb among the polo shirts and strip malls.

Terrail and I break away from the party and drive to the Victorian house where he and Jackie live. As with many homes I visited while writing this book, certain rooms and passageways double as shrines to the owner's glory days, festooned with photographs and framed letters from celebrity clientele. We climb a flight of stairs to his cluttered office and sit across his desk from each other. Terrail has a gravelly, purring voice and gangster's eyes. He's an interviewer's dream, an open book, unruffled by any question and generous with his contacts, even offering an email address for his friend Robin Leach, bombastic British host of the 1980s and '90s syndicated TV series *Lifestyles of the Rich and Famous.* We talk for almost five hours as he paints me a picture of his life and of Ma Maison, including that crossroads that took him to the French Riviera.

"I realized that the future was not in me, but in who was going to be cooking," he says of that time with Outhier. "I may be the gallery, but the gallery is only as good as the art." He always knew that on a gut level, as well as the fact that retaining a good chef meant making him some kind of partner, but his family's outdated attitude retarded his thinking. "My uncle was totally against that," says Terrail. "And he *hated* Paul Bocuse. He said, 'Paul Bocuse is *not* a restaurateur; he's a cook that's going in the dining room.'"

At Maxim's, says Terrail, somebody gave him a name: Wolfgang Puck, an alum of the restaurant who had also cooked at L'Oustau de Baumanière in Provence and was now at the Arco Towers, in downtown L.A. Returning to Los Angeles, Terrail tracked him down. Puck was living in a decidedly unfashionable hotel, a poster of Just Jaeckin's softcore flick *Emmanuelle* pinned to the wall, sheets serving as curtains, and just one bed, shared (platonically), says Terrail, by Puck and his co-chef, Guy Leroy—a professional wingman who had shadowed him in his prior jobs. Terrail couldn't afford to employ either Puck or Leroy full-time, so he contracted them both, for twenty hours per week each, to do four-hour shifts in tandem with their other jobs, and gave them a car to shuttle themselves back and forth. Puck soon distinguished himself as the better cook, so Terrail assigned him the dinner shifts.

"FUCK! FUCK! FUCK! THE FOOD IS *SO* GOOD."

That this diminutive, shy, Austrian-born, thickly accented whisk would come to define the very concept of celebrity chefdom was, appropriately enough, the stuff of Hollywood. . . .

Fade in on the south-central Austrian town of St. Veit an der Glan, where we meet Wolfgang Puck as a boy who harbors kitchen ambitions, born of his love of cooking with his mother, a professional pastry chef. But his stepfather, a coal miner and onetime pugilist, scoffs at him, tells him cooking is for sissies, that he should go into construction. Puck has skills enough to win a national culinary contest, but he's also a klutz; at one interview, he steps into a row of cakes cooling on the floor. At fourteen, Puck boards a train from Klagenfurt to take an apprenticeship at the Hotel Post in Villach. His stepfather shouts after him: "You'll never amount to anything!"

That all really happened—and amazingly, it got worse. Arriving at his destination, Puck set himself up in a rented room in a septuagenarian's apartment, close enough to walk to work. "I was basically like her kid," he says. At the hotel, it was less than a month before he screwed something up, allowing the restaurant's stash of potatoes to run out. "[The chef] told me I'm good for nothing; I should go home," says Puck. "That was the worst day of my life."

A well-known story goes that he thought about killing himself, but today he says it was only a passing, abstract consideration that flitted in and out of his mind that night during an hour spent lingering on a bridge. His professional devastation paled alongside the prospect of returning to life with his stepfather. "I'm not going to go home and prove him right," he vowed.

At home, he tossed and turned until morning, then devised a Hail Mary plan: return to work and see what happened. The apprentice who had had Puck's workload heaped on top of his own was so happy to see him that he hid him in the cellar, where he snuck him staff meals so he could stay out of sight. "I'm sure some people knew," says Puck. "But everybody was scared to tell the chef because he was a crazy guy. And then one day, he comes down and sees me there and says, 'You got fired. You have to leave.' I said, 'I can't leave. I'll kill myself before I leave.'" (When Puck tells this story today, he seems to channel his younger, feral self: His eyes tear up, his muscles tense, and he sets his jaw as if ready to fight. It's intense.) The owner took pity on Puck, sent him to his other property, the Hotel Park. There the chef was a woman with kids Puck's age; she coached him that if he just did his work and kept his nose clean, everything would be fine. And it was.

When he was eighteen, Puck wrote to several of the Michelin two- and three-star restaurants of France until he was hired on at L'Oustau de Baumanière, a three-star affair in Les Baux-de-Provence, in the South of France, where he fell under the spell of chef Raymond Thuilier, perhaps the most unlikely of the band of French chefs who rose to fame in the mid-twentieth century. Though Thuilier came from a family of *aubergistes*, he had spent two decades climbing the ranks of an insurance company before opening his restaurant, in equal partnership with Madame Moscoloni, in his mid-forties, in 1946; the restaurant ascended to three-star Valhalla in 1954 and remained there for thirty-five years. After three months, Puck told Thuilier he couldn't afford to work for free any longer, but the old man had taken a liking to him and put him on the payroll.

"He was my mentor," said Puck of Thuilier. "Town mayor, painter, and a great chef who cooked from the heart without recipes. A real Renaissance man." Years later he would write that Thuilier's "robust and poetic approach to all aspects of his life touched and deeply influenced me." On his rare day off, Puck grew fond of the decidedly French pizzas served at nearby Chez Gu et Fils, especially their *pissaladière*, a cheese-less rectangle topped with anchovies, black olives, and caramelized onions.

From there, he progressed to La Réserve in Beaulieu, the Hôtel de Paris in Monte Carlo, and Maxim's in Paris. In 1973, he relocated to New York City, to become the chef at La Grenouille in Midtown Manhattan, but was discouraged when he got there, concerned that he'd grow bored cooking what he considered bistro food after having been to the nouvelle mountaintop. So owner Charles Masson arranged a job for him at La Tour, atop the Indiana National Bank Building in Indianapolis. Puck, a racecar enthusiast, jumped at the chance to live in the home of the Indy 500, but immediately realized that Indianapolis was no Monte Carlo, and became quickly frustrated by the restaurant's conservative continental fare. In 1975, he and Leroy migrated to Los Angeles and the Arco Towers, two office buildings with subterranean shops, which was where he was slaving when Terrail tracked him down.

At Ma Maison, Puck and Terrail collaborated on a new menu, cribbing from Outhier's, which Terrail had retained from his recent travels, and from Puck's copy of a menu from L'Oustau de Baumanière. Puck quickly proved himself talented enough that Terrail let Leroy go and hired him full-time.

Just as Terrail saw his fortunes reversing, a pall of disillusionment fell over Puck. "I didn't know the restaurant was bankrupt," he says. "My first paycheck bounced. Everything was COD. I went to the fish market: Scandia bought lobster meat for lobster cocktail; I bought the *shells* to make lobster sauce and lobster soup. Ma Maison had no money at all. Maybe three or four refrigerators outside, like home refrigerators. There was no walk-in."* Even worse was the food: "They had on the menu: sardines, radishes with butter. Everything was precooked and everything was terrible. They had mashed potatoes in cans, powdered potatoes to make soup."

Though only twenty-five years old, Puck knew he could do much better. He started to make his mark, phasing in his own dishes like cream of sorrel soup, lobster terrine, and grilled squab with thyme and honey.

"All of a sudden people started to say, 'Shit, the food is so good today,'" remembers Puck. Actress Suzanne Pleshette, Bob Newhart's husky-throated first TV wife, came into the kitchen swooning over a salad. Producer Larry Spangler burst in one day, crying, "Fuck! Fuck! Fuck! The food is *so* good." Before long, say both Puck and Terrail, the chef had become a minority partner, to the tune of roughly 10 percent.

The resourceful Puck made the most of what ingredients were available in the pre-enlightened food days of 1970s Los Angeles. Mark Peel, a San Gabriel Valley native who was hired by Terrail as

* Industry shorthand for "walk-in refrigerator."

a prep cook and was quickly promoted by Puck, remembers, "Wolfgang became somewhat famous for beurre blanc with fresh tarragon. He loved using fresh tarragon all over the place. And the reason he loved using fresh tarragon was because it was really the only fresh herb you could get other than parsley. It wasn't that he discovered tarragon, was in love with tarragon. There was one place out near Pomona that was growing it." Peel was still in school out that way and Puck tasked him with exploring what else the tarragon farmers might grow for him, but the farmers only spoke Chinese and Japanese, so the mission was a failure.

Peel vividly remembers Puck's early repertoire such as a potpie-like sweetbread dish, a duck in two courses, leg of lamb *en croûte*, and fish *en croûte*, which he eventually learned were borrowed from Puck's stints overseas. "It was all straight from Baumanière," says Peel. "But it was a revelation for Los Angeles."

Puck wasn't a kitchen screamer, which he says was trained out of him at Maxim's, where it wasn't tolerated. But he could be stubborn with Terrail and his customers. Freed to cook as he desired, he wasn't in the mood to make concessions. "I was very tough. If somebody wanted their steak well done, I told them to eat the chicken."

Word spread quickly, and Ma Maison was on fire. Cue the montage: Terrail was hosting a who's who of the day: Burt Reynolds, Sylvester Stallone, Johnny Carson, Elizabeth Taylor, Frank Sinatra. In time, film legend Orson Welles would lunch there daily; Carson's *Tonight Show* sidekick Ed McMahon would become a constant presence, dropping by on his way to Burbank every morning to hang out in the office, sit at Terrail's desk, and make phone calls. The restaurant became a hub for openings, gatherings, private-room celebrations, and rituals like a waiters' race based on a Bastille Day tradition in France. Anything could happen at Ma Maison, like the Friday afternoon when opera soprano Carol Neblett burst into an aria, or the night David Bowie bought out the place and a paparazzo leaped from roof to roof along Melrose until he could get a shot of the rock star, in violation of the restaurant's privacy policy; Terrail smashed his camera. All along, Terrail milked the glamour, directing his valets to park Rolls-Royces, sometimes dozens of them, closest to the entrance. The restaurant was also among the very first to employ an unlisted number, although Terrail insists it was only to avoid a crush of "men in leisure suits" after an anticipated *People* magazine article. (The story was delayed so long that it was revised to mention the detail.) He also found himself welcomed into local French hospitality royalty, participating in a weekly Tuesday meeting among the owners of other well-regarded restaurants that had opened within a few years of each other—Bernard's, L'Ermitage, Le Dome, Le St. Germain, and L'Orangerie—at which trends, charities, opportunities, and concerns were bandied about.

To describe the food at Ma Maison, Terrail began employing a variation on *nouvelle cuisine: California nouvelle cuisine.* "I think we were the first people to use the term," he says. "Probably in 1976. I think at that time in France they were referring to *nouvelle cuisine,* and then Roger Vergé came out with the term *cuisine of the South.** So we kind of bastardized both of them and did *California nouvelle* because we wanted to be nouvelle and we also wanted to be California and we also wanted to be the South." To him, the phrase meant baby vegetables, local products, and minimalist presentations. There was also a lightness that suited the Hollywood lifestyle: "In L.A. they're very health conscious. At lunch it was the warm lobster salad, the chicken salad—a lot of salads. Dinner we went heavier."

To obtain more parking, Terrail bought three buildings adjacent to Ma Maison—rented one out to a gallery, turned another into a jewelry store for his mother, and converted the third into a cooking school, Ma Cuisine.† He and Puck imported nouvelle cuisine head-

---

* Actually, *cuisine du soleil*, or cuisine of the sun.

† In time, as he and Puck became too busy to manage Ma Cuisine, Terrail handed the running of the school over to Judy Gethers, whose family owned Ratner's restaurant in New York City.

liners, American icons such as Julia Child and an about-to-ascend Martha Stewart, as well as other chefs from around town who were famous or getting there, such as Ken Frank and Jonathan Waxman.

Puck wasn't born in the United States, but set the stage for much of what would happen to his profession in his adopted country, starting with his kitchen at Ma Maison, which began attracting young American talent, many of whom were enjoying a backroom version of the fun times in the dining room. Susan Feniger, a Culinary Institute of America grad, remembers it as "just sort of this wild time. Most of the waiters were French and we would be doing things, like at four o'clock in the afternoon, we might go upstairs and have a glass of wine and hang out. It was just one of those things that doesn't happen anymore, sitting around and having a glass of wine at the end of the shift. It was such a cool time, because you'd be cooking at lunch for Orson Welles, Paul Newman, Jane Fonda. You knew who was in the restaurant. It was definitely star-studded. I'm still starstruck. I had just moved from Chicago, and seeing all of these people that I'd seen on movies and TV was mind-boggling. And we were partying at that time. Jesus Christ. We'd finish our shift at eleven, we'd all be going out to Moustache Café and party all night long. That was the late seventies, the days of lots of pot, and lots of coke, and lots of drugs, and we would party all night and I'd come back into work at seven in the morning."

Despite the Dickensian dichotomy of their upbringings, Terrail and Puck had much in common: lost boys, far from home, with links to three-star French restaurants, and an arrogant streak. Both had at one time in their lives contemplated or at least been low enough to reflect on suicide; both had been uncomfortable enough with their true selves to take on other identities with L.A. women.

But one was living off the other. Terrail's star was ascending; Puck was the dutiful soldier, thanklessly toiling away, unknown to many—if not most—of the customers. (In Terrail's defense, this was common practice.) And even if Puck did crave the spotlight, some say he wasn't ready for it. Remembers Jannis Swerman, who worked for Puck in the front of the house in the 1980s: "Donald Sutherland ate there all the time. And Patrick came in to say that Donald Sutherland wanted to meet the chef. Wolfgang came out, and his English wasn't very good then. He stood there and he said, 'Hello.' And then he walked away. That was it. It was very, very awkward." (Puck chalks that and other encounters up to an innate shyness that he's more than overcome. "I don't think my English was that bad," he says. "I didn't know what to tell them. *How are you? How is your family?* They are private people and I don't want to ask them that. If I knew what movie they were in, it was okay. If I knew what they were interested in, like I remember later on I met Paul Newman in London and I knew he was into racecar driving, and I love racecars, so we talked for three hours. But if somebody's not outgoing right away, asking *you* questions, I didn't know what to tell them.")

More vexing was the economics. Puck says the restaurant was grossing $18,000 a month when he arrived; now—thanks to his cooking—it was pulling down $350,000 monthly. And there was something else: "What bothered me with Patrick was that he didn't trust me," says Puck. "When he left on vacation or somewhere, he did not let me sign the checks. I was supposed to be his partner, even a minority one, eight or ten percent or whatever it was. He had the maître d' sign the checks. It annoyed me so much, but I said, 'Okay, it doesn't really matter.' Then I ordered Villeroy & Boch plates, like $5,000 or $3,000 worth. He was so upset. *What do we need these plates for?* 'Because I don't want to have this ugly plate and have my food on it.'"

Terrail feels Puck got plenty out of the arrangement: "I was the key person who transacted making a chef a star," he declares. He also claims to have put Puck's name on the menu (unheard of at the time). Some customers would disagree with his characterization. Marcia Nasatir, a United Artists executive during the Mike Medavoy era, who lunched weekly at Ma Maison with the studio chief, says, "I never knew there was a Wolfgang." Terrail also claims to have been the first person to put Puck on television, featuring him on his local cable show *Dining with Patrick Terrail*, produced by sitcom revolutionary Norman Lear. Each episode featured some travelogue footage from Terrail's adventures, a celebrity interview (for example, Suzanne Pleshette, Ed McMahon, Orson Welles), and a recipe: "Wolfgang would do the cooking, and I would explain what he was doing because he couldn't speak English."

"I FELT LIKE AN IDIOT."

"Everybody remembers history differently," says Puck today. We're having coffee in the bar of his preferred Midtown Manhattan hotel. He's sixty-six years old, in New York City for one night only, to participate in the annual Citymeals on Wheels benefit at Rockefeller Center, and he's making the most of his twenty-four hours in Manhattan. He touched down midmorning, ran an errand in Brooklyn, then checked up on the site of Cut, an outpost of his steakhouse concept, in construction at the time and, after all these years, his first Gotham restaurant.

When it comes to Puck and Terrail, he's not kidding about different memories. Those Villeroy & Boch plates Puck bought? Terrail says he purchased them of his own volition as part of the upgrade undertaken when Puck came on board, but Mark Peel shares Puck's recollection: "They only got good china ultimately when Patrick went on vacation and Wolfgang took it upon himself and bought all new china so when Patrick came back it had already been used. Couldn't return it." Remember how somebody at Maxim's gave Terrail Puck's name? Puck says Scott Miller, a Ma Maison cook he had once fired in Indianapolis, actually connected the two. And there's plenty more where those came from.

It's taken years to land this interview, eventually requiring an introduction from a chef contemporary. When I finally shake hands with Puck, he's every bit as affable as he's been described to me over the years; en route to our banquette, he lights up the place, shaking hands with all the busboys and bartenders, who know him from previous stays. The welcome is an apt reflection of Puck's place in the industry: Nobody, it seems, has a bad word to say about him, and he's managed to keep a team of talented chefs and administrators in his orbit for decades. The next day, he tells me, he'll be jetting back to California. At week's end, he's headed to Florida, then to the Far East. The roughly half dozen espressos he knocks back during our time together only enhance his aura of inexhaustibility. Toward the end of our meeting, his son Byron, an aspiring chef and student at Cornell University's School of Hotel Administration (yes, Terrail's alma mater), drops by. How sweet it must be for Puck to encourage a young cook in the family, given the derision with which his own culinary ambitions were met. He himself plans to go back to school: "I'm going to go to Harvard for a three-year period for about a month each year," he tells me. "To learn, with a group of CEOs from different places."

Puck wears a dark, exquisitely tailored suit with no tie. I don't know what he's worth personally, but his companies—which own and operate restaurants and retail food-service concessions and a catering operation; produce supermarket products including a line of frozen pizzas; and manufacture cookware and other equipment—generate hundreds of millions of dollars *annually*. He's completely unaffected and perfectly engaged. "I love the unpredictable," he says. "When I go to one of our restaurants, I say, 'Make me something I never had.' And if they don't and the chef says, 'Why don't you come visit?' I say, 'Because you always make me the same old shit.' I love change and always have."

How in the world do you reconcile this confident, impossibly successful, preternaturally positive mogul with that kid standing on the bridge in Villach, with the young cook being exploited by Terrail, whose benevolent memories are alternate-universe versions of Puck's? Yes, he went on *Dining with Patrick Terrail*, says Puck, and yes, Terrail did the talking, but Puck feels he could have performed just fine. "I hated it, because I couldn't talk. I felt like an idiot: I was cooking and he was explaining."

Puck also believes Terrail went out of his way to deny him other opportunities: "When *Los Angeles* magazine was doing Orson Welles for the cover of the dining guide, they were supposed to take a picture of Orson Welles, me, and Patrick. And Patrick gave me two days off when they were shooting. I think he never admitted it was on purpose."

Then there was the time Dinah Shore, hostess of *Dinah!*, a syndicated daytime television show, asked Puck why he never came on her program. Puck told her all she had to do was invite him.

"Patrick, that son of a bitch!" said Shore. "He said you don't want to do TV."

"THE ELECTRICITY IN THE ROOM JUST WENT STRAIGHT UP."

The same year that Wolfgang Puck arrived in Los Angeles, a brash, moneyed maverick from the East Coast blew into town. But unlike Puck, who came for work and was happy to do it anonymously, Michael McCarty parachuted in with big dreams and the confidence, sense of entitlement, and vision to realize them.

McCarty grew up in Briarcliff Manor, New York, a Westchester suburb about thirty miles north of New York City, in what he describes as a *Mad Men* existence: dad was a GE exec; mom raised the kids; the family summered near Watch Hill, Rhode Island. Westchester was bereft of quality restaurants, so McCarty's entertaining instincts were founded on the stream of parties thrown by his family and their friends, on accessible food, and the conviviality of the table.

At sixteen, McCarty—already smitten with gastronomy—spent his junior year of high school in Brittany, cementing his decision to pursue a life in hospitality. He learned to cook at Le Cordon Bleu in Paris, then like Terrail matriculated at the Cornell University School of Hotel Administration, before lighting out for Colorado, where he earned BAs in business and art of gastronomy from the University of Colorado, Boulder.

McCarty loved food, but was fascinated as well by hospitality. In particular, he was mesmerized by front-of-house men, the impresarios charged with ensuring everybody's good time, floating amongst the tables, monitoring comfort levels, regaling guests with a quick story. He often relives a September 1969 dinner at Laurent, in Midtown Manhattan, the night before he decamped for the Andover-Exeter School Year Abroad at the University of Rennes in Brittany: "In walks the owner to work the floor, and it was like a dimmer, the electricity in the room just went straight up," says McCarty. "It got more intense, people got more excited, it was a very exciting moment, and it was very reminiscent of the feeling I felt as I watched my parents entertain." McCarty calls the dinner an epiphany, centered on the notion of "throwing a party every night and having [the customers] pay for it."

In December 1975, after his year in Europe and time in Denver, where he also consulted and taught cooking classes, McCarty moved to Los Angeles, which he considered a corrective to the snootiness of his home region and that other West Coast food town up north: "San Francisco abhorred Sodom and Gomorrah (L.A.). San Francisco was like an East Coast, Boston, New York kind of a town. Very preppy. Very uptight. Very sophisticated in their minds. L.A. was the exact opposite. It was full metal jacket. It was crazy. Los Angeles really didn't start until '65, culturally speaking. So it was always considered a backwater by Northern California and everyone else. La-La Land."

Like Terrail before him, McCarty rang up Lois Dwan, asked her to point him toward the epicenter of Los Angeles dining. She named Jean Bertranou, chef-owner of L'Ermitage on North La Cienega Boulevard. McCarty beelined for West Hollywood, introduced himself to Bertranou, hung around L'Ermitage, and before long the two had become best of friends and a bit of an odd couple: American McCarty in his early twenties, a well-dressed, energetic prepster eager to make his dent in the universe; Bertranou in his late forties, French, and established. He's also one of the figures in this story who was doubly cursed, historically speaking—Bertranou died at age fifty from brain cancer, long before the Google era, and so faded away, unable to extend and promote his legacy. But for anybody who cooked professionally in Los Angeles in the 1970s, he was a barrier breaker and guiding light.

"L'Ermitage was the most important restaurant to open in California in the seventies, *period*," says Ken Frank, one of the first young Americans to chef around Los Angeles during that decade, and whose fate would soon intersect with McCarty's. "Bertranou was the first chef that opened a restaurant that was a chef's restaurant with a personalized menu that reflected his style of cooking," says Frank. "He was the first one to embrace nouvelle cuisine, the first one to bring seeds from France and plant real haricots verts instead of settling for little tiny green beans that were just picked early. He tried to breed ducks that would be the right ducks. He was flying in fresh fish from France, damn the price. He invited Bocuse and Vergé to come cook at L'Ermitage and he inspired a whole generation of cooks."

"He was the benchmark," says Peel.

Even Puck looked up to Bertranou, whom—though less famous than, say, André Soltner at Lutèce in New York City or Jean Banchet at Le Français outside Chicago—he considered the best chef working in the United States at the time. "Jean Banchet was on the cover of *Bon Appétit* magazine and stuff like that, and Jean Bertranou never got that because he was shy, maybe? Maybe it was not the right time. I think he was a little early, too, in the seventies."

"'This was the revolution," says John Sedlar, a young cook from Santa Fe, New Mexico, who worked for Bertranou at L'Ermitage, and was impressed by his devotion to not only nouvelle cuisine but also state-of-the-art kitchen technology, which could be expensive, such as a refrigerated marble tabletop or a $3,000 sorbet machine. "Preposterous! *You're going to spend $3,000 to turn your sorbets? Do you really need a refrigerated marble tabletop?* He was buying wines first growth, and futures where you had all the first growth, the Haut-Brions, the Margaux, the Latours, all six cases deep. He got me in a lot of trouble because he would change his china with the season. When I began working there, he had the basket pattern,[*] which was very nouvelle. I was garde-manger[†] and I had colorful fruits and lettuces, and the most magnificent red salmon would go on these. They were gorgeous, and they were geometric and architectural, and they had to be placed a certain way. And he had silver cassoulets lined up above the pickup pass-through."

In the incestuous L.A. chef community of the time, McCarty's fast friendship with Bertranou rubbed some people, like Ken Frank, the wrong way. "McCarty was like a barnacle at L'Ermitage," says Frank. (McCarty replies: "I take umbrage at that. Jean and I were good friends and fifty-fifty partners in our company, Mad Ducks, Inc.")

"BEING FROM CALIFORNIA, RATHER THAN FRENCH, I DIDN'T HAVE TO BE THAT WAY."

When Bruce Marder first saw the space that would become home to his West Beach Cafe, he took it as a sign. The restaurant there had

---

[*]   Villeroy & Boch produced a "basket weave" plate that was a sensation in nouvelle cuisine restaurants in the United States at this time.

[†]   The cook charged with cold preparations such as salads.

been Casablanca Café des Artistes, a connection to his formative days in Morocco, where he'd spent that fateful Christmas in 1972.

After Europe, Marder began his formal education under chef John Snowden at Dumas Père School of French Cooking near Chicago, Illinois, where he developed his sense of where food was headed: "Well, first of all, being from California, rather than French, I didn't have to be that way," says Marder of the classic French style. "I could do whatever I wanted. But I picked a certain part of that. Classic French cooking, in reality, is based upon serving a lot of people versus serving a person. You walk into wherever they ate in the castle and they were serving everybody. That's where roux* came from and all of that. Extending everything out in flavor. This is where I kind of got the realization: You cook a steak, you take it out of the pan, you put some shallots and red wine in, you deglaze the pan, you put some butter in, and you pour it over the steak, or you can put a little stock in. But essentially you're eliminating this mass thing and you're cooking to order. If you think about it, that's basically what ended up being nouvelle cuisine, or the beginning of it. You can poach a piece of fish in some white wine, put a little cream in, reduce the cream, and pour it over the fish. That was the beginning of all the froufrou nouvelle stuff. And then I just decided that I didn't need to make sauces and whatever it is. And not knowing anything about anything, I just decided that was the best way to go."[†‡]

Marder returned to L.A., worked a year and a half at the Beverly Hills Hotel, then did a brief stint at L'Ermitage, where his time was cut short when some fellow cooks sabotaged him. He worked

---

* A thickening agent made from equal parts butter and flour.

† In other interviews, Marder has referred to this as "sauté-reduction cooking."

‡ In their book *Cooking the Nouvelle Cuisine in America*, authors Michèle Urvater and David Liederman observe that pre–nouvelle cuisine, sauces "which are an essential part of *haute cuisine*, were being treated with cavalier contempt . . . sometimes heavily laden with flour to give them a body they did not have on their own, enabling them to stand for hours in a steam table without separating."

as a private chef to Richard Perry, album producer for Carly Simon, Barbra Streisand, and others, then took over the kitchen at Carol Lorenz's restaurant Fatherees on Abbot Kinney Boulevard in Venice, but found the rest of the team unserious, left, then returned when Lorenz begged him to come back. They changed the name of the restaurant to Café California and Marder began cooking according to his "sauté-reduction" principle, doing double duty as chef and waiter. He made his customers an offer some found irresistible: If they had any special requests, he'd happily accommodate them. There were takers, like the man who told him he'd return the next night if Marder would make him veal scaloppine. He also staged special dinners, like an Indian feast complete with sitar player, only rather than cooking, say, lamb in vindaloo sauce, he spooned the sauce *over* a rack of lamb. "That's like nouvelle cuisine, really," says Marder. "It's really fucking around with food."

Marder grew tired of partnering with Lorenz. "She wanted to put yellow-checkered tablecloths and place mats on the table," he said. "She always wore muumuus, homemade dresses, things like that. It wasn't working for me." When he told her he wanted to strike out on his own, she was infuriated and bought him out. He set his sights on Venice, desolate at the time, where real estate was dirt cheap. He raised $25,000 in one day from artists and other friends and became partners with Werner Scharff, a German immigrant who owned the Casablanca space, a block from the sands of Venice Beach.

Marder didn't have much to work with. The space was little more than a cinder-block shoebox with gray carpet, so he started borrowing art from whomever he could. Venice was an art hub, with the L.A. Louver gallery just across North Venice Boulevard. Before long, Marder was ensconced in the scene, palling around with architects, hiring a curator for the restaurant, displaying early Jean-Michel Basquiat, Keith Haring, and Donald Judd on the walls. All of this—the minimalist space, modern artwork, and Marder's stripped-down menu—was groundbreaking, and the West Beach drew a devoted following, for both the regular menu and his Mexican breakfast (he also integrated his take on Mexican dishes into the main menu on "Mexican Monday" nights).* Says Kazuto Matsusaka, who cooked for Puck at Ma Maison, "[Marder] was an oddball. He never blended into the chef circle. But he's a very interesting guy. He does it his way and he can get away with it. All the restaurant people used to go there because he was doing something different."

"Oh my God. The best Mexican breakfast ever," recalls Evan Kleiman. "It was just really clear, clean, vibrant flavors. There was no muddiness. There were no extraneous sauces. There was a lot of grilling. Bruce was looking more south. Everybody went. There was a real chile for the chile relleno. It wasn't a canned Ortega chile. Everything about that place was notable. And also the light. The fact that it's also a period of time where the architecture is starting to change, so instead of having these restaurants where you walk in through a door and you're in a completely dark space, very continental, very European, all of a sudden now things are starting to be created for the life we live in California. So there's glass. And especially West Beach. I mean, he's on the beach. So you'd go there on a Sunday morning and there would be light wood and the light would be streaming in and you'd have an amazing cup of coffee and just a killer breakfast. And you would feel like you were at the center of some brand-new thing."

"It was the only truly local restaurant of any interest," says filmmaker Tony Bill, producer of *The Sting*, who went on to open the Venice restaurant 72 Market Street in partnership with comic actor Dudley Moore, with former West Beach cook Leonard Schwartz as chef. "Anything else in Venice that I can remember was cookie cutter; it was so good that it didn't wear out its welcome. It wasn't stuffy, and it was personable."

---

* Marder would go on to open Rebecca's, a Mexican restaurant, just down the block from West Beach Cafe, and stunningly designed by architect Frank Gehry.

"He wasn't flashy, his food was just good, it was just tasty," says
Sedlar. "If it'd be a bean puree for huevos rancheros in the morning, it was a very good bean puree with good cooked eggs and some
good salsas that his dishwasher probably made. Bruce was one of
the first chefs to ever serve a tortilla in an upscale restaurant. These
tortillas came and it was like, *Tortillas? In this übercool Hollywood-
crowd, high-quality restaurant?* It threw me. And then all of a sudden
I had a duck taco there and nobody had served a duck taco. Bruce
has a very intuitive sense about food and cooking, and it was always
very, very good."

"IT WAS LIKE A CAPER MOVIE."

Another early and devoted customer of West Beach Cafe was
Michael McCarty, who frequented lunch when there was a buffet
served at the bar. After about two years of California and Bertranou,
the restaurant muse had descended on McCarty, who envisioned a
place of his own—Michael's—and his quest for the right space kept
"creeping west," until he ended up in Santa Monica, "a ghost town"
in those days, and The Brigadoon, a shuttered Third Street bunga-
low bar in a 1930s pink stucco house. McCarty planned to create a
restaurant unlike any other: alive with flower arrangements, half-
outdoors to emphasize the California climate. It would be a stark
contrast to West Beach Cafe with one exception: He had by this
time met and married artist Kim Lieberman and planned to adorn
his restaurant with artwork, which also made him a regular at L.A.
Louver.

Though he was an unabashed Francophile, McCarty was hell-
bent on creating a "modern American" restaurant rather than an "old
French" one. Michael's would have Americans in the kitchen and on
the service floor, and the food would sing with an American spirit.

Hoping to avoid partners, McCarty approached twelve banks for a Small Business Administration loan, got turned down by eleven. At the twelfth, he found a sympathetic food enthusiast loan officer who requested the recipes that would produce the dishes in McCarty's sample menus. McCarty pointed him to the best purveyors in town, became his cooking coach, wined and dined him at the reigning French restaurants, introduced him to Bertranou. The bank was just two blocks from The Brigadoon and McCarty brought him there as part of the seduction, painting a verbal picture of his fantasy restaurant. The bank turned down the application, citing the vicissitudes of the hospitality industry, but McCarty begged his go-between to replead his case. Miraculously, he came back with a $275,000 loan.

Construction began in the early fall of 1978. As the restaurant was spruced up, the garden planted, the walls painted a rosy cream, McCarty plotted every detail. Friend Jerry Magnin, whose family owned the I. Magnin stores, put him onto Ralph Lauren, still relatively unknown (though he had designed the costumes for the 1974 film version of *The Great Gatsby*). At Magnin's Rodeo Drive boutique, McCarty put together pink and green ensembles for the service team, a clean break from tuxedos—a literal shift from black-and-white to color.

McCarty, only in his midtwenties, was made for Los Angeles. Like the producers in his midst, he was brimming with outside-the-box ideas and the pluck and tenaciousness to realize them. He, too, adored the Villeroy & Boch basket weave plate favored by Bertranou, but not for the pattern. It was the *size*—twelve inches, as opposed to the standard nine-inch plate available in the States—the perfect, audacious frame for the food he had in mind. To get it, he traveled to France, asked Villeroy & Boch to sell him the plates before decaling them. They refused because the decals covered imperfections, enabling them to use almost every plate they manufactured. McCarty explained that he didn't care. He'd even take

the most imperfect plates; the food, with the sauce *under* the protein after the example of nouvelle cuisine, would mask any flaws.
Eventually a deal was struck. "There are hundreds of those kinds
of stories about this restaurant," says McCarty. (His wine director,
Phil Reich, was instrumental in developing what most believe was
the industry's first computerized wine inventory system, and Mc-
Carty was also among the first to institute a tip pool that included
the kitchen.)

Of course, to make the food, McCarty needed cooks. Word of
the project spread so quickly through the small society of young
American whisks that while he was sleuthing out contact information for rising West Coast talent, they were hearing about him,
showing up like mercenaries at his door. McCarty admits that his
memory may be seventies-impaired, but remembers the staffing up
as a *Dirty Dozen*–type affair. "It was like a caper movie," he says.
"People just sort of walked through the door. Even though I didn't
know any of these guys, I knew it was right. I got a vibe that said
yeah, yeah. They were exactly who I was looking for. Four Americans
who wanted to be cooks, wanted to be chefs, didn't want to do what
they did wherever they had worked, for the Frenchies."

When a young bohemian named Jonathan Waxman, fresh
from a stint at Chez Panisse and en route to New York City with
dreams of working for André Soltner at Lutèce, showed up at his
job site, McCarty exclaimed, "I have been looking for you." Seeking candidates, McCarty had called La Varenne culinary school in
Paris, where Waxman had trained, and they had coughed up his
name. McCarty enlisted him as a sous chef. Mark Peel, tipped off
to the opportunity by a Ma Maison bartender, joined the squad
as broiler man. There were also Billy Pflug and pastry chef Jimmy
Brinkley, who had been at L'Ermitage. And McCarty also recruited
an old pal from his Cordon Bleu days, Brit Sally Clarke.

McCarty hired Ken Frank as head chef, though he remembers
fellow restaurateurs waving him off. "He had a notorious reputation

for getting into fights all the time," says McCarty. "Everybody said, 'Don't even talk about it with him, it's a waste of time, he's just a problem, blah, blah, blah, and he only wants to do his stuff.'" McCarty pursued Frank anyway because he had a utopian vision of the key kitchen staff collaborating on the menu, which he refers to today as "the laboratory."

"I believed that assembling a team was the only way we could do this correctly," he says.

Frank was a controversial character in 1970s L.A., but also an unmistakable talent with greater chops than his American contemporaries because he had committed to the pro kitchen earlier than most. A child of the San Gabriel Valley, east of Los Angeles, Frank was the oldest of five children in a family with farming and food roots: His paternal grandfather owned a butcher shop; his maternal one, a dairy business. There were no great cooks in the house, but everybody prized good ingredients. Even as a kid, Frank was drawn to the kitchen: He made flapjacks, grew obsessed with perfecting the art of flipping the disks in the air; grilled burgers by age ten; improvised pizzas with bread, grated mozzarella, and ketchup.

His father, a teacher, won a grant that enabled him to work in Europe for two years, so he relocated the family to Yvoire, a fishing village on the French side of Lake Geneva. Frank went to a local school, hooked up with a French girlfriend, and fell in love with French food. Even at school, lunches were sophisticated, if rustic: stews, sausages, roasts, fresh pasta, an occasional cheese course. He turned sixteen there, had zero interest in returning to California and "seven hamburgers a week." His father told him if he could find a family to host him, and a job, he could stick around. This is how it began in this transformative era. Though he couldn't have known where it would lead, Frank secured both that very day, and was on his way. He started as a dishwasher in a local hotel, then moved to the kitchen. "I learned kitchen French, learned some knife skills, and learned how to work my ass off," he says. Back in the States, he landed a job in the kitchen of a local ski resort, earning the nickname "Frenchie," then toggled back and forth between France and Pasadena, where the chef at Chez Paul restaurant took him under his wing.

Even after all of that, stuck in the tractor beam of conventional thinking, he matriculated at UC Irvine, on a premed pathway, but within three months he was miserable. "I realized I hated school. I hated premed. I hated the kids who wanted to be doctors and be rich. But I was really liking this cooking thing." So Frank moved to L.A. intent on becoming nothing less than the first great American chef, a Yankee Doodle Paul Bocuse. In this way Frank was prescient, leapfrogging the college and backpacking steps undertaken by many contemporaries before finding the vision or courage to dive headlong into the kitchen. He cooked at Ambrosia, a French restaurant in Orange County's Newport Beach, then Perino's, also in Newport Beach, then La Chaumière, where Bertranou had worked before L'Ermitage, though Frank never worked for the budding legend. In 1976, at twenty-one, he assumed command of his own kitchen for the first time at the archly named La Guillotine. He became the city's first famous homegrown toque of the nouvelle era, partially on the strength of two compositions that broke away from the Escoffier repertoire (duck with apples, and a sweetbreads dish)—such a rare move that the menu required asterisks alongside the dish names; a footnote explained to confused diners that those entrees were the chef's original compositions.

Frank's food also evolved at Club Élysée, where he worked immediately after La Guillotine, in part thanks to actor Gene Wilder, on top of his game in fellow food-fan Mel Brooks's *Blazing Saddles* and *Young Frankenstein*. "You know, Ken, your food is so good, you shouldn't put the same vegetables with every dish," Wilder told him one day. "You should really figure out what vegetables go best with each dish and do something specific to each plate."

Frank decided that Wilder was right. "That was when I moved

the protein to the center of the plate and started doing vegetables that were specific to each dish," he says.

In addition to his nationality, youth, and talent, Frank became known as a sort of beta version of the rebel rock-and-roll chef that would soon become emblematic. Wrote Ruth Reichl in the *Los Angeles Times*: "He bragged about driving his Lotus under garage gates at a cool 50 m.p.h., bought his pastry weights in head shops and devoured sushi while others still shuddered at the sight of raw fish. He was the bad boy of the kitchen brigade." He earned the nickname "The Sinatra of the Stockpots," and loved every notorious second of it. "It was awesome," says Frank. "I was driving a Lotus. I was making good money. I was meeting famous people all the time. People were writing great things about me in the newspaper. It's not any healthier for me than it is for Lindsay Lohan or Miley Cyrus. When you're in your early twenties that kind of attention goes to your head; there's just no two ways about it. I don't regret it. It is what it is, but you have to grow out of it." Frank sums up his 1970s attitude as: "*I'm the chef. I'm doing things my way. Fuck you.*"

"I am not an asshole," says Frank today. "But I used to be. I made Gordon Ramsay seem like a nice guy."

Frank was famous, but he wasn't popular. He blames his enfant terrible reputation on an article published after he departed La Guillotine, where he had unsuccessfully lobbied the owners to reduce the number of covers (meals served) so he could cook more consistent food. As a parting shot, he gave an interview to Bruce David Colen of *Los Angeles* magazine, in which he discussed his "heartburn with the restaurant status quo in L.A., my reasons for leaving, my passion for doing it my way, which is quality and ingredient-driven or I'm not interested. I don't just need the money. But I made the mistake of talking about labor practices and truth-in-menu practices—calling things fresh when they were frozen. Or, in more blatant cases, actually substituting things and not being honest about it, and the public really didn't know any better. 'House-made' when it wasn't, or restaurants would soak pork in milk and try to pass it off as veal because it was cheaper. Never any places where I had worked but I knew of it. It was rampant. Fresh-caught today? Go get another one out of the freezer. Fresh duck? It was all frozen, with very, very few exceptions. The restaurant industry was pretty dishonest; not all of them, but there was a lot of that. That made me a lot of enemies in the restaurant business, especially those that I had talked about for their unsavory practices. And that's where a lot of the enfant terrible came from, my willingness to speak out against what I saw as terrible wrongs.'"*

There was another reason Frank believes the establishment had their knives out for him, one that foretold the coming power shift: "The path I was advocating, which was *chef-driven* restaurants . . ."

"*CHEF* IN FRENCH MEANS *THE CHIEF*. AND THAT I WAS. I WILL ALWAYS BE THAT."

When Frank came on board, McCarty already had a direction in mind for the Michael's menu. According to Frank, "It was the ingredients and the fact that it was very much French food at the time but in English with local ingredients. The first menu was very much what Michael wanted it to be. He had some young chefs that he had met in Paris that he idolized that he brought some dishes from. A lot of it was from L'Ermitage. Some of it was from me. The opening menu was pretty well written by Michael and me—mostly by Michael—because he knew what he wanted it to be and I was okay with it."

---

* While the article does quote Frank's reasons for leaving La Guillotine, it does not explicitly detail his opinions of dishonesty about ingredients throughout the industry.

In the months before Michael's opened, the laboratory mind-set was in full flow: The kitchen crew tasted samples from various fish and meat purveyors, tested recipes, and conferred with Mc-Carty. In the background, a young Ruth Reichl, reporting for *New West* magazine, stood with notebook and pen, documenting the goings-on. (Construction was so prolonged, she ended up spending about a year on the story.)* McCarty owned a house in Malibu where he, Reich, Waxman, and Clarke lived. "It was crazy," says McCarty. "We would use Waxman's van to go to work every day. And right at the same month that we opened the restaurant, the Pacific Coast Highway closed. A huge landslide. It was even funnier because you would drive to one end of the slide, get out of the car. I'd put mine on the other side of the slide. We would all walk through the slide on the PCH and get in the van and go to work in Jonathan's crazy van."

Today, McCarty freely admits that while the menu was largely his creation, he never worked on the line during service. "I didn't want to be in the kitchen, be the fucking chef on the line. Ever." Yet in a famous preopening black-and-white photograph circulated by publicist Burks Hamner, McCarty is grouped along with Frank, Peel, and Waxman, in full kitchen regalia.†

---

* I've often wondered why so much of the general public assumes that the chef and food revolutions of the 1970s and 1980s belong exclusively to California. A theory: Reichl's coverage of the key players in *New West* magazine (often assigned by Colman Andrews) and the *Los Angeles Times* profiled chefs and restaurateurs in a way that's common today, but was prescient at the time, showing these characters in ways that nobody thought to in other cities. Imagine if John McPhee's "Brigade de Cuisine" piece in *The New Yorker*, described in the next chapter, were one of a series of such pieces rather than a one-off, and what the effect of that balance might have been. "Ruth made everything happen," says Evan Kleiman.

† Of the photograph, featured on the cover of this book, Peel says, "It looks like The Band. Michael looks just like Mick Jagger. And Ken Frank looks like very early Eric Clapton. I'm the bass player nobody can quite remember the name of. Jonathan Waxman looks like the drummer that is going to overdose in a few weeks."

There are those, like veteran L.A. diners Manny and Wil-lette Klausner, who don't recall Michael selling himself as the chef, but some Michael's veterans make a point of telling me he didn't cook—as if righting the historical record, some explicitly so. "For so many years, he called himself the chef," says Peel. "When I was there for the first year and a half, Michael did not cook once. But I understand why he would want to do that."

"Michael, you should know, was never in the kitchen," volunteers Frank. (Reichl supports all of this: "He was not in the kitchen. I spent most of my time with Jonathan. I spent very little time with Ken. I don't know why. Jonathan was just really nice to me. Even though Ken was the chef, Jonathan was the one who seemed to be spending a lot of time playing around in the kitchen. Michael was dealing with the furniture, with the carpenters, with the digital guys, with supplying, but I never saw him do one thing in the kitchen.")

McCarty's take? "*Chef* in French means 'the chief.' And that I was. I will always be that."

McCarty doesn't volunteer this today, but Reichl remembered that he considered it a coup to have Frank on board, even as he—perhaps sensing the industry's ground shifting beneath his feet to-ward a chef-centric template—worried that the restaurant would become known as Ken Frank's place.

"I THINK HIS NAME SHOULD BE ABOVE MA MAISON."

Things had plateaued between Puck and Terrail at Ma Maison. Yet, were it not for a chance encounter between Puck and Barbara La-zaroff, a Bronx-born premed student, they might have lasted longer than they did.

Lazaroff, the middle child and only girl in her family, refers to her young self as a "hippy without the drugs." Nicknamed "The

Bohemian" by her mother, she dressed to her own beat, but liked to be in control. She attended Woodstock in 1969. "I remember *everything*. I didn't have a camera then. But the pictures are in my head. Everybody was *so* stoned."

She came to Los Angeles for love. The relationship cooled once she arrived, but she took to the city, especially the weather. "I was always a little sad in New York because I'm one of those people that is affected by lack of light," she says. "It's very hard for me because I'm a visual person. My house is full of color. I love gardens. I grew up very poor. I didn't have an opportunity to have any pets, gardens, or anything. I have four hundred rosebushes on the other side of the house, there from 1927. When they bloom, I'm in ecstasy. I love art. All of that."

Lazaroff wasn't immune to the wanderlust that connected her generation's dots, but couldn't afford to travel, so she settled for New York University, a microcosm of everything that turned her on, especially the arts and theater. When her mother learned that she had only applied to NYU, she chastised her, chasing her around with a rolled-up newspaper. "She never hit me, but she bopped me on the head: *How can you do this?*" Mama Lazaroff didn't yet realize her daughter's powers of self-realization: "I said, 'I'm getting in and I'm getting a scholarship!' And I did."

Lazaroff initially planned to study theater design at NYU. She took courses in puppetry, criticism, lighting design. She painted stages. She designed sets and did makeup. She even acted. But she switched to the more dependably lucrative field of medicine, in part to ensure she could finance a life of travel and adventure, continuing to study at NYU, then Hunter College, then Berkeley, then came to L.A. with plans to finish her studies and become a physician.

In L.A., Lazaroff belonged to a gym, lugging along a massive organic chemistry book and studying between sets. A statuesque strawberry-blond Frenchwoman, Gabrielle, found the Gilda Radner–like spectacle unbearably sad and invited Lazaroff to a private party at a local club. When a French gigolo art forger (Lazaroff's description) hit on her, she turned to his diminutive friend and asked him if he'd like to dance. It was Puck.

Breaking with his newly adopted MO, Puck revealed himself to Lazaroff as a chef, asked her if she liked to cook, and invited her to his class at Ma Cuisine. He was mid-demo when she arrived, late, and the sight of her caused him to drop his butter on the floor. Next, she came to lunch at Ma Maison decked out in a stretchy white suit and purple blouse but wouldn't let him hold her hand because she was still with her boyfriend. (Puck was technically still married at the time, to Marie France Trouillot, an old love from France who had joined him in L.A., but both relationships were on life support.)

Hand-holding or not, they entered into a courtship. Within a week and a half, Lazaroff was helping Puck write *Modern French Cooking for the American Kitchen*, a planned Ma Maison cookbook to be published by Houghton Mifflin. Presented with a rendering of the cover at a creative meeting, she insisted, "You know, I think his name should be above Ma Maison, because he's leaving Ma Maison. He's going to be more important than Ma Maison, and this is his book." Puck kicked her under the table. After the meeting, he fretted aloud that they wouldn't publish. "Oh, don't be silly," she told him. (Told the story, Reichl says: "I think that is a perfect example of the two of them then. She was just, *You are going to be famous and I'm going to make this happen any way I can.*")

Lazaroff was right: The book came out with Puck's name inscribed in script above, and larger than, the title. The subtitle, lodged beneath a David Hockney watercolor drawing of the restaurant, was *Recipes from the Cuisine of Ma Maison*. And Lazaroff was right about something else: By the time the book hit store shelves, Puck was gone from Ma Maison.

"YOU WEREN'T THERE IF YOU CAN REMEMBER IT."

Michael's opened in April 1979 to mixed reviews; *Los Angeles* magazine's Bruce David Colen savaged the restaurant, directing his rage primarily on McCarty, whom he found insufferably haughty and insincere on his first visit. When Reichl's *New West* piece broke, she quoted McCarty saying, "I'm not a fifty-year-old Frenchman who owns the restaurant and is mean." Referring to his kitchen team and why they came to him, he said, "They've all been working with these crusty old bastards who treat them like assholes and won't let them do anything creative." McCarty, fearful of offending Bertranou, called Colman Andrews demanding a retraction, but Reichl had it all on tape, so *New West* refused.

"Michael's was a very magical place," remembers John Sedlar, who checked it out with fellow L'Ermitage cook Roy Yamaguchi, who now presides over a chain of more than twenty Roy's restaurants around the United States. "It was brash and he was sassy and he had modern art and great wine. It was a party. It was youthful. Everything was European up until that time, and this was something *Californian*."

(Kleiman delineates the subtle differences between California native Marder and East Coast transplant McCarty: "They were both very, very attached to the whole art scene, but I saw Bruce as being more outsider, more edgy. Because the hippy thing has ended. The disco thing hasn't quite started yet. So there's this period of time where it's, like, who are the edgy people? Well, they're the artists. Michael's, that space was just so thought out and so slick and yet it had this huge patio in the middle of it. It had all this amazing art on the walls. It was filled with light. They were both very prescient at the time.")

For all the bonhomie in the dining room, behind the scenes tension between Frank and McCarty was growing. One early incident that rankled Frank had to do with a duck farm that McCarty said he and Bertranou had started in Acton, just north of the San Gabriel Mountains. McCarty promoted it in the press, including in the *New York Times*, but according to Frank, he misrepresented it.

"Michael is very loose with the truth," says Frank. "I remember sitting in an interview with Lois Dwan from the *Los Angeles Times* and Michael was telling her about the ducks he was raising, and the partnership and the farm, and it was just a flat-out lie. . . . They never succeeded in producing foie gras and they never succeeded in having a very viable duck farming operation. Michael would claim of course that he was a partner in this, and he would claim of course when we were at Michael's we were serving ducks that were grown on his farm, but in fact we were buying the same frozen ducks from Harvey Gussman at Guss Meat Company that Jean Bertranou was buying for L'Ermitage, which was a particularly good Pekin duck with a large breast; it was a particular breed from a particular farm that we all decided was the best."

When the two sat for an interview with *W*'s Mary Rourke, says Frank, McCarty spoke of an illegal restaurant he'd owned in Paris and was forced to close, and of how he longed to return to France and try again someday. "And of course, he had never owned a building in Paris, or had a restaurant in Paris," says Frank. (McCarty explains that he didn't *own* Xavier's, a Paris restaurant that today would be considered a "pop-up," operated in a friend's building, without permits, where he was the chef.)

Many interview subjects expressed skepticism about that duck farm, and Colen, in his *Los Angeles* magazine review of the restaurant, wrote: "McCarty *claims* [italics mine] to be partners with Bertranou in the duck farm the latter underwrote several years ago." To this day, McCarty resents Colen's implication that he wasn't partners with Bertranou, calling it "ridiculous," and adding "I can only tell you how much duck shit Jean and I shoveled." Terrail helpfully explained to me that he bought the ducks for Ma Maison, but that they were too small to use—but neither McCarty's involvement in the farm, its success in breeding usable ducks, nor McCarty's other possible acts of self-mythology seem to rankle anybody the way they do Frank. The prevailing affection for McCarty is summed up by Melvyn Master, a British-born wine expert, marketer, and restaurateur who knew McCarty in his Denver days: "Michael was a great marketing guy. He was passionate about food. He talked the talk. He was the real deal. There was a lot of BS to Michael but it was *genuine* BS, if you will."

Frank didn't share the charitable view of McCarty, nor did he socialize with him or the rest of the Michael's crowd at his Malibu house, which he found "incestuous."

"They'd ride to work together, go home together, stay up at night, get high, talk about food, and hang out," says Frank. "And I went home to my house after work."

Like Terrail and Puck, McCarty and Frank had much in common: both among the very few in their generation who committed early to a life in restaurants. And both were American, both Francophiles. But they couldn't get along, largely because both craved credit, and dominance. Another gem from Colen's review: "The official billing in the PR program notes read, 'Chef owner: Michael McCarty. Assisted by Ken Frank.' Given the egos of both men, I wonder how long that association will last. For the present, at least, McCarty seems content to do his mixing out front." McCarty denies it, but Frank says that he was eventually banned from the Michael's dining room because he knew so many customers from past gigs. (Similarly, Puck recalls that when he began to get over his shyness at Ma Maison, "If I talked to a customer, Patrick went right away there, too, to talk to them.")

Frank departed Michael's, after just four months, but deciphering the reason why is a quandary for which the word *Rashomon* seems to have been created.

Remembers Waxman: "After about two months of this, Ken goes, 'I don't want to be the head chef anymore; I want you to be the head chef. I am going to open my own restaurant but I can't afford to leave right now, so can I be the sous chef and you can be the head chef?' So we switched. And I became the head chef."

"That's a flat-out lie," says Frank. "A figment of his imagination. I got *fired* from Michael's because I was tired of taking shit and didn't take shit anymore and knew I had this other deal working. I got fired from Michael's and I can tell you the date. You can go look it up in the employment records. It was August 5. It was because Michael was charging us; he had a manager named Carl who was counting the number of espressos we drank in the kitchen so he could deduct the cost of the espressos from our paycheck and I said it was bullshit. If I'm working fourteen hours a day and you are going to charge me for the espresso I drink to stay up, *fuck you*. And I probably told it to him just like that.

"That is specifically what triggered it. But the restaurant was broke when it first opened and he missed a number of payrolls. He finally got them caught up because he was busy paying money for other things. He very much took advantage of his cooks. So I called him on that, too, and he didn't like that either."

"That I have no recollection of," laughs McCarty of the espresso charge. But he does offer: "It was a madhouse and if anything, so many fundamentals were broken in those days. For example, I would take them all out to dinner. We would have the wildest times. Everything about that first year, even the first *ten* years, are fundamental rules that you do not break between employer and employee. Lines were blurred. I mean, the stories in my restaurant at two o'clock in the morning, what was going on in the walk-ins. Remember, blow was in the eighties. Blow was a big deal, and a big deal amongst our clients. And it was a raucous time. So if you are going to hear different stories you are going to hear different stories. As they used to say, 'You weren't there if you can remember it,' and it was true." McCarty also blames Frank for terminating his tip pool. "A labor department person came to my restaurant a year plus one day after he left and said this complaint was filed saying that he didn't get paid what he was supposed to get paid. And I said, 'Well, I have a computerized payroll system; here's all of his records.'"

"I think Michael actually fired him after six months," says Peel, who doesn't remember Frank being banned from the dining room, but says that it rings true and imagines the espresso contretemps "was a symbol for Ken of diminished stature. Thinking about it now, with years behind me, thinking about it from Michael's perspective, I do understand that. Here he had put in a lot of his own money, his reputation on the line opening this place—the restaurant cannot hinge on the chef because if the chef leaves it's like sticking a pin in a balloon."

With Frank gone, Waxman was elevated to chef. He introduced what would become a signature dish for decades—a half chicken with fries and tarragon butter—and changed the menu regularly, experimenting. He found the Los Angeles dining public remarkably open to new ideas, even unsuccessful ones: "They were the most enthusiastic audience you could ever imagine," says Waxman. "They were so enthusiastic they were overly enthusiastic. They loved everything. They tolerated the mistakes. I knew they were mistakes as soon as they went out of the kitchen, but they weren't horrible mistakes; they were mistakes of youth." The freedom was intoxicating: "I remember going to see Wolfgang Puck for the first time at lunch at Ma Maison. He had worked at all these famous restaurants in Paris, more classically trained than anybody I knew at that point except for Jean-Pierre Moullé at Chez Panisse. He looked at me and it was like, 'This is great, right? This is cool, right? We get to do what we want now. We get to be the chef. There aren't any rules anymore.'"

But an excess of anything, even enthusiasm, can backfire. Once, when Waxman was away on vacation, Peel ran sixteen specials: four cold appetizers, four hot appetizers, four meat main courses, and four fish dishes. Just reciting them caused delays on the service floor. "I had all of these things I wanted to do, so I just did all of them," says Peel. "I had to promise the waiters I would never do that again."

The restaurant became a beacon for young American talent,

though many, according to Peel, "left after a little while because they got sick of the turmoil. It was not a buttoned-down kitchen. At all. It got a little crazy sometimes. After the restaurant closed, people would stay up and drink Champagne and talk and do cocaine."

One of those drawn to McCarty's flame was Nancy Silverton, a young cook who had grown up one of two daughters of an attorney (father) and writer (mother) in Los Angeles. She first entered the kitchen pursuing a flirtation at Sonoma State University.

"I bought a cookbook and I started cooking out of it. It was quite early on in following these recipes and realizing how much I enjoyed, first of all, just kind of being by myself, but also how much I felt comfortable and enjoyed using my hands. And it was that first semester that it was like a lightbulb went off. It was that memory of standing behind the stainless-steel double-shelved worktable where it hit me that this is what I want to do. This is what I want to be when I grow up. I don't know if I thought *chef*, but probably I thought *cook*." That was 1974.

Silverton, who initially thought she'd follow her beloved dad's footsteps into the law, changed majors a few times, then shifted to Sonoma State's Hutchins liberal arts college. She spent her summer breaks in kitchens, where she was often the lone white girl amongst a crew of Latino career cooks just there for the paycheck. A watershed moment came in 1976, her senior year. "I was studying for my finals and I was having a very hard time focusing and I didn't want to take the test that I was studying for. Didn't want to write the papers I was writing because I knew that there was nothing I was going to be doing with a degree. I called my parents up and I said, 'I'm dropping out of school. I want to cook.'" Unlike most parents of the day, hers were supportive.

She spent a year cooking at 464 Magnolia, a chef-owned restaurant in Marin County populated, like Chez Panisse, by charter members of a new generation of California cooks, college-educated Francophiles who worked from recipes out of books by Julia Child, concert-pianist-turned-cookbook-author Michael Field, Frenchman (and nouvelle cuisine loather) Raymond Oliver. It was also a distinctly California kitchen where gender dynamics were concerned: "It was a very supportive kitchen. People ask me what are my horror stories of being a young woman on her way up in a kitchen, and I had none of those experiences," says Silverton, who recalls an idyllic environment where she talked movies, books, and politics with her coworkers.

In 1977, at her father's insistence, she matriculated at Le Cordon Bleu in London, then returned to L.A., where she dined at Michael's with her parents shortly after it opened.

"The place was busy and vibrant, with beautiful people, and there was great art on the walls. Michael was running around very well dressed but casual, kissing and hugging. You knew that you were in a place to be, and to be seen. The dining room of 464 Magnolia and the dining room of Chez Panisse were much more subdued in a Northern California way. This was *Hollywood*."

Silverton, touting her Le Cordon Bleu credentials, hit McCarty up for a job. She wanted in so badly that she settled for a position managing the restaurant's computerized program during lunch.

"I was so terrible at it," says Silverton. "And the cooks were so angry with me because I would very often put in the wrong order and I didn't know how to do all the things you do on a computer. Well, Jonathan found out somehow that that's not what I was there for; I think he was relieved because he couldn't believe someone as incompetent as me had that job—I probably did it for three weeks. He found out that I wanted to be in the kitchen and so he approached me and he said, 'Look, I don't have anything on the hot side'—because that's what I applied for—'but our pastry chef, Jimmy, is about to walk out the door. I need you to go in there and learn every single recipe you can.'"

Jimmy Brinkley had what Silverton calls "a very fragile temperament." Because his assistant, a friend of Ken Frank's, had departed with him, Brinkley was flying solo and not happy about it.

Again, Silverton accepted a suboptimal assignment, even though she describes herself as having been "less than a C student" in pastry at Le Cordon Bleu, where she found the adherence to dogma suffocating: "There was no flexibility, no humor, no smiles. You did it by the book and you didn't ask questions. Whatever I made just didn't come out because I felt I was so constricted by the precision of it, because they said, 'No, nothing will work unless you do it exactly that way.'"

Pastry was also scarcely a consideration for a young cook in the United States. "It was a time in Los Angeles and possibly the country where it wasn't a given that all restaurants of a certain level had a pastry chef," says Silverton. "In Los Angeles especially, most of the restaurants bought their pastries from two people: One was La Mousse, so you had a frozen mousse cake with all different flavors as a choice, and another was I think called L.A. Desserts or something, and you had a choice of pecan pie and apple pie and things like that, and everybody had the same menu. The few restaurants that made their desserts in-house only made desserts that had French names: chocolate mousse, apple tart, crêpes Suzette. Things like that. So L'Ermitage was one of the first restaurants that not only had a beautiful dessert table, but the desserts did not have classic names; Jimmy brought that over to Michael's."

Under Brinkley, Silverton found a new world of pastry open to her: "As I watched and learned from Jimmy, I saw how the pastry world was not restrictive, that there were certain scientific principles you had to adhere to. If you pour boiling milk all at once over eggs, they are going to scramble. If you cook something at six hundred degrees, it's going to burn. Things like that. But as long as you stay within those guidelines there's a lot of room for creativity. So not only did I just find that so exciting, it was the first time I saw somebody in the dessert world actually taste things and change as you taste. That was really eye opening. I also loved the fact that we had our own little corner of the kitchen and we would come in at four in the morning when nobody was there and we would leave by lunch service. I don't have to tell you that that's the part of the kitchen that I became the most happy at. I didn't want to do anything more to the hot side."

Silverton was fond of a chocolate-caramel tart that Brinkley created, based on the flavors of a Heath Bar, and of a chocolate-raspberry mousse cake, which she loved for its unconventional pairing. Like his L'Ermitage repertoire, Brinkley's Michael's desserts didn't have names, which Silverton found thrilling. "You weren't making *pecan pie*. And all the desserts on the menu were named by the ingredients in the dessert."

Though Silverton doesn't remember it, McCarty vividly recalls encouraging her to bring a boldness to her desserts; specifically he remembers whipping cream aggressively to produce a superfluffy result—he considered the effect to be distinctly American.

Brinkley didn't leave Michael's, as was feared, and Waxman and McCarty sent Silverton to France for six months to deepen her pastry knowledge at Gaston Lenôtre's school in Plaisir, and to work in a bakery. "I came back with so many ideas and I started to make them for Michael, the things that I had learned and really impressed me. And Michael didn't like them. He thought they were too French. His flavor preference was some of the things that Jimmy was making that in truth were much more flavorful. They were much more condensed. So I'd take that chocolate-raspberry mousse cake and I'd say, 'I know how to lighten that. I could take that and if I add more egg whites it'll be just like foam, right?' I mean, egg whites don't have any flavor, so I'm sacrificing flavor for an airiness. And Michael was very gentle in his critique of what I had brought back. And he was right. And I think my success, maybe, was the influence and the technique that I learned in France merging with Jimmy's great knack for making flavorful things, and the two became my style."

Ironically, despite McCarty's redirection, Silverton believes that one of her key contributions to the evolution of restaurant desserts in America was the importing of French techniques that weren't common in the United States at the time, "whether it was certain chocolates that I brought back or certain ways of whipping cream or making a buttercream or making a *pâte sucrée**—then people would go work somewhere else and they would take my recipes. That's just the way the food world works."

George Barber, a Scottish actor and front-of-house man who had worked at restaurants in London and Paris, found his way to L.A. in a "drug-and-alcohol-infused" period in his life, went to work at L'Orangerie, then migrated to Michael's in 1980, at age thirty. "They were young Turks," he says of McCarty, Waxman, and company. "They were hot, they were on fire."

For Barber, McCarty's dining room was a world apart from others he'd worked in. He remembers McCarty drilling him on food during his interview, which surprised and impressed him because waiting tables was largely seen as a rent-paying enterprise for actors and other creatives.

"Listen," McCarty told him. "I'm only hiring people that are really interested in what we're doing. I'm not interested in bullshit."

Despite his experience, Barber took a job as a busboy because McCarty insisted all staff work their way up the chain. Barber was also impressed that the Armani-clad McCarty trained him personally. "He took me through that restaurant from the color of the paint on the front door, to the telephone lines on the side, to literally everything. The data and information that he gave me as we went along was just mind blowing. *Mind blowing.* Then he went into the art. And of course you know the whole story about the art: 'This is Richard Diebenkorn. This is his playing card series.' Then we got into the food, then we got into the service.

"One of the things that I learned about from Michael is that

---

* Sweet pastry crust.

he's so thorough. He was so into what he was doing. But it was a total involvement of everybody. Everybody was connected. And I have to say it was my first real experience with really great integrity of what we were doing, that we were elevating the dining experience. But we were also putting the edge on it, the California edge. Have you seen *The Player?* You know that scene where they're like, 'I'll have my Pellegrino, two blocks of ice with lemon on the side, please.' This is California. Now, we're talking about the top restaurants in California that I worked at where people were mollycoddled. They got what they wanted. There was no question. And they would alter the menu. They were very used to dismantling a menu and saying, 'I'll have this, I'll have this, I'll have this.' Michael wouldn't do it. He would encourage them and say, 'You've got to try *this*.'"

McCarty was also willing to back his team, dramatically if necessary. Remembers Barber: "Once I had these people in the terrace and they were real Hollywood assholes, spoiled people. And we were used to reporting to each other what was going on so everyone knew what this table was like. So you know, of course there's all that 'the customer's always right,' you want to break through and make them happy, so you've accomplished something with them. And finally he says to me, 'Okay, George. I'll take over, dude.' He goes over to the table. By this time they're on their second bottle of Montrachet. Some big wine. They had the apps and it was just going nowhere. So he went up to them, he said, 'Look. Everything that you have consumed and drunk up until now is on me. We can't help you anymore. We can't make you happy. We're never going to be able to make you happy tonight. So good night. I'm sorry it didn't work out. No hard feelings. Bye.' And he goes, 'Clear this table.' And that was the end of that. Might be [a] $400, $500 bill, thirty years ago. I thought, *Wow.* I'd never seen that happen before. It impressed me because he really stood by what he said and felt. It's not that I'd kick anybody out of anywhere. I'm not an employer. But it gave me something to stand by, like a value, that what I'm doing is very right."

McCarty also pioneered a practice that is now de rigueur in restaurants, the nightly staff meeting. "Now that's a given. That was new," says Barber. "Michael would be there. Jonathan would be there. Everybody was there. It took place at five, in the dining room. Dishes would be brought out. We'd be tasting. We were discussing it. It was a really involved part of the night. And that was a new thing."

Around this time, Jeremiah Tower, at the behest of friend Cecilia Chiang, who had ventured south to open an outpost of her groundbreaking San Francisco Chinese restaurant The Mandarin in Beverly Hills, made a tour of some L.A. hotspots, including West Beach Cafe and chef Michael Roberts's Trumps, a hypercreative West Hollywood restaurant and late-night industry dining destination. When he tasted the chicken at Michael's, he burst into the kitchen and demanded, "Who is able to do *that*!" It was, says Tower, "just the most perfect reproduction of the best effort the French had ever done. . . . I just went, 'Oh, my.' It wasn't a verbal thing; it just hit me like a nine-millimeter soft-nosed bullet." Years later, R. W. Apple would call Tower's San Francisco restaurant Stars, launched in 1984, the most democratic restaurant he had ever seen. "But it was only because of that inspiration that came out of L.A.," says Tower.

Things in Berkeley had changed in the intervening years. Tower had become a gun for hire, teaching at the California Culinary Academy, taking over the kitchens of existing, struggling restaurants such as the Balboa Café. Mark Miller, who had become a cook, and eventually chef, at Chez Panisse, departed the restaurant in September 1979 to pursue his personal passion for world cuisine, especially chiles and spices—turns out you can't take the anthropologist out of the chef; he had made it his mission to visit two new countries each year and couldn't fit his developing style into Chez Panisse's resolutely French construct. When Susie Nelson, Chez Panisse's manager, felt the restaurant was becoming too snooty and left to open her own place, securing a space on Fourth Street, she invited

Miller to join her as partner and chef. He matched her investment, kicking in $35,000, and they launched Fourth Street Grill that October. The restaurant drew a crowd immediately, and Nelson and Miller were repaid their investment in four months. The menu drew on influences from you name it: America, England, Italy, Morocco. Miller kept up old relationships: His old Chez Panisse buddy Jonathan Waxman was a frequent visitor; one of his cooks, David Mahler, also recalls how Miller would sometimes bring his crew to Chez Panisse after hours, let himself into the unlocked kitchen, and fix them a snack.

In December 1980, they opened Santa Fe Bar and Grill in the old Santa Fe railroad station in Berkeley. In his book *California Dish*, Tower quipped that the location was "an area more comfortable for prostitutes and drug dealers from Oakland than for Volvo and Saab drivers from the upper Berkeley hills." (That didn't stop him from dropping by on opening night and offering to lend a hand in the kitchen.) Miller explored the food of the Yucatán at Santa Fe, boasted of being able to sell two hundred orders of Peruvian beef hearts en brochette. But it was too much for him and Nelson, and after five months, he sold out his share to focus on Fourth Street Grill.

"ONE OF THOSE ONCE-IN-A-LIFETIME THINGS."

Back in West Hollywood, Patrick Terrail rang up Ken Frank with a new possibility: "La Rouche is going down in flames, they need a chef partner, and I think you can make a deal." The restaurant had occupied the former La Guillotine space on the Sunset Strip, with a sous chef and the original maître d' from L'Ermitage.

"Patrick sat me down and showed me how I could line up twelve investors at $5,000 apiece and pay them back in food," says Frank.

That October, still just twenty-three years old, Frank launched a restaurant with a name that was as cheffy as it gets—La Toque, a reference to the tall white cylindrical hats worn by chefs in formal kitchens—on the Sunset Strip. (Mel Brooks and Gene Wilder, in a sign of the growing interest in food and chefs, invested.) The restaurant was well received, but in spring 1980, says Frank, his partner and maître d', Henri Fiser, left a candle burning in the dining room, causing a fire. While the restaurant was closed for repairs, Terrail invited Frank to be a part of what might have been the first pop-up: Because Ma Maison's clientele decamped to Cannes every May, Terrail decided that rather than stay behind pining for the absent Rolls-Royces and movie stars, he'd open a Ma Maison Cannes for the duration of the festival. Terrail, Puck, Frank, and a skeleton crew assumed command of the dining room of Château de La Napoule just outside Cannes, and not coincidentally across the street from Terrail's North Star: Outhier's L'Oasis.

In Cannes, Puck—in an early demonstration of his innate versatility—cooked a traditional American dinner, which he knew would be exotic to the predominantly European crowd: "I brought my butcher, Harvey Guss[man], with me, he was cutting the steaks."

Functioning out-of-house has become a part of every modern chef's skill set, but for Puck it was uncharted territory, and led to mishaps: "I brought three hundred, or five hundred, avocados but they were way too hard and I freaked out," he says. "I said, 'Shit, they are still like stone! What should I do?' And somebody gave me a stupid idea: They said, 'Put it out in the sun, they will ripen.' So I went up to the president of the festival and he had a big balcony. I laid them all out there and they got black and soft. So then I had to go to the farmers' market in Nice and buy avocados from Kenya or wherever, and then put it with sour cream and caviar. So we served this and then we put our steaks, the New York steaks, which was very hard to get out of customs. Jacques Médecin, the mayor of Nice, helped us to get them through customs, and then we brought baked potatoes. They confiscated them. They didn't let the potatoes in. And corn on the cob. And then cheesecake for dessert. So it was all new but it was a traditional American dinner. I think they loved it. People never saw a fourteen-ounce steak on a plate in France at that time; you got half of that, maybe."

Ma Maison's customers flocked to the temporary outpost. Bob Fosse's autobiographical fever dream *All That Jazz* starring Roy Scheider and Jessica Lange showed at the festival, and was feted with a party in its honor for which a local pastry chef, an old friend of Puck's, created a special cake and a fireworks display was put on over the Gulf of Napoule. "It was an epic party," says Frank. "One of those once-in-a-lifetime things."

Terrail rented out the luxurious Château de La Napoule and gave each member of the team his own bedroom. Between and after services, the crew cooked in the château kitchen, dined at Vergé's Moulin de Mougins, toured a cheese *cave*, enjoyed local specialties like *soupe de poisson* cooked for them by friends of Puck's, and partied at local nightclubs.

It remains a cherished memory for all three men, but it would be one of the last good times for Puck and Terrail.

"HE OFFERED ME A JOB AS A HATCHECK GIRL AND I CRIED."

As Terrail, Puck, and Frank depart Château la Napoule, we pan across the street to L'Oasis, and into the kitchen, where Puck's former cook, Susan Feniger, is working a one-year *stage* under Outhier's auspices, arranged for her by Terrail himself.

Feniger had been raised in a Midwestern Jewish family that valued good food; mom could cook anything, from noodle kugel to lasagna to fudge brownies, and was uncommonly attuned to the seasons, making vibrant salads in an iceberg wedge era. Feniger's first kitchen job was at Smith's Cafeteria in Toledo, Ohio. She loved it, but started college, dropped out, then found herself working for a cabinetmaker in Vermont. Returning to college, this time in California, to study economics, she took a job in the school's cafeteria, learned rudimentary preparations, and *loved* the environment. Her boss pulled her aside one day, told her she should be studying cooking. She convinced her economics professor to let her spend her senior year in a customized, independent-study program at The Culinary Institute of America in Hyde Park, New York, where Feniger became hopelessly devoted to kitchen life: "I loved the camaraderie of it, I loved wearing uniforms, I loved eating and creating. It fit for me."

Feniger was the only woman in her class, but didn't feel the crush of sexism: "Here's the thing: When I was in high school, I was this total Ayn Rand freak. I was this total libertarian to the fullest. I was studying philosophy and psychology and I was reading Nathaniel Branden and then I ended up reading John Hospers." The libertarian bent toward self-sufficiency bucked Feniger up against the chauvinism and harassment of the time: "I probably was in total denial to thinking that was happening. I was, I think, pretty strong and confident. I was a tomboy as a kid. I'm sure it was there. I just didn't feel it. It clearly still is there but it's just not one of those things that came into my consciousness."*

Feniger shifted her attention to cooking. Her family, unlike many of the time, supported it, but her father had one requirement:

---

* This experience contrasted sharply with that of other women such as Helen Chardack, who attended the CIA around the same time and remembers: "You wouldn't walk into the cooler on your own. There were a lot of chefs, kids, or guys who would walk in after you. And then you'd have to do the whole I'm-being-cornered routine and squirrel out. Even in some of the kitchens in New York. Passing by the dishwasher station could be tough. You'd get lots of comments." And Napa Valley chef Cindy Pawlcyn recalls that when she applied to the CIA in the 1970s, "I got rejected because I was a woman and they'd filled their quota for three years. I got a letter."

that she learn the business of running a restaurant. Feniger worked for a hot second at The Quilted Giraffe, a new restaurant in New Paltz, New York, in its formative years, then other jobs in upstate New York and for Gus Riedi's La Bonne Auberge in Kansas City, and gave up novels and philosophical treatises for cookbooks. After two years, she moved to Chicago and took a job at Le Perroquet, a nouvelle cuisine restaurant and one of Chicago's finest, where she became the second-ever woman in the kitchen; the first, still there when Feniger arrived, was Mary Sue Milliken.

Milliken grew up the youngest of three sisters in an East Lansing, Michigan, family, discovered cooking during high school in home ec classes and working in a pizzeria and a donut shop. She also had an epiphany when "I met a guy who was a chef in Chicago, a friend of my sister's, and he cooked dinner in, like, forty-five minutes before my very eyes. I was sixteen, and in that moment, at that dinner, I decided I wanted to be a chef. And I went back to East Lansing, graduated from high school, and moved to Chicago. I really had no idea what kind of a career it was going to be." She went to what she calls "chef school" in 1976 or 1977 at Washburn Trade School, which she describes as "a trade tech on the South Side with a bunch of plumbers and pipe fitters and auto mechanics." To ready students for the rigors of the industry, the school was open every day except Thanksgiving and Christmas. She supplemented her classes with restaurant work at night.

Milliken was, she believes, one of two women in a class of one hundred. "I think when you're in the middle of that kind of a situation you don't allow yourself to acknowledge that it's harder for you than it would be if you were a different gender. So you just barrel through and try to make it happen," she says. "But in retrospect you look at it and you can see that it was definitely challenging and hard. But I have the kind of personality that likes a challenge and likes to be a little bit of a rebel. So I think it fit me. But I had to go to the tequila bar after school and drink as much as the guys. I had to prove myself in kitchens. I had to lift heavy things. I was trying to really be as competitive as I could on that stage."

Milliken had heard of Alice Waters, but only vaguely. As with most people east of the Rocky Mountains—and with Californians, for that matter—her attentions were focused on France. She found direction when Madeleine Peter's *Favorite Recipes of the Great Women Chefs of France* was published in 1979. "I read it, like, five times. I couldn't believe it. *Finally I've found some role models.*" This was typical of the time. With scant coverage or even real awareness of chefs, aspirants were hard-pressed for industry knowledge. "There was no Internet. There were very few of us, and chefs in those days, we worked sixteen, eighteen hours a day, every day, day in and day out. And you didn't read lots of newspapers or magazines. Where were you going to get intel?"

Milliken worked for the Conrad Hilton Hotel, then did a *stage* at Maxim's in Paris. Returning to Chicago, she wanted to work for Jovan Trboyevic at Le Perroquet, which had never employed a woman in the kitchen.

"He said, 'I can't hire you because you're a woman and you'd cause havoc in my kitchen,'" says Milliken. "I said, 'How will I do that?' He said, 'You're too pretty. All the men would go crazy.' I just couldn't believe that. He offered me a job as a hatcheck girl and I cried.* And

---

* The hatcheck job offer was extreme, even by the standards of the time. A more common act of chauvinism was to confine women to pastry or garde-manger (salads and cold prep). The great Boston chef Lydia Shire recalls the summer day she auditioned for a position at Maison Robert as it was preparing to open in the early 1970s: A self-taught, divorced mother of three at the time, she produced an elaborate seven-layer cake from a recipe by Raymond Oliver, called herself an air-conditioned taxi, and arrived at the restaurant unannounced. Her artistry and "chutzpah" earned her a spot in the kitchen, but "as a salad girl, because I'm a woman and I was young and American. I was part of the opening team, in garde-manger, opening oysters and slicing pâté, watching cooks cooking and thinking that's what I wanted to do; that's when I decided that's what I wanted to do." (She eventually decamped for Le Cordon Bleu cooking school in London, returning to

then I started a letter and phone call campaign where I called him every five minutes, wrote him letters. And he finally said, 'Are you going to sue me?' I said, 'No, I just want a job.' So he said, 'All right. Come in tomorrow. It's three twenty-five an hour, minimum wage.' Of course, now he would get sued over it. But then, you know, there were times when, like, seventeen-year-old boys would be making twelve—I can't remember, maybe it was eight dollars an hour, and I would be making five fifty, and I was two years older, with four years more experience. But that stuff happened and you just persevered and kept going."

Feniger arrived about eighteen months after Milliken. "I think he thought he had the best deal on the planet because I was working circles around all the guys in the kitchen and I was so cheap, so he took another," says Milliken. "I had never worked with anybody who had the same sensibility, the same work ethic. We really enjoyed working together."

"The chef there at that time was a total asshole to me," says Feniger. "Complete. But he was a great chef and I felt like I learned a ton from him. It was a totally great restaurant. And it was a great experience, it was the beginning of nouvelle cuisine and they were just doing amazing things. We both learned a ton there."

Feniger moved to Los Angeles, and Ma Maison, in 1978, and fell right away for the laid-back culture, calling Milliken to breathlessly report: "I can't believe you can wear tennis shoes here, you don't have to wear a chef's hat." She also shared a detail that amuses Milliken today: "'You're not going to believe this weirdo who's in the kitchen here. He doesn't even know how to do the ordering. We have three cases of avocados and he orders three more. They're just going to spoil.' We chuckle about that, because it was *Wolf*."

Around the same time that Feniger pushed off from Ma Maison to work at L'Oasis, Milliken embarked on her own *stage* under chef

---

Maison Robert as a line cook and working her way up to chef of the main dining room, then moved on to the more progressive Harvest restaurant.)

Dominique Nahmias at Olympe in Paris. The two kept in touch that year and, when it was over, met up at Milliken's apartment in Paris's Fourteenth Arrondissement, killed a few bottles of wine, and as a rainbow appeared in the sky, came to a conclusion: "We decided that we had to open a restaurant together," says Milliken. "I think being a woman in a man's field, you kind of quickly learn that if you want to call the shots, you're going to have to start out small and do your own thing because trying to work your way up through the hierarchy in a male-dominated field is just pretty hard." (Milliken, along with Lazaroff, New York chefs and restaurateurs Lidia Bastianich and Anne Rozenzweig, Providence's Johanne Killeen, and California's Elka Gilmore, helped start Women Chefs & Restaurateurs, spearheaded by chefs Barbara Tropp and Joyce Goldstein, in 1993. A similar organization, the New York Women's Culinary Alliance, was founded by Sara Moulton and Maria Reuge at Sally Darr's La Tulipe restaurant in 1981. Both continue to thrive today.)

Both cooks were broke—Milliken had even sold her car to finance her European adventure and lived off her savings overseas—so they went where the short-term money was: Milliken to Chicago and a private chef gig; Feniger back to L.A., where she picked up lunch shifts at Ma Maison. By night she moonlighted, running the kitchen for the owners of an espresso bar located next to their L.A. Eyeworks shop, also on Melrose. It was modest, to say the least, a nine-hundred-square-foot cafe with nine tables, eleven barstools, a pastry case, an espresso machine, and no proper kitchen. The owners, over the novelty of running a food-service business and frustrated by the daily grind, asked Feniger if she'd like to run it. She seized the opportunity, shortcomings of the space be damned, setting up two hibachis, a hot plate, and a prep table in the parking lot out back.

"The first special I ever ran was veal tongue with lobster sauce and sautéed pears. I made it *on a hot plate*," said Feniger. "We were two years into it before the health department came by to say we really couldn't do that."

Milliken came to L.A. in February 1981, overcame her Midwesterner's wariness of California—known back home as "the land of fruits and nuts"—went back to Chicago, packed up her things, and by early spring she and Feniger were together in the kitchen at what became City Café, drawing primarily on their French backgrounds, with an emphasis on country over nouvelle: "Confit of duck on a salad with pickled cabbage. Or we would do cold poached salmon with tomatoes and herbs and olive oil and salt. Or we would do grilled turkey. We couldn't afford veal so we were really into turkey for some reason. We'd slice it thinly and pound it and make turkey escalope with lemon and shallots and brown butter." Because they had no refrigeration and required a daily delivery, local purveyors didn't want to service them. Puck, flexing his growing muscle, intervened on their behalf.

Feniger and Milliken found their customers as open-minded as Waxman did, so they began adding organs such as lamb kidneys to the menu. "There was a dialogue and an interchange between the customers and the kitchen," says Milliken. The interaction was enhanced by the fact that the bathroom was through the kitchen. "Whenever a movie star would come in, we'd tell the busboy, 'Give them lots of water so they have to come in the bathroom.'" (Highlights: Gilda Radner, Stevie Wonder, and the giraffe-tall Julia Child, who bumped her head on the pots and pans hanging like a mobile over the kitchen.)

"They would ask about the food," says Milliken. "They'd sit at the bar. They'd look through the window to the kitchen, and we were just bursting with excitement about cooking. We would cook from morning until night, every day, six days a week, and then on Mondays we would just sleep all day. We had so much fun. We'd write the menu on a chalkboard every day. We'd be out there filling the pastry case with homemade desserts. We had a huge pastry menu, too; as soon as I got in the cafe, I was like, 'We're not going to buy any desserts from the outside.' There was a lot of excitement around the food. And I would do things like lamb's tongue salad that people loved. I was just very impressed. It was an artistic thing, eating in L.A., more so than it was in the Midwest."

Emboldened, the women began expanding their repertoire into unprecedented eclecticism: Feniger returned from a trip to India, added potato samosas with chutneys, a vegetarian plate with dals, and lamb curry to the menu. Milliken returned from Thailand and on went a Thai sausage salad, duck red curry, eggplant curry, and pickled tomatoes. A trip to the Japanese fish market was followed by monkfish liver. They persuaded a garden in Brentwood to grow organic produce for them, including black mustard sprouted from seeds Feniger brought back from India.

"We weren't making it accessible," says Feniger. "We were just doing the food we loved. As long as people were buying it, we never thought about it. We never thought about what the press will say; we didn't go there."

One day, it hit Feniger in a flash—the same way it had hit Waxman and Puck in that passing glance at Ma Cuisine—that step by step, imperceptibly as it had happened, she had entered a new world. *"Oh my God,"* she thought. *"We can do whatever we want!"*

"THIS IS VERY SAD, WOLF. THIS IS NOT OKAY."

Barbara Lazaroff, then a stranger to the restaurant industry, saw the inherent injustice in its power structure. Puck had saved Ma Maison but Terrail was reaping the spoils. The dynamic was symbolized in the paycheck Lazaroff found in Puck's bathroom one day, an amount so meager she assumed it was a week's pay, and insufficient at that. When Puck told her that's what he earned every *two* weeks, the New Yorker within was unleashed: "You've got to be shitting me," she snapped. "I earned more than that when I was eighteen years old. This is despicable. You need to go talk to Patrick and tell him to double your salary."

"What?"

"Double it!"

Says Lazaroff, "Wolfgang had transformed Ma Maison. It was going to go out of business. And Wolf transformed it and made it a huge success with a great name. So, yeah, I said, 'This is very sad, Wolf. This is not okay.'"

"The next day I went to Patrick," says Puck. "I said, 'We have to talk. You have to double my salary or I'm going to leave.' He said, 'Go talk to Sid.' Sid was the accountant. He had a little office there. I said, 'Sid, you have two choices: You have to double my salary or else I'm leaving. This is ridiculous.' He said okay."

Lazaroff also helped the newly single Puck clean up his home, hammering ice blocks out of the freezer, sorting through storage boxes piled up all over the place. (He also only owned one fork; in time she'd convince him to do a $35,000 renovation of his kitchen.) One of the boxes contained what Lazaroff calls "faux shares."

"What are these?" she asked him.

"I'm a partner in Ma Maison," he said.

"No you're not," insisted Lazaroff. "These are not real."

They went back and forth but Lazaroff insisted "they were bullshit. And sure enough," she says, "they were bullshit. He just printed out shit, a thing that looks like a bond.

"Wolf is very naïve," says Lazaroff.*

Puck was working lunch and dinner six days a week, and dinner on Sunday. She'd pick him up in the afternoon, and the two drove to her place and hit the sack between services.

One afternoon, Puck turned on the television, saw one of his waiters on the small screen, promoting an industry charity marathon.

"What is he doing on TV?" Puck exclaimed. "He's not even a cook."

---

* Both Puck and Terrail maintain that Puck was indeed a partner.

"Do *you* want to be on TV?" asked Lazaroff.

"Well, yeah."

Lazaroff worked her burgeoning L.A. network, eventually reaching independent casting director Lillian Mizrahi, and pitched her Puck.

"That's really funny," said Mizrahi (according to Lazaroff). "We wanted him to come on to cook something on one of these shows but Patrick Terrail said, 'Oh, no, no, no. I go on,' or somebody else. 'He doesn't want to do that. He doesn't like doing that.'"

Lazaroff pushed her luck, asking if there was a national show that might book him. Mizrahi made some calls, came back with *Hour Magazine*, a syndicated features program hosted by Gary Collins that aired in 117 markets. Puck did a cooking demo the next week.

All the while, Lazaroff was training Puck for stardom. Despite Puck's protestations, according to her (and others), his English was substandard so he'd rely on a meager set of shticky one-liners in customer interactions. A diner might say, "How are you?" and he'd respond, "Not as good as you!" In their limited time together, Lazaroff read *Time* and *Newsweek* to him to punch up his fluency.

Many of their contemporaries say that Puck wouldn't be where he is today had Lazaroff not come along. Puck, before we began recording our interview, groused that this impression annoys him, and Ruth Reichl understands why: "There's nobody like Wolfgang. He's incredibly talented. He's the best manager. People love him. People who work for him love him. Even people who have left, nobody will say anything bad about him. And he's got an amazing palate. He loves to cook. I watched him once in the kitchen at Spago, this is when Sherry Yard was there as the pastry chef. And he was going through, tasting. He just stuck his finger in the ice cream and said, 'Why did you use different ginger?' And she was like, 'How do you even know that?' He's unlike many businessman chefs who start hating to cook. He is always there. It's like I said: I never saw Michael [McCarty] in the kitchen. I never *didn't* see Wolf in the kitchen. He'd invite you to his house. He loves cooking. He'd get in the kitchen and push people aside. I once asked him, 'Why do you open so many restaurants?' And he said, 'Look. You develop these chefs and they're really good, and at a certain point they're going to leave you.' So he said, 'Instead of letting them leave, I open up a restaurant for them to run.' Every chef in America should know that, right? That you become partners. You develop people, and you become partners with them. I mean, the idea that Tom Kaplan [senior managing partner of Puck's corporation] is still working for him, what, thirty-five years later? It's amazing. In this business, how many people have that tight organization that people stay and stay and stay and stay and stay? That's what I mean when I say he's a genius." That said, Reichl does believe that Lazaroff accelerated the process.

So I believe Puck when he tells me that he had concluded that the only way to get what he wanted at Ma Maison was to become a partner, and the only way to accomplish that was to create a second restaurant, force Terrail to join forces with him and create a management company as fifty-fifty equals. (Puck says that Terrail promised him they'd take over La Tour d'Argent someday. "My uncle is so old, in five years we're going to run La Tour d'Argent," Terrail told him. "Then we went to La Tour d'Argent, the uncle comes over and says hello, shook everybody's hand at the table. Did not say, 'Oh, Patrick. So good to see you.' He was like a stranger. I said, 'Shit, we're not going to own La Tour d'Argent!'")

With all of this percolating, Puck commented to Lazaroff one afternoon at her apartment that he longed to have his own restaurant, something like you see in the South of France, in particular Chez Gu et Fils, where he used to enjoy those Sunday afternoons in his Les Baux-de-Provence days.

"But you probably couldn't have a pizza oven," he sighed, resignedly.

Lazaroff picked up the phone, dialed the fire department, asked to speak to an inspector.

"We're thinking of doing a restaurant and we want to put a wood-burning oven in it," she told him. "And we want to make pizzas in the wood-burning oven."

The inspector asked if customers could come into contact with the oven. She assured him that there'd be a counter to act as barrier.

"It sounds okay, lady."

That was enough for Lazaroff. She and Puck began conceiving their restaurant, a casual pizza joint, both filling a longing to replicate the magic of Chez Gu et Fils and to fill a void in the burgeoning L.A. dining scene. He initially envisioned a by-the-numbers joint with red-checkered tablecloths and candles stuffed into straw-wrapped Chianti bottles.

Puck was also spurred by a visit to Bertranou—his head swollen in the full throes of his brain tumor—at his hospital bedside. "I used to bring him the duck salad," says Puck. "I said, 'Jean, look what I'm doing at Ma Maison now.' And he said, 'You should open your own restaurant.' He said, 'Get away from this guy. He's not good. Open your own restaurant.'"

Puck and Lazaroff went through a few possible partners: Seattle SuperSonics owner Sam Schulman came and went, followed by composer Giorgio Moroder, known for his synth-heavy 1980s-defining soundtracks to *Midnight Express* and *American Gigolo*, who suggested the name Spago, but they couldn't come to terms. (According to Puck, Moroder wanted 60 or 70 percent of the profits in perpetuity instead of a more standard 65-35 model that would flip once he recouped his investment.)

The solution presented itself in the same place where Puck and Lazaroff began their courtship: Ma Cuisine. Donald Salk, a dentist from Chicago and fledgling food enthusiast on his second marriage, was a frequent student there. It was easier to score a spot in the classes than a table at Ma Maison—in fact, Salk had never dined there—and cheaper, too, so Salk became a regular and bonded with Puck, who confided his discontent and desire to open what he was still describing as a pizza place. Salk offered to help him raise money, although his wife, an L.A. native, told him he was crazy. But Salk was turned on by the idea of owning a restaurant, or even just part of one. He connected with Michael Roberts's attorney, devised a limited partnership concept, began going after thirty-four investors at $15,000 a pop. To entice them, Puck hosted brunches and Salk wined and dined them at Ma Maison. Despite the love for Puck, there were fund-raising challenges: In time, Spago would become a shining restaurant on a hill, but its predecessor in the space, Kavkaz, was anything but: a Russian Armenian restaurant overlooking a hooker-rich Sunset Boulevard. Memories differ on the final number of investors; the consensus puts it in the midtwenties. Down the homestretch, Puck and Salk put their houses up as collateral to surmount a funding gap. They raised a total of $510,000, which Puck supplemented with an equipment loan. It was barely enough: "I had $10,000 or $12,000 left and I put it in three different banks, and wrote checks on all of them," Puck said, the intention being to give the impression he had more money than he did.

With the financing in place, Puck says he approached Terrail: "I said, 'I found this location up there, we're going to do this Italian bistro. There's only one condition: We have to form a fifty-fifty partnership and we have to spruce up Ma Maison, to get it a little more luxurious, not to have Astroturf and plastic chairs.' And he looked at me after a second and says, 'You know I will always own fifty-one percent; I will never do fifty-fifty.' So I said, '*Me too.*'" Puck realized that it was time to leave. He gave Terrail three months' notice, but after two weeks, people were openly gossiping.

Unsurprisingly, Terrail recalls a different version of events, insisting that he would have taken a fifty-fifty split on both restaurants—the new venture and Ma Maison—but that Lazaroff, not Puck, did the negotiating; that he was turned off by the fact that she would be running the new place; and that she invited him to *invest* in the new restaurant, not be a partner. He also says that he learned about Puck's plans, including the name Spago, when he phoned his office from vacation and his assistant told him it was in the *Hollywood Reporter*. She also told Terrail that television producer Bob Stivers, of *Circus of the Stars* success, had been trying to help Puck and Lazaroff, bringing a steady parade of potential investors—mostly dentists and doctors—to Ma Maison for lunch while Terrail was overseas.

"I come back and obviously I'm a little furious," says Terrail. "Probably short-tempered, probably came to some rash decision . . . but I guess I was young, egocentric, and everything that goes with that. And I probably said, 'Absolutely not. I can't do both.'"

The ensuing breakup was, says Puck, "like a bad divorce." Terrail cut Puck's access to company assets: One morning, he woke up to find the company car missing. He went to the store to buy supplies, and the cashier confiscated his credit card, cut it in half. Puck retaliated in his own way: "Cat Stevens used to come to the restaurant all the time and he used to eat soft-boiled eggs. Patrick comes into the kitchen ranting and raving, 'I need soft-boiled eggs for Cat Stevens!' Finally I took a ladle out of the eggs and said, 'You want the eggs, here they are!' And *bang*. The eggs were on the wall and he had the egg yolks and everything on him."

Puck had become a bit of a known quantity since his first days at Ma Maison, but when he cut the cord with Terrail, he was overcome with self-doubt. "I was so nervous . . . I put on twenty-five pounds," he said. It didn't help that Terrail, his L.A. papa, was—according to Puck—telling anyone who'd listen that he was a bad manager. "It was a terrible time," Puck said.

"THERE WAS NO RECIPE."

Puck and Salk made a visit to Chez Panisse, where Puck connected with his old cook Mark Peel, told him about his new concept, which he was still describing—despite Lazaroff's protestations—as a pizza place that was also going to serve pasta and salads. He painted Peel a picture that would have horrified former set decorator Lazaroff: checkered tablecloths, candles stuck in Chianti bottles, a guitar player on Saturday nights. Because Puck wishfully thought he'd do Spago without leaving Ma Maison, he asked Peel to become the chef of Spago. Peel returned to Los Angeles, took a job back at Michael's to pay the rent for the months when Spago was being built.

Before he left Berkeley, Peel obtained the name and number of the contractor who'd built Chez Panisse's oven, a German, and persuaded the man to move to Los Angeles, where he parked his rig at the construction site, living there and insisting on being paid in cash. He built the oven, but also drank too much, had temper tantrums, fired people. One day, Salk received a panicked call from Lazaroff: the contractor was going to walk if he didn't receive one hundred dollars immediately. Salk rushed over, cash in hand, handed it to Puck, who passed it up a ladder to the man. (Lazaroff fibbed to the Board of Health, telling them it was a fireplace, which was more true than she knew: "We found out later that he built them rather badly," says Peel. "He built them like a fireplace—they were really inefficient when it came to burning our wood.")

Lazaroff brought all of her design capabilities to bear in creating a space like no other, with wire chairs and what she called an "exhibition kitchen."

Spago came together crazy fast; when it was ready to go, there was no waiting. Peel departed Michael's, as did Nancy Silverton (with whom he had coupled up and would eventually marry, then divorce), who signed on as pastry chef. Silverton didn't leave Michael's lightly, because it was established. "None of us went to Spago because it was *Spago*," she says. To seal the deal, Peel pulled an all-nighter, pleading his case to Silverton's mother, earning her blessing.

As the restaurant came to life, Puck—who'd gradually been migrating further and further away from traditional cuisine—decided he wanted the cooks to reflect the changing times. If they were going to be visible to customers, he didn't want them to look formal, staid, the way they did in, say, Soltner's kitchen at Lutèce in New York City. "I said, 'We're going to make baseball caps.' White baseball caps with the word *Spago* on it in our color, the pinkish color. The cooks loved it. Everybody loved it. Then it became a fad all over. It didn't make it so starchy."

The same impulse led Puck to design his own menu, to avoid the formality of a leather-bound tome. David Hockney had designed Ma Maison's menu but Puck couldn't afford him or his peers. So he drew a collage of images depicting casual dishes and scribbled the phrase *California Cuisine* on the cover. The dishes weren't exact templates of what would be served, and that was fine by Puck, who intended the images as "a blueprint."

"When we started, I said, 'We're not going to have a big menu,'" says Puck. "'We'll change it as much as we can, whatever we get.' So we had like six appetizers, a few pizzas, and grilled and roasted food. It was very simple."

The day before opening, Peel began prepping at ten in the morning and worked straight through the night, all the way up until the doors opened. Puck put off writing the menu, a major production in the precomputer/pre-email era requiring typing, proofing, printing, and laminating.

"One day he just sat down at this crappy little desk we had downstairs, four sheets of paper, and wrote the menu. In pen. No cross-outs. No erasing. Nothing," remembers Peel, who was allowed one menu item: He scribbled a Chez Panisse golden oldie, angel hair pasta with goat cheese and broccoli, in the margin.

"I like it that way," says Puck. "I like the pressure and in a way I like the surprise."

Construction continued until the last possible second as well. Says Peel: "They hammered the last nail at four; we opened the doors at six." There were no dry runs, no practice services, known today as "friends and family" dinners. The kitchen team hadn't cooked the menu a single time before opening. "We cooked the first night with the menus propped in front of us so at least we could remember to get all the listed ingredients into the dishes," says Peel.

"There was no recipe," remembers Kazuto Matsusaka, another Ma Maison alum who joined Puck at Spago. "I went up to Wolfgang: 'How do you make this tuna sashimi salad?' Wolf goes, 'Cut it up. Just make it up. Just make it whatever you think is good.' That's how it was."

"IT FELT LIKE BEING AT A PARTY ALL THE TIME."

Spago opened on January 16, 1982. Puck was so insecure that he told Salk to invite his wife's enormous extended family to ensure a somewhat full house. But when the dentist and his family arrived, they were confronted with eighteen Rolls-Royces in the parking lot and had to wait hours for a table. The restaurant did 170 covers that night.

"When the doors first opened," remembers Lazaroff, "I was still shoeless standing on top of the kitchen counter getting the track lights correct. I thought of it as a stage. I used to study theater lighting and design; that's what I did. So I said, 'That's my star. These are my stars. I'm lighting them up.'"

"I never even got to realize what I was in the middle of because who would have thought Spago, which became what Spago was overnight, would become *that*?" says Silverton. What Silverton calls the "floods" came the minute the doors opened. Because there was only the open kitchen, she had to clear out by 4 p.m., when Ed LaDou, the pizza maker, came in. She'd prepped days' worth of ingredients prior to opening night, but it was all gone by closing time.

Things were even more discombobulated on the hot line. Of that first night, Matsusaka remembers: "The timing was horrible. And nobody knew what to do. There's no system. There's no preopening meeting or preopening discussions. There was nothing. And the food started to run out. That was the craziest opening I've ever done. Mark was next to me; he was on pasta. He was making a pasta at six. Later, he was cutting [more fresh] angel hair pasta."

Puck was a draw, which was great for business, but a double-edged sword. Continues Matsusaka: "Wolfgang was in the kitchen, so when we opened Spago, everybody came to see him. That means they're going to start talking to him. So he was on the grill. Then the food has to go out together. So Wolfgang starts talking, nothing is coming out. So I told Mark Peel, 'Mark, we have to kick Wolfgang out of the kitchen.' That's what we did. Because he loves to cook and he loves to talk. He has to be out of the kitchen so he can schmooze those people, talk to people, whatever he wants to do, then we can run the kitchen a little more smoothly."

"It was so crazy we could not get a handle on it at all," said Puck. Famous customers denied a table "screamed at me and said they were never going to talk to me again." If he tried to accommodate them, resulting in a wait, "then they screamed again. It was so hard."

Between Puck's Ma Maison fan base and the restaurant's heat, Spago began drawing a celebrity clientele. Before long, two paparazzi were stationed like snipers along the hill that ran up from the parking lot to the restaurant.

"I had just come from five years working in a beauty salon," says Wendi Matthews, a childhood friend of Silverton's who became an office manager at Spago. "Lots of cocaine and lots of Quaaludes. Lots of hip, cool, young people. Everybody was sleeping with everybody. And it was sort of that same feeling at the restaurant. There were customers coming upstairs and sneaking off into the storage area to get high, and employees and people sleeping with everybody. It was that same sort of feel. It felt like being at a party all the time. I mean, even though during the day we weren't open and it was work, but everybody was sort of having fun."

"You knew who was holding, who was high, who wasn't. But definitely there was a lot of substance going on," says Jannis Swerman, who helped run the dining room. "You couldn't get into the bathrooms. People were going two at a time, so it was either sex or drugs or both." Swerman thinks Puck and Lazaroff were largely oblivious to it, but Lazaroff, who maintains she was an abstainer, was routinely offered coke and pot by customers, as a tip or just to share the good times. She told them owners don't accept tips, to give it to the staff at the door. Sometimes the sheer volume of self-abuse so overwhelmed her that she'd go home at the end of the night, throw open the door, and sob into the living room of the house she and Puck shared on Fifth Street.

"We knew we were on this new wave, this niche of people wanting to have a place that was their own little casual playground that was exclusive in certain ways but was also inclusive, because actually you had a lot of people who were very well known in different fields, a lot of them in entertainment, but in different fields," says Lazaroff. "And some of the most powerful weren't known by the other people in the restaurant, like the studio heads and whatever. I mean, the stars knew who they were, but there were loads of people. Our postman who delivered our mail would come there and dine."

Of course I can get a table; Wolfgang is a close personal friend of mine.
    —Richard Thornburg (William Atherton),
        Die Hard (1988)

All of Hollywood came to Spago, from an intergenerational mix of above-the-line names such as Michael Caine, Teri Garr, Dolly Parton, Burt Reynolds, Sylvester Stallone, and Barbra Streisand, and "everybody who ever played James Bond"—as onetime dining room manager Swerman puts it—to icons like Johnny Carson, to wunderkind directors George Lucas and Steven Spielberg, and emerging industry power brokers like Mike Ovitz. Naturally, no special requests were turned down. Puck also found creative ways to flatter VIP guests, such as automatically sending them a smoked salmon and crème fraîche pizza, known colloquially to staff and guests alike as "the Jewish pizza."

Like the crowds, the fame just came. "All of a sudden *Entertainment Tonight* was there," remembers Matthews, who transitioned into a PR role. "I was getting phone calls: 'We want to do a segment on *ET.*' I didn't think, 'Oh my God, we've hit the big time.' It just sort of *was*." (It should, however, be remembered that Spago didn't monopolize the entertainment business. Morton's and The Ivy, to name just two popular old-school canteens, still drew bold-faced names, and Chasen's retained its popularity among the over-fifty set, reinvigorated by recently elected President Ronald Reagan's fondness for it.)

Maybe, too, the populace was simply ready for something new: In 1981, nearly thirty years before the likes of Eataly in New York City, Jane Erickson, the punk-coiffed companion of notorious art dealer Douglas James Chrismas, opened Charmer's Market, a combination open-air market and restaurant with more than twenty-five Champagnes, under a stucco tent in Santa Monica, a stone's throw from the beach. Dustin Hoffman, Warren Beatty, Ali MacGraw, and Goldie Hawn were regulars. Charmer's bridged nouvelle (scallops with raspberry sauce) and California (hot barbecued duck salad) cuisines and forecast one of the defining characteristics of Spago: dinner as entertainment, for the entertainment set. "I didn't set out to get the Hollywood crowd," Erickson told the *New York Times*. "But I guess there's a certain atmosphere of theater here."

Lazaroff was the embodiment of Spago's theatricality. As her bank balance grew, she began realizing those childhood fashion dreams with a loud, colorful, and unmistakable style that extended from head to toe: "I wear twinkling clothes, Tinkerbell clothes that glisten with beads and sequins," she said. "My style is my own dream as a five-year-old of what I'd look like when I grew up." (That five-year-old must have also loved animals; circling around Lazaroff like cartoon butterflies were twenty-eight of them: parrots, rabbits, cats, and dogs.) Her wardrobe, housed in a twenty-foot-long closet that she kept locked, even from Puck, comprised more than one hundred dresses and more than a hundred pairs of shoes; just two examples: a purple taffeta Karl Lagerfeld minidress with a full, circle skirt, and a black bolero Rifat Ozbek suit with white passementerie. Often, she tied primitive objects into her hair and emphasized her eyes with exaggerated black eyeliner that extended the edges. ("I paint my face as if the audience were looking at me from fifty feet away," she said.) She maintained that it only took her twenty minutes to prepare such a getup, but hours to dress casually.

Puck, too, flowered into fame: He was gifted at making the most demanding guests feel special. He says that because he came from a small town, where the nearest cinema was five kilometers away and they had no car to get there, he didn't see movies as a kid. They didn't even own a TV. As a consequence, "I was never impressed by them," he says. "I wasn't like most of the people were if somebody was a movie star: *Can we get an autograph?* Because I didn't watch the movies. Most of them I never saw." When he became friendly with director Billy Wilder, "I had to lie to him," faking appreciation for his classics such as *Some Like It Hot*, while privately thinking, *"I hope he doesn't ask me who was in that!"*

Tables were hard to come by, but in theory the restaurant was democratic, with one exception—Terrail was forbidden. One night around 1989 while Puck was in San Francisco, his maître d' called telling him that Terrail had shown up unannounced with good pal Ed McMahon. "You know what to do," Puck told him, and hung up.

"HE'S WAY AHEAD OF ALL THE CHEFS."

In 1983, Puck and Lazaroff settled on their sophomore effort, presenting Puck's take on Chinese food. They secured a space in Santa Monica, named the restaurant after the location, Chinois on Main.

Things went more smoothly this time, though there was a hiccup when the Department of Health and Safety withheld a permit from the contractor, prompting Lazaroff to call the inspector. The problem, it was explained, was that brick is porous. The DOH didn't know who they were dealing with: Lazaroff said she'd put a polymer over it. When the inspector said the polymer would burn off, former med student Lazaroff explained that it wouldn't: Bonds strengthen when polymers are subjected to heat. When the inspector insisted she didn't know what she was talking about, Lazaroff exploded into action: She fished her old organic chemistry textbook out of the attic and went to his office early the next day dressed for success in a ruffled black-and-white dress. She insisted on seeing her tormentor, sat at his desk, and read to him out of the book, in a raised voice, so everybody could hear the schooling. Then she leaned in, whispering, "Mister, if you don't sign my health plans right now I'm going to sue you." He stamped his approval and Lazaroff returned to the restaurant, holding the paper aloft, triumphant once again.

Chinois on Main was another seamless Puck-Lazaroff collaboration: The kitchen turned out beef sauté with a honey-chile sauce; mesquite-grilled Santa Barbara shrimp with miso; crab with black bean sauce, butter, and scallions; sole with caviar, ginger, and a vodka-spiked shrimp sauce; and—influentially—a trio of assorted crème brûlées including ginger. Puck showed that he was no one-trick pony in the kitchen, and Lazaroff did the same with the décor: In the center of the dining room were two seven-foot enameled-brass peacocks; on the green lacquered walls was Pop Art; shiny black chairs surrounded green tables; and adorning the room were gargantuan flower arrangements. (Ironically, Puck had to let any Chinese cooks go. "They couldn't cook as we wanted," he said. "They were making gooey sauces with MSG." Any Asian cooks in the kitchen were Japanese.)

As an example of just how many tumblers have to fall into place for success, consider that a year before Chinois opened, chef Susumu Fukui was offering a more formal combination of French and Japanese cuisine, in a prescient but premature tasting menu format at La Petite Chaya in the Los Feliz neighborhood. In nearby Silver Lake, another ahead-of-his-time chef, former L'Orangerie toque Tadayoshi Matsuno, offered his version of "FrancAsian" cuisine at Lyon, a fifteen-seat counter restaurant.

Puck understood the importance of timing. "There are a lot of other restaurants like Spago," he said years later, "but we were first. . . . That's probably the most important thing. It seems like there are a lot of other very talented chefs, good-looking, very articulate . . . but . . . it's hard to get as well known if you're not first."

The sentiment is echoed by a still-admiring Terrail, with whom Puck buried the hatchet after his old boss got into a tussle with throat cancer, even throwing him a seventieth birthday party. "The most important thing about Wolfgang, in my eyes, from my perspective, he's way ahead of all the chefs. He has great vision of when to change and how to adapt. And the only one that I know that has that kind of vision is Jean-Georges [Vongerichten, who came to New York City in 1985]. . . . Wolfgang for some reason has the ability to be at the right place at the right time with the right package. And if you look at all the chefs . . . Joachim Splichal, Jean-Georges, and Wolfgang, I think they're the only guys who really see the world from their perspective and are able to grow with it."

The king and queen of Hollywood dining staged themselves an appropriately regal wedding in spring 1984, a medieval ceremony at L'Oustau de Baumanière, where Puck began his career. Approximately 130 guests made the trip. Lazaroff produced the ultimate fantasy wedding: horse-drawn carriages, three costume changes, and seventeen hours' worth of festivities. But she couldn't escape her role as hostess. When guests complained about the accommodations, she balked, "I'm the bride, why do I have to deal with this?" (They had actually been married by a rabbi in a private secret ceremony in 1983; Lazaroff wanted something that belonged to them alone. And who could blame her—the Baumanière wedding was covered by *Lifestyles of the Rich and Famous.*)

Through it all, Puck relied on Lazaroff for guidance on anything nonkitchen. Asked to cameo in a Shelley Long comedy, he deferred to her. "Yeah, this is cute," she said. "But tell them we can write a funnier line." (The scene ended up on the cutting room floor.) Before consenting to wear a suit for a *Los Angeles Times Magazine* cover story, he had to gain Lazaroff's approval.

Lazaroff didn't resent Puck's fame, but it peeved her to no end that her contribution was often overlooked. Lazaroff wanted credit for everything she did, which should have been news to nobody; the copyright page of *Modern French Cooking for the American Kitchen* features this note: "Introductory material written in collaboration with Barbara Lazaroff."

"When it started to take off at Spago, probably in the second year, and Wolfgang got so in demand and everybody wanted him for a different event and travel and to do different charities and stuff, there came a point where Barbara came to me and said that I had to run everything by her as well before I could just go to Wolfgang and get an okay," says Matthews. "I think that part of it was that Barbara was a partner in it and nobody really considered her. Wolf was in the forefront. He was the chef. He was charming. He had this personality. People really didn't know what Barbara's place was there."

"I know that everybody looks at me like I'm a publicity-hungry society climber," she said. "But the one thing I will not do is all the work on something and have somebody stick their name on it, even if it is my husband." (Though they filed for divorce in 2002, Wolfgang Puck's corporate website features a biography of Lazaroff on the Our Team page, naming her as cofounder, and she still spends time at Spago Beverly Hills.)

Eventually, Lazaroff couldn't take it anymore and began writing letters to reporters who she felt didn't properly credit her in print. Just as Puck had kicked her under the table in that publishing meeting, he worried that she'd alienate the media and their life-giving ink.

Says Reichl: "Wolf used to call me and say, 'Please make sure you get Barbara's name in when you do this story or it's not going to be worth going home.'" When uniforms were being produced for Chinois on Main, Lazaroff had the manufacturer create a jacket for her that had a message embroidered on the back: "I'm not Wolfgang Puck's girlfriend. He's my boyfriend."

"We had a major disagreement," said Lazaroff. "And we finally fought it out. I said, 'Look, Wolf, you do what you have to do. This is what I need to do.' . . . I would rather have somebody say she's bitchy, she's this and that."

Her contributions to the restaurants might have been the least of it, and the true source of her ire. Ventured one reporter: "Lazaroff's most ambitious undertaking . . . has been the making of Wolfgang Puck."

One Halloween, Lazaroff made a Batman villain of herself, naming her costume "I Am Woman"—a black dress to which she sewed "my animals . . . a washboard, models of the restaurants and a drafting board, hammers, nails, cooking utensils, financial papers . . .

all this shit was hanging off me. I wore a big crown and these black gloves that said SISTER, MOTHER, DAUGHTER, WIFE, SEX KITTEN. That is what I feel like all the time."

While Puck and Lazaroff were still living out their dizzying success, a *New York Times* rundown of L.A. restaurants reported the *Sunset Boulevard*–worthy decline of Ma Maison. "Now the Astroturf carpeting is frayed, the flowers are wilted, and the service creaks," wrote Marian Burros. "Without Mr. Puck, Ma Maison is living on its past." (It didn't help that in 1982, when Ma Maison's new chef, John Sweeney, was accused of murdering actress Dominique Dunne, daughter of writer Dominick Dunne, many believed Terrail stood by Sweeney, even enlisted legal counsel for him. In his book *A Taste of Hollywood*, Terrail insists that he merely asked a friend in the public defender's office to make sure he had a good lawyer, and has had no further contact with the man since. Terrail writes that it was one of the most stressful periods of his life, and no doubt cost him customers.) Whatever the reason, Ma Maison closed for good in 1985. The divorce metaphor comes up often in the recounting of industry breakups and, as with the real thing, it's the children—in this case the restaurants—who suffer the most.

2

THE OTTO SYNDROME

The fact that you were doing it for the public was something of an afterthought.

—Karen Puro (formerly Pritsker)

THE STORY OF HOW AN ANONYMOUS CHEF TWEAKED THE
NEW YORK CITY FOOD ESTABLISHMENT WHILE BECOMING A
FOLK HERO TO YOUNG COOKS ON THE EAST COAST, AND A
CONSTELLATION OF AMERICAN RESTAURANT COUPLES WENT
THEIR OWN WAY WITH MIXED SUCCESS AND LONGEVITY, IN
AND OUT OF THE KITCHEN

Six weeks into 1979—about the same time Michael McCarty
was putting the finishing touches on his nascent masterpiece on
the other side of the republic—a mythic figure rose over the eastern
culinary landscape. His name was Otto, and he was a chef unlike
any other, first because he wasn't French, but that was the least of
it: He favored T-shirts to starched whites; owned his own restau-

rant in partnership and collaboration with his wife; and toiled in bucolic bliss in the countryside beyond New York City, where he kept a small garden and a trout pond and whipped up a broad range of eclectic offerings that changed daily and so spontaneously that he couldn't dream of scribbling the menu before three o'clock in the afternoon. He was also a mystery, a puzzle: Otto wasn't his real name but rather a pseudonym dreamed up by *The New Yorker* magazine's writer John McPhee, who introduced him to the world in a sprawling 25,000-word profile in the magazine's February 19 issue. The article spun the tale of how Otto, with wife Anne (also a pseudonym) serving as pastry chef, sommelier, and hostess, ran a fifty-five-seat country restaurant in a rustic farmhouse-inn where the author claimed, audaciously, to have eaten the twenty or thirty best meals of his life, despite the fact that he'd dined in "the fields of Les Baux" and "the streets of Lyons [*sic*]"—sly references to, respectively, chefs Raymond Thuilier and Paul Bocuse. McPhee, known for his extravagantly detailed reporting (he had written a definitive piece on Greenmarkets for the magazine the year prior), stuffed the article so full of minutiae that Otto all but sprang to life and walked off the page: He was a man of mixed Austrian and British extraction who spent his life in utter servitude to his restaurant, poring over cookery books and scavenging for ingredients everywhere from Manhattan markets to his local Grand Union. He began his day at 6 a.m., prepped until the dinner hour, then cooked from an open kitchen for his customers, who might range in number from as few as two to a little more than forty. The chef shopped from local groceries and supermarkets, and had, according to McPhee, developed a repertoire of about six hundred appetizers and entrees (main courses) of his own devising, things like veal and shrimp quenelles; sautéed scallops with pesto; paella à la marinara; and a signature dish he dubbed Chicken Coriander (chicken breasts marinated in yogurt with lemon juice and cilantro). Even when he went classic, he broke with French convention, making bordelaise with boiled pork rinds instead of marrow, béarnaise with green peppercorns rather than black. This was no small matter: Most chefs still adhered to Escoffier (recall those asterisks on Ken Frank's early menu denoting his unique dishes); to do otherwise was an act of rebellion.

McPhee's story was titled "Brigade de Cuisine," an arch nod to the fact that there was no *brigade*; Otto worked alone. "There is no way to get qualified help," lamented subject to biographer. "You'd have to import kids from Switzerland." (The article boasts many such markers of the culinary times, such as Otto's observation that "when you can buy bean curd and eggroll wrappers in a supermarket in a town like this there's some sort of quiet revolution going on.") Decades before the term *food porn* would come into vogue, before series such as *The Mind of a Chef* would dissect generations yet unborn, "Brigade de Cuisine" trafficked in what might be termed *chef porn*: McPhee relates Otto's every step and sentiment, leaving nothing but his name to the imagination. The lingering journalistic lens produces a gauzy, slo-mo literary effect—he devotes an entire paragraph to a day in the life of Otto's kitchen towel and five columns to a Manhattan shopping expedition, laced with Otto's ruminations on everything from ingredients (chorizo, lobster, sea urchins) to the most rudimentary of equipment (whisks). Readers found themselves parked in Otto's restaurant galley as he crafted new dishes, observing him in his home, where he packed school lunches for his children. They were even introduced to his customers, a utopian and eclectic lot that included a bridge toll collector, a plumber, a state senator (from another state), and an international tennis star, left tantalizingly unnamed.

McPhee also reported that "the center of attention, and the subject of a good deal of table talk, is the unseen man in the kitchen." The customers present as groupies as they relate, in rapt terms, their admiration of him and his skills, in language usually reserved for artists and musicians. As if that weren't enough, Otto—in the piece that catapulted him to a sort of postmodern fame—expresses his distrust of the limelight: "He prefers being a person to being a personality," writes McPhee. "His wish to be acknowledged is exceeded by his wish not to be celebrated, and he could savor recognition only if he could have it without publicity." So per McPhee, he deserved attention commensurate with the kings of nouvelle cuisine, but was too modest to covet it. He was, in other words, perfect.

The issue landed like a hand grenade. Otto—in part because of his anonymity, in part because of McPhee's rhapsodic appraisal—was an overnight sensation and a one-man generational demarcation line, received differently by two very different populations. The larger, more entrenched, more vociferous of them—the culinary establishment—wasn't nearly as taken by Otto as the author was. No sooner had the piece hit newsstands than it was, in *New Yorker* parlance, the talk of the town. In hindsight, it was perfectly engineered to be that: McPhee opened with a bang, putting his best-meals-of-my-life claim in the first paragraphs, and compounded the mystique by not divulging the restaurant's location, only teasing that it was "more than five miles and less than a hundred from the triangle formed by La Grenouille, Lutèce, and Le Cygne," three of the most celebrated French restaurants of the day.

Some muckety-mucks granted the unknown toque the benefit of the doubt—"His range is fabulous and his ideas are awfully good, too," said Joe Baum—but most industry honchos and media bigs treated him as a curiosity, possibly even a fraud. *The New Yorker's* editor William Shawn had inadvertently softened "Brigade de Cuisine" up for attack, when in an unprecedented break with the magazine's policy, he allowed McPhee to perform his own fact-checking in order to preserve Otto's identity. Nonetheless, the magazine's offices were inundated by calls seeking the truth behind Otto, spurring an internal guessing game. Some industrious staffers, long before the conveniences of Google, researched the woodland critters name-dropped in the story, hoping to discover that one of them thrived in a particular locality.

The fact-checking anomaly sparked accusations that Otto was pure fiction, or a composite of multiple chefs, but the author's sterling reputation denied those any oxygen.

Still, there was no shortage of criticism. Four Seasons co-owner Tom Margittai balked that Otto wasn't "in the restaurant business really. He's an eccentric doing his own thing." One observer, former Culinary Institute of America president Jacob Rosenthal, suggested the piece was a gambit by *The New Yorker* to make up for lost ground in the restaurant-coverage war with *New York* magazine, where critic Gael Greene, an early proponent of nouvelle cuisine, whose sensual reviews and articles (she also wrote erotica) were tailor-made for the emerging times, was making waves.

Reporting at the time only hinted at the anti-French sentiment woven into "Brigade de Cuisine" and whether Francophilia might therefore have motivated the article's detractors. As if Otto's not being French and McPhee's claiming that his food lapped France's best weren't bad enough, in the piece Otto refers to the most celebrated New York City French restaurants derisively as "frog ponds"; bristles at the snobbery of the captains in their dining rooms; reveals that he once found ice crystals in his meat at the well-respected La Caravelle. There's also no question that, whether intentional or not, McPhee's claim that his meals at Otto's were superior to those he'd enjoyed in the nouvelle cuisine temples of Les Baux and Lyon casually called into question the palates and knowledge of the city's reigning tastemakers. Then there was the handful of words buried in the piece in which Otto, dining with McPhee at Lutèce (the absolute pinnacle of French food in New York, if not the country, at the time), deduces that the turbot they are eating must have been purchased . . . wait for it . . . *frozen*. ("Why should the story be taken seriously?" asked Raymond Sokolov, former food editor of the *New York Times*. "Why should we accept McPhee's reaction to food and an unknown, unnamed chef criticizing the fish at Lutèce?")

Mimi Sheraton, the *New York Times* restaurant critic from 1975 through 1983, believes that effrontery might have provoked some of the attacks on Otto: "I think that's partly true and especially in the food world," she says. "Food writers loved Lutèce. I don't think it bothered me any more than the fact that he was taken around to all kinds of restaurants and critiqued them [to McPhee during the writing of the piece]. I minded that whole part of it. Something about that rankled me. Craig [Claiborne] and Frank [Prial, the *Times* wine critic] and I all thought it was bullshit. Craig, of course, on the part of Lutèce, because he was even closer to André [Soltner] than I was. They didn't think it sounded that good." (The gentlemanly Soltner declined to criticize Otto but chafed at the notion that he served frozen fish. The Lord of Lutèce fired off a mailgram to *The New Yorker*, offering to produce ten years' worth of ichthyologic receipts and demanding an apology.)

After a week of Otto mania, the establishment smackdown came from Prial and Sheraton herself, who'd had no plans to cover him until the paper's managing editor, Al Siegal, sent them individual notes that read, "I hope you guys are looking for this [guy]."

"Oh shit," Sheraton recalls thinking. "Let's find him. And in three days we did."

The writers dispatched a stringer to out Otto, and they ID'd him as Alan Lieb of The Bull Head Inn in Shohola, Pennsylvania, and prior to that, through November 1978, of The Red Fox Inn in Milford, Pennsylvania. The clever sleuth poked around political circles, leading to a Pike County Republican pol who happened to be president of the bank that gave Lieb and wife Anna Rozmarja, nicknamed Ronnie, their mortgage. Sheraton, Prial, and Prial's wife made a pilgrimage to The Bull Head Inn. Sheraton was unimpressed. (She still is. As I sat with her in the living room of her Greenwich Village house nearly four decades later, she scrunched up her face and said, "The food was really bad. I still remember a something filled with something that was all wet bread. I have in my mind a vision of a lump of wet bread.") On February 26, 1979, just two weeks after the Otto feeding frenzy began, Sheraton detailed the trio's disappointment in a piece headlined "Dinner at the Elusive Otto's: The Disappointing Details." What's striking is how personal the takedown seems as Sheraton turns Lieb's own words, as quoted in "Brigade de Cuisine," against him: In McPhee's piece, Lieb rails against canned foods; Sheraton describes the artichokes he serves as having "pale yellow . . . bottoms of the type usually canned." She also echoes the Lutèce slight: "The block shape of the duck and the precision of the straight cut through the breast bone hinted that the duck might have been purchased frozen." (Ironically, given the fact-checking scandal attached to "Brigade de Cuisine," the *Times* verifier let one detail slip: Lieb's first name is printed as "Allen" when it was in fact spelled "Alan.") "While it is true that one cannot make a definitive evaluation of any restaurant on the basis of a single meal," Sheraton concluded, "it is equally true that there is a minimal level of quality below which a great and experienced cook cannot sink even on his worst day." This criticism would sting today; at a time when the *New York Times*'s power was absolute, it was devastating.

"I have a little roadhouse in which I try to cook fairly good food," Lieb said that March. "That review was like dropping a hydrogen bomb on a small island."

Adding to the melodrama, McPhee was tipped off to the impending unmasking and phoned Sheraton at home around midnight the very evening she dined at The Bull Head Inn to entreat her not to out the chef. When Sheraton returned the call around four the next morning, things got heated: "I said, 'You know how hot a topic food is, you know how hot a topic restaurants are, do you think you could write that in *The New Yorker* with all the signposts? It was like a scavenger hunt.'" Then she informed him the point was moot: Unbeknownst to McPhee, an initial appraisal had been phoned into the *Times* by Prial from a roadside phone booth and was in that morning's paper. (Sheraton's longer piece ran two days later.) The ensuing crossfire was worthy of a Quentin Tarantino shoot-out as many of

Sheraton's fellow writers publicly criticized her decision. Around the same time, *Village Voice* photographer Fred McDarrah sold a picture of her to *Newsweek*—depriving her of *her* anonymity—which she believes might have been retaliation for her exposé. As *New York Post* gossip columnist Cindy Adams used to sign off: "Only in New York, kids."

"I guess the press can't stand a vacuum," concluded Lieb. "This time the vacuum was me."

"YOU DON'T HAVE TO BREAK INTO THAT TRIANGLE."

Chefs and the journalists who cover them live in surprisingly different worlds. For all the offense "Brigade de Cuisine" caused, to a subset of young Americans considering a life of chefdom, Otto was an instant folk hero and North Star. The same temerity that offended the establishment bolstered them, showed them what was possible, and—perhaps because Otto's true identity was initially unknown—allowed them to imagine themselves tracing his footsteps. They no doubt also related to his off-the-grid anonymity, since none of them would have been sought out to opine in the flurry of Otto stories. They were the rebels waiting to spring on the public.

David Liederman, who with his wife, Susan, would open Manhattan Market the same year the piece ran, and would go on to strike gold with his business David's Cookies, calls it "probably the best food article I ever read in my life. It was seminal to the food movement in the United States." (Like many who came up at this disconnected time, when Liederman speaks of "the United States," he means his corner of it, just as when some refer to the California food revolution, they omit contemporaneous goings-on across the rest of the country.)

"Everybody wanted to be Otto," says Liederman. "Everybody

wanted to cook like Otto, have the repertoire of Otto. This is when there were not a lot of people cooking. Otto was self-taught. He was a genius cook, according to John McPhee. He had impeccable technique. He totally freestyled, which at the time was totally new. This guy had total freedom to cook whatever he wanted to cook with no rules. He was an absolute artist."

"It was everything that I was dreaming of," says Peter Hoffman, who was then cooking at La Colombe d'Or, a Provençal bistro, owned by George and Helen Studley, in New York City, and would go on to open the SoHo mainstay Savoy. "Here was a guy who was writing a daily menu, working off of what was available to him, improvisationally, living out in the country. His wife was the pastry chef. It was a beautiful fortune and I completely loved it."

"It was like, you don't have to break into that triangle," says Hoffman, referring to the trio of French restaurants name-dropped in the article. Hoffman so related to Lieb that when Sheraton unmasked him, "I was like, I'm going. I went with my girlfriend at the time. And we spent the weekend out there. I was there to make a pilgrimage. I wanted to see the trout pond in the back and I wanted to walk the grounds."

Hoffman's Bull Head Inn experience counterbalanced Sheraton's. It was, he says, "very good, not perfect. It was still incredibly exciting and creative and well executed. It was a menu that wasn't trying to be traditionally French at that point in any way." Thirty-eight years later, Hoffman still remembers the meal starting with a risotto ball with molten cheese in the center and thinking, *They [aren't] going to have* that *at Lutèce*.

Not all young American cooks loved Otto: Bob Pritsker, who with his wife, Karen, would open Dodin-Bouffant in New York City, also in 1979, found it all very suspect: "The production by two people of food which seemed intricate, and smoked in the house and ground in the house and shopped for inefficiently at Grand Union. It's not real. You don't conduct a restaurant that way and hope to come out the other end whole, financially or mentally," he says. Nonetheless, when Google coughed up a phone number for Pritsker and I cold-called him for an interview for this book, he chuckled, then asked me if I'd ever read McPhee's piece, a printout of which was spread before me on my desk. It seems I had caught Pritsker precisely at a moment when he was remembering it, nearly four decades after the fact. Alan Lieb has long since faded from the spotlight, but for those he touched, Otto still looms large.

American food, as I saw it, was as much about who was in my kitchen as anything else. We'd start with a southern dish, fried chicken or pan-blackened fish, which Able would perfect. Wasabe would take it over, adding a daikon or seaweed salad. Valentine would add a package of rice wrapped in banana. . . . Together we made an amalgam that was as American as shoofly pie.

—Karen Hubert Allison,
How I Gave My Heart to the Restaurant Business (a novel)

"YOU WERE LIVING IN YOUR OWN LITTLE WORLD."

In a quirk of timing on par with the Jane Fonda–Michael Douglas nuclear cautionary film *The China Syndrome* being released, coincidentally, in March 1979, just two weeks prior to the Three Mile Island accident, "Brigade de Cuisine" reflected and predicted a very particular species of chef evolving throughout the Northeast around this time. Before 1979 drew to a close, five American couples would open restaurants in the Otto and Anne—or Alan and

Anna—mode. Only they would do it right in New York City. They were, in order of opening in New York: Bob and Karen Pritsker's Dodin-Bouffant, Len Allison and Karen Hubert's Huberts, Barry and Susan Wine's The Quilted Giraffe, David and Susan Lieder-man's Manhattan Market, and David and Karen Waltuck's Chante-relle. (It was also the year that another couple, Tim and Nina Zagat, who had met working in Paris, started a New York restaurant sur-vey among friends that would lead, three years later, to the first of their slender burgundy-hued publications that would be updated annually, and then appear in other cities and eventually online. And another couple, Brit Keith McNally, who would go on to build a res-taurant empire founded on Balthazar and other classics, and Lynn Wagenknecht, whom he would marry, then divorce, opened the styl-ish bistro The Odeon in Tribeca the following year in tandem with McNally's brother, Brian. The restaurant launched the career of one of the few prominent African American chefs of the 1980s, Patrick Clark, a cook's son from Brooklyn who had trained under Michel Guérard and fashioned a menu that fused French finesse and Ameri-can must-haves like burgers in a retro, casual setting trumpeted by a neon sign that became an iconic image of the 1980s.)

The restaurants were far from clones but had much in common, especially considering the paucity of American chefs at the time and the relatively small number of standout restaurants—most of them French—in New York City. All were operated by couples who were also owners; most of the couples had, at most, limited formal training, and learned or sharpened their cooking and hospitality chops on the job; and they favored or aspired to a nouvelle style over traditional French cuisine. (Yet another couple, Sally and John Darr, opened La Tulipe in the West Village that same year with a gender reversal—Sally was the chef and John, who left academia for the restaurant, the multitasking partner—but the restaurant served classic cuisine. Nevertheless, by the time she got around to review-ing La Tulipe in 1980, *New York* magazine's restaurant critic Gael

Greene, connecting Sally Darr to the trend, fretted that she might have been "another victim of The Otto Syndrome.")

Two of the restaurants gestated outside New York City well before 1979: Dodin-Bouffant, which opened at 405 East 58th Street just weeks before Otto was introduced to the masses, began life in Boston in 1974, a labor of love by Karen and Bob Pritsker, and The Quilted Giraffe debuted in New Paltz, New York, in 1975, strictly as a business venture by the Wines. All of the restaurants had been conceived before Otto was introduced to the world, but they were all of a piece with McPhee's subject, showcases for a very specific subspecies of American chef when *American chef* was scarcely a species to begin with. The restaurants also represented some of the first attempts by young Americans to interpret the nouvelle cuisine sensibility in the United States, a reflection of their open-mindedness and of the breakaway barrier to entry: The idea that couples with scant, if any, formal training could even contemplate becoming chefs and restaurateurs in Manhattan would be laughable today, but at the time it was a reasonable enough prospect that several successfully attempted it.

"It was a very happy time," says Josh Wesson, who briefly served as sommelier at The Quilted Giraffe, then filled the same role for about three years at Huberts. "There was a group of like-minded individuals who were all doing different things but had a kind of shared vision when it came to experimenting, innovating, playing with different culinary traditions and different techniques, and creating things that were uniquely theirs. The first wave of nouvelle cuisine had broken over the shores of the States, so there were techniques and an appreciation of freshness and lightness, informed as much by Japan as it was France, but the directions that each of those couples took were quite different."

Of the restaurants, three proved short-lived and two endured to help define the ensuing decades in New York City dining.

The first of the short-lived duets was Dodin-Bouffant, the love-child of Karen (née Cooperman) and Bob Pritsker, who were, respectively, an advertising copywriter and an attorney by trade, though Bob never got around to actually practicing; when they met he was working for Hotel Corporation of America. (Three of these couples' husbands were law-school grads, and two never practiced, demonstrating both the force of conventional career paths and how strong and sudden was the kitchen's lure.) Bob was a native of Providence, Rhode Island, who grew up in Pawtucket; Karen was from Westchester County, New York. In Boston, sometime around 1969, he spotted her—a Boston University student at the time—and went right for her. They fell in love, and his enthusiasm for food and cooking swept her away in its undertow. Julia Child was an abstraction to most Americans, but to the Pritskers, she was a very real, local presence. "Julia Child had come back from France and moved to Cambridge and was the doyenne, suddenly, of food," says Bob. "Right there in Boston, this shithole of a microcosm for food, except for the fish, perhaps." The Boston food scene in the early 1970s was minuscule: Karen remembers it as Child, cooking instructor Madeleine Kamman, French restaurant Maison Robert, and nothing else. Jack Savenor, Julia Child's go-to butcher, was a hub for local foodnoscenti—"a bit of the glue," says Bob—and the Pritskers hung around his shop, networked. "There was a lot of fanaticism at that counter, a lot of intensity," remembers Bob. "I'd never seen anything like it."

Years before *Julie and Julia* author Julie Powell conquered the Internet doing the same in a blog that led to the book, the Pritskers cooked their way through Child's *Mastering the Art of French Cooking* (volumes one and two), and also leaned heavily on Richard Olney. "I don't think there were that many books that were written clearly enough for people who weren't formally trained," says Karen. They bought their meats from Savenor, their fish from Legal Seafood's George Berkowitz, and produced so much food in their low-rent Back Bay apartment, prepping on a half-collapsed Ping-Pong table, that they gave most of it away to neighbors.

And just like that, they were cooks. "It must have been a feeling within some of us that what we were doing in our lives wasn't particularly satisfying," says Karen of the zeitgeist. "That we were doing what we were preprogrammed to do. It was way more fun to find something that you loved and go with it as far as it would go."

In time, they developed finesse, could whip egg whites to perfection, stopped breaking their béarnaise. When they married at the Regency Hotel in New York City in May 1971, they dictated the menu to the more seasoned hotel chefs. Back in Boston, they began catering parties for "a very old, suburban crowd," remembers Karen. The husband of a Wellesley couple, frequent clients, was president of two stock exchange companies and offered to back the Pritskers in a restaurant. If they were good enough to attract a benefactor, they figured, they should go into business for themselves. They borrowed $50,000 from Karen's stepfather, about $50,000 more from a bank, and in 1974 opened Dodin-Bouffant, a prix fixe dinner-only restaurant on Boylston Street. The name nodded to both novelist Marcel Rouff's *La vie et la passion de Dodin-Bouffant, gourmet* and a Paris restaurant of the same name.

Of taking the restaurant plunge, Karen says, "The way I think we saw it was if you're doing it with your life partner, what a support system you have. You were living in your own little world. I don't know that it was thought about; it just felt natural to share with your spouse or your partner something you enjoy. The fact that you were doing it for the public was something of an afterthought."

Following the French model, Bob marketed each morning, but the similarities ended there; the kitchen team was largely unrefined. "It was pretty haphazard at the beginning," says Karen. "There was Bob and myself and two other cooks in the kitchen. We placed an ad in probably the *Boston Globe* and we hired people whose personalities we liked who had done some cooking, but there were no professionals around. It was just sort of fun. Everybody was cooking and talking about food and other things as well." Because the restaurant was dinner-only, the schedule suited people with other careers, especially photographers and artists.

The university-rich city echoed the politics of Berkeley, but Bob says that he and Karen weren't part of protest society, but "we were counterculture as to the frogs in Boston, however few they were, who had French restaurants. Most importantly, there was a guy who owned a restaurant, Maison Robert. Maison Robert moved from a less-important place to the old city hall. And it was such a snobby act and he looked down his nose at these two American kids who started cooking French food, of all heretical things, that we weren't entitled to even be cooking."

The Pritskers, in another commonality amongst many of the couples, learned on the job. Karen says that except for the size of the industrial stove, in Dodin-Bouffant's first months, they cooked as amateurs—Karen in a T-shirt and clogs. Customers were few and far between: The staff played hearts during service while Karen and Bob used the lulls to master the fundamentals of timing. But there were other unanticipated challenges: They wanted to be more creative, but lacked the technical foundation that expressiveness demands, so were stuck in the classicism rut, especially after a 1976 tour of France that included visits to Alain Chapel and Troisgros. Boston tastemakers weren't receptive to the prix fixe concept or to the European-style service charge they employed, which in September 1976 prompted local critic David Brudnoy, on his *Nightline* radio show, to comment that "the food is fine, the people who run it are pigs." (The Pritskers sued him for defamation.) They were unprepared for the scrutiny, or the criticism, especially Karen, who developed a reputation for haughtiness. (Gael Greene, who is friendly with Karen today, attributed the reputation to misread shyness.) By 1977, the Pritskers were at a crossroads: The restaurant was straining the marriage to the breaking point and they separated; then the media picked up on the separation, dealing them another blow.

"Everyone knew personal information that was written in the press," says Karen. "I could never put myself through anything but food scrutiny."

"The restaurant didn't close," says Bob. "I continued on without her there. . . . We had to separate. We were in deep trouble interpersonally."

Karen retreated to New York City. Eventually, Bob shuttered Dodin-Bouffant, sold it to Moncef Meddeb, who transformed it into the French restaurant L'Espalier. The Pritskers reconciled, decided to try their hand at re-creating Dodin-Bouffant in Manhattan, enlisting an attorney so that they could pounce when the perfect space presented itself. In January 1979, the Pritskers opened Dodin-Bouffant 2.0 in a single-use residential brownstone that they transformed—largely by their own hand over eight months—into a street-level fifty-seat dining room painted pink, white, gray, and blue. The kitchen was subterranean. (While they were in construction, Barry Wine, an attorney turned chef, strolled in, introduced himself, told them he was thinking of relocating his own restaurant, The Quilted Giraffe, from New Paltz to Manhattan.) The Pritskers' budget blown, the restaurant opened with walls bereft of artwork, freighting the pink tulips that adorned the tables with a tremendous atmospheric burden.

Establishing what would become a commonality among the Five Couples, the Pritskers had by then broken free of traditional cuisine to cook in their own style. "Once we knew what we were doing in terms of how long it took to sauté a veal kidney, we could play with the concept," says Karen. "It was a combination of that and the trips we began taking to France. We closed the restaurants in both Boston and New York every July and we spent a month traipsing through France and seeing what other people were doing. Frédy Girardet [at his self-titled restaurant at the Hôtel de Ville in Crissier, Switzerland], Jacques Pic [at the three-Michelin-star Maison Pic in Valence, France]. Interestingly enough, at Taillevent the creativity wasn't as abundant as it was at Chapel or Crissier, [though] the execution was so perfect. But we also learned a lot about service and what guests expect when they get to a great table.

"We had changed as cooks and we knew that we wanted to have more fun with the food," says Karen. "We didn't want to do classic food anymore although we did do certain classic preparations. We knew that if four people came to dinner, three of them may have had fun with our fun, the fourth might have been more conservative."

The Pritskers also incorporated an amuse-bouche,* which Karen believes they were among the first to do in New York City. "We felt it very important because we had seen it in our travels and thought it was a nice way of welcoming." There was also a less altruistic reason: "We sometimes got backed up in the kitchen so we knew if we had something on the table, that and bread gave you a little breathing space." Diners on the American side of the Atlantic had some catching up to do: "We served rillettes† a lot. People would be very circumspect about the fat on top so we changed it up.

"We ran with our intelligence," says Karen. "I think all those couples who were running restaurants in New York at that time were smart, and curious. And I think our curiosity got most of us to where we eventually wound up."

And what did they cook? "I did a sort of a take on steak au poivre, but it was calf's liver. I also did a vegetable sausage. I know the Waltucks did a seafood sausage and I did a vegetable sausage and nobody

---

* A one- or two-bite offering from the kitchen, common today in upscale restaurants. When David Waltuck introduced amuse-bouches at Chanterelle, he explained to the staff that it was like getting nuts at a bar. Front-of-house team members would order them by saying "Nuts for two," or for however many people were at their table.

† Potted meats, often duck or pork, usually spread on toast.

had ever done a nonmeat sausage until then. There was a chicken forcemeat that bound it, not much, and anybody who was vegetarian, we never told them and they ate it anyway. Chicken forcemeat, egg white, broccoli, carrots, and peas all blanched carefully, not pureed, very finely minced, put into casings, poached, and then sautéed and served with a beurre noisette and chopped hazelnuts. We also did our own duck pastrami; we used a *magret*. Took the legs and cured them and hung them in the kitchen in cheesecloth, no temperature control. We monitored them and we used them. We also did gravlax garnished with smoked potatoes and smoked leeks. Mixing what we knew classically with really interesting changes."

As in Boston, staffing was catch-as-catch-can: "We had one Czech, who had worked in Europe and had good butchering and charcuterie skills," says Karen. "We hired a young man who had worked in Long Island whose parents owned an Italian restaurant. He had some kitchen skills, but everybody else we hired, I don't think any of them had professional experience. Year two of the restaurant, we did start hiring people who had graduated from The Culinary [Institute of America] and had more developed prep skills or sugar skills." One of the Pritskers' catches was Mark Chayette, a graduate of Michel Guérard's kitchens at Les Prés d'Eugénie in France, and Régine's in New York City. "A very gifted guy," says Bob. "An unusual guy. A Williams grad. Very cerebral. Great hands. Knives were sharp. Workspace clean. The towel was always in the apron."

Bob didn't bother with French kitchen conventions, and was so unconcerned with appearances that he thought nothing of visiting the dining room in blood-spattered whites, which became an inadvertent sartorial signature. "I didn't change my apron. I didn't put on a toque. I'm a Jewish kid. *Toque?* What does that even mean?"

New York magazine's Gael Greene praised the food at Dodin-Bouffant as "original, strikingly personal, even eccentric at times." She adored the calf's brain fritters with house-pickled cherries, lamb over arugula with baby beans and root vegetable purees. She found the desserts similarly idiosyncratic, breaking with what Greene described as "French restaurant cliché," such as ricotta-pepper tart with nutmeg ice cream. In 1980, Greene put Dodin-Bouffant atop her list of favorite French restaurants of the moment. Mimi Sheraton, in an early iteration of what would become a repeating pattern between her reviews and Greene's, was more measured: She found much of the food excellent, awarded Dodin-Bouffant two stars, but was frankly critical of some dishes, and of what she saw as the restaurant's pretensions, including the menu, written in French with no translations.

"The Mimi review irked the hell out of us," says Karen. "I found it difficult. [Bob] found it unbearable. He railed at every review that wasn't perfect. There was something obsessive about the way he looked at the press. The night that the *New York Times* calls you in advance to fact-check, you knew. The fact that Mimi only gave us two stars threw him for a real personal loop." (Today, Bob says, "It's an expectation thing, I guess; while she praised the food, she didn't give it the third star. That happens. It was a long review. I thought it was enthusiastic.")

Regardless, Dodin-Bouffant did a solid business, so solid in fact that it was omitted from the 1981 *Gault Millau Guide to New York* because the critics had one "catastrophic" meal and the restaurant was so solidly booked they were unable to return for a second dinner. "The economy was good. Wall Street was rolling," says Karen. "A lot of expense-account people coming to dinner. Woody Allen and Mia Farrow. It was the kind of restaurant where you got to see everybody." Another regular was an increasingly omnipresent Michael McCarty, keeping tabs on the evolution of the food scene on his native coast.

Dodin-Bouffant, and the marriage, would last less than four years in New York City. But let's leave the Pritskers in bloom for a moment; the end will come soon enough.

"I'M SURE IF HE WERE DOING IT NOW
HE'D BE INTO SOUS VIDE AND LIQUID NITROGEN."

Huberts began life as a Brooklyn dinner party when Len Allison, an English teacher, who along with girlfriend Karen Hubert, a writer, got it in their heads to make a documentary about a clothing store in Brooklyn, New York. The unlikely odyssey to the professional kitchen began in 1977 when, in a sort of culinary Kickstarter campaign, they staged a series of dinner parties in their Cobble Hill home to raise $10,000 to buy a movie camera.

Two years later, in 1979, the movie hadn't been made (it never would), but Allison and Hubert—who were regulars at John Novi's Depuy Canal House*—had taken the plunge into the restaurant business, launched the twelve-table Huberts on Hoyt Street in Boerum Hill, in an 1880s house that had been converted to a tin-ceilinged saloon space (it now houses the popular, though resolutely unvarnished, watering hole Brooklyn Inn). In addition to regular service, the couple hosted a cookbook author series, celebrating new publications by writers such as Edna Lewis and Paula Wolfert. The *Times*'s Sheraton was an early fan: "There was something very dear about the one in Brooklyn," she says. "None of the plates matched, different silver, and it was very sweet, more personal in a way." She also admired Allison's tendency toward experimentation. "I'm sure if he were doing it now he'd be into sous vide and liquid nitrogen. He had that kind of mind."

With time, Allison and Hubert developed their technical skills, and a repertoire of recipes. By July 1981, seeking sufficient clientele

---

* So were Barry and Susan Wine of The Quilted Giraffe. "John Novi was our Otto," says Susan Wine. "He did totally innovative, amazing things. I could never understand because he never got out, didn't know other chefs, didn't travel. My God, I wondered, is he speaking to the ultimate source above us?"

to maintain their business, they relocated to larger quarters at 102 East 22nd Street in Manhattan. The space, in what would become a minor design trend, celebrated the street scene outside by omitting curtains in the windows. (The restaurant would move again, to 575 Park Avenue at 63rd Street, in 1989. Patrick Bateman, the antihero of Bret Easton Ellis's *American Psycho*, dines there in the film version of the book.)

Allison and Hubert (the couple married in 1984, whereupon she affixed his last name) were unique among the Five Couples, and among most of their contemporaries, in that they did not come at food and cooking from a French vantage point.

"Where did people get their sensibility from?" says Peter Hoffman, who cooked at Huberts from 1981 through 1985. "They didn't travel to Europe; they were getting it from intellectuals. We were an early participant in what became New American Cuisine. It was a combination of local ingredients but it was also about native ideas— native cooking. What's in *our* tradition? Why are we always looking to Europe? What are the traditions *here* of great dishes?

"New American Cuisine was both about recipes and about source," says Hoffman. "So we began buying direct from producers and being involved with the [Union Square] Greenmarket at Huberts."

As with many of the Five Couples, technique wasn't the Allisons' strong suit, or priority. "They didn't know from technique," says Hoffman. "So we all brought to it what [we] brought, and where [we] had been, so that's part of the trajectory."

Allison and Hubert's food was even more idiosyncratic than the Pritskers': In their first year in Manhattan, there was a starter of smoked salmon pâté flavored with dill and aquavit. There was chicken soufflé with morels; turkey potpie; bourbon-braised pork loin with prunes and assorted purees; sautéed fillet of beef with mushrooms, scallions, and crème fraîche. There were also daily specials, including a rotating selection of fish stuffed with fish mousse. (In her two-star *New York Times* review, Sheraton—who remains an ardent fan—chided that "the most consistent culinary flaw is a tendency to sweetness where it doesn't belong.")

Of the kitchen's intellectual bent, Wesson, sommelier there from 1983 through 1986, says: "It was always a therapy session with spatulas and tongs. There was a lot of introspection, a lot of analysis, a lot of looking back and looking forward, a lot of putting things in context. This is how everybody talked about everything in those days. . . . I think that's because Karen and Len were particularly self-aware. All of these restaurants are defined by their couples. And it's not just their professional experience that defined the way that the restaurants felt if you were working, but it was the whole gestalt of the place.

"The glove was pulled inside out at Huberts," says Wesson. "They still wanted to create a great dining experience and do things that were worth doing and different from what other people were doing, but they didn't approach it from the very top tier of existing restaurants. They were kind of doing it from the ground up." The couple also built on the program that was a fixture of the Brooklyn iteration, welcoming chefs and cookbook authors.

Len Allison's personality was, according to Wesson, "*The Dawn of the Dead*. There were different sides of the brain. Karen was very right hemisphere, emotional, soft, extraordinarily kind, almost poetically kind. Len was much more uptight and controlling. And I think he was both enamored of and threatened by people who were more skilled than him."

Wesson raises an important point: In a theme that would repeat itself in various restaurants around the United States throughout the 1980s, many of the chef visionaries were dependent on more technically proficient subordinates to realize their ambitions. According to Wesson, Allison wasn't at peace with that reality: "He was self-trained. And when he would get in the kitchen with some-one who was formally trained, had better skills than him, he would learn, of course, but depending upon who that person was, he could be intimidated by them. And sometimes the concrete expression of that tension made for a difficult environment in the kitchen."

"Len, I thought, was driven to the point where maybe something at a moment in time wouldn't be so pleasant," says Bob Pritsker. "But, God, to know him socially was a joy. I enjoyed him. He was bright, giving." Says Sheraton: "Len was sort of a luftmensch, but she was so darling and simple. They went very well together."

Allison's personality quirks aside, Wesson recalls Huberts positively. The couple, he says, shared "a love supreme," and also gave him a wide berth in devising his own wine list, which paralleled the open-minded attitude toward food. "It was an exciting time to be a somm, because there weren't very many people who were doing that. So it was a tight little group of folks who would commune with one another in the service of finding deliciousness. There was excitement coming from all over the place. The wine world was expanding the way the food world was. If you followed along you were able to transcend the traditional hierarchies of French fine dining and French wine lists and boldly go where nobody had gone before."

Huberts closed in 1991. The Allisons tried another restaurant, Onda, in SoHo that same year, but it was gone by 1992. Len Allison taught at The Culinary Institute of America for three years, then the couple moved to Maui, where he took up Chinese medicine and acupuncture. Both Allisons are deceased; Karen died in 1997, at age forty-nine, from breast cancer; Len died several years later.

"I WAS IN LOVE."

The second lawyer of the group, David Liederman—a quick-witted and confident nonconformist—was struck by lightning as a young man. Born in New York City, raised in Princeton, New Jersey,

Liederman was first turned on to food by Julia Child, but was by no means a sophisticate. In 1969, touring France at age twenty, he and a girlfriend visited La Maison Troisgros, the Roanne restaurant run by brothers Jean and Pierre.

"As soon as I walked in the door, I said, 'What the fuck is this?'" recalls Liederman. "They were serving food that was so far beyond my wheelhouse I didn't begin to understand it." When his girlfriend, who spoke some French, saw foie gras on the menu, she exclaimed, "I'm not eating anybody's liver!"

"That's how unsophisticated we were," says Liederman.

"I remember the first day. They invented something called *La Grande Dessert*. And I remember watching this dessert working its way around the dining room, because when we got there, we were kind of the last people in line. And these two gigantic trays of pastries and ice creams and berries and everything you can imagine that I wanted to eat would come. And they put it down on the table and then the waiter would ask the guest, 'What would you want?' I watched everybody take a little bit of this and a little bit of this. One or two things, no more. When the guy came to me, I said, 'I'll take a little bit of *everything*.' You know, the thing was still full. He cleared the table, opened up the wings in the table, and he served me almost thirty little plates of dessert. I was in love."

The brothers, as they were apt to do, invited Liederman to return the next day for lunch on them. By the time he left, "I made it my mission somehow, some way, to get back in that place and work there."

Back in the States, Liederman attended cooking school with an eye toward the food business, not necessarily cooking, but just to learn. Whenever he could, he returned to Roanne and Troisgros, hung around for a few days, spent time in the kitchen. He won his bet with Jean Troisgros that if he could beat him in tennis, he could work there—an unprecedented proposition for an American. On completing law school and taking the bar exam, he flew to France in 1975. Troisgros scarcely remembered the wager but put him to work doing perfunctory tasks. Liederman's big break came in August, when half the staff went on vacation, just as the country was flooded with American tourists. Liederman leaned into the work, became indispensable, experienced what he calls the "three-star high" of working, sleeping, and participating in soccer games against rival restaurants such as Alain Chapel.

Liederman didn't want to go into the restaurant business, because he witnessed often the spectacle of Jean Troisgros in agony at the end of a service. But fate had its way with him. After a stock-reduction enterprise, Saucier, failed—"Twenty-five years ahead of its time," says Liederman—he decided to go into the cookie business. In order to secure a production space at 1016 Second Avenue near 59th Street, he took the space next door. He enlisted the help of Bobby Shapiro, who with stockbroker Giancarlo Uzielli owned Hoexter's Market restaurant, and launched Manhattan Market in September 1979.

Manhattan Market, a gray-walled space decorated with black-and-white photographs and adorned with chandeliers rescued from a Philadelphia train station, served what Sheraton, in a one-star review in the *New York Times*, termed *aggressively* nouvelle cuisine: salmon mousse with snow peas, vegetable terrine and chicken with cold tomato sauce, chicken breasts with lemon-lime glaze, calf's liver with a sherry vinegar sauce. As the nouvellians were doing in France, Liederman made room for pasta on his menu, such as fettuccine amatriciana. There were pear mousse, lemon-almond tart, and a selection of David's Cookies for dessert.

As the Pritskers and Allison and Hubert had done before them, Liederman had gone full Otto, creating his own, distinct oeuvre. As much, if not more, businessman as chef, he was also among the first of his generation to expand beyond the kitchen: In addition to his cookie business, he coauthored a cookbook, *Cooking the Nouvelle Cuisine in America*, written in collaboration with Michèle Urvater and published by Workman in 1979. For anybody seeking insight into this woefully misunderstood movement, especially on this side of the Atlantic, it's indispensable. He and Urvater add their own three amendments to the infamous Gault-Millau ten commandments: the emergence of the chef into the public eye; a focus on plating over platter service; and the fetishizing of vegetables as a thoughtful garnish, which recalls Ken Frank's Gene Wilder–inspired epiphany around the same time. He also coauthored *Running Through Walls* (about starting a business) with Alex Taylor III in 1989, and *David's Delicious Weight-Loss Program* with Joan Schwartz in 1990. Additionally, he sold his cookie empire to Fairfield Gourmet Food Corp in 1996.*

In 1985, the Liedermans, fans of L'Ami Louis in Paris, recast Manhattan Market as Chez Louis, an homage of sorts to the original, finishing the walls a lacquered red and specializing in roast chicken. The restaurant endured until 1991, then was briefly resurrected near Rockefeller Center in 1999.

"AN OPTOMETRIST WHO WAS WILLING TO SHELL OUT $200 ON WHITE TRUFFLES—NOBODY KNEW SUCH A CREATURE EXISTED."

Of the two restaurants in this pack that survived for decades, one tells a tale of uptown opulence, the other of downtown artistry. The Quilted Giraffe came first to Manhattan: Barry Wine's conversion from attorney to chef was more swift and unpredictable than either Pritsker's or Liederman's. A Detroit, Michigan, native who had

---

* Liederman declines to disclose the amount of the sale, but was reported to have earned his first million by 1982, and as early as 1985, David's Cookies boasted 178 stores nationally, mostly franchises, and anticipated annual sales of nearly $60 million.

practiced law in Milwaukee, then New York City, he and wife Susan, a Barnard College grad, paralegal, and hobbyist baker, relocated to the Ulster County village of New Paltz, about eighty miles from Manhattan, in 1970. Taking the ground floor of their home for his office, Barry hung out a shingle and became a self-described country lawyer, with a decidedly seventies caseload: "Most of my practice was wills and criminal work for the students arrested for marijuana," he said.

The Wines bought three Victorian houses on Academy Street, converted them to shops, including an art gallery and toy store (specializing in children's quilts) run by Susan. One was slated to become a restaurant, financed by a group of dentists backing a Culinary Institute of America instructor. When they got cold feet, Barry—having invested about $10,000 in the buildout and obtained a coveted New York State liquor license—decided to proceed with the project himself, seeing an opportunity in the "ladies who lunch" who would no doubt be in need of sustenance after patronizing the Wines' other businesses. A press release promoted The Quilted Giraffe as "French country" dining, promised a violin duet playing "everything from show tunes to Vivaldi!"

Wine had come to know and love good food as a law student in Wisconsin, where a summer in the employ of a Milwaukee attorney and bon vivant meant field trips to Chicago's best restaurants. He and Susan had also taken full advantage of the culinary riches of New York City, shopping at the Upper West Side gourmet emporium Zabar's, supping at Lutèce and other French restaurants.

The Quilted Giraffe, which opened in June 1975, with a boyfriend-girlfriend team running the kitchen, didn't live up to the Wines' standards: "On opening night, nobody remembered to wash the spinach," Barry says. "The terrine was still in the refrigerator and you just opened the refrigerator door, took a slice, and put the terrine back. Nobody knew it should be warmer."

Nonetheless, The Quilted Giraffe lurched forward. In February 1976, Brian Van der Horst reviewed the restaurant in the *Village Voice*. He found the décor "godawful quaint" but rhapsodized over the food, awarding it four Vs. (In a harbinger of Wine's future chef-dom, he had made the blueberry ice cream mentioned in the review, something he still points out today.)

Most people can't pinpoint the exact day and time they became a chef, but Barry Wine can. By December 1976, another CIA grad, Robert Johnson, was running the kitchen. On New Year's Eve Day, he phoned to report that his car had died en route back from a ski jaunt. Wine and his brother-in-law, an orthodontist, went into damage-control mode.

Says Wine, "Believe it or not—it seems absurd today to think we did it—we sat at a table and said, 'How are we going to serve these people?' There were only fifty people coming for dinner, [maybe] seventy-five. And there were other people working in the kitchen. And we figured out the system that became the Quilted Giraffe system and what I think made The Quilted Giraffe what it was. And that is: Everything was supposed to get cooked in less than ten minutes, and if you counted backwards and you knew there's a clock on the wall, and said you wanted to serve the main course at ten after eight, which is ten minutes after they cleared the apps, you just said, 'Scallops take four minutes. Let's wait until six minutes after eight to throw the scallops in the pan and they'll be done.'"

Wine survived his trial by fire, realized it wasn't rocket science, and thought he might like to become the chef. "I decided I could do a better job," he says, even though, he admits, "I didn't know the first thing about cooking."

Shifting gears, the Wines modeled their new life on mom-and-pop French convention: Susan baked and managed the reservation book and dining room; Barry oversaw a crew of CIA grads and took a three-week night course himself. The Wines made weekly pilgrimages to New York City to shop for food and flowers, sometimes crashing in town and taking in a fancy French dinner.

The Quilted Giraffe was a Sisyphean labor of love: "Today it's very easy to open a restaurant," says Barry, contrasting the deep bench of front- and back-of-house talent and management-worthy veterans currently available to restaurateurs with the scarcity that confronted his generation. The Wines made a fact-finding trip to France, hit a number of Michelin three-star restaurants, and Barry, a dreamer and opportunity-seeking missile, saw one in the regard of nouvelle cuisine's front men. "The first chefs who came in the dining room, that was a new thing," he says. "And I saw the appeal of that." They returned from France freshly charged to take the restaurant to another level.

More reviews followed. In July 1977, Gael Greene trekked to New Paltz, essayed a love letter in *New York* magazine, dubbing the restaurant a "celebration of amateurs," though warning that "amateur passion often lurches into silliness"—in particular, she was turned off by giraffes everywhere, from swizzle sticks to a four-foot-tall inflatable one in the restroom, and some culinary overreaches such as duckling with bananas, banana brandy, and light caramelized banana sauce.

The Quilted Giraffe, already popular with upstaters, developed a Manhattan following. The Wines visited France, returning with new ideas—some of them outright lifts, which in the politics of the kitchen is closer to cinema's homage than literature's plagiarism. A signature offering, his beggar's purses—crepes filled with crème fraîche and caviar—were borrowed from Les Jardins de la Vieille Fontaine in Maisons-Laffitte, a Parisian suburb. Eventually, inevitably perhaps, they couldn't resist bringing their regional hit to Manhattan. They took over a space formerly inhabited by The Bonanza diner at 955 Second Avenue, between 50th and 51st Streets, and deepened their Gallic model (and the one followed by André and

Simone Soltner at Lutèce), living above the restaurant. The Quilted Giraffe opened there in June 1979. By now, the Wines had two children, Winifred and Thatcher, and a dog, Eloise, and the family piled into the car on weekends after the last service, driving upstate to their old home, now a weekend retreat.

Over the ensuing years, the Wines grew The Quilted Giraffe into one of the city's powerhouse dining destinations. One of their secret advantages, shared by several members of the Five Couples, was that they had routinely experienced the pinnacle of food *and service*, both in the United States and abroad. Many aspiring American cooks came from working-class families, had never dined in those restaurants; the Five Couples were people of relative means, seasoned diners who might have been less proficient than formally trained cooks but had taste memories and a highly developed sense of hospitality that informed their efforts. Not only did they have the funds, or the ability to raise them, to open their own restaurants, but they were well traveled enough to have a vision of what the experience of eating there should be.

Of these trips, which all of the Five Couples save Allison and Hubert took, Hoffman—who briefly worked at The Quilted Giraffe before switching to Huberts—says, "They went and ate, and so they were there as an intense crash-course education on what fine dining looks like, of which food was an *element*. And they came back and said, 'Here's how we're going to do wine service,' or 'Here's a dish we want to work on.' They were on par, those two ideas, whereas other people were just in the kitchen doing their work."

Says Barry Wine: "It was people like Bobby Pritsker and David Liederman who would go to Europe on these monthlong tours. And you might even run into them on the same Michelin three-star route. That's what we did. We took the Michelin three-star route. My perception—the view of American cooking began with nouvelle cuisine, of all things. It showed us all that you didn't have to follow the rules. If those guys weren't following the rules, if Michel Guérard was making leg of lamb baked in hay and it was in his cookbook, we could have leg of lamb baked in corn husks from New Paltz cooked on a Weber grill on the front lawn of the restaurant."

"It *looks* different," says Sheraton of nouvelle cuisine. "The presentation, the plate arrangement, was something that was different about nouvelle cuisine, and that's something that kicked off a lot of the thinking of these American chefs like Pritsker and Wine. 'Oh, if the French can do it, we can do it.' People took a whole new look at how food can be presented, more personal and freer."

Sheraton, who describes herself as proudly antihype, saw a weakness in the approach favored by many of the couples. "I was very skeptical of these guys," she says. "Some more than others. The fact that they were so conspicuously creative, that everything had to be different. And what I didn't like and what I was always wary of in reviewing was that they wanted to be given credit for their *goals*, for what I am *trying* to do—my concept, my philosophy—and to me it's *my* dinner. And if it isn't good, I don't care what your goal is. So they were often taken aback by a review that said, 'This doesn't work.' And then they would say, 'Do you know what I'm *trying* for?' And I felt, 'You're not Picasso, going through a rose period or a blue period at my expense!"

The Five Couples were also, with the exception of Susan Liederman (a former actress who was the daughter of a Presbyterian minister), it must be said, all Jewish, although it might be something else that set them off from other young cooks in town. "I don't really think it's about Jewish as much as I think it's about class," says Hoffman. "There was the money and the sophistication to be comfortable in the dining room, to appreciate sitting in the dining room as an aesthetic experience; some people were cooks and some people were into the restaurant business."

"I can only speak for myself," says Karen Pritsker, now Karen Puro. "I think I had an innate understanding of the clientele we had, especially in New York because I grew up [there]. My parents, had they still been married, were in a social situation where they would have come to a restaurant like mine." Echoes Susan Wine: "All of the French chefs who grew up in the kitchen, they really did have the apprenticeships, the blue-collar background, but they hadn't been to these restaurants, they didn't have the diner's perspective. We had the American perspective: The customer's always right. We were putting the pieces together from this perspective. That was the one-up that we had on these guys."

As if to make Karen Pritsker's point, Gerry Hayden, a young cook in New York City at this time, visited The Quilted Giraffe in the mid-1980s, when he was working at The River Café in Brooklyn, and recalls: "I was blown away by The Quilted Giraffe because it was the first time as a cook in New York I started looking at the *entire* experience, not just the food. I started looking at the bathrooms, which were phenomenal, the atmosphere of the restaurant, the waitstaff, the linens, the plates."

Loren Michelle, who began cooking at The Quilted Giraffe in the mid-1980s, remembers a key lesson Barry Wine taught her, one that flowed from his experience as a diner: If dishes didn't arrive at the pass simultaneously and at optimal temperature he'd say, "I'm not serving a table. I'm serving *customers*. We're not serving this table. There are *people*."

The Wines assembled a front-of-house team who could bring his vision of a Michelin three-star-level experience to life. Of the Five Couples, the Wines were the superior capitalists, proudly, repeatedly, deliberately driving their check average north of the highest ones in town.

As the eighties, with all of their excesses, unspooled, the restaurant became synonymous with unbridled luxury, bordering on hedonism. Wine served the beggar's purses to customers, instructing them to eat them off the plate or platter without their hands, sometimes handcuffing their hands behind their backs to ensure compliance. The restaurant maintained a humidor, which housed

Cuban cigars (illegal at the time) and kept a '77 Rolls-Royce Phantom V idling outside between the neighboring Irish bar and Korean fruit stand to shuttle VIPs to postmeal destinations. Wine recalls the chauffeurs as "characters," including a Chinese man who packed a gun, and a six-foot-tall woman. In accordance with the Wines' democratic instincts, rides were offered to every guest, from "Joe Blow to Warren Beatty [to] the Rockefellers."

The excess knew no bounds. One cook who trailed there, Arnold Rossman, remembers, "All night long they were waiting for the truffles to come. And the truffles are coming. The truffles are coming. The truffles are coming. And at about ten-thirty, ten-forty-five, all of a sudden there's this aroma. They'd come in the front door. They'd landed at JFK, they came to Quilted Giraffe first. A woman walks into the kitchen—a woman or a man—walks into the kitchen with this beautiful woven wicker basket with a big handle and a damask linen napkin over the top. The aroma is overwhelming and she pulls the napkin and the thing is filled like *this* with white truffles. Huge, perfect, gorgeous white truffles. I had never seen anything like that before. And Barry says, 'Give me a piece of chocolate cake.' And they had this gorgeous, triple crazy chocolate cake and they put a piece of chocolate cake down and he takes out a truffle slicer, and he slices white truffles over the cake and he takes a bite out of it. And he's like, 'What can we do with this?' I just thought, *There's no fucking way I'm going to work in this place.* It was too much for me; it was overload." But there was no shortage of people willing to be overloaded. Andy Birsh, restaurant critic for *Gourmet* magazine through much of the 1980s, credits Wine with helping create, or unearth, a new clientele. "Until The Quilted Giraffe there was no such thing as a Quilted Giraffe–type of customer," which Birsh defines as "an optometrist who was willing to shell out $200 on white truffles—nobody knew such a creature existed."

In the kitchen, Wine developed a reputation for playfulness: He had a fondness for puns, such as serving vegetables cut like shoelaces as an accompaniment to sole crepes (get it?), and once created a visual riff on breakfast with a dessert of chocolate "sausage" and poached, sweetened eggs.

In 1984, at a time when just a handful of restaurants in the city, none headed by an American, held four stars, the *New York Times*'s Marian Burros—acting critic while the paper searched for a replacement for Sheraton—showered the restaurant with a quartet of them, cementing the restaurant's place as the pinnacle of fine dining at the time.

Wine's palate changed with the times. Instead of serving duck with Armagnac or a cherry sauce, he might pair it with fried plantains and hot peppers; lobster and monkfish might find themselves napped with ginger and scallion. As the restaurant drew top talent, a centrifugal force pulled the kitchen toward greater heights. Not unlike Michael McCarty, Wine took a collaborative approach to running the kitchen and had a knack for showmanship. (Both McCarty and Wine, says Bob Pritsker, "knew how to massage the whole show.")

"Everybody was smart," says David Kinch, today chef of the Michelin three-star restaurant Manresa in Los Gatos, California, who began working at The Quilted Giraffe shortly after the review. "Everybody was a lot smarter than me. I went to culinary school but there was a lot of—Katherine Alford, she's a UC Berkeley grad. There are a lot of people who had second careers but their careers were academic and they were attracted to cooking. It was almost like a Chez Panisse kind of thing going on. But the food was completely un–Chez Panisse; it was really the ultimate in luxury."

"This is what sociologists term *genius culture*," says Wayne Nish, who began cooking at The Quilted Giraffe in April 1984. "Where you have an enormous amount of talent that's attracted to one particular place so there's an explosion of activity." He describes a culinary *Saturday Night Live* scenario: "Everybody's bouncing ideas off each other. We were trying to outdo each other on a daily basis, whether it was conscious or not. People were vying to get things on the menu. You have this close-knit community at a point in time where there are influences that are shared in common with a bunch of people and a high degree of interest. All of a sudden, there's a lot of interaction and, boom, you get something new."

"You weren't pantry and sous chef and all this stuff," says Tom Carlin, who started at The Quilted Giraffe in the mid-1980s. "We were all 'associate chefs.' And [Barry] was open to hearing what everyone wanted to do and selecting different ideas. David Kinch and Katherine probably had the most influence. A few others. He created an environment where we could come up with things. I think he was probably one of the first people to start doing the Asian fusion thing. That was really new, his love of Japanese culture and cuisine." (At the invitation of a sake importer, Wine took a transformative trip to Japan in 1985, saw a connection between *kaiseki* and nouvelle cuisine tasting menus, and took The Quilted Giraffe in an Asian direction.)

"I'm not a chef," Wine told Carlin (according to Carlin). "Picture this as the *New York Times* and I'm the editor. I've got a lot of great writers and I'm going to pick the stories. I'm not writing the stories. I'm not out there doing it, but I know what I want and I try to hire talented people and pick it up." (After relocating the restaurant to New York City, Wine began employing a formally trained first lieutenant to help realize his ideas; Mark Chayette, a graduate of New York Technical College, was named as chef, along with Wine, in a *Food & Wine* article profiling rising American toques from around the country in May 1983.)*

---

* I had a firsthand glimpse of a number of Wine's enduring traits—from the creative to the managerial—when, in the summer of 2014, my family and I visited his and Susan's old home, now Barry's weekend retreat, in New Paltz, so I could interview him and raid his Quilted Giraffe archives. He made his famous tuna-wasabi pizza as part of Saturday-night dinner. When I woke up early Sunday morning and wandered into the kitchen, I found him alone in his gym clothes,

Josh Wesson contrasts Wine's openness with Len Allison's fragile ego. "I think that Barry was more secure in his role than Len was, and the dynamic in the kitchen was quite different," he says.

"We used to get scared when [Barry] picked up a knife to use it," says Carlin. "Because he didn't know how to use a knife. We thought he was going to cut himself or something. Like me and Tom Colicchio [who started at The Quilted Giraffe in 1985], we were really into, like, how fast can you fillet a fish? Or how perfect is your diced shallot? That type of stuff. Barry couldn't do any of that stuff. But he could do a four-star restaurant."

In fact, Wine's lack of formal training, like Jeremiah Tower's at Chez Panisse, might have been his greatest strength: "One of the great things about Barry was his kitchen was collaborative," says Kinch. "He wasn't a French guy who's like, 'This is my way or the highway, fuck you,' kind of thing. Barry, because he was self-taught, would say things or suggest things. He'd go, 'Let's make a béarnaise. Let's use duck fat.' Those of us in the kitchen that had been classically trained, we were like, 'Why do you want to do that? You don't do it that way.' He'd be like, 'Why don't you do it that way?' This sounds quaint nowadays but back then, it was a big deal. And we'd be like, 'Barry, we can't do it.' And he'd be like, 'Just do it. Just do it

---

layering slices of mozzarella over a round of leftover pizza dough. He topped the cheese with blueberries, then powdered sugar. "I'm going to make a blueberry pizza," he said, grinning beneath his shaggy gray bedhead, then shrugged and said delightedly, "Why not?" He popped the pizza in the oven and gave it a long ride. Meanwhile, as others roused and joined us, he assigned them tasks: His niece, in her twenties, prepared shirred eggs; I was instructed to cube leftover tuna, spread it on a sheet tray, and freeze it to replicate a Japanese breakfast dish he'd read about. When the cubes were cold, again at his instruction, I piled them in little pyramids on bread-and-butter plates and topped them with a speck of wasabi. Meanwhile, sugar, blueberries, mozzarella, and dough had improbably fused into a wonderful breakfast pizza. We all sat around his kitchen island and dug into the eclectic meal, which, while not perfect, was mostly delicious, and doubled as a conversation piece.

and see what happens.' And of course it wouldn't break. Of course it'd be great. That would be something different. Of course he could think outside the box like that."

"His eyes were a little more wide open and could see that there's different ways of doing these things, and he used that," says Carlin. That inventiveness extended to the dining room, where, like Mc-Carty and Waters around the same time, Wine attempted to replace the tipping system with a service charge, including the cooks in the pool. "I know he got sued and lost," says Carlin. "But I liked the concept. No one else had done that. He ran his restaurant like a business. That was new. Things were organized. The food went out on a nine-minute schedule.* 'Pick up salmon in seven.' 'Got it. Salmon in seven.' Everyone's writing down. That kind of organized way. I don't think anyone was doing that."

Chris Majer, who cooked at The Quilted Giraffe in the 1980s, recalls the digital watches the cooks used to ensure compliance with the nine-minute timing ritual: "I was watching all these people work on digital watches because every course had to be sequenced in ten-minute streams, plus or minus within a minute at the most, and so the level of service was unlike anything I'd seen before. It was almost militaristic."

"There was a rhythm," says Michelle. "It was almost like a dance in the kitchen where food was in harmony and synchronicity. We basically talked through every technique: 'Chicken in the pan, sear-ing, flipping, saucing. Veg in the pan. Up in two, up in one.' We were walking through. So if the food for a table of four was coming up, there was somebody saucing; the expediter was there; there were two or four waiters there. Their hands were on those plates ready

---

* Quilted Giraffe cooks recall a nine-minute system; Barry Wine, often stationed at the pass, remembers it as ten, and Susan Wine, honchoing the dining room, recalls an eight-minute span between one course being cleared and the next being dropped.

to go. . . . That was unbelievable, the communication. I've never seen that anywhere else, ever. It's so chaotic in every other restaurant. There's a lot of yelling, a lot of blaming. There was none of that."

Wine also welcomed team members to make technical improvements that helped the kitchen organism evolve. Kinch recalls that Colicchio came to work at The Quilted Giraffe after a *stage* in Auch, France: "That's duck and foie gras territory. And Tom said, 'We used to cook duck this way.' And if Tom had said that in any other kitchen, they would have said, 'Shut the fuck up.' Barry said, 'Everybody gather around Tom. Show us how you did the duck.' And if it turns out it was a better way of cooking duck, Barry would say, 'Okay, this is how we're going to do it now. This is great.' And in fact, it was. And in fact, he did. And we started cooking the way that Tom saw in France. And I was like, 'What just happened? What just happened?' I would have been kicked. You're always taught you learn how to do things and you learn how not to do things, and you keep your mouth shut and then you apply your data points elsewhere. Barry wasn't like that. And the things that most affect me now from Barry are that sense of collaboration and the sense of trying new things."

Colicchio remembers his training earning him resentment: "The ten-minute system, which was really a nine-minute system, was run by the sauté position. That's the position they gave me. And I had apparently pissed off a lot of people in the kitchen because that was the position everybody wanted. That was the sous chef's position. And I came in and jumped ahead of everybody. But I could work circles around most people in the kitchen because I had a lot of experience prepping and with the knife. So when a baby lamb came in, everybody kind of looked at it. I was like, 'Give me it.'"

In addition to staffing his kitchen exclusively with Americans, Wine also helped break another barrier: "Barry had a lot of women in the kitchen at that time," says Kinch. "There would be periods of time where fifty percent of the kitchen were women on the line and nobody did that then. That was pretty amazing back then."

"When I worked at The Quilted, it was almost like a devout respect Barry had for the women in the kitchen," says Michelle. "He came in a couple of times a year with earrings for the girls. We had Lipstick Night: Go downstairs, get ready for service, put lipstick on, put your earrings on, and cook. We all kind of got into it because it was like, okay, we're getting ready to cook. And we were taking charge in the kitchen."

The Quilted Giraffe is not without its detractors. Colicchio describes resentment in other chef circles for the Wines' achievement. "A lot of the guys who worked in the French restaurants were, like, 'Whatever.' Because he wasn't one of them. He got four stars and came out of nowhere to do it but it was the idea that Barry would go to France and rip off some dishes and bring them back, like the beggar's purses. So people knew where they came from. But the critics didn't know; the chefs did. Barry got shit for knocking off people's dishes."

Terrance Brennan, a young graduate of Alain Sailhac's kitchen at Le Cirque who had also cooked for Roger Vergé in France, was hired in 1986 as chef de cuisine. He'd never eaten there but was enticed by the restaurant's four-star status and stratospheric $65,000 salary.

"I just came from such a strong French background. Michelin-star restaurants and technique and structure and everyone's serious. And there, not one person was professionally trained. Noel Comess [one of Wine's chefs at The Quilted Giraffe] came up through the ranks. Barry wasn't professionally trained either. Some people got together and they happened to get four stars. And they would do stuff like the fish came filleted already. I just thought it was a quality thing. You can still get great fish filleted but at that time my mind was like, *Oh, that's terrible.* They would cut the steak right after they cooked it and all the blood would run out. You know, *rest it.* Stuff like that that perhaps a professional cook would know about, they would do. I was like a fish out of water. Barry, the way he managed, he had cooks run food up, and he would just come back and play with the food.

"I remember one time we had an awesome chocolate soufflé. There was a food critic out there and he wanted something and something else went out, crème brûlée or something like that. I can't remember exactly but he was telling the food critic, 'This was this.' And it wasn't; it was something else. He was insisting. 'No, it's *this*.' And he came back and he found out that it wasn't that. And then he'd come by and put orange confit on caviar or something. I just found that he wasn't a good chef. Within two weeks I had to sit down and I said, 'This is not going to work.' So it was just a brief stint."

Rossman remembers of his trail: "The food to me was too bizarre. I remember them serving roasted rack of lamb with mustard ice cream, which I thought was the craziest thing ever. Hot and cold; you don't do that. You can have a mustard sauce, but you can't have mustard ice cream." He also remembers the chef de cuisine and a lead line cook discussing lasagna for staff meal. "He goes, 'So we need some béchamel, how much do you need?' And he goes, 'I don't know, like two or three cups.' All right, great. Béchamel: you make a roux, [add] milk. So the guy comes back with a gallon of milk, three cups of flour, two pounds of butter. And I'm looking and I'm going, you've got to make two cups. I'm like, these guys have no connection [to classical cooking] because they're new American cooking. . . . I just thought, that's weird; it just gave me a weird feeling."

And while Marian Burros's successor, Bryan Miller, upheld the restaurant's four stars in 1986, Sheraton included the restaurant on her list of America's most overrated restaurants in a *Vanity Fair* piece in 1985.

"Not to take away from it," says Brennan, offering a glimpse into the resentment many classically trained cooks directed at The Quilted Giraffe, "that's great that he could do it, be a lawyer, open it up, and be four stars and all of us had to work our asses off and get all this training and get our balls busted and we still don't achieve that. So more power to him."

That was mere background noise, though. The Wines were on

top of the world, and made the audacious decision to close the restaurant on Saturday and Sunday nights.

"The reason for it was that Barry didn't want amateur diners," says Nish. "The bridge-and-tunnel crowd* were too difficult to deal with. And as a matter of fact, our cooking was so precise that Monday through Thursday we'd pull a rack of lamb [out of the oven] at 117, 118 degrees; on Fridays, we'd pull it at 120. It was too rare the other way. We had to make some adjustments on Friday night."

Wine's calculation was that since the restaurant was always fully booked, they'd make as much on a weeknight as they might on a Saturday. "The place was a machine," says Nish. "We did one hundred fifteen covers every night. Like clockwork. The highest American Express average in the country. It was a money machine. I know he had topped $3 million in sales. He was doing pretty good."

"YOU GUYS SHOULD OPEN A RESTAURANT."

If the Wines offered the Midtown equivalent of a French three-star restaurant, David and Karen Waltuck, with their SoHo jewel box Chanterelle, created a uniquely downtown translation.

David Waltuck grew up the son of two New York City social workers in a middle-class Jewish family on a steady diet of American and Middle European home cooking.

The Waltucks occasionally splurged on a Broadway show, treating their children to dinner beforehand. The meals were French, not the rarefied air of Lutèce, though he had been there, but one of the unheralded restaurants that dotted the West Forties and did a steady business feeding theatergoers. He was swept away by the elegance and the food. "By the time we ordered dinner," David wrote

---

* A derogatory term for people from the outer boroughs and New Jersey.

in the *Chanterelle* cookbook we coauthored, "I had the sensation that I was no longer in New York City, but in some otherworldly place devoted entirely to the comfort and contentment of its guests."

Those bistros and their cuisine, especially the sauces, seduced the boy. Before long, David was consumed with food, became a voracious reader of culinary tomes. He started baking, quickly shifted to savory, began taking himself through a progression of exercises not unlike a cooking school curriculum, making stocks, mayonnaise, and other basic preparations. He began amassing equipment; his experiments grew more ambitious. Before long he was making fish mousse, terrines, confit, cassoulet, then combining them into meals. In time, he found his way to Richard Olney's *Simple French Food* and *French Menu Cookbook*, which became guiding lights.

Waltuck had studied marine biology at City College, graduating in spring 1975, then swiftly course corrected and matriculated at The Culinary Institute of America. His relationship to the CIA epitomizes much about the Five Couples: Most of them had no formal training, and Waltuck himself ended up leaving the CIA prematurely; the school bored him. He was caught up in Gault and Millau's reports of the derring-do of nouvelle cuisine and had already begun discovering his voice. Here's a small matter: He didn't care for celery, found its flavor "peculiar," and so began leaving it out of his mirepoix at home, despite the teachings of his instructors. While training at the school, he worked as the brunch cook at The Empire Diner, a trendy Art Deco restaurant that combined coffee shop grub with creative cooking.*

Bronx boy Waltuck was plunged into a new, predominantly gay world: "It was an eclectic group of people . . . and the chef was this guy named Sophronus Mundy. He had no restaurant experience as

---

* The restaurant has closed and reopened multiple times since 2010; it had a brief renaissance in 2014 with chef Amanda Freitag in the kitchen, and at the time of this writing has reopened once again with chef John DeLucie at the helm.

far as I could tell. He was a private chef. He was Aaron Copland's chef or had been. The people that owned it had owned this place on the Upper West Side called Ruskay's. I'm pretty sure most of those people are dead now. This was pre-AIDS so I'm sure a lot of them died in that epidemic. They were opening this thing that was supposed to be kind of a diner but also a somewhat ambitious restaurant in the sense that they had diner-ish food, but then every night, there was supposed to be a four- or five-course prix fixe menu that would change every day. And nobody was really in charge because Sophronus was in over his head, he used to go out to all the gay bars at night and I would come in in the morning and he wouldn't be there and the food would start arriving. So I was thrust into this place where I had to kind of figure it out without a whole lot of support. And that was fun. I was doing stuff that I had no business doing in terms of designing the menu." This was doubly true because Waltuck was learning kitchen basics as he was creating those menus: "All of a sudden soft-shell crabs were there and I had to ask somebody, 'How do you clean soft-shell crabs?'"

Though Waltuck grew up in a place and time where "gay was just like an insult that you called somebody," he adjusted quickly to the Empire scene, thought Mundy was "a great guy. He had like two personalities and he would go to his favorite bar . . . and he would roll in at like four or five o'clock in the afternoon the next day."

In the summer of 1977, Waltuck—a shy string bean—began dating Karen Brown, a brassy free spirit capped by a Sally Bowles hairdo who worked in an East Side women's boutique. They were polar opposites, in just about every way: Karen was more well traveled than David, having spent extended time in Europe and South America, and was also fearlessly extroverted. They fell in love between meals at Café des Artistes, La Côte Basque, and Lutèce.

Waltuck dropped out of the CIA, went to work for Charles Chevillot at La Petite Ferme, a rustic French bistro on the Upper East Side. But he was bored there, too, wanted to start rule-breaking.

He and Karen, who had by then begun entertaining ideas of perhaps opening a restaurant with him, visited France, dined at Taillevent in Paris; Karen was especially inspired by Fernand Point's widow, Mado Point, and by Maguy Le Coze at the original Le Bernardin in Paris.

Back in the United States, the Waltucks began hosting dinner parties in their studio apartment on East 77th Street. David cooked dishes such as lobster *navarin* in a cream sauce, squab mousse fortified with Cognac, soft-shell crabs with sorrel, lobster with apple and cider, and rack of lamb with whole cloves of garlic and garlic jus. He also devised a seafood sausage, inspired by reading of Taillevent's *boudin des fruits de mer* in a piece by Gael Greene. There was real value in not having an Internet: As a creative exercise, Waltuck often challenged himself to create dishes based on the names he'd see in print. The apartment essentially became a pop-up: Karen would procure flowers and shop for wines at 67 Wine & Spirits on Columbus Avenue.

As it happened for so many of the Five Couples, guests began to echo a shared refrain: "You guys should open a restaurant."

The Waltucks decided to give it a go, inspired in part by the Wines and Allison and Hubert. They hashed out a budget of $35,000 (which would prove far too low), and went to work seeking a space, settling on a shuttered bodega in SoHo, at the time an urban wasteland. They were there for budgetary reasons (the rent was just $850 per month) but the neighborhood, where artists lived legally in city-subsidized lofts or illegally in industrial buildings, brought out the rebel in them. Waltuck continued to essay dishes with abandon, while Karen staffed up her dining room with a cast of characters who could not have worked in Midtown restaurants: dancers, photographers, and other creatives, many boasting facial hair that would have been a deal breaker north of SoHo and the Village. She also hired women when there was scarcely a woman on any dining floor in town; at one point, a troupe of four dancers who lived together around the corner worked as servers.

A number of aesthetic decisions were groundbreaking. Bill Katz, a designer of stage sets, came up with the name Chanterelle (leaving off a *Le* or *La* was itself considered audacious), and the Waltucks elected to write their menu, which Karen rendered by hand in a script that imitated Mado Point's, in English, something that even The Quilted Giraffe didn't do in its earliest New York City incarnation. Katz also, as Allison and Hubert did before him, left the restaurant's windows unobstructed—diners were one with the undeveloped environs that retained their nineteenth-century facades and cast-iron accents.

The Waltucks hit a speed bump when they realized they were going to fall $30,000 short of what they'd need to open. In a moment that could have happened only in the 1970s in New York City, they were sitting in their job site late one evening when Susan and Louis Meisel, owners of a nearby art gallery, came by on roller skates, en route home from the Roxy nightclub. An impromptu conversation followed and the Meisels arranged a dinner for investors in the restaurant space, securing the remaining funding.

Chanterelle opened in November 1979 with ten tables and no liquor license. The Waltucks didn't want art on the walls to distract from the food and their company. Katz came through again with the idea of featuring artwork on menu covers, which became a signature of the restaurant as a who's who of artists from Ross Bleckner to John Cage to Francesco Clemente to Eric Fischl donated artwork, usually in exchange for a dinner. The restaurant also had no dress code, at a time when Midtown dining palaces would have loaned gentlemen a sport coat if they arrived in shirtsleeves.

The effect, wrote Waltuck, was "our idiosyncratic take on a three-star French restaurant, such as could only exist below Houston Street in 1970s New York." The restaurant became a magnet for the slow-growing community of foragers and purveyors, including a young couple from New Jersey proffering mushrooms and George Faison, who was just launching the foie gras business D'Artagnan with partner Ariane Daguin.

Within a month, Greene had penned a review in *New York* magazine titled "The Daring Young Man on Grand Street." Though she found the restaurant to be a work in progress, her enthusiastic appraisal declared, "David Waltuck is not yet as brilliant as he intends to be. But when he is good, Chanterelle is astonishing." It was an apt study in the contrast between Greene—a cheerleader for the new—and proudly clinical Sheraton, who essentially panned the restaurant in an early review.

"Mimi was about what's on the plate and how good is this dish," says Peter Hoffman. "Gael was into the theater and the experience and the cooking as an expression—the plate as an expression of the whole dining experience."

Chanterelle continued to develop over the years, eventually earning four stars from Bryan Miller in 1987; it moved to a new home, on Harrison Street, in Tribeca, in January 1989, where it remained in business until 2009. Of the restaurants started by the Five Couples, the two that survived the longest rose the highest.

"YOU'RE THROWN INTO A POT OF BOILING LIQUID."

In an era when cooks and chefs improvised their careers, often in isolation, with no professional community outside of their immediate workplace, this cast of characters knew each other, with varying degrees of intimacy. "I got to know Barry Wine very well and I got to know Pritsker very well, and all these guys who all turned out were lawyers, they had the same stories," says Liederman. "They kind of just organically fell into it. They wanted to cook. They thought they wanted to run restaurants. None of us knew what was involved in running restaurants until we started to run a restaurant."

Even those who weren't friends frequented each other's restaurants, seeing in the others kindred spirits, though not all of them felt a kinship with the group: "I did [feel a part of something], but not in a huge way," says Karen Puro. "We were aware that we were in the forefront of change that was taking place in New York, and in the U.S. In Boston we'd felt pretty much alone." (Puro was also keenly aware of Chez Panisse having been featured in a *Harper's Bazaar* article about, per Puro, "two women who were making it in the culinary world.")

The business also deepened some of the relationships, while straining others. The Waltucks are still together today, as are the Liedermans. The Pritskers broke up for good in 1982.

"It's very hard to work with somebody twenty-four hours a day, seven days a week, and find that you have enough left to have an interpersonal relationship," says Puro. "Bob and I used to beat each other up a lot verbally in the kitchen. It's just a hard life. We didn't always see things the same way. Bob was very bottom-line oriented, and I hadn't really grown up enough to realize you own your own business for a profit. We used to argue over how many covers we'd do a night. I'd say we can't do more than sixty a night, let's say, because the shit's going to hit the fan, and then what. And he'd say, 'Look, we have four loins of veal sitting in the fridge.' Couples in the best of situations don't have to see eye to eye; when you're working together with someone, you really have to toe the line the same way and we didn't."

Of running a restaurant with his partner, Bob Pritsker says, "You're thrown into a pot of boiling liquid; swimming together in it is not for everyone. Swimming alone in it isn't for everyone. And it's a forum for differences. There's so many things to disagree on suddenly."

The friction showed in the dining room. "I was very friendly with Bob and Karen until they were getting divorced," says Liederman.

"That became uncomfortable. The last time we went to that restaurant, we walked in and Bob sent us a bottle of wine and Karen came to the table and took it off." (He and Bob did remain friendly enough that after Dodin-Bouffant closed, Bob helped out in the Manhattan Market kitchen during a staffing shortage.)

Things boiled over in summer 1982: The Pritskers separated in June and closed the restaurant for the month of July. Pressured by friends and fans, they reopened in the fall with a schedule designed to keep the peace: They hired a maître d' to take over some of Karen's front-of-house responsibilities, Karen prepped all day, then Bob showed up and honchoed the kitchen at night. "We did that for three months and it wasn't viable and we were in the process of getting a divorce," says Puro. "And the press picked it up again, they'd have to, at that point. I was over the marriage so I didn't take it personally."

Puro went on to work for restaurant consultant Barbara Kafka's Star Spangled Foods, then became pastry chef at Tavern on the Green. Bob went all in on the bachelor life. "I was suddenly a liberated New Yorker, and I acted like one with women. That was fun," he says. "I burned both ends. I worked twelve hours a day but I found women everywhere, often in my dining room. I don't know that chefs were in their great moment at that time, but if you were in your basement kitchen and some lady or two ladies were at a table and one was delicious-looking, as the chef thanking them for coming and hoping that they enjoyed everything, that was not the last sentence. That was not the last question, you know? There's an awful lot of stuff that could happen."

The Wines, too, had a tempestuous relationship. "Barry and Susan were often at one another's throats," says Josh Wesson. "If you worked on the floor you were stuck in the middle. Her role there was running the front of the house but Barry also did some of that. She never went into the kitchen but he came out and would butt heads with her."

Of the dynamic, Susan Wine says, "We were married for twenty-nine years. If we hadn't been in business together, living three shifts a day, we'd still be married. We burned it out." She also says that it was only on their day off that she could reflect on or enjoy their success. "When we were out of the restaurant, or out in New York City, or rebuilt our country house and had people out there, then there was a certain amount of basking. But never when we were in it."

Until 2009, when Chanterelle abruptly shuttered just shy of the restaurant's thirtieth birthday, David Waltuck used to crack that of the Five Couples, he and Karen were the only ones that were still in business *and* still together. The marriage endures, as does the Liedermans', the last gasps of that enchanted moment when a couple could cobble together a restaurant from pluck, passion, and a few dollars, hone their craft for paying customers in the public eye until, suddenly, improbably, they had all of New York City eating out of the palms of their hands.

3

ON THE WATERFRONT

"My dear fellow, who will let you?"
"That's not the point. The point is who will stop me?"
—Ayn Rand, *The Fountainhead*

HOW, AND WHY, BUZZY O'KEEFFE, AGAINST ALL ODDS, BUILT
A RESTAURANT ON THE BROOKLYN SIDE OF NEW YORK CITY'S
EAST RIVER, AND—JUST AS IMPROBABLY—DISCOVERED A
SUCCESSION OF GREAT AMERICAN CHEFS (LARRY FORGIONE,
CHARLIE PALMER, DAVID BURKE), CONTINUING TO THRIVE AS
THEY GRADUATED TO MANHATTAN

Buzzy O'Keeffe was a fussy (his word) kid with a passion for quality that informed everything he did. How fussy? Well, most of his friends made slingshots from any old Y-shaped branch and a bicycle tire. Buzzy fashioned his from maple, stained and lacquered it, fit it with a length of medical tubing, sheathed it in a leather pouch.

He decorated his boyhood bedroom. He built himself a dock, one that could withstand any storm, kept a boat there, varnished it to perfection.

"I was always into getting the best," he says.

In 1977, O'Keeffe—who had owned several hospitality businesses by then—completed his crowning achievement, a glittering European-style restaurant that floated on a barge just off the fringe of Brooklyn Heights, with a peerless panoramic view of Manhattan. The restaurant became a runway for three of the defining American chefs of the 1980s—Larry Forgione, Charlie Palmer, and David Burke—who succeeded each other, in that order, each setting forth his own distinct style of contemporary American food. All three attracted significant media coverage, then alighted to successful careers as chef-owners in the Promised Land of Manhattan, across the East River. The chefs became household names; O'Keeffe did not. But don't be confused: The story of The River Café is ultimately Buzzy O'Keeffe's story, and the chefs—while unmistakably talented—owed their big breaks to his good taste and keen palate, and to his unquenchable thirst for perfection.

"FINDING THE PEACH AND NOT MESSING WITH IT IS THE REAL PROBLEM."

O'Keeffe was born in the northeast Bronx, an Irish American kid in an immigrant-rich community. Don't ask him where the nickname Buzzy comes from—it was conferred on him as an infant; he didn't know his real name was Michael until grammar school.

His family didn't have much money but O'Keeffe recalls a comfortable childhood. His mother kept a garden that he admired, and they could afford an occasional restaurant meal. He found the hospitality business early: At sixteen, he worked at Schrafft's on

Fifth Avenue, one in a chain of candy shops and lunch counters, where his mother had been a waitress. By the time he was halfway through Fordham University, he had eaten at La Caravelle and La Grenouille—his favorites—and at The Four Seasons and the other dominant restaurants of the day. He loved their physical beauty, especially the murals at La Caravelle, painted by Versailles native Jean Pages, whose brushstrokes also graced the walls at Le Manoir and Le Cygne, among many others. O'Keeffe served in the United States Army, then took a job as a sales rep for a California-based food products company for which he was willing to fly coach, stay in cheap hotels, rent a Chevy instead of a Cadillac as long as they would foot his bill in the finest restaurants. His supervisor got the better end of the deal because outside New York City, O'Keeffe couldn't find destinations that met his high standards, usually settling for a steakhouse.

O'Keeffe prided himself on being a gentleman. He threw parties to which he invited more men than women, but if the men got fresh, he'd banish them: "He's out!" he says today in imitation of a baseball umpire, jerking a thumb to indicate the door. He resisted drugs, even at parties where crystal sugar bowls brimmed with cocaine, and he wanted his establishments to be drug-free. In everything he did, quality was paramount. Years before brand-name chefs and blog-inflated butchers elevated burgers, O'Keeffe made a study, soliciting wisdom about the optimum fat content, and embarking on a personal odyssey in search of the best bun: "I tested every hamburger roll from Philadelphia to Boston," he says of that road trip. "Who had the best hamburger roll? It turned out to be Arnold. Just a little sweeter."

He was also a dreamer: In the mid-1960s, he hatched a scheme worthy of Bugsy Siegel—to open a restaurant on a barge on the East River, on the unfashionable outskirts of the Fulton Ferry landing on the Brooklyn side, with a panoramic view of New York City, before the Twin Towers, which would be completed in 1973, were added to the landscape. (Appropriately enough, another restaurant visionary, Joe Baum, ran Windows on the World atop the North Tower, with views that stretched to the horizon line.)

"I always wanted to serve good food, nice surroundings," O'Keeffe told me over a breakfast interview at The River Café, after he miraculously brought it back from the pounding it took by Hurricane Sandy in 2012. "I only did this because I could have a garden, too. I was into gardens. The city's pretty harsh. So I figured I'd make an oasis where New Yorkers could escape without having to drive fifty miles."

O'Keeffe is a lean man of indeterminate age. (A fellow writer warned me not to ask him his birthday, which is a well-kept secret.) He's an immaculate, conservative dresser and as exacting about that as he is about everything else; he was actually forty-five minutes late to our interview because, he said, he hadn't been able to locate just the right cuff links for his ensemble.

During the years he lobbied the city for permission to build The River Café, he opened other restaurants, including Bowden Square, a nightclub in Southampton, Long Island, which he operated from 1973 to 1978. Drug use was peaking, and he didn't care what people did in their Ferraris or Lamborghinis or in the potato field across the road, but he did care what they did in his joint. It didn't take narcotics to put him off: If a party of ten showed up in tuxedos and evening gowns and one member was chewing gum, the entire reservation was canceled on the spot. To this day, The River Café, just minutes from where you can tuck into three-star *New York Times* meals in shorts and T-shirts, requires that gentlemen wear jackets after 4 p.m. (O'Keeffe had a shot at the space that became Studio 54 in 1977 but turned it down because "I didn't know that many nice people.")

After a decade of persistence, the city relented and granted O'Keeffe permission to build his dream restaurant, but he couldn't find a bank to back him until a childhood friend, an executive with a New Jersey bank, helped push through a loan. "All you need is somebody with some balls," says O'Keeffe.

O'Keeffe had traveled to London and Paris, eaten in their finest restaurants, modeled The River Café on those settings: stone flooring, rattan chairs, flower arrangements, fine china.

His culinary leanings were almost Californian in their purity, the default being to fete great product: "If I give most young chefs who want to do peaches, say, in August, a peach dessert, the biggest problem we have is finding the perfect peach with just the right sweetness and juiciness. It's hard to find. Some seasons you don't get them at all. Ninety-nine chefs out of one hundred will take that fresh peach and poach it. They can't leave it alone. They must put some magic to it, which I disagree with. And they will make it taste exactly like a *canned* peach with all their magic. I said, 'You take it, you slice it, you lay it out like flower petals, a tiny little bit of sugar on top, sprinkles of water, just let it sit there for a little while, develop its own syrup, and you serve it with a very high-quality double cream. You get high-quality heavy cream, shake it halfway between whipping, just pour it on.' People might say, 'That's all it is, a peach?' *Yeah.* Try to find a peach. Finding the peach and not messing with it is the real problem."

To satisfy his lofty demands for great product, O'Keeffe developed a network of purveyors, including a fisherman in Everglades City, Florida, who periodically shipped him stone crabs on ice via Eastern Air Lines, and another on the Peconic Bay who sent him scallops two or three times a week. He even sourced venison from the Rockefeller estate in Sleepy Hollow, New York, instructing the hunter where to shoot the poor beasts, and how to hang them and for how long before he sent his man to pick them up.

He hired Rick Stephan, a Culinary Institute of America–trained chef, but by 1979 was on the hunt for a new toque.

"WHY WAS THIS NOT TAKING PLACE IN AMERICA?"

Larry Forgione, then going by his more formal name, Lawrence, grew up in a different borough than O'Keeffe, but had been on his own compatible evolutionary path as a chef while O'Keeffe was making his bones as a builder and restaurateur.

Forgione was born on Long Island, spent his early life in Queens, New York, one of four children in a middle-class family. One set of grandparents was Italian, the other Irish, so family gatherings were a fixture of his childhood. His Italian grandmother had a self-sufficient five-acre farm on eastern Long Island, where Forgione spent every other weekend and extended time in the summers. His Irish grandmother was a devoted home cook, "one of these women that got up at six and went to church, came back, put an apron on, and didn't take her apron off until she went to bed at night. She just loved cooking," says Forgione, who was especially fond of her "little dessert buffets," featuring at least five home-baked pastries, cakes, and pies. (His Irish grandmother had been a farmer who moved to Queens to raise Forgione's mother; the Italian grandmother was a Brooklyn seamstress who ended up on Long Island in later life. The upshot was that both sides of the family knew good food and good ingredients.) Even as a kid, Forgione understood that he had it better than his friends, with Sunday feasts regardless of which grandmother hosted. His Italian grandmother was good at sneaking in foods like snails and rabbit and not revealing what they were until they were in the kids' bellies.

Much as he loved food, it never occurred to Forgione to become a chef. As a child, he considered the priesthood; after graduating high school in 1970, he went to college with plans to become a physical education teacher because teachers were exempt from the draft. When pneumonia put him down for a semester, he killed time working for a cousin's Brooklyn catering concern. He loved it;

when the next semester rolled around, he skipped school and kept the job. He worked at The Breakers Hotel in Palm Beach, Florida, took to the professional kitchen setting, learned some classic techniques like ice carving, came back north intent on becoming a chef, and applied to The Culinary Institute of America.

Two years later, after graduating the CIA, Forgione wanted to get to Europe, mailed a letter to Michel Bourdin, chef of Maxim's in Paris. By the time the letter got to Bourdin, he had migrated to London's Connaught Hotel, and offered Forgione a job there for twenty-five pounds a week. Forgione signed on for six months and took a room in the staff dormitory. He ended up staying two and a half years, working his way up to *chef de partie*, doing time on every station except pastry in the resolutely classicist kitchen.

In London, Forgione experienced something he'd never witnessed in the United States: the direct link between farming and foraging and restaurant kitchens. "It was the first time I had seen baskets of wild mushrooms showing up at the back door, brought by the foragers. We would get a load of lamb from Kent every, say, Thursday. Fish that was just impeccable. Produce that just was the most perfect things that you could want. The Connaught bought only the best. And it started to make me think: America is so big, has so many different regions and terroirs. We have mountains; we have streams; we have rivers; we have oceans; we have hot climate, cold climate—why was this not taking place in America? Why were even the best French restaurants in America using canned chanterelles from France? And in my stupidity, naïveté, it was: Don't chanterelles grow in America?

"It just started to bother me. Why were they getting such great ingredients and back in America we weren't getting great ingredients? You were getting a sheet of paper handed to you by your purveyor and if it was on the paper, you could get it; if it wasn't on the paper, you couldn't get it. You never made a request because he didn't have it. You always got cauliflower wrapped in plastic. The food universe was very small in such a huge, magnificent country. So the real thing came to me when there was a shipment of *poularde de Bresse** and all the French guys, everybody, were acting like we were about to have a religious experience. The chef cooked it, he sliced it, and gave everybody a piece. I just remember putting it in my mouth and saying, 'Wow, this tastes like my grandmother's chickens.' It tasted like what chicken *should* taste like. It was at that moment that something popped. . . . From that moment on, when I tasted a strawberry, all of a sudden I could recall the flavor of my grandmother's strawberries. Or my other grandmother's sweet peas. It was almost a cosmic thing."

When Michel Guérard blew through London to promote his new book *Cuisine Minceur*, Bourdin set Forgione up with a gig helping the great man. Guérard offered him a job at Eugénie-les-Bains, but it was scuttled due to a government crackdown on foreign workers in Michelin-starred restaurants, a response, according to Forgione, to complaints that there was a shortage of quality jobs for young French cooks because of a new phenomenon—the influx of American and Japanese aspirants willing to work for nothing. So Guérard dispatched Forgione to New York and Régine's, for which he was a corporate chef.

In 1977, Forgione reported for duty at Régine's, a nightclub co-owned by Régine Zylberg (dubbed "Queen of the Night" by the *New York Post*) and situated in a 20,000-square-foot space in the Delmonico Hotel at 59th Street and Park Avenue. For the young chef, it was a culture shock: "Régine's was something I had never seen before: It was what I would consider a three-star restaurant up until ten o'clock at night, and then the walls opened and it was this international disco." There were a Lucite dance floor, neon hearts, and a nonstop parade of bold-faced names: Jack Nicholson, George Hamilton, Mick Jagger, Brooke Shields, future United States presi-

---

*   French chickens raised and slaughtered according to strict guidelines.

dent Donald Trump. Andy Warhol mingled about, tape-recording conversations with the in crowd.

"When celebrities came in, they always snuck them in through the kitchen," says Forgione. "So we had this constant parade of celebrities coming through: Cheryl Tiegs. All the bad boys of tennis: Björn Borg, John McEnroe, Jimmy Connors. The Mick Jaggers. Everything from musicians to sports figures to movie actors to television stars like Telly Savalas."

Forgione cooked food right out of *Cuisine Minceur*. The book was a sensation, but some customers would complain about portion sizes. "We had problems with the one little stuffed chicken leg. People would complain that it wasn't an American portion, even though the leg was stuffed with truffles and sweetbreads."

At Régine's, Donna Summer hits—*Mmmmmm, love to love you, baby*—throbbing the walls, his disappointment over the state of American product boiled over into full-blown frustration. He decided to do something about it, no small feat in a pre-Internet age: "My process of looking for ingredients was to first think about where they would be grown, or could be grown. I knew that my grandmother grew delicious basil and so on. By trying to sort of be local, I would find someplace on Long Island that grew herbs. I'd say, 'Well, can you grow these herbs?' And they would grow these herbs. I think the first things I started working on were mushrooms because it really bothered me that we didn't have mushrooms. And so I would research chanterelles, where would they probably grow in America? What matched that scenario? Morels, same thing. And then, the process—since you couldn't type in online "morels in America"—you would have to do some research. What I would then do is, say, find out that wild hickory nuts grow in the groves—the biggest part of where they grow is Indiana. So I would actually call a town in Indiana, speak to their Chamber of Commerce, say, 'Hey, do wild hickory nuts grow in your part of the state?' And they'd say, 'No, it doesn't grow in our part, but you should call such and such.' And then you'd call them and they'd say, 'No, but call this person,' and then you called that person. And then you finally got to somebody who said, 'Oh, yeah, we have more wild hickory nuts than we know what to do with. You should call John Dolan and talk to him.' And then next thing you know, we had true American wild persimmons or hickory nuts or true American chestnuts from a little grove of chestnut trees. Morels came from the Pacific Northwest. And then I learned that the people that are interested in mushrooms are what's called the Mycological Society, so I'd start calling mycological societies and they would put me onto people who they knew went out and did it. It was a process.'"*

This was, no exaggeration, the beginnings of the extravagant sourcing network that's just a mouse-click away from today's East Coast chefs, and Forgione says that he spent good chunks of most workdays in this pursuit, but it wasn't with history or legacy in mind: "At the time, and I think you'll find this universally amongst all the chefs of that era . . . I just wanted great ingredients for myself. I wasn't thinking of it as, *Oh, this will make me rich and famous.* I wanted the best possible ingredients I could get so I could cook the best food that I could make. And I always had an inquisitive mind and I was dogged in my pursuit of things. It kind of sounds corny but it's that expression that Fernand Point is famous for: 'You can't have great food without great ingredients.' I don't think any of us were doing it to become famous; it just happened. We were doing things that we believed in, that we loved."

Forgione eventually became chef at Régine's, fashioning his own menus after the master's guiding principles. When Guérard vis-

---

* André Soltner had followed a similar path ten years earlier. When he first arrived in the United States in the early 1960s, he was so horrified by the ingredients that he almost did an about-face back to France. His hunt for better produce led him to, among others, a mushroom forager in Oregon who told him that he usually sold his mushrooms to a company in Germany that put them in cans, topped them with a preservative liquid, and shipped them back to the United States.

ited, he was shocked: "He couldn't believe that we had great fresh herbs . . . ducks that were not the processed American, standardized Long Island duck. That we had some game birds. That we had some incredible vegetables and fruits and so on. He was blown away that this existed in America." Forgione remained there for close to a year and a half, then, through Lynne Bien, a pastry chef he used for catering gigs, who also supplied The River Café with its superlative pies (as in L.A., house-made desserts were not a given in New York City restaurants), heard from Buzzy O'Keeffe about the prospect of taking over the kitchen at his Brooklyn restaurant.

They met at O'Keeffe's Pear Trees restaurant at First Avenue and 49th Street. O'Keeffe shared his aspirations for The River Café, that he wanted it to—says Forgione—"be a world-class restaurant, a very important restaurant. He thought that it was one of the most beautiful restaurants in the world but hadn't discovered any culinary voice or tradition. . . . I told Buzzy that if he'd leave me alone, 'I will give you one of the best restaurants in New York within a year.'" O'Keeffe hired him.

"When I first got there, it was kind of helter-skelter," says Forgione. "It was the type of kitchen where people would be running over here and putting salad dressing on. It wasn't where the chefs designed and created everything and served it to you. To quote Craig Claiborne, 'The River Café is at best continental cuisine, but from a continent that we have not discovered yet.'"

Forgione wasn't kidding when he told O'Keeffe he wanted to be left alone: He painted a box on the floor from which he expedited during service. "I didn't want anybody coming in my box," says Forgione. "The front of the house couldn't enter my box. If they wanted to talk to me, they had to talk to me from outside the box." (Though there's often a tension between cooks and servers, the "box" was *not* normal kitchen protocol; Forgione himself laughs sheepishly when reminded of it today.)

Forgione and O'Keeffe differ about who deserves credit for the

American vision that took hold at The River Café and quickly came to define the restaurant. "Larry is also very fussy," says O'Keeffe. "When Larry first came, his training was all in French, CIA, and then he went to work in the Connaught Hotel in London. And it was a famous French chef, Michel Whatever-His-Last-Name-Is. I met him a few times. It was all French. We told him we were building an American restaurant. So Larry's menu was all in French. . . . He's here practicing for a week . . . and I said, 'Larry, *American*. Same thing, just in English. We were trained by the French, great culinary artists, but we're an *American* restaurant. We're going to use the best we can of what's in *America*.'"

"He and I disagree on a number of things that happened in the beginning," says Forgione. "I can hear the conversations. He must have heard a different conversation. Yes, Buzzy always wanted it to be an American restaurant, but there's American restaurants that serve prime rib and O'Brien potatoes, and there's American restaurants that serve some of the best food in America. So it was true that Buzzy—the only thing he knew was American food. He was using this woman that made pies because she made great apple pies and cherry pies and, you know, really old-fashioned American desserts. So, yes, he did want it to be an American restaurant."

Concurrent with his change of venue was an evolution in Forgione's vision for his own cuisine, which he decided to take in an American direction, in part because he was jingoistic, but there was another reason: "You listen to so much shit from everybody when you're in Europe about how Americans don't know anything about food, they don't know how to cook, that American cuisine is hot dogs and hamburgers and haute American cuisine is steaks and lobsters. And as I started to research it and read about it, it was just so full of incredible ingredients, things that you didn't hear about anymore. It was a cuisine of great home cooking. But so are a lot of other regional cuisines. So I always felt that I could take something as simple as mashed potatoes and make *great* mashed potatoes and they would be fine on a menu at a three-star restaurant, a high-caliber, serious restaurant. That it was okay to do that. That really was the backbone of what was going on with myself and Buzzy. . . . I think that it really solidified The River Café as one of the great restaurants."

As part of his mission, Forgione wanted to develop a relationship with James Beard. "I thought that if I was going to get involved with American cuisine and take this position that I think American food and American cuisine can be world class, I should know the person who I feel is the most important figure in American cooking." Mutual friend Stephen Spector, co-owner of the Japanese-inflected nouvelle cuisine restaurant Le Plaisir, where chef Masa Kobayashi ran the kitchen, suggested that Forgione simply ring up the icon, pointing the chef to the white pages.

"There it was: James Beard, West 12th Street. So I called him up. He actually answered the phone. I told him a little bit about what I was doing. I don't know if he got these calls all the time, so what I started to do was, as I was getting in ingredients, I would make this little basket and then have the driver deliver it to him. I'd send him a basket of morels or I'd send him some wild hickory nuts—just different foodstuffs that I know that he hadn't seen in a while, with a note: 'Wonderful morels from northern Michigan. Have fun with them.'" Eventually he picked up the phone and called me and said, 'I'd like to come over and have dinner.'"

Forgione was so blinded by Beard that he doesn't remember who joined him the night he first came to The River Café. He sent out significantly more food than was promised by the prix fixe four-course menu. "I had happened to just get a shipment of illegal bear meat in from a Native American tribe in northern Michigan," says Forgione. "Native Americans in northern Michigan up in the Upper Peninsula, they were allowed to trap and hunt freely but they just want the pelts and the skins and so on; they didn't really want the meat. So my [future] partner at American Spoon Foods before we had American Spoon Foods* was a wild-foods forager and he would get the meat from the Native Americans and send it to me. So I happened to have some bear meat. I cooked it up, and he just went crazy because he hadn't had bear meat in God knows how long. The River Café became the first restaurant to serve buffalo in New York since buffalo became extinct. I think he enjoyed tasting things that he hadn't tasted in a long time, and that excited him.

"He seemed to have a good time. We talked a little bit. He left. He said, 'Let's talk again.' And one thing led to another and we started talking all the time on the phone and in person. Instead of sending the driver over with the little basket, I'd go over with the little basket and we just developed this great relationship. . . . Jim was bigger than life. He had fun in everything that he did. 'Is that fun?' was a common statement of his. Or he'd taste something and go, 'That's fun. This is really delicious. It's so much fun.' He equated happiness with fun and he got so much happiness and joy, particularly, out of food. I was so excited to have the opportunity to meet him, and then connect with him and then have this ongoing relationship with him until he passed away, that I feel very fortunate.

"I used to sit with him at his townhouse in Greenwich Village and we would just pull down books and read them and talk about recipes. He also had an incredible memory: Say you were talking about an antique apple; he could say, 'Oh, I remember having that at such and such restaurant back in 1955; that was just so incredible.' It was like he could taste it as he was talking about it."

Forgione continued to expand his network, buoyed by the restaurant's brisk business and buying power, which enabled him to make greater commitments to farmers and producers than he could at Régine's. He also began serving chickens from Paul Kaiser, a farmer who raised them in a cageless environment. In one of their

---

* A fruit preserves and condiment company.

periodic meetings, searching for a succinct way to explain them on the menu, he and O'Keeffe came up with a designation that became legendary: free-range chickens.

Helen Chardack, a young cook from Buffalo, New York, who had spent time at Chez Panisse, then returned to New York City, came to work for Forgione, found him a "big, generous, gentle man. This is not the chef who's walking around yelling at everybody. This was a man who knew what he was interested in, knew the kind of food he wanted to make." Having spent time in California, she was especially impressed by his sourcing: "When you walked into the little office there, there were reams of papers of who was making what, where the mushrooms were going to come from. I kept thinking, *Oh my God. This is gold. If I could somehow get all of these purveyors, this is where it's at.*"

Eleven months after Forgione took the helm at River Café, Gault and Millau's New York guide came out, naming The River Café one of the best five restaurants in town. It was the only American restaurant on the roster. "I'm not sure if I felt shocked since I was so completely overjoyed—mission accomplished kind of thing. It was hard to believe that I was accepting an award standing next to André Soltner, who was the biggest chef in New York, the king of kings in New York."

Forgione began meeting other members of his generation who were making their names around the country: Jonathan Waxman, then cheffing at Michael's in Santa Monica, popped in for brunch with fellow Chez Panisse alum Mark Miller. Alice Waters, on Beard's recommendation, appeared for dinner one night. Waters and the New Orleans chef Paul Prudhomme had bonded in 1979, at a Food & Wine magazine first-anniversary event at Tavern on the Green, at which Prudhomme stole the show, and he and his army of cooks bailed Waters and her sous chef Jean-Pierre Moullé out, helping them cook and plate a lamb dish. Waters, Forgione, and Prudhomme developed an ongoing telephone support group. Ed

Fertig, a Culinary Institute of America extern at The River Café in the early 1980s, remembers Forgione gathering the troops around, speaking to them of contemporaries such as Waters, whom he himself was learning about for the first time.

Just as Forgione had had an epiphany in London, Fertig was awestruck by the foodstuffs delivered daily to Forgione's door: "I saw things I had no idea about as far as product. When guys would show up, like Paul Kaiser with the chickens. I was like, *Wow, you mean he just drove up here like at five thirty this morning and brought us chickens?* It was surprising to me. I worked with the butcher for a while. I was the guy eviscerating these things and breaking them down at seven in the morning; they were still warm."

If nouvelle Americana doesn't seem like the foodstuff of hip New Yorkers, Forgione didn't think it was either. "The River Café under any of the chefs was still a highly tourist restaurant," he says. "Our main clientele was people not from New York City. And I don't mean that it was a tourist attraction, but in a certain sense it *was* a tourist attraction. Where else could you sit and look at New York, this beaming, glistening New York, the lights of downtown, at the time the World Trade Center and the Statue of Liberty off to the left. It was a postcard."

Forgione felt that he had helped put the restaurant on the map, though he admits that was "only in my ego; nobody else's." Nonetheless, he wanted to be made a partner. O'Keeffe's reply: "How much is that worth? . . . It's like giving somebody a couple million dollars, you know? I don't know how you'd calculate it," says O'Keeffe.

"Maybe you have to go on your own," O'Keeffe told him.

This, to borrow a phrase from O'Keeffe, took balls. The fate that befell Patrick Terrail at Ma Maison in its post-Puck period typified the emerging industry dynamic. Restaurants closely associated with, or dependent on, one chef rarely maintained the same level of prominence after the chef departed; those that survived risked being engulfed by a fog of anticlimax.

The moment presaged what would become a recurring theme at The River Café, as chefs inevitably wanted to become owners.

"I would always be happy to see them succeed," says O'Keeffe. "Some owners got mad when the people left. I said, 'I'm providing the stage. This is like Carnegie Hall, Lincoln Center. You dance and then people see you and you're finished.'"

After Chef Kobayashi decamped Le Plaisir for California, owners Stephen Spector and Peter Josten didn't need the money and didn't want the headaches of maintaining the restaurant. They came into The River Café one night and told Forgione to fork over half his life savings and he could have the restaurant. A deal was struck, and Forgione began planning his next restaurant with a name suggested by Beard himself, An American Place.

"IT WAS THE WILD, WILD WEST."

The River Café sputtered along for months with one of Forgione's sous chefs stewarding the kitchen, until O'Keeffe was put onto a new prospect: Charlie Palmer, then going by his more formal given name, Charles, chef of Westchester County's Waccabuc Country Club, where he'd been recruited by members seeking something more refined than the typical continental fare.

Palmer, a broad-shouldered, Hemingway-esque former high school football player from the dairy community of Smyrna, New York, had first discovered cooking thanks to a neighbor who was also his school's home economics teacher. From a young age, purely out of necessity, Palmer found himself at her house, making pies and such, "because we were hungry, not because we had any interest in cooking. Back in that day, the guys took shop, did woodwork and machinery and stuff like that, and the girls took home ec and they learned how to keep a household," says Palmer. "So she came to me with this idea: 'Hey, take this class. You're just going to cook. You don't have to do any sewing. And think of the possibilities: It's you and twenty-six girls. Not a bad thing for a high school football player. And you get to eat everything you make. So you can bring in all the stuff that you hunt and we'll cook it. We'll learn how to cook it together in class. We'll bring in rabbit, bring in venison.'"

The classes led Palmer to a job at the Colgate Inn, just for money, really, but the teacher convinced him to consider The Culinary Institute of America, driving him there for his interview. After the CIA, Palmer worked at La Côte Basque in Midtown Manhattan, then for Georges Blanc in Vonnas, France, an hour north of Lyon. The enterprising Blanc, whose reach extended beyond his eponymous restaurant, opened Palmer's eyes to the possibilities of his chosen profession. "Seeing a guy that was literally running a hotel restaurant, owned other businesses in the little town, kind of owned a town, in a sense. I was really impressed with that whole thing."

Palmer, who started at the country club in 1982, followed the goings-on in the New York City restaurant scene, and identified with Forgione's River Café MO. Because he was given free rein in his new position, "I thought this is a chance for me to experiment with kind of incorporating this Americanization of French cuisine and make my own style."

After a year and a half, Palmer missed New York City too much to stay away. He had met O'Keeffe through Marc Sarrazin, of De-Bragga & Spitler, a meat purveyor, who told him to expect a call from the restaurateur about the River Café job. The call never came, but Palmer pursued O'Keeffe. Months of thwarted meet-ups and interviews followed—a canceled dinner at The Quilted Giraffe, a planned dinner at which Palmer found himself dining alone with O'Keeffe's girlfriend. "It was to the point where I thought this guy's crazy," says Palmer. "This is not going to happen. It's not intentional with Buzzy. Knowing him as well as I do now, it's very hard for him to make a decision. It's very hard for him to move on from something. I love

Buzzy. I would say I'm probably one of his closer friends-slash-chefs over the years, but he's a different animal, man. But I think he always struck me as, like, an interesting guy and obviously successful guy. I always thought it was just a genius move to put a restaurant at the foot of the Brooklyn Bridge looking at New York. I always thought that takes real foresight, especially at that point when he first did it because it was literally the ghetto over there."

Palmer persisted, arranged a face-to-face meet-up, told O'Keeffe to give him a shot and fire him after four months if he wasn't happy. O'Keeffe agreed. When Palmer showed up to work two weeks later, nobody in the kitchen knew he'd been hired. It was, says Palmer, "very rough." The chef, who still hadn't negotiated his own salary, fired four cooks in the first three weeks, brought on his own trusted lieutenants, some from as far away as Westchester County, promising them he'd work out a good situation. "We basically turned over the whole kitchen in the first four months," says Palmer. "There were three guys that stuck with us out of the whole crew. It was not a good scene. And there was a lot of animosity. I don't know how it all started, but I suspect it was a lot of communication breakdown. And it was dysfunctional. But here was a restaurant with people coming in every night so it *had* to work."

The saving grace was Palmer's quick rapport with maître d' Rodney Garbato and his front-of-house team. "Some of those people really embraced me because they had not had that relationship with Larry. When I showed them some respect and said, 'Look, we're going to make this place better than it's ever been,' they bought into it." When Palmer broke out the turpentine and had the box erased from the kitchen floor, it was taken as a symbol of solidarity. Palmer carried the lesson into his future endeavors: "It doesn't take long when you're a chef and you become a restaurateur to realize that your money is made out there," he says.

Under Palmer, the River Café kitchen underwent a constitutional transformation, morphing into one of the most macho upscale backs of house of 1980s New York City.

"I always hired these young, smart-ass kids from New Jersey or Long Island because they always had the best attitudes," says Palmer. "They could take a lot of shit. They could work hard. They were good, young, smart kids. I just filled the kitchen with these guys."

"It was the Wild, Wild West," says Palmer. "And we had that reputation, too." He's not kidding: The crew became known as hardworking, hard-drinking, rambunctious.

"I wouldn't call it a serious kitchen in the sense that you don't look at the guy next to you," says Palmer. "It was more: Let's work on things together and throw ideas back and forth. It was an incubator. There was an idea a day that made it onto the menu. There was no stopping that process. I think everybody had the feeling that we could do anything. We just had to put our marks to it. I didn't feel at that point that we had any boundaries. You know, in French cooking there's the classical recipe. You follow the recipe. You respect it. And there we had this good understanding of cooking but we didn't have any boundaries. There wasn't anything that said you couldn't combine this ingredient with that ingredient.

"It was a time where—maybe to a fault—almost every plate had [to have] two different cooking methods. It was rare beef with fully braised something-or-other. Or lamb or veal, that kind of thing. We'd hear about something, read about something. We'd bring in monkfish liver. We'd make monkfish liver pâté—cure it. We were curing sausages. We were doing all that stuff way back then."

A young cook named David Burke, referred to Charlie Palmer by chef Waldy Malouf of Bedford, New York's La Crémaillère, where Burke had been a sous chef, came to The River Café as a sous chef in 1985, on the same day Gerry Hayden, a student at the CIA, began an externship there. Burke and Hayden were fast friends, trashtalking each other's place of origin: Hayden from Long Island versus Jersey boy Burke.

Hayden was a bit swept up in the image of Palmer as a coach: "I never saw Charlie in anything but his whites," he says. "He came to work in his whites, and he left in his whites. He was all business. And he loved the fact that women loved to see men in a chef's jacket." He found Palmer's lifestyle aspirational. "He was all of twenty-seven, and he was living in Brooklyn Heights on Hicks Street in this fabo apartment with Roederer Cristal and great art hanging on the walls."

The days of the career grunt, just there for the paycheck, were starting to phase out. Every cook in the kitchen, it seemed, wanted to be a chef, creating an addictive relationship to cooking.

"I swear, all we did is get up in the morning, get coffee, go to work, leave that night, go to bed, get up," says Hayden.

"From the day I went in there, every day was amazing," says Neil Murphy, a self-described "knucklehead" and fine-dining know-nothing when he was hired. "Every day I learned dozens and dozens of things about cooking, about myself, about other people, about equipment. The food was amazing. The camaraderie that we had over time was amazing. If I wasn't with that group of guys, I probably wouldn't be where I am today because we were so into our craft and so into cooking that it just took over our lives. It was more important than our girlfriends or our wives. It was more important than getting stoned. It was more important than drinking, although that was a priority as well. I never experienced that really in life that much. Nothing was as intense as that."

Murphy credits Burke as a catalyst at The River Café: "As fun as it was working for Charlie, Dave Burke was really the guy who brought it all together," he says. "He was the guy who would go out and talk about food, talk about different things that we could do. He always had an active imagination. It was fascinating to hear somebody talk about food this way. Then we'd come in the next day and try some of these things and we were actually able to get them on the plate."

"It was still European technique," says Burke of the American style at The River Café. "It was different names. They call it *steak au poivre*; we called it *black pepper steak*. We're serving local fish instead of Dover sole. Cooking is cooking. It's still cooking the European way. We're sautéing. We're grilling. Instead of a brandy sauce we're making a bourbon sauce for the steak. It's not that much different at that stage. We're buying fiddlehead ferns. You'll never see that. Charlie's buying stuff from local [purveyors], stuff which Larry started. Charlie's putting some menus together. They're not hypercreative yet. Him and I together—I'm doing specials, but not all of them. Charlie writes them, too. But then I get to write them and as time goes on I start writing more. We made a very good team."

"We were making Maxim potatoes—overlapping slices, brushed with clarified butter and baked—back then, we were trying to do them and it was so hard to do; we had too much oil in the pan and it was so hot and there were no Silpats,"* says Murphy. "Dave was fascinated with consommés; we made all kinds of consommés; who even *makes* a consommé now? I remember, doing brunch, he would have six mini English muffins with six quail eggs and six types of hollandaise. Can you imagine prepping for that? But we were down for that. It didn't matter. We'd come in early for that. And we got paid a shift rate, nothing was hourly, so it was seventy-eight dollars a shift, and the shift could be eight hours or the shift could be sixteen hours, it didn't matter. This is now becoming our life. If you were worried about the money then you didn't fit in, and the universe was going to kick you out."

Of the English muffins, Hayden recalls that "one day at brunch, early in the morning, we decided we were going to do quail eggs Benedict. So we started making English muffins. Nobody in that kitchen had ever made an English muffin. Okay, you pull out the books, you figure it out. So we're making this little griddle. It wasn't on the menu, so anybody that ordered anything we sent out a few

----

* Silicone baking mats.

quail eggs Benedict, as a starter, just to see if people liked it. Just this little half muffin with a little tiny over-easy or sunny-side-up quail egg on the top with a piece of bacon we were smoking in the back. Stuff like that would happen all the time."

"I was a *why not* guy, not a *why* guy," says Burke. "*Here's why we do onion soup with Gruyère cheese.* I'm like, well, why does it have to be only onion soup that has cheese on it? Why can't I do a minestrone with cheese on it?"

Hayden recalls Palmer and Burke as something of a Lennon-McCartney duo: "They would always try to outdo one another," says Hayden. "I remember Charlie made a cold lobster soup. It was made with shells, cream, tarragon. It was fucking phenomenal. But it was cold. And he served it with poached lobster and a beautiful, almost like a tarragon timbale, like a custard. It was so elegant. It was very reminiscent of something you'd see in a Georges Blanc cookbook. That blew me away. That's when I knew he was the chef that everybody thought he was . . . and there were a lot of times where the cooks on the line would say, 'Hey, Charlie, I was reading this article last night about morels. Do you think we could get some morels in?' And the next thing you knew, morels showed up. It took chutzpah. You told Charlie what you thought, then he took it and then he would draw it up on the plate. We just had so many rotating specials. Charlie would have specials written up for the entire week so you knew every minute of every day what you were doing. Nothing came from left field. It was all well thought out. We ran like a machine. It was the best. The best learning experience anyone could have. I went back to school after my internship, and before I graduated, I was like, *I can't wait to get back to New York. I'm wasting my time at school.*"

The unbridled energy and adventurousness of the Palmer years at The River Café are summed up by many who were there by a smoker the crew built: "We built a smokehouse in the building," says Palmer. "We got this huge, basically walk-in cooler and piped in the smoke source. And this is all out of a book, you know? A DIY project, totally. But it was great because we're going to smoke all our own salmon. We're going to smoke sausages. We're going to do all that stuff. We created a curing room. You didn't even think about it. You just said, *Okay, there's some space over there.* I remember we sent Neil Murphy out to this place out in Brooklyn and he brought back this walk-in cooler for nothing. It was out of a junkyard. I don't even know how he found it. We knew we had to have a big, big container."

"The locker room was thirty or forty feet from the side of the restaurant," says Murphy. "We got an old double-door fridge, took the guts out, popped a hole in the side, put an aluminum manifold in it. We wanted to cold-smoke. We smoked everything: salmon, squab, quail, shrimp. One time we must have left twenty sides of salmon in there and we overcooked them, hot-smoked them. We had twenty sides so we made consommé, raviolis, rillettes. We never let any of that go to waste."

"Charlie—you know, you want to try something? We'd try it," says Burke. "And you had the manpower to do it. And you could sell anything at The River Café. I made smoked kidneys. I made kidneys taste like bacon, served it with calf's liver. Instead of bacon and onions, I'd do leeks and kidneys. We could sell anything because we had forward-looking customers but also a lot of tourists. We had a lot of Japanese people that came in. You wouldn't make something in vain. It would sell."

All of this was undertaken in addition to the daily demands of the kitchen, and the crew wore the workload as a badge of honor.

"We were inundated with prep," says Hayden. "It was unbelievable, the amount of work it took that we had to get ready for service every single day.... We were better than other kitchens because when I heard about all the people that would do the vegetable blanching, that was all *our* responsibility. There was no guy that blanched the vegetables. Every cook was responsible for getting his veg, sauce, and proteins together. That's why I had a big head."

The long hours and like-mindedness produced a pack mentality:

"We were like a gang," says Murphy. "I loved that. You never had to worry that somebody was going to take you down because other guys were going to watch out for you. That was the vibe. If one guy couldn't get set up on time, somebody's going to help you. If the grill guy gets fifty orders and the sauté guy gets ten, he had your back, you didn't even have to ask. . . . We all loved each other. *Love* is a strong word. To where you'll fucking almost die for that guy for whatever reason, that's how we felt about each other. . . . It was a pretty amazing feeling. You rarely get something like that."

Hayden remembers the restaurant as fiercely supportive and friendly competitive: "There were times where we would race each other from the minute we got in the door to see who could be set up with their station, all their *mise en place*,* everything they needed to do for that day. Because I worked a fish station and the fish station at The River Café was two people. Then there was a sauté guy and a grill guy. And so me and Neil Murphy, we would bet that we could set up faster and better and be outside a half hour before service started."

The long days, punctuated by peaks and valleys, created an extraordinary need to blow off steam. Between prep and service, Murphy and Hayden would knock back multiple double espressos, meet out back on the barge, and while the other cooks sucked down cigarettes, get each other pumped up for service, wrestling and pinning each other down and screaming "Are you ready!" in each other's face. It was extreme, even by River Café standards: "I think the rest of the folks thought we were crazy," says Hayden.

After hours, as with most kitchens (then and now), alcohol was a must. Most of the time, says Murphy, the crew would hit a bar. "We would go out every single night and suck down a bunch of beers," he says. Occasionally, "we would sit out on the deck at The River Café and we would drink all night for free, sometimes till four in

---

* Ingredients prepared ahead of service.

the morning. I never wanted to leave." (Murphy recalls the bridge as a presence: "This big, looming, ugly-beautiful, historic piece of art." He also recalls that "when there were jumpers, they would close the bridge and we would be slow for several hours.")

Once or twice a month, says Murphy, Burke might arrange for the team to meet with another restaurant's crew across the river in Manhattan, and "we would drink and do blow all night." (The drinking actually began at the start of service. "There were two cases of beer put on the line, on ice, at the beginning of the night," remembers Murphy, who found himself "half-hammered by the end of the night," which impaired his cleanup: "You'd just dump everything into the garbage.")

"That's one thing that brought us all together," says Murphy. "If you didn't come out and drink with us you were on the outside."

They were magical times at The River Café, but as for Forgione before him, Palmer's days were numbered from the get-go, because—mostly due to the example of the French nouvelle cuisine titans—he had realized, "Hey, we're the engine in this business, we should own it or be a partner in it." He told O'Keeffe that he needed to become a partner or push off. O'Keeffe, not one to make decisions quickly, considered it, and considered it, and considered it, until Palmer realized it simply "wasn't in his DNA." Over lunch at La Grenouille, Palmer told him about an offer he had to become a partner in another restaurant. "I said I thought it was too good to pass up," says O'Keeffe, letting another future all-star slip away.

"WE WERE DOING THE FLAVORED OILS FIRST."

David Burke's path to The River Café was longer and more convoluted than his predecessors. Known as a wild man to this day, his reputation has obscured his chops, which were among the most impressive of any of his contemporaries.

Burke grew up in Hazlet, New Jersey, a better-than-average student for a cook, blessed with the ability to retain information and mentally organize it; in time, he'd graduate early from high school. He was also industrious, with a bruising paper route, and competitive, especially in wrestling, which could bring out the beast in him. Like many tri-state-area kids, his first interest in cooking came not from food but from the kitchen environment, discovered in a dishwashing job in a local hotel at age fourteen. There he was mesmerized by the chefs and cooks, their butchery skills, and the camaraderie of the kitchen.

In 1980, when he was eighteen, came The Culinary Institute of America and a weekend gig private cheffing for a hotel owner at his Catskills home. Burke simply couldn't stop screwing around with food. In the private chef gig, he made snails bourguignonne, but wrapped the snails in chicken tenderloin. He externed at the Fairmont Hotel in Dallas, Texas, taking a night job in another restaurant to pay the rent. Then it was back to New Jersey and the Fromagerie in Rumson. Though just the broiler man, Burke was beginning to experiment in earnest, and the owners, Hubert and Marcus Peters, were open-minded, put his dishes on the menu—the first was a riff on *poularde demi-deuil* with a stuffing of ricotta and spinach between skin and meat creating a three-layer effect when roasted.

In his second year at the CIA, he dabbled in cooking competitions. After graduating (named Most Likely to Succeed), he cooked for a family in Norway. In the interview, his prospective employer asked him if he could make certain dishes; he rattled off the recipes and approaches he'd take to create them, from memory. He got the job, traveled around Europe, too poor to eat in the best restaurants, but made a study of the menu boxes out front.

Back in the States, he took a saucier position under Waldy Malouf at La Crémaillère. He was swiftly promoted to sous chef, stayed on for two and a half years, then took a job (with the assistance of André Daguin) at La Rapière in Mauvezin, France. He dined at Michelin three-star restaurants, catching the attention of the chefs with his enthusiasm and appetite, ordering dishes beyond those featured on the degustation menus. (Bocuse joined him for a glass of wine; Pierre Troisgros gave him a kitchen tour.) Back in New York City, he took a job as fish cook with a young, newly arrived chef named Daniel Boulud at the Hôtel Plaza Athénée.

Bored with the style of the food there, he jumped when mentor Malouf recommended him to Palmer at The River Café, where Palmer's laboratory style absorbed Burke's burgeoning creativity, and on the menu went such dishes as shrimp and ginger wontons and oysters with watercress on roasted peppercorns. After a year, he took six weeks to return to France, work for Georges Blanc, Troisgros, and Marc Meneau.

One day, when eating a slice of pizza, Burke noticed the red oil that oozed onto the plate: "Oil from the cheese and tomato. It was red. It looked pretty on a plate. I'm like, I can flavor oils, man! Then we started making them colorful. Curry, tomato. Now I've got a lighter sauce." The flavored oils were deployed for economy and elegance: "I had tuna tartare on the menu and I had horseradish with ginger in it and I didn't want the pieces. I wanted it to be smooth. So I took the peels and made oil. I didn't throw shit away. I was using the peels and made oils. Now we pour that oil in the tartare, you get the flavor." To this day, Burke maintains that he was employing flavored oils before Jean-Georges Vongerichten, who came to New York City in 1985 and took over the kitchen at Lafayette, became famous for them among many other flourishes and innovations.*

---

* Burke was also an unacknowledged precursor to the molecular movement of the early twenty-first century. He discovered Harold McGee's *On Food and Cooking: The Science and Lore of the Kitchen* relatively early, reading and citing him in the

"Now I've got a pretty plate. I got color. Listen, I worked at River Café. I had to get people's eyes on the plate, not out the window."

In December 1987, he discovered that Palmer was on his way out. Burke was supposed to leave with Palmer, become his lieutenant in his new venture, but O'Keeffe offered him the chef's position.

"Buzzy, I can't take this job. I'm not qualified," said Burke.

"You're qualified," said O'Keeffe. "Everyone in the building says you are."

Burke felt that before he could assume command of the barge, he needed to know more about pastry. He reached out to Michel Richard at Citrus in Beverly Hills, offered to work for free, but Richard refused him. Burke told O'Keeffe he wanted to go to Gaston Lenôtre in Paris, and O'Keeffe backed him.

"I came back to the River as the chef. I brought a pastry chef back with me and then we just started rocking and rolling," says Burke. "We put twenty-four desserts on the menu.

"I knew how to cook classic food. I knew a little bit about what modern American ingredients were. And then I just said, 'Listen, I'm going to do it my way. I'm going to take chances. I'm going to twist it. And I'm going to craftsmanship the hell out of some of this stuff, too.' And listen, I made the chocolate Brooklyn Bridge."

The bridge was one of the great pieces of cleverness in restaurants

---

mid-1980s. "I worked at some flavor houses out in Jersey," he says. "People that create what a lot of molecular guys use. The xanthan gums, the extracts." He's referring to companies like Lipton who employed these additives for industrial purposes. "When I went to Park Avenue Café after The River Café, in the early nineties, I created cheesecake pops. That had some science to it, xanthan gum and all that stuff, and modified food starches and all that crazy [stuff]. I created pastrami salmon, packaged it. And you know, swordfish chops. So the creativity, some of it was [realized] with the help of some of that." He's quick to emphasize that the science was a means to an end, a method of bringing ideas to life, not an end itself. Does he see a dotted line between his food during that era and the work of a chef like Wylie Dufresne? "Absolutely. One hundred percent. There's a dotted line to a lot of stuff."

at that time—a miniature chocolate replica of the restaurant's neigh-boring landmark. "They sell $25,000 worth of Brooklyn Bridges a year. Maybe more. And Buzzy will never take it off the menu. They make it smaller but—because I had some pastry knowledge then, I said, 'Listen, that's what I want. I want to sell it for two. I want it to be the iconic dessert of this place.' . . . I'm not a pastry chef, per se, [but] I like to be in that. I like theater desserts. I like people to take that Instagram, [or] mental shot before Instagram, take it home, you know? Because it ends your meal with a smile.

"I think I was one of the guys that was more concerned with entertaining the public with presentation and great combinations and *ahas*," says Burke.

Burke was so proud of his food he once asked O'Keeffe to drape the windows so diners could focus on it. "He thought I was fucking nuts," says Burke, who recalls O'Keeffe simply walking away, shaking his head, unwilling to even dignify the request with a verbal response, though Burke does recall a moral victory the night Chicago chef Jean Banchet and La Côte Basque's Jean-Jacques Rachou came to dinner and turned their chairs away from the windows, telling O'Keeffe, "We came to look at the food."

Burke ran a demanding ship at The River Café. Paul Zweben, a young cook from New Jersey who had been working in restaurants and bakeries for almost ten years, graduated The Culinary Insti-tute of America, interviewed with Burke, told him he had been an executive sous chef in his last position at the Pavilion Hotel in Miami Beach, Florida. Burke, himself just twenty-four at the time, was unmoved by his status and offered him a cook's position at $8.75 an hour.

Zweben was all too happy to take the demotion. On his way into the office, at the tail end of lunch service, he'd been mesmerized by the kitchen, which he described as "magical. I saw all these cooks moving around like it was a ballet." He also sensed the machismo that had been a defining characteristic of the Palmer era: "There was a tremendous amount of testosterone in the room. You could just feel it. You could feel that this was a competitive kitchen, and if you were going to survive in it, you had to do whatever it took to survive."

"We all worked six shifts a week, so you basically worked four days or four nights and then you did a double. So you could work literally from, you know, two in the afternoon to one or two in the morning, then you would be back the following morning at seven and you would work literally eighteen hours and then you would be off for a day or two. And that's how it was," says Zweben.

The drinking culture also continued. The only moment that presented itself for Zweben to talk to Burke about becoming a sous chef was after hours. "We were at a bar and it was four in the morning and everyone had left and I was like, *This is the time for me to talk to him about becoming a sous chef.* And we went to a bar that was closed that actually opened for us at four a.m. So the gates go up and the bartender's like, 'Hey, David.' And I'm completely wasted out of my mind. And I think we drank until, like, seven in the morning. And he drank gin and tonics, and I think I actually tried one that night and almost vomited. But it's just how we did it. So you know, we would work—basically we would get into work if we worked the night shift anywhere between twelve and one or two. You would be completely wired at midnight. By midnight we would start drinking. As we were shutting down we would have a couple beers in the kitchen, and then it was time to go out. And we would go out and drink hard pretty much every night." (Diane Forley, one of the few women to work at The River Café in the 1980s, recalls the kitchen: "That was like walking into The Culinary Institute of America; everybody had their toolbox. It was very intense," she says. "Not many people came in off the street, the way I did. It was very hard." Forley began as a prep cook, but lobbied for the position of *tournant* [roundsman], who fills in on every station as needed. "David finally put me there and that for a woman was a big deal. There weren't any women line cooks. It was just guys, even garde-manger, so I became one of the guys.

I was there for so long, they ignored that." Forley abstained from the after-hours binge drinking, but even at the restaurant, during working hours, she remembers The River Café as "more of a wild kitchen. It had an army-like, military feel to it. I think they liked the regimented part of it because it kept them in order; people liked feeling like they belonged to that.")

"We all sort of paid our bills," says Zweben. "But no one worked there to get rich; we worked there because this was a place to work where eventually we were going to be like, 'You know what, Daddy? It's time for us to be a chef. We're out of here.' And then he would let us go." (A fringe benefit of being a sous at The River Café: O'Keeffe gave sous chefs a fifty-dollar-per-week dining allowance to try other restaurants around town.)

"I MAKE BIG-NAMED CHEFS; I DON'T HIRE THEM."

If there was a common trait among the chefs, O'Keeffe says it was that "they all had to have some kind of an ego to pursue excellence. You have to want to pursue that somehow." It's a make-or-break trait for him. He once told a sous chef who wanted to fill in for a chef on leave that he was a good enough technician but that he lacked the pursuit of excellence. "You have to be crazed to make it perfect."

He knows of whence he speaks: To this day, O'Keeffe remains a stickler for detail. He can tell you the perfect way to serve Perrier (well chilled, in a chilled glass, rather than with ice, which threatens the minuscule carbonation bubbles when it melts). From day one at the restaurant, he kept dairy, meats, and fish in separate coolers, so they wouldn't absorb each other's odors ("Cream is like a sponge," he says). His idiosyncratic perfectionism and taste extended to his choices of chefs. Forgione, says O'Keeffe, wanted a name chef to replace him when he left, but O'Keeffe had other plans. "I make big-named chefs; I don't hire them," he said.

"I was the only one of my staff who wanted to take Charles Palmer. He was a big country boy. I said, 'No, this is the guy it's going to be because I think he has the pursuit, the energy, and *he's* pursued me.'"

Eventually, Burke, like the others, left The River Café, for the Park Avenue Café in Manhattan. "I don't like to see them go," says O'Keeffe. But go they do. It's been an inevitability, a fact of life at The River Café.

4

FRENCH RESISTANCE

*I don't think it bothered us that we thought they didn't
respect us. I don't know if we respected them.*

—Tom Carlin

HOW THE FRENCH GUARD AND A GENERATION OF YOUNG
AMERICAN COOKS LEARNED TO LIVE TOGETHER IN NEW YORK
CITY, AND THE "CULINARY UNDERGROUND RAILROAD" THAT
HELPED BRIDGE THE GAP

David Kinch, chef-owner of Manresa, a Michelin three-star restaurant, plies his trade in the affluent placidity of Los Gatos,
California, an hour south of San Francisco. Kinch exudes West
Coast tranquility—he even surfs on his days off—but he has been
in one fistfight in his life. The year was 1984, and the Pennsylvania
native, then in his early twenties, was working a *stage* at Hôtel de la
Poste in Beaune, France, an ancient, walled town in the heart of Bur-

gundy country. Late one night, after most of the *brigade* had cleared out, Kinch found himself alone with the pastry chef, brother of the restaurant's sous chef.

Kinch considered the brothers "the definition of douches," who laid rubber on their way to and from work in a Citroën sports car, a flaming eagle emblazoned on its hood. As was the case in many kitchens of the day, the French masters rode the Americans in their kitchens harder than the rest of the crew, seasoning the punishing workload with a pinch of prejudicial ridicule. Kinch usually brushed it off, but that night was different.

"He pushed me too far," remembers Kinch. "He was deriding me: '*Américain, Américain.*' He was saying some really derogatory things. I just snapped and pushed him against the wall."

With action-movie convenience, a pile of egg flats was stacked within Kinch's reach; he began chucking the orbs at his tormentor.

"He went down," says Kinch. "I was hitting him hard; I was throwing them like baseballs. He was cowering in the corner and I emptied the whole fucking tray on him, just one after the other, maybe sixty eggs as hard as I could from fifteen feet away."

Kinch fully expected to be fired but when he returned the next morning to face the music, the place was spotless and his nemesis, humbled, greeted him as if nothing had happened. He had proven himself worthy of fear and respect, and his reward for taking that leap was peace—and survival.

The showdown illustrates the love-hate dynamic between a subset of young American cooks desperate for knowledge in the 1970s and '80s and the French chefs who possessed and, in many cases, hoarded it. This complex relationship acts as an overlay to the story of the Five Couples and to The River Café and other boundary-breaking restaurants of the time, and also defined the formative years of many cooks who came up seeking little more than a mastery of French cooking technique.

"YOU HAD TO LEARN FROM THEM, THEY HAD THE KEYS."

The United States and France had long enjoyed a warm relationship, but the professional kitchen was French territory, and when Americans began infiltrating that sacred ground it often led to friction: The French, generally speaking, considered the Americans talentless, with palates honed at McDonald's; the Americans considered the French haughty, exclusive, and oftentimes abusive.

Neither camp was entirely right, or wrong.

This culture clash was mostly an East Coast phenomenon reflecting the Atlantic Seaboard's inherent conservatism, predilection for French food, and relative proximity to Europe. The Five Couples and other Ottos were the exceptions. Generally speaking, young Americans in the tri-state area sought to emulate the French, and also coveted their approval.

It made sense: France continued to dominate and define what for most was the epitome of Western cuisine; tourists hadn't yet discovered or developed a respect for the pleasures of Italy's regions in droves as they would in the coming decades. Those who ruled the roost in France—especially nouvelle cuisine honchos like Paul Bocuse, Michel Guérard, and Alain Chapel—still towered like deities over the gastronomic universe. And the touchstones that united American home cooks pointed toward France and its cuisine as well: Julia Child, Richard Olney, and Elizabeth David were all culinary Francophiles; French restaurants were the only venue for fine dining in America's major cities; and, of course, the language of the kitchen itself—*sauté*, *flambé*, *julienne*—was French.

One book resonated more than most to these young cooks: *Great Chefs of France*, by food critic Quentin Crewe and photographer Anthony Blake. A collection of portraits, profiles, kitchen layouts, menus, and recipes, it depicted the culinary chieftains of every three-star restaurant outside Paris at the time of its publication in 1978. The fascination with a tome devoted to the professional kitchen highlighted a key difference between this subset of cooks and many of those who took up professional cooking in Northern California, and the Five Couples, who were devoted to the likes of Child, David, and Olney. (French culinary supremacy was such a given that *Great Chefs of France* author Crewe could include the following sentence without irony: "The relative indifference shown to its chefs in the past only compounds the mystery of why France is the only Western country to have made cooking into an art and raised its appreciation to the level of connoisseurship.")

Terrance Brennan, who grew up in Annandale, Virginia, and would go on to open his own Picholine restaurant and Artisanal bistro in New York City, remembers receiving the book as a gift from a friend's mother after he catered a party for her. "That was the turning point. When I opened that book, my mouth dropped. I saw those Michelin-starred kitchens, all the copper and silver and the chef's tie underneath the suit. Louis Outhier and Bocuse, and seeing them squeeze sauce through cheesecloth. I was like, *I've got to go to Europe!*"

"I was always fascinated by that book and what they were doing. I would just stare at it and read it. I had the menus memorized," says Kinch, who was born in Pennsylvania and started cooking as a teenager in New Orleans, where he worked for Paul Prudhomme. "These were French guys who grew up in this amazing gastronomic tradition. There wasn't Spain or Scandinavia or everything else back then. France was the glowing epicenter where we all strived to work."

John Doherty, an Irish American from Long Island who became chef of the Waldorf-Astoria in the 1980s, gave the book to his cooks and says it gives him goose bumps to talk about it. In the Internet age, it may be difficult to imagine a book having such widespread impact, but those were the times. It's like rocker Brian Eno's line about the first Velvet Underground album, released in 1968; it sold a mere thirty thousand copies, but everybody who bought one started a band.

A prelude to *Great Chefs of France* had been Bocuse's American star turn on the cover of *Newsweek* magazine in August 1975, a moment recalled by many future chefs who were in their teens at the time. The article, titled "Food: The New Wave," didn't merely profile Bocuse, but encapsulated the entire nouvelle cuisine movement, including an appealing evolution from the anonymous, kitchen-bound chefs of the past, reporting that "Bocuse and his friends habitually stroll from the kitchen to chat with the clientele."

The article went on to summarize nouvelle cuisine's ripples in the United States and how a new strain of gastronomic connoisseurship was taking hold: Supermarkets had begun stocking fresh herbs and organic produce; specialty shops were doing a brisk business in cheeses, pâtés, and escargots; and kitchen supply shops were selling out of such exotic equipment as woks, which the authors took the time to define as "a Chinese cooking pan," all in spite of an economic recession.

Seeing a chef in the space usually reserved for national and world leaders, entertainment phenoms, and athletes sparked the imagination of young Americans who enjoyed cooking but would never have considered it a viable—or desirable—career. More and more of them began to consider chefdom as a profession, but with no homegrown toques to mentor them, they quickly realized that a necessary rite of passage was to get next to a French (or European) chef and soak up as much knowledge as possible.

"You had to learn from them. They had the keys," says Mike Colameco, a working-class Philly native, amateur boxer, and gym rat who cooked around New York City in the 1980s. "They *knew*. Making consommé, the first time you actually made that clarification, or the first time the chef took you in and showed you how to make a pâté or a pike quenelle, it was like you were being handed something special, a knowledge skill set that not a lot of people had. And the only way in there was through them."

"IT'S LIKE PRISON."

To many of these young Americans, culinary schools beckoned, offering a crash course in the fundamentals of cooking and proximity to French, or at least European, masters. (That same *Newsweek* article touted an increase in enrollment at these schools, helping plant a seed that would lead to further matriculations; many readers had never heard of such a thing as a "chef college" until then.)

Traditionally, culinary academies had been trade or technical schools, a notch up from where you might become an auto mechanic or hair stylist. The most well-known U.S. cooking school was, and remains, The Culinary Institute of America, though it was hardly the only one of note.* With dreams that went beyond merely learning a marketable, menial skill, a new, more ambitious breed of young Americans began mixing in with the traditional student population at The Culinary Institute of America throughout the 1970s, with a steadily escalating concentration of aspirants toward the end of the decade and into the 1980s; some were, by traditional standards, a bit

---

* Other prominent U.S. cooking schools founded in the 1980s and earlier include the California Culinary Academy (San Francisco, California); the French Culinary Institute, now the International Culinary Center (New York, New York); Johnson & Wales University (Providence, Rhode Island); Kendall College Culinary Arts School (Chicago, Illinois); and the New England Culinary Institute (Montpelier, Vermont). The French Culinary Institute offers a unique underscoring of the blue-collar roots of the trade: It was founded in 1984 by Dorothy Cann Hamilton, daughter of John Cann, known in the New York metropolitan area for his television ads for his Apex Technical School. Just as Cann promised in commercials that "you get to keep your tools," an early pitch for the FCI enticed students with the prospect of graduating the school with a knife kit in tow.

old for school, but were swept up in the food craze. Doherty, who trained there from 1976 through 1978, recalls, "One or two guys were career-change people in their thirties or forties. They were old dudes. They had struggled in their career; now they're chasing their dream, going after what they really want to do, because they can. But most of the people were coming out of high school with very little experience."

The evolution of The Culinary Institute of America, commonly referred to as the CIA or "The Culinary" by students and graduates, helpfully traces the evolution of the profession and of the ever-changing landscape of restaurant food in the United States. The school was founded in New Haven, Connecticut, in 1946, as a trade school for World War II veterans. The driving force behind its creation was Frances Roth, known to Connecticut society as a strong-willed woman with a talent for achieving ambitious goals: She was the first female member of the Connecticut Bar Association and central to efforts to tamp down vice in New Haven. And so, when a group of restaurant owners sought to improve their establishments' food, they turned to her with the idea of developing a better class of cook culled from the ranks of returning GIs. Roth found a passionate backer in Katharine Angell, wife of Yale University president James Rowland Angell, whose oldest son was killed in the waning days of World War II and who subsequently poured herself into veterans' causes.

In May 1946, the school kicked off as the New Haven Restaurant Institute with fifty students and a modest faculty comprising a chef, a baker, and a dietician. The six-week or ten-week curriculum (sources differ on the length) pumped out worker bees proficient in making American staples such as beef stew and apple pie. By 1950, the institute had gone through a name change, becoming the Restaurant Institute of Connecticut, and, according to the school, graduated six hundred veterans hailing from thirty-eight states. A year later, it took on a name reflective of its burgeoning national stature, The Culinary

Institute of America. The resulting monogram, CIA, drew curious stares when it began appearing on student sweatshirts around New Haven, implying a class of aspiring spooks, rather than the annual influx of cooks, had infiltrated the college town.

Throughout the 1950s and '60s, the school's reputation grew. The *New York Times*'s Craig Claiborne held a special fascination for it, and for Frances Roth. In a 1958 article lamenting the state of classic French cuisine in the United States, Claiborne swooned, "There is one person making a valiant effort to perpetuate classic cookery in this country. She is Mrs. Frances Roth, a handsome grandmother and lawyer, who until twelve years ago, had never seen the inside of the kitchen of a public dining room."

By 1960, the CIA's curriculum had evolved into two courses of study: The first was an extension of the original program, conferring instruction in making the jingoistic grub prepared, carved, and ogled by Norman Rockwell subjects—roasts, gravies, pies—the eighty dishes most requested by American diners at the time. The advanced course was open to the top half of each graduating class and was devoted to the canon of French cookery, everything from cream and wine sauces to baking and desserts. Instruction in special disciplines such as ice carving and pulling sugar were available to those with the aptitude. By this time, some foreign students had begun to matriculate, as had a few women (a very few—just two in a class of two hundred that year).

Despite the incorporation of an auxiliary campus to accommodate overflow, as 1970 approached, the school was straining beyond its capacity. After a search for new homes that stretched as far west as Chicago and as far south as Atlanta, the school landed relatively close by, at the St. Andrew-on-Hudson Jesuit novitiate, a seventy-five-acre enclave in Hyde Park, New York. Within a decade, it had begun to morph into today's state-of-the-art facility boasting eleven production kitchens, a research kitchen, two pantries, four bake-shops, three student dining rooms, a wine-tasting room, a meat-cutting department, and a fourteen-*thousand*-volume library. And it was thriving, welcoming approximately fourteen hundred students into a two-year course into which had been folded such disciplines as advanced pastry, banquet planning, ice carving, and business law. The average student age was twenty, and the school remained predominantly male with a ratio of six men to each woman.

The CIA experienced some turbulence in the late 1970s, burning through two presidents in as many years. To the rescue came Ferdinand Metz, installed as president in 1980. A native of Munich who had apprenticed at Café Feldherrnhalle and been chef at the Deutscher Kaiser Hotel, Metz immigrated to the United States in 1965. He worked for Henri Soulé at Le Pavillon and as banquet chef at the Plaza Hotel, and had most recently been developing new products for H. J. Heinz. Tension between his immediate predecessor, J. Joseph Meng, and the school's twenty-five-member board of trustees had reportedly sunk Meng. Since Metz was a member of that board, many believed he would be able to navigate the politics of the job.

"It was also an exciting time for the school, since Metz was beginning to take the institute in new directions, attracting high-profile instructors and rounding out the curriculum," recalled Alfred Portale, who graduated the CIA in 1981.

The CIA mostly trained Americans, but reflecting Europe's culinary supremacy, most of the school's instructors were Swiss, German, or French. The school required that prospective students have some professional experience, but memories of people who were there vary about what the minimum was—most remember that it was one or two years. (Current CIA president Tim Ryan, himself a graduate of the school, believes there was no prerequisite, but ironically he is in the minority.) For the most part, though, the experience was limited to casual restaurants in the students' hometowns. When they got to the CIA, many were exposed for the first time to the phenomenon of chef as drill sergeant—the prototypical, absurdly demanding, occasionally red-faced, border-line abusive European taskmaster. Some became legendary among the legion of cooks who attended the CIA, such as Fritz Sonnen-schmidt and Roland Henin.

"Henin was this tall French guy with these big hands and really long nose," remembers Colameco. "And he would fuck with you: He'd turn your oven off and not tell you, to teach you that you should check your oven every fifteen minutes. Because you know what happens in commercial kitchens? That kind of shit happens. Maybe the pilot fucking blew out. Maybe the thermostat's wrong. Maybe some guy just doesn't like you. It's like prison."

John Kowalski, who graduated the CIA in 1977 and is now an instructor there, believes that many instructors just wanted to see if newbies could "hack it." He also fondly recalls that each of his instructors had at least one off-hours diversion that would allow him to decompress and that revealed another, softer side of his personality: Out in the country, or returning from a weekend with exquisite, fresh, uncultivated oysters from Rhode Island, "they were like little babies," he says.

The instructors were also the embodiment of the students' ambitions. As they observed European maestros butchering whole animals, pulling sugar, demonstrating more potato preparations than any American knew existed, whipping up every conceivable sauce from memory, and displaying an exquisite touch with puff pastry, they got their first taste of the Everest before them, and an insatiable desire to summit it. And one of the first realities for culinary school graduates to digest was the gap between cooking school and real pro kitchens. And so French kitchens, and more generally European kitchens—whether in New York City or abroad—became the unofficial finishing schools for cooks, the places where blanks were filled in, skills were honed, real-world chops were earned, and acceptance was conferred.

"The way I looked at school was that when I graduated, that wasn't the end of my education; it was the *beginning*," says Larry Forgione, one of the first of the prototypical modern-day chefs to matriculate at the CIA. "When I left, I was probably the only person I know that was taking jobs for experience and not for position or money." Forgione's approach—prizing knowledge over mere employment—was ahead of its time when he graduated in 1974, but by the early 1980s was becoming the norm for a portion of each graduating class.

"Cooking schools are fine," says Colameco, who graduated in 1982. "But I'm not sure cooking was ever meant to be taught that way; it hadn't been, historically. You do an apprenticeship—that's how it is in France and that's how it is in most of the world. You start at thirteen or fourteen and you just learn how to do the craft from someone that's good at it." What you can't get in school, says Colameco, is "the reality of a working kitchen; a restaurant is not a laboratory. It's not conceptual."

Indeed, there was an entire class of Americans who followed the European model, never attending a culinary institute, the most notable example being the most celebrated chef of that generation: Thomas Keller. Another chef who forwent culinary school was Stephen Lyle, an American who trained in France in the late 1970s, and cooked for fellow American Leslie Revsin at Restaurant Leslie, a well-respected nouvelle cuisine outpost on Cornelia Street in Greenwich Village. "I'd worked with some CIA grads," remembers Lyle. "And they were great with jargon and they'd talk about their *mise* a lot, but they just didn't really know what the hell they were doing. Not so unusual for a kid straight out of school, but they thought they knew everything. We would kind of laugh about that. People I worked with, a lot of them had been trained in France. We just knew a hell of a lot more than these kids did." Lyle describes a rivalry between those who came up in pro kitchens and the cooking school grads, whom he and his colleagues saw both as pretentious and as "rubes. There's obviously some very talented people but there were also a bunch of idiots."

A contrast between the East and West Coasts was how few cooks in the Golden State even contemplated culinary school. Traci Des Jardins, a spitfire who had become a protégé of German-born Joachim Splichal in his L.A. restaurant Patina, explains that "Joachim wasn't oriented towards them. He was looking for hard-core French experience." Fellow Californian Jonathan Waxman expresses a more Zen version of this attitude: "When people say they go to school to learn how to cook, I always laugh. Where you go to school is in the street. Where you go to school is going to other people's restaurants or going and working at other people's restaurants or going to people's homes or going to the supermarkets. Cooking is so much about just living, you know?" For another sign of California's distinct sensibility, consider that one of the head instructors at San Francisco's California Culinary Academy in the early 1980s was Jeremiah Tower, who had been chef at Chez Panisse, but had no formal training.

"THE KITCHEN WILL ALWAYS EMBRACE YOU."

Whether or not they attended culinary school, many who set their sights on the professional kitchen during these years had more in common than a desire to learn how to cook: They were almost meta-bolically incompatible with traditional classroom education. Which is not to say that they were not intelligent. As Bruce Springsteen once said: "One problem with the way the educational system is set up is that it only recognizes a certain type of intelligence, and it's in-credibly restrictive. There's so many types of intelligence and people who would be at their best outside of that structure get lost."

Frances Roth felt the same way as The Boss. She was said to be upset at the American attitude toward "those who work with their hands rather than in white collars."

Very often, cooks are among those lost boys and girls, and this was especially true before the alphabet soup of syndromes and disorders—ADD, ADHD, OCD—applied to today's children was available to the mainstream.

A number of influential chefs hail from the halls of academia, especially those who began cooking in Berkeley in the 1970s and '80s, but for every higher-educated chef and cook, there were—and to some extent still are—scores of cooks who didn't do well in school, who zoned out or fell asleep during class.

"If I was a kid nowadays, I most likely would have been diagnosed with ADD," says Tom Colicchio. "I had all the classic signs of it. I had report cards saying, 'Tom should be doing X and Y, and he's doing Z. Seems always distracted.'"

Colicchio's distractions extended even to his first kitchen forays at home. "I remember serving this particular recipe and it was clear that I didn't read the whole thing because when it was served, the family was like, 'Where's the rest of the meal?' It was clearly only an appetizer and that's all I made. So my mother had to get up and bail me out."

"I was not a great student," says New York City chef Scott Bryan. "I didn't really apply myself. I was bad at math, not great at English. But social studies, remembering stats, things like that? Very good at them. It's ADHD. People who can't concentrate or focus. A lot of cooks I know, they're bored at school. They can't pay attention. They pay attention maybe for a minute or something. Unless something catches them, then they become idiot savants in a way. People joked about me as, like, Rain Man. I'd do the same things over and over. Say the same quotes and verses. It's OCD *and* ADHD, in a way."

"I know a lot of chefs who are dyslexic," says author, producer, and television personality Anthony Bourdain. "A lot of chefs who tell me—because I heard this from people who read [my book] *Kitchen Confidential*—that they hadn't read another book since high school. I think for a lot of people who were uncomfortable in their verbal comprehension skills, reading comprehension; who felt awkward speaking or who struggled with language; here's a business that's nonverbal, that's sensual, where you can express yourself without using language. Reading skills not needed, really. You could get around it."

None of which is to imply that these are unintelligent people: "I would say that there are one thousand ways for smarts to represent themselves," says Mario Batali. "Some of which is in developing management skills and some of it is developing your own interpersonal ability to somehow participate and help run something good. And it's in a very physical way, whether you're building a house and you're suddenly a journeyman adding bricklaying. Someone who starts as an introductory knucklehead on a construction job—there is a way for that person to eventually become a general contractor much faster than people who have been there a lot longer than them. And it's because they possess a faculty for understanding the larger picture while they're doing the same hand movements.

"It's the same way with cooks; you look at cooks and maybe these cooks hadn't made it in the military or hadn't made it in a place where somehow they hadn't accepted whatever authority was going to lead them. In the world of cooking you can work outside of the authority in your own mind while watching everything being done. And that allows you, if you're a quick learner and attentive and watching, to learn a lot of the tricks from the very best people in the field or in your restaurant or within ten feet of you because you are able to mimic their actual hand motions."

A majority of these cooks discovered the kitchen almost by accident, taking a high school job as a dishwasher. They came for

spending money, then fell in love with the atmosphere, the characters, the physicality, structure, and craft.

"The dishwasher position of course is an entry-level position into
the restaurant because you don't enter as a skilled cook, even as a
journeyman cook," says Christopher Lee, onetime co-chef of Chez
Panisse. "You start at the bottom, which is a dishwasher. That's the
way into the kitchen and that's the first station you hit when you
come in the back door. You've got your toe in and then the guy says,
'Hey, can you help me with these onions?' And it sort of accrues
from there, it builds from there."

What's more, those who found their way to the kitchen were
often treated as, or considered themselves, misfits or outcasts in
"normal" society: "I also think there are a lot of people who just
sensed in themselves a general discomfort with polite society," says
Bourdain. "I mean, working in an office, interacting with others in
a larger situation, interacting with a room full of equals. Awkward.
Difficult. You don't see the high school quarterback in a kitchen that
much. People who feel adrift, at odds . . . shy people. Some of the biggest shouters are actually very shy, insecure, tenuous people outside
of the kitchen."

"The kitchen will always embrace you," says Batali, whose first
job was as a dishwasher. "If you're there to do, and do, a good job,
the cooks will eventually throw you a fucking steak every now and
then because they appreciate you doing the good job and you saved
them."

It wasn't long before Batali moved on to the kitchen line: "The
cohesiveness of the team was something that I grew to like. It was
something I had never seen before. People that you loved, and people
that you didn't even like, had to come together as a team and work
through the dinner service that you would eventually conquer, and
it was about concentration. It was about precision. It was about mastering your hand movements and thinking around the room while

226 CHEFS, DRUGS AND ROCK & ROLL

you were trying to make sure that everything was going to come up in the right way. There was never anything that took longer than eleven minutes to cook so there wasn't a lot of complexity to it. But there was certainly the high point of the adrenaline buzz of when it's working and you're working together in a team and everyone's doing their job. It's very much like a ballet or like a football team playing an excellent play."

Boston chef Jasper White recalls his first impressions of the kitchen: "My mother had moved to Arkansas and I was nervous because I heard she was going to get married and I actually packed up and went there for a little bit and I got a job cooking breakfast in a hotel. And that was my first real cooking job. I only stayed for six weeks but within three days I met the first openly gay women I'd ever met in my life. I worked with a German chef who had a Peruvian crew. My mentor was a guy named Uncle Charlie, who was a black man who grew up in Louisiana. Within a week, I said, 'I'm home.'

"I could be who I was. I didn't have to pretend. It wasn't a job where I had to dress up. I just threw on my uniform and went to work. I loved the contrast of the humans I was working with. The different personalities. I felt there was compassion at a level I wouldn't find anywhere else. At that particular hotel there was a dishwasher named Robert, and I don't know what was wrong with him, but he would try to drown himself in the sink when he ran out of work to do. He was handicapped. Uncle Charlie said to me, 'Make sure Robert always has stuff, even if you have to give him clean stuff to wash again.' And that was part of the daily routine. But it wasn't like, 'We've got to get rid of this guy.' It was: 'We've got to take care of this guy.'

"You know," says White, "behind the screaming and yelling and all the tough stuff that chefs can do, there was a lot of compassion."

"THIS WAS NOTHING SHORT OF A METICULOUSLY TIMED FOREIGN INVASION."

Like the founding of the CIA, the establishment of a community of French chefs in New York City was a footnote to World War II. The unintentional catalyst was the French pavilion at the 1939 World's Fair in the borough of Queens, New York. To honcho France's restaurant there, the French government tapped Henri Soulé, who had worked his way up from busboy at age fourteen to assistant maître d' at Café de Paris. A front-of-house man, never a chef, Soulé assembled a team that included Pierre Franey as assistant fish cook.

As they bobbed across the Atlantic on the SS *Normandie*, key kitchen personnel met daily to plan how they'd feed the one thousand visitors expected to dine every day at the French pavilion. "This was nothing short of a meticulously timed foreign invasion," Franey would later write of the enterprise. "All of the equipment, from ovens to pots and pans, was brought from France. That meant we had to construct a kitchen from the ground up."

Upon arrival, the Frenchmen devoured New York City at a time when the metropolis swayed to the big bands of Benny Goodman and Glenn Miller, fraternizing at the Vatel Club (an organization for French in the hospitality industry), sunning themselves at Jones Beach, and visiting the cinemas and nightclubs of Times Square. They were to return home after two spring-summer runs in America, but with the occupation of France by the Nazis, most elected to stay put. By 1941, their leader, Soulé, had opened his own restaurant at 5 East 55th Street in Midtown Manhattan, naming it Le Pavillon, and many of his fellow refugees flowed into his employ.

The French pavilion was intended as the ultimate showcase for haute cuisine, and with that DNA, Le Pavillon quickly rose to the ranks of the finest restaurants in America. Ferdinand Metz, the future president of The Culinary Institute of America, worked there as fish and vegetable cook in the mid-1960s, and commented, "I think it gave people the understanding of what cooking and service at its very best could be."

Le Pavillon became a fixture in New York City and Soulé became one of its most well-known dining room impresarios, welcoming Manhattan's aristocracy, its Kennedys and Rockefellers, though he wasn't considered gracious by all guests; he regularly offended Columbia Pictures mogul Harry Cohn, also his landlord, by seating him in the back, prompting Cohn to more than double his rent, from $18,000 to $40,000. Rather than pay it, Soulé moved Le Pavillon to the Ritz Tower 57th Street, eventually returning and reopening on 55th Street as La Côte Basque, a less expensive restaurant.

Le Pavillon became a sort of university for French front-of-house men and cooks in New York City. "Le Pavillon was my alma mater, my Princeton, my Yale," said assistant head waiter Fred Decré, who left in 1960 to launch La Caravelle. Another who worked there before becoming a restaurateur in his own right was maître d' Charles Masson, who would go on to launch La Grenouille at 3 East 52nd Street in 1962. Throughout the 1960s, a constellation of additional French restaurants proliferated in Midtown Manhattan, such as Lutèce on East 50th Street in 1961, where André Soltner rose to four-star prominence, and Le Cygne on East 54th Street in 1969, where Alain Sailhac did the same.

"I REALLY BELIEVED THAT THE DINING EXPERIENCE COULD BE SOMETHING SPECIAL, AND CERTAINLY AT THAT TIME IT WASN'T."

One of the defining threads of the evolution of the American chef in the late 1970s and early '80s in New York City is the story of these three worlds—aspiring Americans, the CIA, and the French-European old guard—colliding, becoming acclimated to one another, and eventually unifying.

First, the colliding: Although many young cooks revered the French, some were rubbed the wrong way by them, regarding them as more haughty than haute. The Quilted Giraffe's Barry Wine cherished his dining experiences in France—one even brought a tear to his eye—but loathed French restaurants in Manhattan (most especially their snootiness) and delighted that his business was right around the corner from the most fabled French restaurant in town, Lutèce.

"The Quilted Giraffe had printed on the menu from day one the quote from Brillat-Savarin: 'There is no place like the table for reconciling body and spirit to the anguish of a life that is necessarily too short and too imperfect,'" remembers Wine. "I really believed that the dining experience could be something special, and certainly at that time it wasn't. In the French restaurants, it was stilted and it was looking down on Americans. And so the goal of The Quilted Giraffe was to show that Americans could run a four-star restaurant."

Wine's attitude animated his menu: "You couldn't cook American food unless you knew who Howdy Doody was," says Wine. "In 1985, you could say that because anybody of cooking age had seen Howdy Doody. But if you grew up in France, you didn't understand the Howdy Doody experience. It had to do with looking at things in an American way. And this was the beginning of serving chili for seventy-five dollars, fried chicken for seventy-five dollars."

It wasn't just the American accent in the food; Wine also eschewed the French tendency toward authoritarianism and abuse as the default style of kitchen leadership. Remembers Tom Colicchio: "It wasn't about just being a brute and yelling and screaming and carrying on, doing everything by force. This was all about finesse. It was more cerebral."

Colicchio explains how Wine's collaborative approach led to

distinctly *American* compositions: "One day, Barry said, 'I want to do a dish but I want it to be American. What's really American?' We were throwing some ideas around. I said, 'How about a clambake?' He went, 'Yeah, that's exactly what I'm talking about. Now, how do we get that on a dish?' He didn't mean a clambake that goes on the dish; how do we turn that *idea* into a dish? I think we worked it into a lobster ravioli with corn, something like a butter sauce with corn and tarragon. That's the kind of thing that he would think of."

Even when The Quilted Giraffe received four stars from the *New York Times*, Wine got no recognition or encouragement from the top French chefs in town, such as Lutèce's Soltner or Sailhac, who moved from Le Cygne to Le Cirque in 1978. "They did not come to look," says Wine. "Some of the French from France actually came to look. Some guys from Lyon, ultimately Paul Bocuse, they all came." Wine says that even earning high marks from Gault and Millau didn't break the ice: "When you went to the awards luncheon, still the French chefs wouldn't give you respect. They'd stand together and speak French." But he insists that the cold shoulder didn't sting him in the least. "In fact, it made for competition. It was motivating," he says.

Even those who worked for Wine felt the French chill toward The Quilted Giraffe. Kinch, who overlapped with Colicchio there, received barbs from not only French cooks, but also Americans who worked in French kitchens, who would chide Kinch and his Quilted Giraffe colleagues if they ended up in the same bar after hours, mocking the restaurant's four-star status.

"Read 'em and weep," Kinch would retort, holding four fingers up over his beer.

Tom Carlin says that although he might have sensed the French guard's indifference toward Wine, it didn't bother him: "We probably felt that they were old school, the classic French had already peaked and was going down. For us they were passé, so I don't think it bothered us that we thought they didn't respect us. I don't know if we respected them."

Colicchio believes that Wine's great appeal to diners of the day, his outside-the-box thinking, was the very thing that turned off the French. "I think that's why a lot of the chefs didn't like it. Sometimes that experiment would backfire, like asparagus ice cream and sweetbreads, but Barry was always thinking. He was always looking. He was the first person I know that took a trip to Japan, came back from Tokyo, and said, 'We're going to start moving in that direction.' And a lot of it was very good."

It didn't take four stars to get the old guard's back up. Chef Alfred Portale, a native of Buffalo, New York, remembers the night in 1985 that Gotham Bar and Grill, where he was the chef, earned three stars from the *New York Times*. When the review broke, "I went to Bud's and met some friends and I remember there was somebody from The Four Seasons there. They were perturbed. 'How can they let this punk . . .' They said something. It was like, 'How can a restaurant that does this get three stars?'"

Phil Carlson, chef Leslie Revsin's widower, tells a similar story: One night, he and Revsin were dining at one of the top French restaurants in town, visiting with the chef at the end of the meal. Discussing the influx of Americans into the profession, the chef sneered, "I know. Anybody can be a chef now. Even cab drivers are doing it," which Carlson took as a not-too-veiled reference to a rising American chef who was known to have driven a taxi at one point.

"When you're breaking away from either traditional French restaurants like Lutèce or La Côte Basque or what was going on at Le Cirque, there definitely was suspicion, in some cases antipathy, especially if the new kids on the block got a lot of love from a critic," says Josh Wesson. "And somehow it was perceived to be coming at the expense of the old guard. No doubt about that. But I don't think the reverse was true. Whether it was the Waltucks or the Wines or Len and Karen [Allison] or David and Susan [Liederman], there was an abiding respect and love for where food had come from, an almost insane amount of respect for what that generation of chefs and restaurateurs had accomplished. It wasn't that people were breaking away for the sake of innovation or to be different; they were *expanding* on the culinary traditions and expertise of old-school restaurants and then combining that with new ingredients, access to new foods, techniques that had been developed both in France and in Japan and places like that, and creating something that didn't exist before. So there was a lot of respect for what was. But it didn't flow in the other direction from many of the great storied restaurants of the sixties and seventies, handing off the baton to the next generation of really exciting, innovative chefs."

The resistance to Americans staking a claim as chefs in their own right was nothing new; Larry Forgione had detected the same hostility years earlier at Régine's. "I wanted to be very respectful to chefs that I felt were important," says Forgione. "I certainly didn't think of myself as important. So I went to La Caravelle and the five or six great restaurants of New York. André Soltner was just an incredible human being, friendly and supportive of, at the time maybe it wasn't of American cuisine, but of a new young chef. Jean-Jacques Rachou [at La Côte Basque] was the same way. Then there were other ones like La Grenouille, where they were basically like, 'You're paying homage, now it's time for you to go.' I was just coming over to say hello. I *was* coming over to pay homage, but I didn't expect to be shown the door after I did it. You didn't have five minutes to talk to me?"

The same tension created a problem for cooking school grads looking to round out their education: "You came out of the CIA and came to New York in the early eighties and there were eight or nine restaurants to work in," says Colameco. "That was it." But most of the great French kitchens in New York City wouldn't hire Americans.

"I wanted to work at Lutèce," says Kinch. "I met with André Soltner for about ten minutes. He kind of laughed me off." (Kinch eventually found a foothold in New York City at the bistro La Petite Ferme, where David Waltuck had cooked in the 1970s.) Being declined by Soltner was essentially a rite of passage in New York City. Most describe his rejection in kinder terms than Kinch, but they all believe he turned them down because they were Americans. (Peter Hoffman says he would have washed dishes at Lutèce; Revsin's widower Carlson says she would have worked for him even after having been a chef in her own right but he simply told her, "Leslie, I just can't." For his part, Soltner insists that he had a small kitchen and a loyal crew and so rarely had open positions; and he's quick to point out that he did hire a few Americans, such as Bill Peet and Henry Meer.) And getting hired overseas was, generally speaking, even more difficult.

Daniel Boulud, who came to the United States in 1981, insists that anti-Americanism wasn't to blame for the resistance to employing Americans in French kitchens in New York, but rather that Americans simply lacked the training required to thrive in a French kitchen. "There was a limitation of opportunity for an American to really learn to become a great chef," says Boulud.

"WHAT SET HIM APART IS HE HIRED AMERICANS."

Against this backdrop, a network of U.S.-based French and European figures coalesced to connect American prospects with the experience they craved, a sort of culinary Underground Railroad. The three main operatives were CIA instructors like Eugene Bernard and Leon Dhaenens, who had direct ties to French culinary royalty such as Paul Bocuse and Fernand Point; meat purveyor Marc Sarrazin of DeBragga & Spitler; and chef Jean-Jacques Rachou, who was the chef-owner of Le Lavandou and purchased La Côte Basque from Henri Soulé in 1979, and was the first high-profile French chef willing to enlist a predominantly American crew.

"Jean-Jacques Rachou understood very early on, not that the French were dying, but if you wanted to get on the right bus you needed to get all these young American guys working in your kitchen because those were the people that were going to move up," says Charlie Palmer.*

In many cases, the Americans were so desperate for opportunity that they took a passive role in their own fate, allowing the elders to pull their strings. Today, Palmer lords over an empire of restaurants and hotels from his home base in Northern California, but in 1979, as a student at the CIA, he was a spectator in his own budding career: One winter day that year, Dhaenens and the young buck headed down to New York City and had lunch at Le Lavandou, a petite bistro on East 61st Street near Lexington Avenue. At the end of the meal, Dhaenens and Rachou spoke in French for about ten minutes, then Rachou turned to Palmer and said, in his trademark mumbled French accent, "Okay, you start March 26."

---

*   Another, less well remembered supporter of young American cooks at this time was Michel Fitoussi, who ran the kitchen at The Palace in Midtown, and then at 24 Fifth Avenue in Greenwich Village. Recalls Diane Forley, who was interested in a cooking career but not in cooking school and worked in Fitoussi's kitchen for no pay: "Michel was a Frenchman in an American house, very different than Rachou. He hired all Americans, only Americans. He was known for blown sugar apples at The Palace. He was there in [the late 1970s]. He was cooking creatively. He was also part of the beginning of the 'media chef'; he was on the news; that's how I first saw him. Other French chefs were not part of the media, but he was flamboyant. He was a kid."

    In addition to staffing his kitchen with Americans, Fitoussi's willingness to hire women was a striking exception to the long-hardened chauvinism that made breaking into French kitchens doubly difficult for American women. Michael Romano, a young American who had returned from six years *staging* in France and Switzerland and was hired on as chef at La Caravelle in Midtown Manhattan in 1984, recalls: "I hired the first woman in that kitchen, Jo-Ann Makovitzky. Roger Fessaguet—who at that point had moved from being chef to one of the owners—comes down in the kitchen, stops dead in his tracks, looks at her, and looks at me, and says, 'What's that?' That's exactly what he said. I said, 'That's a cook.'"

"There was no discussion of what you're going to do," remembers Palmer. "What you're going to get paid, *if* you're going to get paid. And Dhaenens said, 'Don't worry, my boy. Everything is set.' It was a deal. So that's what I did. I showed up and that was it." (Rachou, in need of more cooks, sometimes asked the Americans to recruit their friends, leading Palmer to reach out to his CIA classmate, Philadelphia native Frank Crispo.)

Another hopeful, dispatched by the CIA's Bernard, was Rick Moonen, a restless, raspy-voiced cook from Flushing, Queens, also sent to Rachou in 1979 as Rachou was preparing to open La Côte Basque. Enshrouded in a black cashmere overcoat borrowed from his father, Moonen showed up for an interview at La Côte Basque, then a construction site. He asked a Frenchman in red flannel outside the storefront if he could point him to Chef "Rahoo," mangling the name. The man grumbled, led Moonen inside.

"He opens the door, I follow him, he closes the door, locks it behind him. We entered through the men's room. Now, I didn't know that's where Henri Soulé had passed away, but that's how I first step into La Côte Basque, through the men's room side door."

Turns out the Frenchman was Rachou himself, punking the young American.

"He brought me downstairs into the kitchen. I'm following him around for twenty minutes. He doesn't say a word to me. He stops, he gives somebody some money, talks to another guy, gives some instruction over here, down the stairs, around the corner. Jackhammers. He turns to me, he goes, 'So you want a job?' I said, 'Yeah.' He says, 'Okay.' That was the interview.

"He said, 'Come in on Monday.' He didn't tell me a time. Nothing. I'm getting dust all over my dad's overcoat. I'm stressing out over how I'm going to get through this interview, but Eugene Bernard had made the phone call and I was already hired. He just wanted to see me and tell me I had to come in on Monday." (Palmer, Moonen, and

Crispo weren't the first Yanks Rachou hired. A few had previously worked for him at Le Lavandou.)

Assigning young American cooks hither and yon wasn't the only way in which their European puppet masters demonstrated their benevolent power. A young cook named David Bouley, who had worked for, among others, Roger Vergé, in France, joined the staff at La Côte Basque shortly after it opened under Rachou, remembers that "Rachou used to give me my mail from Vergé opened all the time." A few years later, Bouley was working under Sailhac at Le Cirque. Because of Sailhac's and Le Cirque owner Sirio Maccioni's ties to France, the restaurant was a frequent stop for the likes of Bocuse when they were in New York. On one such visit, the bosses summoned Bouley to their table.

"I went out in the dining room and I remember Paul Bocuse, Vergé, Craig Claiborne, Pierre Franey, they're all sitting there," says Bouley. "And Sirio sat me down at the end of the table. And they told me like they always did, 'This is what you're doing next, going back to Vergé and opening in San Francisco.'* There's no discussion. 'This is what you're going to do. This is going to be the best thing for you and you're going to have a good time. You're going to like it.'"

"When we first opened up we were making these chicken breasts that were hollowed out and stuffed with a chicken mousse and truffles," remembers Moonen. "It was a very big deal. It was poached and sliced and circled with a morel sauce. These are my formative years so these things are ingrained deeply in my taste memory, the smell of the restaurant, the sounds of it, the feel of it. Every living thing about it I remember as if it was yesterday."

In keeping with a trend of the day, the food was served on the Villeroy & Boch basket weave plate, also admired and used by Barry Wine at The Quilted Giraffe and Jean Bertranou at L'Ermitage in Los Angeles.

---

* Bouley was sous chef to Hubert Keller at Vergé's Sutter 500 in San Francisco.

Rachou, who was perennially hunched over, could come off as gruff and introverted. "But he had a sense of humor," says Moonen. "And he loved my sense of humor and Charlie Palmer's sense of humor. He had a love of what he did. He was an amazing artist. But he was very quiet."

According to Moonen, Rachou had moved on from the minutiae of kitchen work and was more concerned with building his empire, carving meats on guéridons in the dining room, especially in the VIP section.

"He wasn't an instructor. He wasn't a mentor, where he would take you and show you. He would say, 'I'll show you tomorrow.' And he never showed you tomorrow. He trusted that you were going to do it on your own. And we did figure it out."

Echoes Palmer: "We could relate to him but he honestly didn't teach us much. We were taught by some of the senior sous chefs in the beginning. And Rachou was—I don't want to say a 'figure-head'—he was always at the restaurant, but he wasn't really in the kitchen cooking with us besides tasting something, and saying, 'Hey, stupid, it's . . .'"

So Americans had to do their homework to fill in the gaps left by cooking school: "I had to make a cassoulet. I didn't know what a cassoulet was," says Moonen. "Fuck, man, I didn't learn that at school. I'm not French. But I'm the saucier, so I'm in charge of making the cassoulet. Cassoulet is many different layers. He said, 'You make a lamb shoe, you take a confit, you make the sauces and . . .' He's saying all these things. I don't know what the hell he's talking about. You make a lamb *shoe*?" Moonen would furiously scribble down whatever flowed from Rachou's mouth, then scurry home and hit the books. "I'm looking up *shoe*. In *cookbooks*. We didn't have the Internet. We didn't have Google." He finally realized that the chef meant lamb *stew*. "The French can't say S-T," says Moonen.

There was also the matter of Rachou's patois, French accented and marble mouthed. "He mumbled like crazy," says Moonen. "I learned how to answer people by inflection." If Rachou's unintelligible statement went up at the end, "that was a question. You had to take a chance. 'Oui, Chef' was mostly the correct answer." If, on the other hand, Rachou furrowed his brow, Moonen guessed that the right reply was "No, no, no, Chef. No, no. Absolutely no."

For quick reference in La Côte Basque and other kitchens, another book became indispensable: Louis Saulnier's *Le Répertoire de La Cuisine*, a pocket guide to six *thousand* preparations. Though published in hardcover, the skinny trim size made it possible for cooks to keep it in their back pockets.

Why was Rachou so open to hiring "the Other"? Colameco offers this perspective: "Rachou was an orphan, he was adopted. His life was very abusive. Whoever his adoptive parents were treated him like chattel. He slept in the barn. He took care of the animals. He had no rights. He wasn't their kid. So at the age of twelve or thirteen he got a job in a restaurant where he actually got to sleep indoors in a bunk with a bunch of other kids. He got to eat. It was paradise. And he couldn't read. He's illiterate. So he comes here to the States, married, had been working in the Caribbean and funky places. And he can't read. So his wife has to read the leases to him, has to read the agreements to him. So he gets what it's like to be the underdog. His whole fucking life he's been the underdog."

"What set him apart is he hired Americans," says Moonen. "He was chastised for it. How did I hear that? I don't know if it was discussions I had with him, or if it was confirmed with other people that were involved with the Vatel Club. It was exclusively run by the French mafia in the beginning, and he was chastised by his peers because he supported Americans. They were wondering why he wasn't being more nationalistic and hiring only the French." (Moonen is quick to point out that the front of the house at La Côte Basque was entirely French, specifically from Brittany, or at least French speaking.) "He got tomatoes thrown at him in Vatel meetings. I don't know literally, but figuratively for sure. He got beat up. He believed that Americans were hardworking and were hungry."

"Rachou one time admitted that he liked working with American cooks better than French," says Crispo. "Because they were easier to deal with. And he got huge criticism from all his Frenchie chef friends. Because he was telling the truth."

"I don't know if this is a fact. I don't know if you can even check it, but for a time, they threw him out of the Vatel Club," says Colameco. "It was the idea that he had crossed this line, and that was considered indefensible. And Rachou said to me, 'You know, I looked at these young American cooks and I watched them work and I thought, *They're as good as the French guys. Equals. Maybe better. Why don't I give them a chance?*' He was the guy that broke the ice. Before Rachou, you couldn't have gotten a job in those kitchens."

As the 1980s unspooled, more kitchen opportunities presented themselves to Americans in New York City, but Rachou's pro-American attitude was a rarity. In most *brigades*, there was an anti-American sentiment; Americans and French worked together but the relationship ended at the stoves.

"We didn't hang out with the French guys that much," says Palmer. "Xavier Leroux was with us. And he was a really nice guy and taught us a lot and was really a good partner with us in the kitchen but we never hung out with Xavier outside of the kitchen." (Bill Yosses, a pastry chef who came up around this time, charitably suggests that part of the reason might have been that many Frenchmen were self-conscious about their English.)

Crispo, who moved from La Côte Basque to The Polo to work with Daniel Boulud, remembers one particular cook Boulud brought in from France: "He hated Americans. We sucked. He came off the plane: 'Everybody sucks.' But he didn't speak much English. So it was great getting back at him because he would ask me how to say something and I would tell him completely the opposite, and he would goof up. Somebody would say, 'Hey, how you doing?' and he would say, 'Hey, you suck.' Then he turned around; he changed. He saw that we were working. Did he ever apologize? No. He's French."

The young Americans were gleaning the knowledge they craved, but at the same time, their eyes were opened to the realities of restaurant life, a far cry from the idealized world portrayed in *Great Chefs of France*, even in French kitchens.

"It was incredibly busy," says Moonen of his days at La Côte Basque. "When it first opened up it was so hot, it was so under-ventilated, that the plastic coating on the outer part of the fluorescent lights melted and fell to the ground. I was swimming in my sweat in my own boots."

"We used to wring our trousers out, never mind our pants, our jackets, from sweat," recalls Bouley.

Details like that, however, were nothing compared to the state of affairs at Le Cirque, one of the most celebrated restaurants of the day. But behind the scenes, the high volume and power clientele—regulars included everybody from Woody Allen to Henry Kissinger—produced a constant pressure that led to flaring tempers and some breathtaking shortcuts.

Arnold Rossman, who began cooking at Le Cirque in 1981, recalls that Sailhac and his sous chefs would often shout, "Dead or alive!" as code to indicate a dish had to be delivered to the pass ASAP.

"It didn't matter what shape that food was in, you got it on a plate and you handed it to him," says Rossman. "I remember the first day. I cut a rack of lamb and they wanted it, let's say, medium. It was bloody rare but I put it on the plate and I handed it to the chef."

The stressful environment also led to frequent turnover. Remembers Rossman: "The first day, my memory is just a blur of screaming, total pandemonium and chaos. The kitchen's not that big. It was never designed for the kind of volume we were doing. So the night crew was not allowed to set foot in the kitchen until two o'clock in the afternoon. That would give enough time for the day guys to get ready, get up and go, and be doing lunch service because there was the backup crew doing preparation for lunch anyway, once lunch was going. And at two o'clock we were allowed in the kitchen. We walk into the kitchen at two o'clock, and Philippe, the *entremetier/sous chef*, he's French, he and the chef are two inches away from each other, screaming at each other in French. I mean the veins in their necks are bulging; they're literally spitting into each other's—I don't understand French at this point and I don't know what they're saying but they are furious—back and forth, back and forth. And at one point, that's it; it's over. Philippe turns around, he grabs his knives, and he makes a very rude gesture to the chef and storms out. And the chef is heaving. And he starts looking around the kitchen, and our heads are down and all of a sudden I hear, 'Rossman!'"

The newbie approached the chef.

"Rossman, you are the new *entremetier*."

"*Oui, Chef*."

"I'm just standing there, and he goes, 'What are you doing?' And I'm like, 'What do you want me to do?'"

"You are the new *entremetier*; get to work."

"Chef, I just started yesterday. I have no idea what to do."

Sailhac directed Rossman to Ralph Tingle, the sauté cook alongside whom he had worked on his first day. "Go talk to Ralph; he will explain to you what to do."

Rossman found Tingle in the back, head down, chopping on his cutting board. He explained the situation and his battlefield promotion.

"Congratulations," said Tingle. "What do you need from me?"

"The chef told me to come to you to explain to me what to do."

Tingle went blank, expressionless.

"What's the matter?" asked Rossman.

"I just started the day before yesterday."

Terrance Brennan, obsessed with getting into a French kitchen, sent letters to eight New York City restaurants. Only one responded:

Lutèce's Soltner succinctly informed Brennan that there was no room in his *brigade*. ("I had to look up *brigade*," laughs Brennan.) But Soltner invited the young cook to visit him next time he was in New York City. Brennan visited, knocked on the kitchen door, and the great man spent close to half an hour with him, then referred him to Sailhac at Le Cirque.

Brennan was through the looking glass: "I went in there and I saw all the petit fours. I've never seen this stuff before. I'm thinking, *Oh my God*. And I'm just so naïve about everything." After a brief interview in Sailhac's famously cramped office—Brennan had to sit in the doorway—he returned to Virginia, then was summoned back within days when an opening presented itself. Brennan didn't even ask how much the job paid; he turned around and came right back.

Brennan replaced none other than Rossman. "I got one day of training from Pierre, the sous chef. *One day*. And they were talking in French. I didn't know any French. The assistant saucier was really the *légumier*, or the vegetable person, doing all the garnishing for all the plates. And I got my ass kicked. Dover sole, I don't even know. I didn't know anything. It was an intense kitchen. This is back when Sailhac was in the kitchen, just to put it in context. And nothing taken away from Daniel [Boulud, who succeeded Sailhac], because he made it great, but there were only eighteen people in the kitchen when Sailhac ran it: one sous chef and eighteen in the kitchen. When Daniel took over, he had three sous chefs and thirty-six people in the kitchen.

"So every single night we're in the shit. We're in the weeds. Every night. Monday, Tuesday—doesn't matter. Six days a week, every night. He's cussing and screaming. And I'm like, 'Holy shit! What did I get into?' And I wasn't physically in shape. Every plate, I had to bend over in the oven, take it out. Every single plate. Making the garnish and running around. Back then you were nonstop. You were running and you didn't sit down. You just barely made it for service.

I'm not exaggerating. And every single night, be it Monday or a Saturday, over two hundred dinners, three people on the line. *Three people!* Saucier, me in the middle, and the grill guy. That's it."

Brennan also recalls that during particularly busy services, "the sous chef would come around from doing a little prep for the parties for the next day and throw *poussins* in the fryolator, throw racks of lamb in the fryolator." Inclined to think only the best of the French, Brennan figured the frying must have been a secret searing technique practiced in France.

"But it was just because we were in the shit and he wanted to get it going fast, just to get it out. That I found out later," says Brennan today.

That same year, disenchantment with Le Cirque, ironically, led to an early alliance between a French-born chef and an American-born contemporary, both of whom would go on to become industry legends: "I generally loved Sirio but I hated the work environment," remembers Bouley, who started at Le Cirque in 1981. "I remember talking to my girlfriend at that time about how I'm going to go back to school. *I can't do this.* At Le Cirque, there were three of us. Philippe, who was the sous chef, and Alain Sailhac was a lot of time in the office. We did two hundred seventy-seven covers one night. The menu was an encyclopedia. And if someone sat down and said, 'Can I have sole Véronique?'—it's not on the menu—you got the Dover sole and you got a can of grapes and you had to make sole Véronique. It was ridiculous. You just could never keep up with the amount of volume. Nothing was cooked to order. You had a big bain-marie with ladles, and a lot of things were cooked in advance sitting up there. When they called for it you threw it on a plate or you threw it on a copper thing and you threw a sauce with it and it went out in the dining room with some vegetables or whatever. It was so hard that you never felt you did anything right."

Bouley developed the opinion that the much-lauded French

chefs in New York City were closed off from modern times. The food at Le Cirque, he laments, "wasn't one hundred percent plated food yet"—a reference to his own nouvelle experiences in France. In time, he'd come to believe that the chefs he was working for in the United States hadn't eaten the evolved food of modern France, let alone worked in one of those kitchens. "They had learned how to French-cook in New York from a group of French people that was very focused, very tight from almost the World's Fair. A lot of the restaurants had the same style. La Côte Basque was a little different, but if you went to Pavillon, La Grenouille, Le Cygne, Le Cirque, Le Périgord, they were pretty much all the same kinds of menus." The contrast between what he'd cooked in France and what he wanted for himself in America and what was available was crushing: "The bodies and the amount of people in the kitchen were not at all conducive to me and my group, which were students of the nouvelle cuisine, so we all felt lost."

One afternoon that year, Bouley prepared a lunch for his friend, the pastry chef Jean-Pierre Lemasson, and two friends of his. "I made a pot-au-feu and I had great cheese and Jean-Pierre made all this food. The day before, he said, 'I forgot I've got a friend coming in from France. Can I bring him?' I said, 'Yeah, sure. Go ahead. I have plenty of food.' So he brought him in. That was Daniel Boulud. He came from JFK to my apartment. And we all were talking about how much there is to do here. And Daniel says that was the day that he decided to make his career in New York. There was a gap of forty years and how are we going to transfer this style of eating into what we were taught, nouvelle cuisine, healthier, cleaner, more detailed, plated food, a whole different structure of cuisine. . . . What was the opportunity? So the possibilities were to team up and try to transfer the cuisine into a different direction. We had a pact." (Asked about this, Boulud—a consummate industry politician—squirms and jokes, "I have no idea what he's talking about." Boulud had come to New York to take over the kitchen at

The Polo restaurant at the Westbury Hotel, but five years later, in 1986, he replaced Sailhac as chef of Le Cirque.)*

"HE WAS THE GODFATHER TO THE CHEFS."

An advocate for young Americans during these years was Marc Sarrazin, a butcher from France's Charolles region who came to the United States in 1954, became a salesman for meat wholesaler DeBragga & Spitler, and bought the company in 1973. DeBragga & Spitler supplied many of the best restaurants in Manhattan. Sarrazin† isn't remembered for his product, but for his vast network and willingness to help cooks and chefs at every level, an unofficial, one-man employment agency for the entire industry.

"He was the godfather to the chefs," says Boulud. "He was the agency to the cooks."

"When we were kids, if you were at Jean-Jacques Rachou's for a couple of years and you wanted to move, you'd say, 'Chef, I don't

---

* The silver lining to the sameness of the menus in New York's French restaurants was that even those who had jobs could pick up extra shifts for money, or knowledge, in other kitchens. A young Thomas Keller, Boulud's sous chef at The Polo, was so hungry that he was in a constant state of motion, and cooking: "At night I would do my *stages* anywhere I could. Most weeks I would spend two or three days at the Maurice with Christian Delouvrier. Alain Senderens was the consulting chef there. I was just totally immersed. I would do some prep for Serge Raoul because I worked at Raoul's in the winter of '81, I believe, or '82, something like that. I'd drive up to Nyack with a buddy after work at The Polo and we would prep galantines and mousses and things throughout the night and drive back to the city the next morning and get five hours of sleep and then go to work. So we'd go to Nyack twice a week, I'd do Maurice three times a week, and working at the Westbury six days a week, so totally immersed in what I was doing."
† Sarrazin was killed after being hit by a car outside Claude Troisgros's New York City restaurant CT, while in the company of Paul Bocuse, in 1995.

want to offend you but I've been with you for three years. I've learned a lot. I want a new job.' He'd probably send you to Sarrazin," says Colameco. "That's what happened to me. You'd go to his office. Go downtown, walk through that little parking lot, up that long step, and in there would be Marc. He was the guy. All the French restaurants bought meat from him."

Sarrazin's office was an unassuming, wood-paneled affair, lined with photographs of chefs. A meeting there was a real "get" for an aspiring cook, and a sit-down lunch with Sarrazin at one of his favored restaurants meant you had arrived, like a comic's first shot on Johnny Carson.

"Being French and being connected with all the French chefs in town, he was the one who helped all those kids from the CIA to enter into La Côte Basque, into La Caravelle, into Le Cirque, into even—not Le Pavillon because that's too old—but into all those restaurants," remembers Boulud. "As soon as somebody would lose a job, he would help him find another job. He was distributing meat in the clubs. He was distributing meat in the restaurants. He was distributing meat in the hotels. He was distributing meat in the major larger caterers. Basically he was covering the entire spectrum of the industry and in a very wide range, also, not only New York but the five boroughs. He was very French and very appreciative of everyone, it didn't matter—and his son was born in America so he had this mentality of an American as well when it came to embracing young talent."

"He was the nicest guy," says Colameco. "It was a different time. If you didn't buy your meat from him, would it have affected your business? Maybe. There was a kind of a criticism that he had a lock on things. I guess he did. It was business. But beyond that, his personal generosity was amazing. Because we were the first generation of American chefs trying to climb a ladder that was in French or in German or in Swiss, but mostly in French. And you had to get past the gatekeepers and you had to work within the system, and he was the guy."

Sarrazin was also known for his indirect interviewing style. "You can learn an awful lot about somebody by the way he dresses, how he or she behaves," Sarrazin said at the time. "What is the handshake like, does the person light a cigarette without asking." It was in these telling details that he formed his opinion of talent and character, and helped make matches between cooks and chefs, chefs and owners. By all accounts he spent as much time administering to the affairs of his business as he did doling out advice and counsel. A typical morning found him working the phones, fielding calls from all over the city, and occasionally the country, followed by lunch in one of Manhattan's grand French restaurants, then came drop-ins on kitchens around the metropolis, where he did business and kept tabs on job openings and other possibilities, and the day was capped with dinner at the likes of Le Cirque and La Côte Basque.

"WE ALL LIVED LIKE RATS."

For newcomers to the city, it was a bizarre double life, cooking refined French food by day, then returning to a squalid residence when the kitchen closed. Line cooks make a paltry living, and the crime-addled New York City of the late 1970s and early '80s brought that reality into high relief.

"I was petrified," recalls Palmer, who took a $78-per-month sublet on West 43rd Street in Hell's Kitchen. "I'd come home from La Côte Basque and there would be hookers sitting on the building stoop. They all knew my name. They were like, 'Hey, white boy's home.' But I adjusted quickly. I became pretty comfortable very quick."

Brennan would leave Le Cirque, return to a place he was renting on Long Island. "I was physically exhausted, the screaming and yelling. I'm beat up and I'm sleeping on a couch with punk rockers. I would stay up until four or five in the morning partying. I'm like, 'Oh my God, what did I do?' Then I got an apartment in Queens. I just signed something real quick. It was a dungeon, one of those illegal dungeon apartments. There was no sunlight. I'd come out at nine, ten in the morning and be like Dracula: 'The sun!'"

"It was exciting," says John Schenk, a cook from Buffalo, New York. "The first day I moved here, I had to go into Williamsburg, to the Hasidic community, to buy futons and I didn't even know what a Hasid was. I came back with the futons. I'm like, 'You won't believe what I just saw.' Didn't even have the idea that that existed. I remember driving up First Street, where it veers off of Houston, goes on that angle, and it was an über ghetto. Everyone was all over the place. There were fires in the garbage cans. We used to live in Brooklyn, so we'd go over the Brooklyn Bridge and there would be all the hookers standing there by Sammy's Roumanian on that block. I remember one having this huge razor blade inside her glove. She took off her mitten—I was sitting in the cab—you see this huge razor blade. It was a different world. It was gritty. I liked it a lot."

"We all lived like rats, you know?" says Traci Des Jardins. "I lived in a living room and slept on a futon. New York was so dangerous. I lived on the Upper East Side on 82nd between Second and Third so I would catch the subway. I almost got my brains creamed in—I was walking to the subway and there was just a bunch of young kids. And I was by myself. It was just one of those moments where you say a little prayer and hope that they don't turn their attention to you. They had baseball bats and shit. They were looking for trouble. And it was just obvious. You're just walking along and you see that and you can't turn around. You keep going and you just hope that they're not going to—you know. So I called my mom. My parents had not been real supportive of what I was up to. I was self-funded and didn't have any help. And I said, 'You've got to give me one hundred dollars a week to take a cab home at night. I'm going to get killed.' Everyone I knew got mugged. It was dangerous. I never did, but I felt that threat all the time. So my mom started sending me a hundred bucks a week to take a cab home at night."

Danny Meyer, who was beginning to envision what would become his first restaurant, Union Square Café, in the early 1980s, recalls of the restaurant's neighborhood, "It was really dicey. I remember very well at least three occasions walking to Union Square Café on a Saturday morning and there would be a chalk outline on the sidewalk of someone who had presumably been shot the night before."

The city could be grittily seductive to French newcomers as well. Boulud remembers New York as "mad, not very safe, not very clean. I was a little bit lost because I was not a New Yorker then." He recalls one night in particular after a private party at the Westbury: "There was this guy who organized the party who said, 'I'm going to show you the town. Let me take you downtown.' So we went to the Meatpacking District. There was the Hellfire Club* there. It was a basement where they were all hanging on ropes and fucking each other. I mean, there were like cabins where you could watch people getting sucked over or fucked over. It was stables, and you peep over. For us it was all about being a voyeur and curiosity. Every time we had a friend coming from Europe, we said, 'Okay, we've got to take you to a place.' It was so fucked up downtown."

---

* A BDSM (bondage and discipline, dominance and submission) club in the basement of a space at the triangle formed by Ninth Avenue, Hudson Street, and West 14th Street.

"YOU HAD TO GO TO FRANCE. THAT WAS IT."

The ultimate immersive experience for a young American at the time was to take the plunge and commit to a *stage* in France. What became a de rigueur rite of passage for future generations was a novelty at the time, and one that wasn't easily accessed. The very concept of *staging* was unique, harkening back to another era, suggesting a quest for knowledge: an unpaid position, undertaken in exchange for the conference of experience and skill.

Says Thomas Keller: "From 1978 until 1983, it was that quest of trying to get somebody to commit to hiring me. And during that period of time, I amassed an enormous amount of information about France. Articles on Gregory Usher, who ultimately started the Ritz-Carlton cooking program; Robert Noah, who was an influential American over there who would do culinary tours. I wrote Julia Child; she introduced me to [La Varenne founder] Anne Willan."

Keller's big break came when Jean Goutal of the Westbury Hotel, where Keller was sous chef to Daniel Boulud, set him up with a job at a one-star restaurant at the Hôtel de Ville in Arbois.

"I was to stay there for three months, I think. I got there and I stayed there for three *days*. I was miserable. The Hôtel de Ville was this restaurant in the basement where my job was to get the coal and fire the ovens at five in the morning. My window was black and I didn't understand it was black until I went down the next morning, realized that the chimney was next to my window. Lightbulbs hanging from wires from the ceiling. It was like prehistoric, Dark Ages. I don't know how many Americans they saw over there. It was kind of a one-horse town. Reminded me of something from a Western movie. I was only there for three days. I was terrified because I was in this environment that had nothing. The image of that environment or the reality of that environment was nowhere in my catalog of images. I'm reading about Noah, I'm reading about Anne

Willan, I'm reading about Taillevent, I'm reading about all the great restaurants, all the great chefs. And I've just come from The Polo. I was like, *This is insane. How could this be? I'm in* France."

Keller called his friend, restaurateur Serge Raoul, owner of an eponymous bistro in SoHo and a Frenchman. His advice? "Go to Paris. Hang out there and see what you can do."

"So I actually did what everybody told me to do five years earlier," says Keller. "'Just go. Go knock on kitchen doors.' But I was much better prepared. I was a much better cook. I had much more knowledge. I had much more information. I made some great contacts. And within a couple weeks I was done, for the nine, ten months or twelve months I was there with my *stages*. I had them all lined up, then floated and got invited back to Taillevent. Everything was just beautiful."

"You had to go to France," says Colicchio. "That was it. For me, it wasn't about going there and learning dishes. For me, it was going there to understand *why*, not how. Like, why certain things just made sense. I ended up going to Gascony."

Kinch felt a similar pull: "The thing was to get out of New Orleans, a town of five thousand restaurants and five recipes, and get to New York, because New York was like the American epicenter, and work there," says Kinch. "And the whole point of moving to New York was to find a place that would be a stepping-stone to get to France. At that time I was hearing rumblings about Chez Panisse and the things that were going on in California, but it really didn't resonate with me at that time; California was another world apart. It's just, work in France, work in France; stay in France for as long as possible. Learn as much as I can about being a French chef so someday I can apply it and be an American chef. That was everything. That was the mantra."

Americans' reception in France was a mixed bag. Some were welcomed as equals in the kitchen; others were treated as curiosities, or with hostility.

"I was sort of this novelty to the French chefs in the restaurant," says Eric Bromberg, who *staged* at Le Récamier in Paris while attending culinary school at Le Cordon Bleu. "They used to call me George Bush or Ronald Reagan, which is pretty funny. Anyone from America they called Reagan. Ketchup and Coke were the two big insults. They called Coke *vin américain* [American wine] and at every staff meal they'd put a bottle of ketchup next to me."

Des Jardins, encouraged to work in France by mentor Splichal, landed a position working with the Troisgros family in Roanne. There, Des Jardins says she was received "as a freak. I was American. I was a woman. I was nineteen. I was so young and so naïve. If I knew then what I know now, I would have never attempted that. It was insane. I'd never been out of California. I just plunked myself down in the middle of nowhere in France. But I had such drive. . . . So I went to Troisgros. Arrived there, met the family. Michel [Pierre Troisgros's son, who had spent time at Chez Panisse] was running the kitchen; it was sort of the beginning of his tenure there. Jean died I think the year I started cooking, so in '83. So this was '86, so Jean hadn't been gone for too long. Michel was entering the kitchen with Pierre. Michel was showing me around and walked in the locker room and he's like, 'You can't change here. You have to come to work in your whites because there's only the boys' locker room.' They didn't know what to do with me.

"It was tough. I came from being *chef poissonier* [fish chef] for Joachim to being an apprentice, so I was knocked way down the rung. I was back to cleaning lettuce and chopping herbs. So it was hard. I understood that that was where my place was in the kitchen but I was capable of so much more. And there was no way to show that. That wasn't a possibility. You didn't do that kind of thing in those kitchens. It wasn't the way things worked. So I humbly kept my place in the corner.

"It was pretty lonely. It was so much more controlled than what we were doing in the States at that point in time. In Michelin three-star restaurants, the same thing happened every day: It was ninety-five covers for lunch, ninety-five covers for dinner, and you got to work at eight and you left the kitchen at three, you came back at five and you worked until twelve and you went out to the discos at night and danced for a few hours then went to the cafe and the boulangerie and had a fresh croissant before you went to bed and you slept for three hours and you got up and did the same thing again and slept in the afternoon.

"You had one day off every week. And it was so interesting talking to the people that you worked with because these were all French boys who were between seventeen and twenty-three. They were young. A lot of them came from royal culinary families. Their fathers had been Michelin two- or three-star restaurant chefs and they were at Troisgros working for their father's friend. It wasn't full of possibility. It was a different world because it was almost like a caste system. These guys were doing this because their fathers and their grandfathers and their grandfathers before them had done it. It didn't have the same feeling of what we were doing in California, which was the world of possibilities. . . . None of these guys had ever eaten any ethnic food. I mean, Italian food was ethnic to them."

"THIS IS GOING TO CHANGE; IT'S JUST A MATTER OF WHEN AND HOW."

Whether they achieved it at home, abroad, or both, a funny thing happened to many of those Americans who mastered French cuisine: They quickly developed a desire to move beyond it, to forge their own style, whether a personalized answer to nouvelle cuisine or—in many cases—the development of a distinctly American repertoire founded on the hard-earned techniques they'd picked up from the French.

As it turned out, what both French and American alike perceived as a weakness—the United States' lack of a gastronomic
tradition—turned out to be a strength: Without eons of history
to constrain them, they quickly grew tired of the norm, and eager to
imprint their plates with a personality all their own, drawing from
regional, cultural, and even familial influences. For Forgione, one
of the first to show the way toward an American style, an early revelation came after making that goodwill tour of New York's great
French restaurants. He gathered menus from all of them, even
those who dissed him, laid them out next to each other: "Say each
menu had twenty things on it, so if you had six menus, you had the
possibility of one hundred twenty things. But there were only about
thirty things that were on these six menus." Just as many of the
restaurants featured murals painted by Jean Pages, "everybody had
ris de veau chanterelles. Everybody had *tournedos*—probably not
Rossini, but a *tournedos* dish that they all had. They were very similar menus at the six great restaurants. It was amazing to me that
that was going on."

In contrast, the sameness of French menus didn't bother younger
cooks like Colameco at the time: "It was such a different world back
then. If you could take a snapshot of the menus at La Côte Basque,
La Caravelle, Lutèce, Le Cygne, in any given month of any given year,
they're identical. Literally, you could be the saucier at one restaurant
one day and move over to another restaurant, because we were cooking from Escoffier. You simply had to know the garnishes and how to
make them, but that was still magic for us. Because we didn't know
that."

Some, like the Five Couples, leapfrogged classic training; others
participated in it. Once that education was completed, though—
perhaps owing to something inherent in the American character,
or to that generation, or a combination of the two—it was almost
inevitable that even the most classically trained cooks began to forge
a style all their own.

"It became obvious to me I was never going to be French, nor did I want to be French," says Palmer. While working for Rachou, he read about goings-on in American kitchens, foremost among them Forgione's at The River Café. "I'm not going to change my name, you know? And I thought, too, classical French cooking, all this cream and butter. I would make beurre blanc by the gallon at La Côte Basque. I was buying the butter, and we were buying literally a ton of butter a year. So I thought, *This is going to change; it's just a matter of when and how.*" (Palmer's arc epitomizes the forces of the time in New York City: educated at the CIA, trained under Jean-Jacques Rachou, and referred by Marc Sarrazin to The River Café, where he forged his own muscular American style.)

Kinch's revelation came earlier than most. Inspired by *Great Chefs of France*, he had a crystal-ball epiphany before traveling to France or working for Barry Wine: "My pride was to create a great American restaurant, to be a great American chef and not try to pretend to be French," he says. "And that was in my mind when I was twenty-one years old. I kept it to myself. If I talked to people about it, they were like, 'What in the world are you talking about?'"

What seemed outlandish to Kinch's friends and coworkers became an accepted evolution in a matter of years. In August 1982, The Culinary Institute of America updated itself yet again in service of its constant mission to keep up with the United States' quick-shifting dining landscape. To complement the Escoffier Room, a student-run restaurant that served classic French cuisine, a new on-campus eatery was developed by 1977 CIA grad and future institute president Tim Ryan, in tandem with fellow instructor James Heywood, who had graduated the school in its New Haven days. The restaurant's name doubled as an apt title for the emerging epoch: American Bounty.

5

THE STANFORD COURT GANG

It was the start of something bigger than we envisioned.

—Bradley Ogden

HOW ONE EVENING ATOP SAN FRANCISCO'S NOB HILL CHANGED
EVERYTHING, AND BROUGHT RISING CHEFS FROM ACROSS THE
COUNTRY TOGETHER FOR THE FIRST TIME

Bradley Ogden calls it "the first gathering . . . the start of the American food movement." Larry Forgione describes it as "a giant tribal council." Jimmy Schmidt says, "It went on for decades."

"It" was a dinner billed simply as An American Celebration. It was held on May 4, 1983, the day prior to James Beard's eightieth birthday, at the Stanford Court Hotel, perched high atop San Francisco's Nob Hill. It was the brainchild of Michael McCarty, Julia Child, and Robert Mondavi, founding members of the American Institute of Wine and Food (AIWF). It was a multicourse, collaborative dinner that would present a sampling of what the new

American chefs were up to from coast to coast. There are probably at least two such dinners happening in the United States tonight; at the time, it was unprecedented.

Most of the chefs, though well known in their home markets, had never met before, and in some cases hadn't heard of each other. They arrived at the Stanford Court skeptical, strangers; they left realizing they were part of a larger movement, and ready to take their craft, and careers, to the next level.

"WE WEREN'T CONNECTED AT ALL."

"I was Michael's chef so I was a little bit his bitch, so I became the one who had to organize it," recalls Jonathan Waxman, who had been chef at Michael's for three years when McCarty told him of his outlandish plan: to bring chefs from around the country together for one night, have each one contribute a course to be paired with American wines, at a dinner for hundreds of guests at San Francisco's Stanford Court Hotel.

Waxman began lining up people, mostly those he knew personally, meaning mostly Californians: Mark Miller, Jeremiah Tower, Alice Waters. He invited his buddy Larry Forgione, but none of New York City's Five Couples or others who were breaking the mold on the East Coast, such as Lydia Shire and Jasper White in Boston, or Norman Van Aken in Florida. That said, Paul Prudhomme had become famous enough that he made the cut.

"There wasn't a real connection amongst all these American chefs at that point," says Waxman. "Everybody had their little citadels everywhere. You had Paul Prudhomme doing his thing in New Orleans. . . . You had people in Boston doing different stuff, and Miami. Everybody was kind of doing their thing in different places but we weren't connected at all. We weren't *aware* of each other at all."

They were so unaware of each other that when Waxman compiled his initial list and somebody (Tower claims credit; McCarty says it was James Beard) suggested adding Kansas City's Bradley Ogden and Detroit's Jimmy Schmidt to represent the center of the country, Waxman had no idea who they were talking about.

Ogden was a Traverse City, Michigan, native who had grown up hanging around his father's rock-and-roll palace, the Tanz Haus ("Dance House"), and enjoying the natural riches of the Midwest— hunting and fishing for ducks, pheasant, quail, ice-cold brook trout, small- and largemouth bass, perch in the winter. He and his twin brother occasionally spent weeks on his Hungarian grandmother's farm, learning what to do with those catches and kills—as well as baking pies. It was, says Ogden, "typical Midwest, but English, Hungarian, a little American Indian—the wild side."

He and one of his brothers started at the CIA together; the brother dropped out, but Ogden graduated in 1977 and went to work for a restaurant company to which Joe Baum's group consulted. He took the reins at The American Restaurant in Kansas City, often found himself face-to-face with Baum, including trips to New York, where Baum, Barbara Kafka, and James Beard wined and dined him, showed him what was up in the Big Apple, took him to The Four Seasons. He always came back dazzled and updated his menu. Ogden incorporated local ingredients, developed a distinctly Midwestern style based on his childhood food memories, and became a local celebrity, making regular television appearances.

Schmidt was doing similar work at the London Chop House in Detroit, but though he also drew on local bounty, he came to his style by way of Europe. Born in 1955 and raised in Champaign, Illinois, the last of five kids on a family farm, he'd always been surrounded by great ingredients, but not great cooking. Dinners out consisted of fried fish sandwiches or a Swedish buffet. He went to college on an engineering scholarship, but followed a quietly rebellious streak, first to New York where he spent time with his sister in the summer, returning to the Midwest decked out in a Nehru jacket and Beatle-ish sunglasses. "That didn't go over very well," he remembers.

In 1973 and 1974, he studied abroad, in Avignon and Aix-en-Provence, where he met legendary chef and teacher Madeleine Kamman. His interest in cooking sprung purely out of practicality. "I took cooking classes because I was a poor student and I wanted to eat. And then I took wine classes." Richard Olney and Simone Beck* were also involved in Kamman's program, so he met them as well. He hit it off with Kamman, and visited several Michelin two-star restaurants as part of the class.

He followed Kamman to Boston and her cooking school, Modern Gourmet. His mother thought he was nuts: "When I was moving to Boston, she was like, 'You're crazy.' So I'm living in Boston, and she sends me a little written note in the mail and inside was a book of matches like you used to get at the tobacco store. And inside it says, 'Learn a career, fix radios.' She kept sending me books of matches to learn how to fix toasters."

After graduation, in 1977, he worked at Kamman's student-run restaurant for two years, then his mentor introduced him to Lester Gruber ("a tough guy, we banged heads a lot"), who offered him a job. The London Chop House specialized in, says Schmidt, "period food that was French influenced, like veal Oscar and béarnaise sauces and asparagus with hollandaise and clams casino, oysters Rockefeller, and all of those kind of standards. And lobster bisque and some of the other classics, Dover sole, all of which was very foreign food to me because it isn't really French food."

Before long, Schmidt was promoted to chef, based on his sensibility, developed in France, and started drawing on what was available locally, in dishes such as mousseline of pike, "because with the Great Lakes you had all the great fish," he says. "I was playing around

---

* A French cooking teacher and food writer and Julia Child's frequent cookbook collaborator.

with mixing components together. I played around a lot with spice levels relative to using vanilla and what's considered dessert spices into entrees, like a breast of pheasant that was cured in vanilla and ginger, that type of direction."

Gruber knew Beard, so Schmidt got to know him as well. "He was pretty dry but he was like a walking encyclopedia. If you'd say, 'Hey, what's the deal about a triple lamb chop, loin chop? Where did it come from?' You could get a lot of information out of him. And he was very forthcoming with it, too. I had a million questions. *How many different varieties of tarragon are there? What's the difference between the French stuff and the American stuff?* He was very calm, really dry, very interested in everything that was going on. Obviously, he was very interested in Larry Forgione with An American Place; he actually told me about Larry's opening."

Gruber also visited France a few times a year, occasionally bringing Schmidt along. Desperate for first-rate product, Schmidt returned from those sojourns with seeds for red peppers, arugula, and herbs, then convinced local farmers' kids to grow them for him, paying them for the harvests in cash. He also introduced a bread program to the Chop House, ordering cookbooks from Kitchen Arts & Letters in New York and other specialty stores, and baking it fresh twice a day.

"PEOPLE HADN'T CONSIDERED THE IDEA OF A REGIONAL CUISINE AS HE HAD PRESENTED IT."

Prudhomme was, paradoxically, at the time the most famous of the group present for the dinner and unquestionably the outlier, a chef who had developed independent of many of the cultural forces that had led many of his professional contemporaries into the kitchen.

Born July 13, 1940, Prudhomme was the youngest of thirteen

children in a poor sharecropping family who lived on their farm out-side Opelousas, Louisiana. The name Paul was entered on his birth certificate by a priest who insisted he have a saint's name, but he wouldn't learn that until years later: Instead he went by Gene Autry Prudhomme.

Since Prudhomme came from a destitute family, his initial impressions of the professional cooking trade were the very opposite of many of those who wandered into the kitchen from middle-class backgrounds; it seemed positively regal to him: In 1949, at age nine, he had heard of a cousin who worked in a New Orleans hotel and earned $150 per week. "It seemed like an awesome amount of money to cook," he said. "I mean, to be a cook, which was fun, and to get paid that much money and be all dressed in white just seemed like a wonderful thing."

When his sisters left home, he helped his mother cook, leading him, as a young adult, to his first forays into the professional kitchen. His inaugural attempt at entrepreneurship was a disaster: In 1957, at age seventeen, he opened a drive-in burger joint, Big Daddy O's Patio, in Opelousas, Louisiana. In less than a year, the restaurant, and Prudhomme's first marriage, had gone belly-up; he tried his hand at three other restaurants and each of them went under as well.

He took to selling magazines, then knocked around the West Coast, mostly in Colorado, cooking in restaurant kitchens. It was at the Elkhorn Lodge in Estes Park, where he had his version of the epiphany that so many of his peers had when he got his hands on some small, store-bought red potatoes. They were a favorite of his, but no matter how he dolled them up, he couldn't reproduce the sensuousness of the ones his mother had cooked for him as a boy. Then it hit him: "I remembered that the first thing we did was we went out to the field and we dug them up. I recognized at that point how important it is to have fresh ingredients," he said.

In 1970, he returned to New Orleans. He did time at two hotels—as sous chef at Le Pavillon, and then at Maison Dupuy, where he began experimenting with Cajun food—and in 1975, he became the first American-born executive chef of Commander's Palace, where he was initially hired as the lunch chef, but took over the entire restaurant within a week. He transitioned the menu to his evolving roster of Cajun specialties such as chicken and andouille gumbo. "The gumbo I did at Commander's was a roux gumbo," said Prudhomme. "To my knowledge it has never been before. . . . It became a staple. It was chicken and andouille gumbo. It was down-and-dirty Cajun. It was what Mama used to do. I'd go into the country and buy the andouille from the guy I'd known since I was a kid. We didn't have andouille in New Orleans until later." He also introduced culinary flights of fancy such as "Cajun popcorn," a real novelty at the time.

Run by the Brennan family, led by matriarch Ella Brennan, Commander's Palace, following the French lead, began touting Prudhomme's food as nouvelle Creole. (They had a point; Cajun food was the marriage of French technique and Louisiana product and soul.)

Prudhomme began to catch the attention of writers, such as James Villas, who profiled him in a cover story for *Bon Appétit*, a rare, Bocuse-worthy bit of publicity for an American toque.

In 1979, Prudhomme and second wife K Hinrichs, a former waitress he'd met when they both worked at Maison Dupuy, opened K-Paul's Louisiana Kitchen on Chartres Street, in the New Orleans French Quarter. The restaurant was cash-only and had only sixty-four seats. It was also a money machine: costing only fifty dollars per month in rent (which included tables, chairs, a counter, bar, and full kitchen) and turning the tables four or five times per night.

Prudhomme continued to work at Commander's Palace, enlisting Frank Brigtsen, a former Louisiana State University student and apprentice from Commander's Palace, to be his chef. There were no recipes; menus were created in late-night confabs and by phone during the day, when Prudhomme would call Brigtsen and describe something as radical as crabmeat hollandaise with enough lusty detail that the latter could successfully whip it up on the fly.

Having the chef from Commander's Palace, one of the fancier places in town, running one of the most casual (dinner ran a mere five or six bucks) was cause for a double take. Brigtsen believed Prudhomme did it for love, and also to create a place where his family could feel comfortable when they came to town. (Eventually, he left Commander's but not until they found a young, unheralded chef named Emeril Lagasse to take his place.)

K-Paul's was, in Prudhomme's own words, a dump. It had communal seating, wobbly chairs and tables, and blue-plate specials.

K was a character and the restaurant was run in her image: "No reservations. No credit cards. No wine list. If you wanted the food, you'd wait in line and pay cash for it. And if you didn't finish your plate, you were probably going to get yelled at," remembered Brigtsen.

"Chef was the cook," said Mary Sonnier, a former K-Paul's cook, "but it was her restaurant. I don't care what anyone tells you. . . . The kitchen was his but the restaurant was hers."

The demand for tables was enormous—one hundred people would be queued up at opening time, and they'd seat sixty people at once, get slammed.

Prudhomme was a true original: Though he hewed to principles of Cajun cooking, the restaurant's repertoire was distinctly his. Both were noteworthy. "People hadn't considered the idea of a regional cuisine as he was presenting it," said Michael Batterberry, founding editor of *Food & Wine*, which brought Prudhomme to that Tavern on the Green event in New York City where he met Alice Waters in 1979.

Prudhomme's insistence on fresh ingredients was also new and drew purveyors his way. Farmers from as far away as Mississippi brought livestock and produce to his door. One, Dan Crutchfield, arrived with everything from fresh rabbits to peanuts to edible flowers. Prudhomme's cooking elevated ingredients like tasso and boudin to national attention.

When Prudhomme went on *Today* for the first time, he demonstrated how to make jambalaya. One of his brothers was outraged, called him to ask how he could cook "trash food" on national television. Cajun food at that time wasn't a source of pride; it was the shameful food of the poor, though Prudhomme was rapidly changing that.

In March 1980 Prudhomme introduced one of the first of what would become known as "signature" dishes to America's culinary lexicon: blackened redfish, made by dipping fillets in butter, coating them with a mixture of cayenne and dried herbs, and searing them in a skillet. (The dish's popularity literally threatened the population of redfish in the Gulf of Mexico, prompting Prudhomme to eventually limit the number of orders per table at K-Paul's.) A prototype of the dish was born at Commander's Palace when somebody's offhand reference to campfire-cooked fish led Prudhomme to experiment, greasing redfish with butter, seasoning it, and cooking it on the flattop used to keep large pots warm. He wanted to put it on the menu, but Ella Brennan insisted on a grilled version, not blackened. At K-Paul's he did the fish in a cast-iron skillet, and it became a sensation.

Prudhomme became a national celebrity, and his gregarious personality and imposing physical stature (he was exceptionally hefty and bore more than a passing resemblance to the comic actor Dom DeLuise, a major star of the day) made him a television natural. The summer following the AIWF Stanford Court dinner, he would take his show on the road, like the Ma Maison Cannes experiment years earlier. It was yet another ahead-of-its-time iteration of the pop-up concept, in San Francisco, in a kitchen-outfitted nightclub arranged by concert promoter Bill Graham. The promotion sold out its entire four-week run, despite the fact that it didn't take reservations;

people waited in line for up to twelve hours for a table.* And the year following the dinner, in 1984, long before it was an expected step for an American chef, Prudhomme published his first cookbook, *Chef Paul Prudhomme's Louisiana Kitchen*, and would go on to create and market a Magic Seasoning Blends line of spices that required a thirty-thousand-square-foot plant to meet the worldwide demand for the product.

"CAN'T YOU GET LAMB IN CALIFORNIA?"

An American Celebration was perhaps the purest distillation and greatest expression of Michael McCarty, who summoned all his producer-like powers to will it into existence, creating an unprecedented happening: an eight-course tasting dinner, each course prepared by a different chef, and—perhaps even more audaciously—paired exclusively with wines from American vineyards. The goal was nothing less than to announce to the world that American food had arrived and to underscore the continued development of wine production in the United States since the "Judgment of Paris"† seven years prior.

"Finding Jimmy Schmidt at the London Chop House, that was through James Beard, because this guy named Lester Gruber owned the London Chop House and he was really into American food," recalls McCarty. "Hallmark had a restaurant called Harvest or American Café or something in their headquarters; it's still there I

---

* Amazingly, Prudhomme would later reveal that he lost $65,000 on the venture.
† The Paris Tasting of 1976, also known as the "Judgment of Paris," was a blind tasting pitting French wines against American. Two California bottlings—Chateau Montelena's Chardonnay (white) and Stag's Leap's Cabernet Sauvignon (red)—won the competition, in the year of the U.S. bicentennial, no less.

think as a restaurant. Bradley Ogden was the chef there [before The American Restaurant]. We only knew Prudhomme by his reputation, of him doing blackened redfish—that was me reading about this guy who was changing Creole and Cajun food and making it modern.

"Who in Northern California is creating modern American food?" says McCarty. "Okay. Alice, at this time, was beginning to shift. You had to do Chez Panisse; she was a big part of us. Jeremiah Tower had his Sante Fe Bar and Grill. Mark Miller had Fourth Street; he was doing the first of Latin, of Southwest. He was the first guy to really begin to use peppers, jalapeños and all that stuff. Those were the three from Northern California. Jonathan and me in L.A. Wolfgang because he had just opened Spago and pizzas were a big deal."

Of course, some of the chefs already knew each other: Waxman and Forgione had met at brunch at The River Café. Waters had been to The River Café, and Waters and Prudhomme had bonded at that *Food & Wine* event at Tavern on the Green. "Prior to that dinner, Alice, Paul Prudhomme, and myself kind of had a little alliance amongst ourselves," says Forgione. "We did talk regularly. We shared a couple of things."

Things were so disconnected at this time that Schmidt didn't even know his closest geographic colleague, Ogden, with whom he was to collaborate on a course. So they connected by phone to begin planning their dish: "Okay, we've got to do a bunch of Midwestern stuff. And he said, 'Yeah, I'm from Michigan.' And it was right at that time of year in May—it's like, 'Hey, we can get morels; we can do lamb.' And I said, 'I've got a great source of lamb, this guy who raises lamb in Michigan; he raises *petits pois* for the Green Giant.' The lamb would clean all the fields, so it's really sweet lamb. He said, 'That's cool.' So I sourced the ramps and the morels and all those ingredients and shipped them out. And then Bradley and I got together and did all the prep work together and knocked it out.

"We shipped everything on the plane to get it there. And obviously, that's a hell of a lot of lamb. So we were schlepping all this stuff around trying to pile it into cars at the airport. And they're, like, 'What's in the box?' 'It's lamb.' 'Can't you get lamb in California?' I thought it was really cool, because using the local, indigenous ingredients from Michigan made a lot of sense. And that was kind of the direction my food was going, using all these local things that I'd seen in France and formulating how I was cooking and what the guests were eating based on foods in season, that taste the best, that are the best for you, probably instinctually what you crave anyway. So we got out there, worked through the Stanford Court—that's like one big mother operation type of thing."

The Stanford Court held a special place in the emerging culture of American gastronomy. The hotel's founder, Jim Nassikas, and his lieutenant, Bill Wilkinson, were known as patrons of the culinary arts. "Jim Nassikas was a founding board member of the AIWF and that's why it was with Robert Mondavi, and that's why it was held at the Stanford Court, because it was a close relationship with the Mondavis and the hotel," says the hotel's longtime pastry chef Jim Dodge, now director of specialty culinary programs for Bon Appétit Management Company. "That's where all the chefs would stay for their culinary events coming into San Francisco." Beard also regularly stayed there when visiting the Bay Area.

If creating Michael's was a caper movie, this event was a heist picture: Every month for a year, McCarty flew to San Francisco for an AIWF board meeting and to plan the dinner. To accompany the food and wine, McCarty enlisted his friend, Paul Gurian (producer of Cutter's Way and other films and a frequent dining companion) to work with him on a series of videos introducing the chefs, and in many cases their dishes, to the audience.

"One thing that impressed me right from the beginning," says Forgione, "was that I had a sense that this was going to be a spectacular evening by the fact that [Paul Gurian] was producing the video that went along with it, that they were going to such lengths to capture the chef and his surroundings. And we were going to be staying in a world-class hotel. We were going to be cooking for the Julia Childs, the Bob Mondavis, the Dick Graffs, all the people that you had heard about and read about and met through your restaurants. You just knew that all the people in this event, whether they were cooking, serving, or dining, were all in a community together."

In a cosmic coincidence, that same month *Food & Wine* published what it dubbed "The Honor Roll of American Chefs," a hall of fame of Americans in pro kitchens who were changing the industry, one of the first such lists ever published, which included the Stanford Court's own Jim Dodge, and most of the chefs participating in the dinner. (Mark Miller was relegated to the "Also Noteworthy" category along with Susan Feniger, Mary Sue Milliken, and Leslie Revsin, who was listed as a "Chef in Transition.") It also featured Ken Frank, who was by then ensconced at La Toque on Sunset Boulevard, but there was no mention of the reclusive Bruce Marder. In a public relations coup, the issue also featured recipes from Heywood and Ryan's menus at American Bounty at The Culinary Institute of America.

The Honor Roll remains a fascinating document that illustrates how quickly people cycle through the industry. It's also a tribute to the power of celebrity: Most of the chefs who didn't participate in the dinner have faded into obscurity, though a few remain in the national—even international—consciousness.

To Waxman's point about people having the same experience around the country, each in their own way, many of the honorees' stories mirrored those of the AIWF participants.

Among several others, there was Patrick O'Connell, who had opened his Inn at Little Washington in Washington, Virginia. There was Robert Kinkead, then working at Harvest restaurant in Cambridge. There were Jasper White and Lydia Shire, listed as a team, at Seasons Restaurant near Boston's Faneuil Hall. From Los

Angeles there were Michael Roberts and Le St. Germain's Patrick Healy.

For all his success and influence, Wolfgang Puck, born in Austria, wasn't included on the Honor Roll. Neither was McCarty, who, alas, wasn't a chef.

"IT'S HAPPENING. WE'RE DOING IT."

The dinner was set for May 4, 1983, a Wednesday. The chefs started arriving the day prior. The hotel, no stranger to hosting industry heavy hitters and ambitious events, nonetheless hummed with anticipation.

"I remember the planning and the detail," says Dodge. "It was extremely exciting. However, none of us in the kitchen really understood exactly what was going to happen to have that many visiting chefs in that kitchen, which was a good-sized kitchen. We always had a big staff because of the focus on the service and the quality of food we served. But to have twenty or thirty extra bodies in that kitchen and have camera cables throughout the kitchen, and *big* cameras, it was amazing. Absolutely amazing."

"Jim Nassikas was one of the greatest hosts in America," says Forgione, who thinks the trip might have been his first to California. "Anything he was involved with was done over the top."

Not only had most of the chefs never met; many of them didn't know anything about the others' food. As they materialized, in addition to sniffing each other out, they also marveled at what the others were cooking.

"As each person arrived, they were bringing food with them," remembers Forgione, who prepared his "Terrine of 3 American Smoked Fish with Their Respective Caviars" in New York and flew it in, leaving only the sauce to be made in San Francisco. "So you would be there checking your stuff and rewrapping it and getting it put away, and next thing you know, Jeremiah would be floating down and then somebody else would come down."

"I was picking up techniques and seeing what other people were doing," says Schmidt.

And there they were: the emerging titans of a new American cuisine, gathered in one room—a kitchen, no less—for the first time: Larry Forgione, Mark Miller, Bradley Ogden, Jimmy Schmidt, Jeremiah Tower, Alice Waters, Jonathan Waxman. (Also present, if somewhat incongruent, was restaurant consultant Barbara Kafka, whom McCarty had invited to participate at James Beard's request; she prepared tripe gumbo for the after-party.)

"Before you knew it, you were having a party in the kitchen," says Forgione.

Wolfgang Puck, the biggest chef of the moment, was absent; at least two major historical accounts place him at the dinner, but he wasn't there. Remembers Mark Peel, who attended on his behalf: "Spago was not given a course at the dinner. We were doing the pizza at the *after*-party. And Wolfgang was pissed. I think it was because—now Michael [McCarty] may deny this—but my feeling was that Spago was the big, hot ticket in L.A. at the time and Michael was a little pissed about it. So it was like him saying, 'Yeah, you make *pizza*.' So Wolfgang was annoyed, but he wanted to be involved in the dinner so he sent Ed LaDou and myself and we made pizza for the after-party." (Video of the event shows Peel and LaDou representing Spago to Julia Child on camera during a post-dinner kitchen curtain call.)* I thought perhaps the reason might be that Puck wasn't American, but when I emailed McCarty to ask why the pizzas were relegated to the after-party, he wrote back, simply,

---

* Puck confirms that he was not at the dinner. Rather he was at the opening of Spago in Tokyo, but he doesn't contest Peel's description of his upset. "Maybe Mark remembers better," he laughs.

"wanted to have something really easy, casual, and fun after the big meal!"

Schmidt remembers his first impressions of the group: Waxman was "earthy, Berkeley, laid-back," even in the kitchen; Forgione was "serious"; Ogden was impressed with his skill and, as a fellow Midwesterner, was the closest temperamentally to Schmidt; Miller was "spicy, very effervescent, he's just bubbling and he's got ten million ideas going one hundred miles an hour"; Tower was "theatrical, very well spoken, very high society," even in the kitchen, and already had the disposition of a star; Waters was "granola, laid-back, really about the ingredients, really very focused, but not overly animated." Even at that point, Schmidt described her as "iconic, at least in my mind."

And Schmidt's impression of McCarty? He sums it up in one word: "Armani."

AN AMERICAN CELEBRATION

DINNER MENU
4 May 1983

The Stanford Court
SAN FRANCISCO

Reception

CULTURED OLYMPIA OYSTERS
FROM PUGET SOUND, WASHINGTON
BELON OYSTERS FROM TOMALES BAY, CALIFORNIA
PORTUGUESE OYSTERS FROM
VANCOUVER ISLAND, B.C.
Schramsberg Vineyards 1977 Reserve Napa Valley Champagne

*

TERRINE OF 3 AMERICAN SMOKED FISH
WITH THEIR RESPECTIVE CAVIARS
LARRY FORGIONE, River Café, Brooklyn
Jordan Vineyard & Winery 1981 Estate Bottled Chardonnay

RED PEPPER PASTA WITH
GRILLED SCALLOPS
JONATHAN WAXMAN, Michael's, Santa Monica
Chalone Vineyard 1981 Estate Bottled Chardonnay

GARDEN SALAD
ALICE WATERS, Chez Panisse, Berkeley
Sanford Vineyards 1982 Vin Gris

BLACKENED REDFISH
PAUL PRUDHOMME, K-Paul's Louisiana Kitchen, New Orleans
Beringer Vineyards 1980 Private Reserve Chardonnay

MARINATED GRILLED QUAIL
WITH POBLANO CHILE, CILANTRO & LIME SAUCE
MARK MILLER, Fourth Street Grill, Berkeley
Iron Horse Vineyards 1982 Sauvignon Blanc

ROASTED RACK OF LAMB
STUFFED WITH MISSOURI GREENS & HAZELNUTS
GRATIN OF WILD ROOT VEGETABLES,
FIDDLEHEAD FERNS & CATTAIL SPROUTS
BRADLEY OGDEN, American Café, Kansas City
JIMMY SCHMIDT, London Chop House, Detroit
Acacia Winery 1980 Pinot Noir St. Clair Vineyard

AMERICAN CHEESE SELECTIONS
Robert Mondavi Winery 1974 Private Reserve Cabernet Sauvignon

PECAN PASTRY WITH CHOCOLATE & SABAYON SAUCE
JEREMIAH TOWER, Santa Fe Bar & Grill, Berkeley
Balboa Café, San Francisco
Joseph Phelps Vineyards 1981 Scheurebe 'Late Harvest'

*

After-Hours Party

SPAGO PIZZA
WOLFGANG PUCK, Spago, Los Angeles
Domaine Chandon Blanc de Noir

TRIPE GUMBO
BARBARA KAFKA, Star Spangled Foods, New York
Christian Brothers Private Reserve Centennial Sherry

An American Celebration was a service like no other.

When the night of the dinner arrived, McCarty, the ringmaster and master showman, gathered the chefs in an ancillary room and ran through the logistics with them. He was brimming with pride at every aspect of the evening, even the fact that computers were used to check people in: "We were trying to accomplish many different things at the same time," says McCarty, still underscoring the then-novelty of a computerized check-in system that allowed staff to print table assignments by keying guests' names into their system. "Each table was a ten-top. Molly Chappellet did the floral arrangements. They weren't flowers; they were fruit. Absolutely spectacular what she did."

"She has a degree in art," says Dodge of Chappellet, who designed special flourishes for culinary events at the Stanford Court. "So what she did at her home in the winery—because she's a phenomenal gardener as well—she liked to bring the outdoors inside. So for table arrangements she would bring in a head of cabbage and peel back the leaves and create it so that it was a beautiful arrangement. And she did that at that event. On every table there was a vegetable that she arranged in an artistic form. Alice was just absolutely amazed. She said to her, 'I've always thought these things were in themselves beautiful, this produce, but I just didn't know how to incorporate them onto the table like that.'"

A few hundred food aficionados gathered in the dining room to see and taste for themselves what was transpiring in restaurants around the country.

In the moments before the dinner, distractions mounted along with the pressure. There were journalists on hand, and many of them made their way through the kitchen during prep, prompting Schmidt to think, "*We're going to get our asses kicked.* I just said, 'It's time to put our heads down and get this thing done. Because we're not going to get all this lamb through all these ovens.' . . . I think it's very flattering. But I've always been of the mind of 'Put it on the plate; let the food talk.'"

After the kitchen work was done, plates were shuttled to four production tables in the dining room, where they'd be finished, then shuttled to guests by the service staff.

Between courses, the videos were shown. The shorts are cheesy, but charming, and capture—in many cases forecast—the iconic images these chefs would attain: Alice Waters is depicted strolling her garden, gathering greens for a salad; Jonathan Waxman, dressed in a wooly sweater, grills scallops on a mountaintop while—no joke—Chalone Vineyards' Dick Graff flies in and lands a small aircraft within shouting distance of him.

"What are you doing?" Graff asks Waxman from the cockpit.

"I'm grilling scallops for my scallops and red pepper pasta dish," says the chef.

"I've got just the thing to drink with it," says Graff, holding a bottle of his vineyard's Chardonnay aloft.*

Since his services weren't required until the after-party, Peel was free to act as a floater, working with the other chefs, getting a first-hand knowledge of their food by helping them prep it. "Alice's course was salads, so I got to plate all of the salads. I got to do blackened redfish with Paul Prudhomme. We had all of these big charcoal grills out on a fire escape. They had prealerted the fire department that billows of smoke were going to be coming from the Stanford Court. They didn't want people calling in. We had to put the cast-iron skillets right on the coals to get white hot and they double-dipped the redfish in clarified butter and then this heavy, heavy spice goes on it, then it gets dipped again, then it goes into this white-hot skillet, and I was nearly poisoned from these billows of smoke."

"Paul Prudhomme was larger than life," remembers Schmidt. "And he was doing blackened redfish, which was the big craze in the world at that time. And he was cooking it outside on this balcony thing and I thought that was pretty cool, because he was dipping the fish in butter and the fish was cold, so the butter would congeal and he would hit it in the spices and do it."

"He almost burned up the joint," says Ogden.

The chefs learned almost as much as the diners: "It was just surreal," says Forgione. "I remember how hard everybody worked and how much everybody helped each other. It wasn't, 'My course is done, I'm going to go get a glass of wine.'" (Waxman provided extra support to Barbara Kafka of Star Spangled Foods, who was recovering from meningitis. "I said, 'Barbara, I have your back,'" says Waxman. "'Whatever you need, I will take care of it.' She was literally on my shoulder the whole night. I said, 'Don't worry, I will do all of

---

*   This segment is painfully ironic today; Graff died in a single-engine Cessna crash in 1998.

the heavy lifting for you. You just look good, girl.' That was my job. It was very special.")

"We all cooked together that whole dinner," says Waxman. "Every course, we cooked with each other. It was the coolest thing in the world. We saw what each of us were doing. It was all different, which was the coolest thing. Some were more classic than others, and some were more crazy than others. That was the sort of culminating moment when we knew that it was a codified American food scene. What that meant, we had no clue, but we knew that even though we were all from different parts of the country we had this very strong bond. We were all trying to change the landscape of what we do."

"I think that was, bar none, where American food started," says Ogden. "It was really acknowledging that we have good cooks in America. And to represent America, represent our sort of history, where we were up to that point in our culinary works. It was the start of something bigger than we envisioned. We had no idea. We were just cooking."

Not everybody was enchanted. "Well, I mean, we accomplished *something*," says Waters. "That we did. But it was a lot of cameras and lights. It felt very Hollywood to me. It felt a little surreal. I just don't feel sentimental about it. Although I felt like I was always cared for by this group of chefs. They've always been my friends. I love that. I was the only woman, but I was their pal. And I loved that they sort of took care of me. I felt like I could count on them."

One of the journalists on hand was the omnipresent Ruth Reichl, who says of the evening: "I was back in the kitchen. And even my editors, when I pitched it to them, it was like, 'Oh, come on. You can't get a bunch of chefs together. It's going to be a nightmare.' We all thought it would be. I mean today, it's so obvious. *Of course* these chefs all work together. Nobody had ever done anything like that. I just remember it was lighthearted in a way. And the AIWF wasn't lighthearted; every program had been very serious. And so to me it was the chefs taking over from the Bob Mondavis, Julia Childs, the Jim Nassikases, and this young spirit coming in. Because people were still thinking of the food business as people who were in competition with each other, nobody thought that this was going to work in any way. And the spirit of camaraderie. I mean, it could have been a nightmare, and it wasn't. It was at the Stanford Court, which was very proper. And it was just an event that was not like anything anybody had done before in that sense of how much fun it was, how lighthearted it ended up being."

The de facto main course, the meat course, came up: Ogden and Schmidt's collaboration, which was ambitious enough without the added burden of putting out several hundred dishes.

"We were struggling just to get it all pushed through, all that lamb," says Schmidt. "And it was new for Bradley and me to work together. So it was kind of just like, 'Let's figure this out. Let's show them what we can do here.' And we did. There were plenty of steps in the dish: We had taken all these herbs and stuff and turned it into a stuffing and put it inside the morels. There were multilayers of flavors and au gratin potatoes and reductions."

In the heat of the moment, Schmidt looked up to see Waters, Tower, and other new friends arranging his and Ogden's food on plates, bringing their dish to life: "Everyone teamed up. There was a whole sense of, not competitiveness, but actually camaraderie, working together and everybody plating food together. We really hadn't seen that before, with people you had just met. It was amazing how it just all accumulated."

Once he and Ogden got the last lamb dish out, Schmidt—who had only really tasted a few canapés and Prudhomme's blackened redfish—stood back and took it all in.

"The quality, the plates that were coming up, the dishes that were being made, was world class. The meal was fabulous, compared to sitting in a three-star restaurant in France. You didn't have to be over there anymore to have that experience. That's what my take-away was, that what was going on those plates, the quality of the ingredients, the style, the culinary technique, the shared philosophies of people working together, was world class. We had entered having a cuisine that could actually be deemed powerful enough to represent the country and not feel ashamed that we're a second-class food [nation]."

It's happening, Schmidt thought to himself. *We're doing it.*

At the end of the meal, an ebullient Julia Child interviewed the chefs for the camera. Then came what has become a de rigueur element of any chef-fueled charity event—the after-party.

"It's a really wide range of personalities," says Schmidt. "The foundation, or the glue, was that that group of people had reached these conclusions of cooking in a certain direction with American ingredients almost separately. We kind of came to the same place. And we also, funny enough, did it not because we were going to get our name in the paper. We did it for the purity or the value."

And there was an added benefit: "We put out the dinner and then it was party like crazy," says Schmidt.

"After everybody left there was another room that was set up," says Forgione. "For the chefs. If I remember correctly, it was basically the whole party came into the after-party, or a good portion of them; certainly the people that were also serving wines at these dinners or donated food or were producers of the food."

"We had the best fucking time," says Waxman. "We were drinking Champagne out of the bottle. We were laughing our heads off."

"That whole [two days were] just celebratory," says Forgione. "We were truly celebrating American food, American drink."

During the postservice release, the chefs also had time to absorb the night, to replay the food they'd witnessed and helped each other prepare, to realize the magnitude of what had happened.

"You felt like you were part of a history-making dinner, that this was going to begin something," says Forgione. "This was going to begin a tremendous movement. I think it reinforced what everybody was doing by seeing everybody else that was doing it. And it wasn't that you were doing it better than somebody else; it was just that we were all doing it. We all loved what we were doing. It was so exciting. We all wanted to work together.

"You feel like now there's other people to talk to," says Forgione. "There's people who want to know about your free-range chickens and I want to know about Paul's soft-shell crawfish, and the bounty of things that are in California."

Ogden gravitated to some chefs more than others. In Forgione, he saw a kindred spirit, "shy, sort of like I was. . . . We just hit it off. When I got talking to him, he sort of had the same background as me a little bit, even though he came from the New York area. And his style is more French than my style. Mine is more American because it's the way I was trained. That's the way I grew up. But we became the best of friends."

Seeing what each other was up to was an empowering moment for these chefs. The crowd was split between chef-owners such as Prudhomme, the absent Puck and wife-partner Barbara Lazaroff, and Tower, who was already hard at work on his new restaurant, Stars. The others all were essentially employees, but they began to see in that weekend a blueprint for the future, a time when chefs could call their own shots, perhaps own their own restaurants.

"I realized that it was time for me," says Waxman. "I was done working for someone else. It was time for me to go and be my own chef. Stake my little claim." The dinner also changed the trajectory of Ogden's career, leading to talks with Campton Place Hotel's Bill Wilkinson that would bring him from Kansas City to San Francisco.

"That day was the beginning of so many careers," says Ogden.

"It was time for me to get out of Detroit," says Schmidt, who ended up partnering with McCarty on The Rattlesnake Club in Denver, Colorado. "He was looking for a chef and I said, 'I'll do it.'"

Moreover, the chefs were keen to stay in touch, to collaborate again, and—whether it was stated or not—to take advantage of the power inherent in their numbers.

Chemistry played a huge role in the evening's impact: Though the group comprised people of different economic, geographic, and social backgrounds—a sort of culinary version of *The Avengers*—somehow they meshed.

"We could have hated each other," says Waxman. "We could have been what chefs used to be—standoffish and secretive and protective."

Everything the dinner foretold came to pass: The chefs became the core group that represented and lorded over the industry for years to come, the go-to interview subjects for the proliferation of national articles on New American Cuisine and the people who were creating it, as well as the nucleus of large-scale fund-raising events. An early example that endures to this day is Citymeals on Wheels, a charity created by Gael Greene and James Beard to deliver meals to homebound elderly in New York City. Many of the chefs also participated in Wolfgang Puck's (unrelated) Meals on Wheels charity fund-raiser in Los Angeles. "I did thirty years of those dinners with Wolfgang," says Schmidt. "I was there from the first year out; I didn't piss anybody off so I got through it."

Before leaving the Stanford Court, though, spare a thought for Mark Peel: "I had a different experience because I was helping everyone during the day and during the service," he says. "The after-party was when I was working my fucking ass off. Everybody else was partying and drinking their Champagne, but I was turning out pizzas like a machine gun. I didn't have the luxury of time to gaze out over the crowd and have this epiphany."

Peel was living out one of the truisms of the chef's life, working while others are celebrating. He was also a metaphor for one of the themes of this era: Those forging this new world were often so consumed by their work that they didn't realize how far they'd come until well after they'd arrived.

6

CALIFORNIA DREAMING?

I like to see a little cooking for my money.

—Alan King

HOW JONATHAN WAXMAN BROUGHT CALIFORNIA CUISINE,
IF THERE IS SUCH A THING, TO NEW YORK CITY, DRIVING A
STAKE INTO THE HEART OF DINERS' EXPECTATIONS, WHILE
EAST COASTERS FORGED THEIR OWN NEW AMERICAN STYLE,
CONFUSING, THEN ERASING, DISTINCTIONS BETWEEN EAST
AND WEST

You're not supposed to light a Weber grill indoors, but there was
Melvyn Master, firing two of them up in the open kitchen of
his restaurant on East 79th Street on Manhattan's tony Upper East
Side. It was only a few weeks into 1984, and Master and his chef-
partner Jonathan Waxman were all set to introduce California
cuisine to New York City at their hotly anticipated Jams, starting

with a preview benefit for Citymeals on Wheels. The party was just hours away but the Montague grill Waxman had specially ordered* had been stalled by a snowstorm in Pennsylvania. No grill meant no California, hence the Webers. Master positioned them under the ventilation hood, loaded them with mesquite, lit them. Within an hour, Waxman and his cooks were pumping out passed hors d'oeuvres. Everything went swimmingly, until the extractor fan gave out. "The room filled with smoke and people's contact lenses were bulging out of their eyes," recalls the British-born Master. "Finally, we got it under control and everyone was fine. That was the birth of Jams."

Improvising had always worked wonders for Waxman and Master. And it would continue to work for them. Until it didn't. Though short-lived, Jams left a deep footprint, exporting California cuisine, and a California management style, to New York City. Along with a handful of other chefs who came east in the mid-1980s, and a smattering of Manhattan restaurants created in the California vein during the same period, the moment would forever blur the distinctions between chefs on different sides of the country.

"THERE WAS NOTHING LIKE IT IN NEW YORK."

Did it all start in the fall of 1979? As Waxman might say with a weary sigh, "Who the fuck knows?" Master thinks it did. As sales director of Sonoma's Jordan Winery, he enlisted Michael McCarty to put on a guest dinner at the vineyard, flying up McCarty, his chef Waxman, and sommelier Phil Reich.

---

* He selected it, in part, for sentimental reasons: He had attended California State University in Hayward, California, where the grill was made, and the design was lifted from Maxim's and other top French restaurants of the day.

Master and his wife, Janie, high school sweethearts from across the pond, had known McCarty when they all ran restaurants in Denver in the mid-1970s, but it wasn't until Michael's that they met and became friendly with Waxman. Both guys were, says Master, "party boys, and we were all doing that kind of stuff that we all did back then." The Jordan dinner was such an A-list affair that *People* magazine was on hand to document every sip and nibble. Waxman gave hostess Sally Jordan fits: When she asked to see a menu that morning, he told her his muse wouldn't clock in until after lunch and a few glasses of wine. Properly lubricated, Waxman began cooking that afternoon, while McCarty—taking charge, as usual—gave the winery's staff, Mexican women costumed in frilly French-style black-and-white maid's uniforms, their hair hugged by bonnets, a crash course in front-of-house elegance. The evening was a triumph, betraying none of the haste of its preparation, or maybe because of it.

(McCarty didn't revere top food writers the way many of his California peers did, as evidenced by an incident that took place during dinner prep: "Sally Jordan comes up to me and says, 'Mike, there's someone on the phone for you,'" recalls McCarty. He took the phone and the caller introduced herself: " 'This is M. F. K. Fisher.* Would you guys like to come over for lunch?' I had no idea who M. F. K. Fisher was. I thought it was just one of the crazy rich people up there. I said, 'Listen, we're really busy, we have this big party tonight. I'm really sorry but we just don't have time. Goodbye.' Boom." [*pantomimes hanging up the phone*] "She lived right around the corner.")

The Masters and Waxman grew close over the ensuing years, dining around the States, traveling to Paris. Waxman was one of those chefs who left the AIWF dinner at the Stanford Court Hotel

---

* A prominent twentieth-century food writer, author of many books, including *Serve It Forth, How to Cook a Wolf*, and a translation of Jean Anthelme Brillat-Savarin's *Physiology of Taste*.

itching to strike out on his own. California was home, but New York City fascinated him, especially Lutèce, which he still had a crush on after all these years. He almost doubled down on McCarty, who was eager to open a Michael's in New York City, with Waxman on board as his bicoastal chef, possibly even a partner, but McCarty—who insisted on a backyard garden to conjure the California spirit—couldn't secure his dream space, on West 55th Street in Midtown Manhattan.*

Meanwhile, the Masters, who owned a stately home outside Litchfield, Connecticut, planned a gargantuan New Haven seafood restaurant to be christened Billingsgate, after the London fish market, but couldn't cobble together the backing. Mel found himself on the phone with Waxman—never lacking for an opinion—who told him New Haven was crazy, they should open a restaurant in New York City. Intrigued, Master invited Waxman to come on board.

Timing is everything. With the McCarty deal stagnating, Waxman said, "Fuck it," and decided to partner with the Masters. And so was conceived one of the seminal American restaurants of the 1980s.

Evolution was swift: The fish eatery mutated into a shared vision of a restaurant that would package light, leafy California cuisine in a bleached-white box and plop it down, incongruously, into the concrete canyons of Manhattan. Billingsgate was shed in favor of the name Jams, an Americanization of *confitures*, as well as shorthand for "Jonathan and Melvyn's" ("or *Janie* and Melvyn's," semijokes the other Master). The idea, says Master, was "to bring a Michael's-type restaurant, Jonathan's food, California cuisine to New York City." For good measure, they poached Michael's pastry chef James Brinkley.

Waxman had a vision for the kitchen and the food: Not unlike Puck, he would eschew the European model that dominated

---

* He eventually nabbed it in 1989 and it became one of the homes of the New York City power lunch.

New York City, the chef's toque towering like a skyscraper, knotted neckerchiefs, a cacophony of whirring blades throughout the prep day, clanging oven doors and pans during service. Those tradition-bound restaurants were fundamentally concerned with transforming ingredients; the California school preferred to fetishize their natural state, or as close to it as could reasonably be sold in a restaurant, and the kitchen would reflect that: "I wanted to have a wood-burning grill, which I never had before," says Waxman. "And I wanted to have no machinery. I had no Robot Coupes or Cuisinarts. I wanted that rusticity."

As for the food, Waxman planned to draw heavily on his menu from Michael's, a document whose DNA included genomes from McCarty's time ghosting Jean Bertranou. Not going anywhere was the chicken: "I wanted to make my own french fries the way I had learned in France. And I wanted to buy the best chicken I could possibly get." (Buddy Larry Forgione, by this time at An American Place, put Waxman onto Paul Kaiser's free-range chickens, and to so many other purveyors that Waxman joked that Jams should have been called *Another* American Place.)

Master was in perfect sync with his partner. "There was nothing like it in New York," says Master. "No one had mesquite grills. No one had open kitchens. No one had baby vegetables."

The Masters and Waxman rented a $400-a-month one-bedroom apartment in the West Village. Waxman, who'd come to town with a Ferrari, a wardrobe, and nothing else, crashed on the sofa. The trio beat the pavement looking for a space until, driving across East 79th Street one day, they spotted one for lease: a restaurant on the lower two floors of a townhouse. An extracted pipe left a three-foot sag in the dining room, but they would've accepted a dirt floor because there was no down payment required. "We didn't have any money," says Waxman. Master summoned an old friend from the L.A. restaurant scene—Larry Shupnick—who in turn corralled Marvin Zeidler, who would go on to become Bruce Marder's partner in Santa Monica's Broadway Deli and other ventures. The two came to New York City, saw the space, and said, "You're both insane but we'll back you."

"THOSE WERE THE LITTLE IDEAS THAT I HAD IN MY HEAD."

Like so many chefs of his generation, Waxman had taken his sweet time finding himself, and the professional kitchen. Trained as a trombone player, he had chops enough to earn a scholarship to the University of Nevada, and gig with the likes of Sammy Davis Jr.

But food was always in the background. In the late 1960s, after returning from Nevada to his hometown area of Berkeley, he moved in with a woman whose parents were passionate foodniks and treated the young lovers to expensive dinners. Waxman left the relationship with a foundation in fine dining that complemented an innate weakness for luxury.

He joined a band in 1970. Rather than eat in crap restaurants on the road, the musicians threw spontaneous dinner parties that descended into bacchanals, cooking out of a copy of Julia Child's *Mastering the Art of French Cooking*, passed down to Waxman by his mother. Like many contemporaries, Waxman had discovered food, in large part, thanks to Child, Graham Kerr, and *Gourmet* magazine. Back in Berkeley, Waxman took, and loved, a class with Le Cordon Bleu's Richard Grausman at a local department store before moving to Maui to study politics at the University of Hawaii. After dropping out of school and a quick stint with yet another band, he found himself stranded far from home and penniless.

"There are two things you can do," counseled a friend. "Sell drugs or work in a restaurant."

Waxman chose the latter, securing a job on Ka'anapali Beach. "It was one of these restaurants with a huge bar that served daiquiri cocktails in snifter glasses and the cocktail waitresses wore basically nothing," says Waxman. "It was right on the beach, open air with a canopy above. People grilled their own steaks and swordfish. My job was to prep all the meats in the morning and bus tables at night. Within six months, I was the manager because I smoked less pot than everyone else."

Returning to Berkeley in 1972, Waxman led a triple life: By day he donned a pair of Gucci loafers and sold Ferraris and Alfa Romeos; by night he played in a jazz band and tended bar. Between customers at the auto dealership, Waxman gabbed about food, prompting the owner's wife—a food lover—to recommend her friend Mary Risley's San Francisco cooking class. This being Berkeley, the shop's head auto mechanic matriculated with Waxman, who proved a natural.

After the last day of class, Risley approached him, asked what he was doing with his life.

"I don't know," said Waxman, then twenty-five.

"Why don't you think about going to cooking school to become a chef?" she asked.

The thought had never occurred to him, but it made perfect sense. Risley secured him a spot at Paris's La Varenne. His parents put up the tuition, and on his birthday, November 15, 1976, he touched down in Paris. He can still taste the duck confit and garlic potatoes he ate on arrival. A Paris virgin, he spent six weeks learning French at Alliance Française, befriended a fellow student—a photographer—and ended up rooming with the shutterbug, a colleague of his, and two fashion models. Then he dove into cooking school, compares it to "dropping acid"; he couldn't get enough. Instructors and the French media were obsessed with the kings of nouvelle cuisine and Waxman lapped it up. He and some friends rented a dilapidated Opel and made a gustatory tour, dining at Troisgros, Bocuse, and other Michelin starlets. The zeitgeist prompted a barstool epiphany: *What if we took all the sort of classic regional foods of America and did what they did in France?* he thought. *Lighten them up? Make them more accessible? Make them different somehow?* "I didn't know what that meant really," he says. "*What if instead of having a big slab of abalone cooked in butter and flour and put on a plate with more butter, you took that abalone and cut it into strips and deep-fried it and tossed it into a salad to wilt the salad?* Those were the little ideas that I had in my head. Those were the things I tried at Michael's."

"IT WOULD BE AN HONOR AND A PRIVILEGE FOR YOU TO WORK FOR ME."

In Woody Allen's *Annie Hall*, released in 1977, protagonist Alvy Singer, a New Yorker, orders "alfalfa sprouts and a plate of mashed yeast" at an outdoor L.A. cafe. Gothamites erupted into peals of laughter at the line—a bite-sized summation of the East Coast's perception of the California diet. How things had changed in seven years: New York food writers and diners anticipated Jams with "the-circus-is-coming" giddiness, and many young cooks, most of them trained in French kitchens, wanted to work there. In an era when there was scant national coverage of chefs, their reputations and legends grew like gunslingers'—by word of mouth—and Waxman's had already swelled to tall-tale status. Forgione, now at his own An American Place, sent his former cook Helen Chardack there to meet "his buddy from California." She interviewed in the unfinished space: "It had wires and lightbulbs and the toilet was sitting in the middle of the room and it was completely undone, but he was going ahead and he was going to open anyway," says Chardack, who, having done time in California, saw through the clutter: "I knew exactly what he was doing with that grill. I knew exactly what he was doing with his food." Ralph Tingle, who'd cooked for Wolfgang Puck at Ma Maison before coming to New York, and had admired Waxman's work at Michael's, had left Le Cirque after a tiff with Alain Sailhac; he strolled into the Jams space one day, asked Waxman for a job, got hired on as sous chef. Ed Fertig, another River Café grad, also interviewed at the construction site. Waxman ended the tête-à-tête saying, "It would be an honor and a privilege for you to work for me." Fertig found it pompous, but figured there had to be talent behind the bluster. The legend grew before he'd served a morsel of food in Manhattan.

Journalists, too, wanted a piece of the action: *New York* magazine's Gael Greene contacted Master about a preopening piece, insisting on a photograph. The restaurant was still under construction, so it was improvisation time: "Janie goes next door to [Rosedale] Fish Market," says Master. "She buys some scallops, Jonathan buys some greens, brings them back, Janie takes her eyebrow pencil out, paints black lines on the scallop to look as if it'd been on the grill. Jonathan does his magic putting the things around it, and—*voilà!*—we have what looks like amazing grilled scallops with little baby greens. That was the photo that went into *New York* magazine."

In January 1984, the month before the restaurant opened, Marian Burros penned a *New York Times* piece titled "Food Accent for the 80's Is Decidedly American," a summation of the action to date: the emphasis on fresh ingredients, the rediscovery and reinterpretation of American dishes, the proliferation of chef-farmer relationships, and the transmission of inspiration from major market to major market. She also traced the movement's echo in the fast-food and super-market realms, and predicted an uptick in "Oriental" and Mexican influence. In the piece, she observed that chefs were opening "their own restaurants instead of going to work for others," citing An American Place's Forgione and Waxman, with his about-to-launch Jams, as role models.

When the restaurant finally opened in February, the dining room could have been plucked right from Santa Monica: a minimalist space with chalk-white walls hung with outsized modern paintings procured by Waxman, and floral arrangements created daily by Janie

Master. There was a petite freestanding antique zinc-topped Parisian bistro bar with a walnut facade. Tables were set with blue-rimmed white Ginori china. The kitchen was—of course—open, barely set off from the dining room by a butcher block–covered Traulsen pass-through refrigerator that served as the pass. To avoid a Siberian stigma, the upstairs was decorated to evoke a clubby setting, an exclusivity Master would offer the anticipated celebrity guests. Ironically, given Master's wine acumen, they had yet to secure a liquor license, requiring customers to bring their own in the restaurant's first days.

The food was everything people had been primed to expect, and more. There was, of course, the chicken. There was a shiitake and oyster mushroom salad with pine nuts and Smithfield ham. There was sautéed foie gras with deep-fried spinach. There was swordfish with blood orange and shallots, and veal with veal stock and limes.

There were also Californians; several West Coast peers were in town around the opening, including Puck himself, who dropped in for lunch.

The restaurant took off fast, despite some good ol' fashioned New York attitude. George Barber, former front-of-house man at Michael's, came to New York City, ran into Waxman on the street, and took a job at Jams. "There was a stay-in-California thing among these tough New Yorkers," remembers Barber. "New York was different in the eighties. It was a lot more cynical. It was a lot more territorial as well. They did a big thing coming from California."

Waxman picked up on it, too: "New York had no idea what I was doing," he says. "So when I opened up they were like, 'What the fuck is this? Where does he get off grilling chicken and serving it with french fries? Where does he get off serving sweetbread salad? Where does he get off serving wilted mushrooms?' They all kind of loved it and they were kind of confused by it at the same time. But everybody seemed to take it in stride."

"I think Gael Greene legitimized a lot of it," says Barber. "She started Citymeals on Wheels, and I think Jonathan was the first one that really helped her and he got a lot of cachet from that."

With Waxman plying his trade in New York City, the legend went full supernova: "Jonathan would come into the kitchen and gather up these ingredients and create this plate. It was almost like he was dancing," remembers Stephanie Lyness, who cooked at Jams. "And that's the way the food was. It was very fresh, simple, alive feeling, and certainly à la minute. Everything was just coming off the grill."

Tingle found the food lacked the "elegant twist that Michael's had; it was more stripped down, more organic," which he attributes to Waxman's time at Chez Panisse. Accordingly, he was knocked out by the ingredients Waxman was able to secure: "It was the first time I'd seen vegetables coming in from these organic farms, like baby carrots, and they were rock-solid fantastic. We had chickens coming in with rigor mortis, with the feet on and the head on. Jonathan was a pretty good forager. He was finding some pretty unique things to bring into the restaurant. And how we treated them was pretty darn simple and straightforward. We weren't making coq au vin through marinades or sauces or whatnot; we were taking this chicken that's beautiful, organic, fresh, and grilling it and putting a little rosemary on it." Tingle, charged with ensuring certain standards, like a crispy skin on the chicken, understood the inherent risk in Waxman's approach: Simplicity leaves "nothing to hide behind so you really have to do a good job with it."

"The grill was hot as shit," remembers future Quilted Giraffe cook Tom Carlin, who came to Jams from 40 Main Street, a contemporary American restaurant in Millburn, New Jersey, where Tom Colicchio also worked early in his career. "It was like working in a coal mine. I'd come home and blow my nose and it'd be black. And if you were standing in front of the grill and then moved your arms forward and your chef's coat hit your back, it would burn you." The minimalist kitchen called for unconventional techniques: The fries were made in a pot on the grill, rather than in a fryolator; the oil sometimes bubbled over, causing fires.

The laid-back vibe extended to the plating. "He didn't want to arrange the food," says Carlin. "His words were 'Don't move things around. I want it to look like it just fell from the sky and landed gently on the plate.'" The price tag for such simplicity raised eyebrows: The chicken and fries were $20 on opening day. (For comparison, it debuted at just $29 thirty-one years later at a poorly received Jams reboot.)

Waxman changed the menu weekly, sometimes daily—an ongoing, unpredictable Jams session by the onetime musician and innate improviser, the only problem being that the maestro operated on his own wavelength, sometimes changing up the setlist at the last possible second. Fertig remembers it as a "free-for-all"; one morning, Waxman blew into the kitchen minutes before lunch service and proclaimed, "It's Beaujolais Nouveau Day, everything has Beaujolais in it!" Never mind that all the food for the planned menu had already been prepped and guests would be filing in any minute. Sometimes Waxman went too far, like the time he tried grilling live lobsters; they (understandably) began crawling off the grate, requiring the cooks to cage them.

Some found the spontaneity stimulating, others maddening. Eric Bromberg, who became chef of Jams during its run, remembers that at the outset of each week, Waxman gave him a typed menu to realize by Friday. Often, it was a puzzle to be solved: "There was no description on anything. Just the names of the dish and a couple of cryptic, sort of weird things. One of them was Onion Surprise. That's how it was written. 'Here's the menu, go make all the food and start the new menu on Friday.' It's, like, three days out, and I have no idea what he has in mind."*

---

* Waxman says he gave more direction for the Onion Surprise dish than Bromberg remembers.

Chardack, who took over the kitchen a few months after opening when Tingle left, says, "Jonathan used to write up a menu every day and we would get it all prepped, and forty-five minutes before service began, he would change it. It was painful. I would tell the cooks, 'Even if you're not ready, look like you're ready.' Because it was an open kitchen." (Incidentally, in these days, a sous chef might have been more akin to what is, at the time of this writing, considered a chef de cuisine, the person who ran the kitchen day to day and/or during service. Tingle and Chardack would have been considered sous chefs in most kitchens at the time, but not at Jams. "Jonathan was not hung up on titles," says Chardack. "He's from California." That said, Chardack did have an unofficial designation: "I was Grill Queen, who controlled the rest of the kitchen, because all the entrees came off the grill.")

"My take on Jonathan is that he's first and foremost an artist," says Lyness. "I feel like he might have been a painter. He might have been a sculptor."

Waxman himself frequently speaks of food in musical terms: Of the evolution of his style, he says: "It's a little bit like musicians, learning the scales like they did four hundred years ago. What you do with them, well, it's up to you, you know?"

"Jonathan's a jazz musician and he thrives a little bit on chaos," says Chardack. "If you can just go with the flow with him, then everything would be just fine."

"IS THIS A MOVEMENT? I DON'T KNOW."

Food as conversation piece, an American chef of burgeoning celebrity, the cachet of California. It was a perfect storm. Savvy diners flocked to the restaurant to experience California cuisine with a curiosity comparable to that of those who visited Wylie Dufresne's wd~50 decades later to lose their molecular virginity.

"All of a sudden the restaurant was so full it was crazy," says Waxman. Before long, Steve Martin (at the height of his movie and stand-up-comedy careers), Paul Newman (late-career peaking, between *The Verdict* and *The Color of Money*), and Mick Jagger (still firmly in the Rolling Stones) were showing up, sometimes simultaneously, as did food titans like James Beard and Paul Bocuse. Being the "it" spot meant there was no end to what Master could get away with, like crowding six to eight people around a four-top, or euphemizing the bathroom-adjacent table as "the kitchen table." Rather than be turned away, Princess Stéphanie of Monaco, Dodi Fayed, and friends deigned to dine in the restaurant's ramshackle office one night. Wine storage was improvised—some bottles went into the fridge, others to the basement, which doubled as the coat check; mink coats were scattered about, slung over stockpots, occasionally finding their way into the soup.

By March, the *New York Times*'s Marian Burros had chimed in with a two-star review: "Cognoscenti and would-be cognoscenti have been flocking to Jams on the Upper East Side . . . eager to be among the first to sample the California cuisine they have heard so much about," opens the review. She goes on: "For the untutored, New York's first restaurant to offer this minimalist style of cooking in a minimalist setting may come as something of a shock." (On one of her four visits, the ventilation system went wonky, allowing smoke to waft into the dining room; by the fall, the owners had spent $22,000 to improve it.) Gael Greene held her judgment until September, then mostly rhapsodized over the food but related a conversation with a friend who tried to sell her on it being "California relaxed elegance." "To me, it looks rather tentative, undone, the exposed kitchen its only dramatic statement, though borrowed canvases and tailored blinds have brought it all together," she wrote. Greene also noted Waxman's use of purslane, common in kitchens today, calling it "an odd herb."

Despite the buzz, many New York cooks disdained the California school and the bohemian chef who personified it. "Jonathan was the devil to me," remembers Bromberg. "I worshipped French cooking. And he was spitting in its face." Bromberg found his Jams indoctrination cultish: "It's California cuisine, which I can't even put together in my mind what that actually even means. Stephanie would use that term: 'We do California cuisine here.' And Jonathan, Jonathan, Jonathan, Jonathan, Jonathan. Jonathan was the deity to everybody. It was Jonathan and Melvyn. And they were having a pretty good time. But they made things totally differently than I had learned how to make things. And so for probably the first two and a half months, I tried to make specials. And I'd make classic French dishes. And that was going fine and then Jonathan showed up; he just walked in the kitchen. He was like, 'Hey.' I don't even know if he looked at me. He looked at this dish that I'd just made. I don't exactly remember what it was, but I know there were tomatoes in it. And he looked at it and he goes—I don't know if he said, 'What the fuck is this?' or 'What the hell is this?' And I turned around and I'm like, 'This is blah, blah, blah,' whatever I said it was. And he said, 'We don't make that here.' And I said, 'What do you mean you don't make that here?' And he said, 'We don't make that here. We don't cook tomatoes,' or something like that. And I was like, 'Oh.' He was in my world and shocked the shit out of me. I just kind of stood there. And he said, 'You know why I don't cook tomatoes? It makes me fart.' And he turned around and walked out."

"It was really a change to work for Jonathan after this hard-core French stuff," says Tingle, who had done time in France between California and Le Cirque. "It was kind of a shock to the system in some ways, and hard to wrap myself around at first, but after a while I began to appreciate the honesty of it."

"We looked at the food and just thought, *What is this shit?*" remembers Mike Colameco, who was working as sous chef to Frenchman Christian Delouvrier at Maurice restaurant in the Hotel Parker Meridien at the time. "'Where's the technique?' All the stuff that we valued so much was nonexistent in that kitchen. Back in the day, one of the great jobs was to be a saucier in a restaurant because it was a huge responsibility. You were the alchemist; you created these wonderful things. And then you get to Jams and we used to joke that the saucier makes vinaigrettes. The saucier there worked with a whisk and a couple of mixing bowls and a couple of olive oils and vinegar. *What the fuck?*"

"The difference was we were trying to create food that was generated from the idea of braising, roasting, sautéing," says Gerry Hayden, at The River Café under Charlie Palmer at the time. "What they said in California about the produce being spectacular: It *can* be spectacular. It doesn't mean you can't still *do* spectacular things with it."

"When I went to Jams, I was like, 'Yeah, it is kind of what I expected. It's real simple and lots of vegetables,'" remembers Chanterelle's David Waltuck. "Is this a movement? I don't know."

"I'm sure that I visited most, if not all, of those restaurants," says Josh Wesson, working at Huberts when Jams opened. "But that was a *moment*, not a movement. I don't have any specific [recollections], just sort of a fuzzy awareness that I went to those restaurants and can't remember a thing about them."

"I THINK IT'S A SILLY TERM."

Waxman was the first to introduce California cuisine to New York City, but only by a hair, as it turned out. In his wake, and within a year or so, came Wolfgang Puck protégé Richard Krause, first at Batons and then at Melrose in Manhattan, and Michael's and Spago alums Mark Peel and Nancy Silverton, whom Warner LeRoy recruited to take over the kitchen at his Maxwell's Plum, an

American restaurant with a legendary hookup scene—"singles bar" in the patois of the time.

The concentrated influx of California chefs to New York City during these years is Exhibit A for those who believe most credit for the American food revolution belongs to the West Coast. Initially, at least publicly, Waxman expressed discomfort with the California cuisine designation: In December 1983, just weeks before Jams opened, he quipped to the *New York Times:* "What's California food—food served on a surf board with sand on it?"

It's a good question: Just what is California cuisine? The term has been used so loosely, even by those most associated with it, that it doesn't have much meaning beyond the sketchiest: a preponderance of vegetables, especially baby vegetables; a scarcity of sauce; the use of a wood-fired grill; salsas, pastas, and pizzas.

Like most such categories, *California cuisine* was coined by journalists rather than chefs. As with *nouvelle cuisine, California cuisine* was created as a convenience, most likely by *Gourmet*'s Caroline Bates, as a hook with which to corral a group of disparate chefs operating on the left coast, to facilitate headlines and reference points. Like most such groupings—*molecular gastronomy* is a more recent example—the terminology ultimately fails, especially in this case because it implies the most populous state in the union is monolithic. But anybody who has been to both Los Angeles and San Francisco knows that the two cities, almost four hundred miles apart, have little in common: L.A. is Hollywood, Sunset Boulevard, and the beach; San Francisco boasts a more intellectual bent, with wine country nearby, and the bohemia of Berkeley alongside. Joyce Goldstein, former chef-owner of San Francisco's Square One and a historian of this era, says, "They were two different *planets.*"

Though many were all too happy to capitalize on it at the time, even the most famous practitioners of California cuisine take issue with the phrase. "When Caroline Bates wrote that Alice and I were doing California cuisine, we talked about it. We didn't have any idea what she was talking about. We just did what we felt like doing," says Narsai David. "Joyce Goldstein and Alice Waters and I just sort of laughed. We were doing what we felt like doing. Now, Alice, of course, has gone far beyond that, demanding that everything be as local as possible. Of course, I chuckle when I think of the exceptions she makes for things like peaches, which must come from three hundred miles away because she likes the farmer. But I can tease her about that a little bit."

"I think it's a silly term," says Goldstein. "I call it the *food revolution*. It was a revolution about ingredients. It was a revolution about wine. It was a revolution in restaurant design. You put in an open kitchen, the hushed dining room goes away. No one is tiptoeing or whispering anymore because the stage is happening. And you put in an open kitchen and things can never be as formal again and yet your staff has to be professional. We changed our menu every day. That meant we had briefings with our staff every day and they tasted food every day. In the old days the menus never changed. They hardly ever had briefings. Now everybody has the briefing. Well, that started here. There's so many things that started here because of the kinds of changes that we made."

California cuisine, says Goldstein, "is undefinable. What it really means is fresh, seasonal, local, preferably grown by people you know."

"For me, a *cuisine* takes the test of time," says Alice Waters. "When you talk about Chinese cuisine or even Italian cuisine, we're talking hundreds, thousands of years. It's sort of presumptuous to think that we could define a kind of cooking in California that has these qualities about it that are enduring. I think what I was thinking about, that's been confused with California cuisine, is a *philosophy* of food. And that's what is enduring, and that is what certainly we've tried to express. It's about what is found locally, what is cooked simply, what is seasonal and ripe, what is pure and grown correctly—that's all part of a philosophy of food and can be applied to any food.

"But *cuisine*, I think there are characteristics of cooking in California that can be talked about because it's warm here and we can be outside and we can make fires and cook over a fire, and we have a warm climate that has fruits, and we grow a lot of vegetables. Those are undoubtedly going to be part of any cuisine that comes into being. And we're close to the sea. We're going to have fish. We have influences from Mexico and Japan, and those are going to be part of what's happening without any question. They were just absorbed into it."

"*California cuisine* is not the right term because it wasn't a cuisine; it was a mind-set which was the only one I knew because I grew up in Europe, which is that the menu is done from the marketplace," echoes Jeremiah Tower. "You have to understand that in 1973, when I started, there was nothing. There were no fresh herbs to buy commercially or wholesale. There was olive oil from the one Italian delicatessen in Oakland. The fish, I would go to the fishing boats in Chinatown and all that. I mean, talk about *foraging*. It took three or four hours for me every morning before going in to cook lunch. So it was really restating what was completely obvious to every French grandmother for the last five hundred years. It was an *approach* to cooking."

Ironically, Spago's menu cover notwithstanding, the first true California cuisine might have been put forth in New York, at Jams, where Waxman and Master made a self-conscious decision to bring that style of food, and restaurant, to New York City.

"He was really taking what he learned from cooking in California and applied it to what was available to him in New York," says Waters. "And he made—if such a thing exists—California cuisine."

"IT WAS ALMOST LIKE A DREAM."

Jams hit New York City when the 1980s were peaking, the high-flying, cocaine-dusted, preposterously prosperous days immortalized by Jay McInerney, whose novel *Bright Lights, Big City* featured a rendering of The Odeon's facade on its cover, and Tom Wolfe.

"That's why I think the whole L.A. movement was so important, because it created a media buzz around these chefs," says Tom Colicchio. "After the seventies and Studio 54, people just finally woke up from that cocaine age and said, 'What are we going to do now?' Restaurants became the place where people would go, and that was the evening. It wasn't about going to a club anymore. That was over and it was done. People were just looking for something new, and there were people who wanted to understand the personalities behind the food."

Jams was made for the moment—tables were hot commodities, signifying status and access. "People wanted to be part of the scene. It *was* a scene. Which is why I say it was a party. They had a real small bar up front and no one was sweating bullets over the fact that people were crowding around it, waiting for the next seating, or coming in or whatever. Because that kind of heat that it generated, of mingling, was part of the whole world," says Chardack.

Amping things up, Waxman and Master were themselves becoming celebrities—appearing in *Life* magazine, and on the cover of *Esquire*. Waxman also famously posed for a New York *Daily News* magazine cover in silk pajamas. Before long, they were breaking the same rules as McCarty, blurring the line between employer and employee, partying with their crew after hours, maybe chowing down 'round midnight across Central Park at Lynn Wagenknecht and Keith McNally's bistros Café Luxembourg on West 70th Street or The Odeon in the depths of Tribeca. "Café Luxembourg was the loudest restaurant on the planet, I think," says Tingle. "Jonathan would bring a truffle in his pocket and shave some onto the plain risotto." They drank Cristal for breakfast and had no trouble running up $10,000 in lunch bills in a month at La Goulue. "Waxman was wild," says Tingle. "He was in and out of the restaurant, and he'd let you hang a little bit. He was just kind of everywhere. He'd be out partying. He was a little aloof."

Chardack remembers Jams as "loose, a party, fun. There was a wonderful relationship between the front of the house and the back of the house. Jonathan's was this great California kitchen with that vibe that we're all working together." It was also a more harmoniously coed crew than in many other restaurants. Claudia Fleming, who would go on to fame as Gramercy Tavern's pastry chef, was the office manager and Gale Gand, who would go on to success with future (then ex) husband Rick Tramanto in Chicago, was in the kitchen.

"He and Melvyn were The Guys," says Bromberg. "They'd just take over the place. It would be like, 'Jonathan's here!' and everyone would bow and people from other places would come over. He was just huge. You'd sit down, Jonathan would go in the kitchen, or whatever, and we'd just get food, get taken care of."

Chardack remembers Waxman being up on the newest restaurants, like Italian Sandro Fioriti's Sandro's or Zarela Martinez's Zarela. "Jonathan was good at going to see who was doing what, and bringing his entourage with him. There's something very hedonistic and wonderful about sitting around and drinking. It was part of his whole thing. It was just an extension of Jams."

In the late 1980s, a young Mario Batali, then working at the Clift in San Francisco, made a fact-finding trip to New York with his chef Kelly Mills. They dined at Jams, Melrose, Le Bernardin. "Wow, this town is unbelievable," he thought. "How elegant and how sexy. The restaurants were cool and the chefs looked like they were gods and they were being adored by everyone that walked near them." There was certainly a cult of personality around Waters, Miller, and

304 CHEFS, DRUGS AND ROCK & ROLL

Tower out West, but in New York City, "it seemed more grown up." California restaurants, Batali felt, were "cas. No one was dressed up. There didn't seem to be any pressure, and in New York you got into a restaurant and everything was palpable. Just walking into the restaurant to try to get something, try to be a part of it: *I've got to taste it, have a glass of something, have a dish.* New York was so much more impressive." (The only San Francisco restaurant that impressed him in the same way, he says, was Jeremiah Tower's Stars.)

Waxman was a known quantity when he arrived in New York but was unprepared for the rapid ascent that awaited him there. "I didn't realize the power of the New York press," he says. "Of New York being the epicenter of the publishing world."

Today, Waxman says he didn't feel that his contribution to Michael's qualified him for such plaudits "because I still had the sensibility of what French chefs had accomplished, and it took them twenty, thirty years to get where they were." But Reichl, writing in the *Los Angeles Times*, recalled an early press confab at Michael's at which a journalist told Waxman she would make him famous. "He smiled and said deprecatingly, 'Don't do me any favors.' He had every intention of being famous, his tone of voice implied, and he wouldn't need anyone's help, thank you."

In any event, Waxman *was* becoming famous. "It was almost like a dream," he says. "It seemed one hundred percent surreal. It happened extremely fast." (Chef Brendan Walsh, who would draw considerable media attention at the Southwestern restaurant Arizona 206, felt a similar sense of unreality during the same years: "My life was a whirlwind. I'm not going to tell you I handled everything perfectly. I was overwhelmed. It went to my head. I was insecure; I was arrogant; I was everything. There was so much shit going on. . . . Nothing prepared you for that. Did you see the amount of press that I got in a short period of time? I was called the American brat by the French guys. The Southwestern guys didn't like me; here I was doing creative Southwestern food but that's *their* stuff. . . . I became friends with all those guys, but they felt like I was co-opting their stuff because all the media's here. I became something I didn't want to be. I was starting to be somebody I didn't recognize.")

Though embraced by the city, Waxman also felt a bit alien. When the *Los Angeles Times* solicited a letter home from L.A. expats living in New York, he wrote that he missed the camaraderie among California chefs and claimed to have toyed with possibly returning to L.A. He also bemoaned the feast-or-famine nature of product in New York at the time, and the demanding clientele: "Californians are so enthusiastic, it got to the point where you'd want to say, 'Can you be a little more negative?' New Yorkers are very skeptical. You have to prove yourself. L.A. people respect experimentation. New Yorkers feel, 'Well, experiment out of town before you bring it here.'"

Mimi Sheraton, who was friends with comedian and bon vivant Alan King, recalls him saying, "I like to see a little cooking for my money," which for her summed up the New York attitude toward restaurant food.

Waxman, who kept an apartment above Jams, couldn't resist the lure of the city. He developed a reputation for being a no-show at his own restaurant, often doing a quick tour of the kitchen, then lighting out on the town. "It was maybe three weeks before I met Jonathan," says Bromberg of his time at Jams. That's not uncommon today, but in the 1980s, most chefs were in their own kitchens most nights of the week.

"It was always a love/hate with Jonathan," says Master. "Everybody didn't want to upset Jonathan because they loved him, respected him, but everybody wanted him to focus."

"He would do a pass-through," says Carlin. "He would come down from his apartment in a chef's coat and he'd do a little lap through the kitchen and then he'd go out, leave in his chef's coat. And he would meet with Larry [Forgione] and they would hang out."

Forgione's An American Place, which opened the year prior, was thriving a stone's throw from Jams on Lexington Avenue, between 70th and 71st Streets. James Beard, with whom Forgione's friendship continued, dined there every Thursday night.

"I remember one night that it was completely filled. Sixteen tables were food writers or critics. And the other table was James Beard. We had a table set aside for Warren Beatty and Diane Keaton. Dan Rather had his table. Diane Sawyer had her table. Jackie O had her table."

Forgione was gaining attention, which he enjoyed, but he says he mostly appreciated it for another reason. "What I was always more excited about was the fact that notoriety was making other young cooks want to follow the same pursuit, that if it wasn't for maybe the notoriety or the fame that myself and other chefs were getting, maybe there wouldn't be so many people who were jumping in and pursuing American cooking."

"REFIRE THREE RED SNAPPERS THAT WERE RAW."

Meanwhile the good times continued at Jams.

"People were partying, and the staff, too," says Bromberg. "There was clearly a hell of a lot of money in New York. There were expensive bottles of wine. There were truffles, there was caviar, there was modern art. You could definitely feel the money in New York.

"The eighties at that point, if you had money and you were going out in the city and you were young enough, you were doing something," says Bromberg. "The staff was doing speed and everything else you can do to stick with the party. It was nuts. It was faster. The whole speed of it was so overwhelming to me, and working eighty, ninety hours a week took me to a whole other place. I used to sleep on bags of rice in the storeroom, between lunch and dinner, and overnight. Just couldn't get to my apartment and back even though it was eight blocks away."

Bromberg lost about sixteen pounds at Jams, kept a bottle of Mylanta or Pepto-Bismol in his pocket, nipped it all day long. But that changed: "Jonathan walks in one night with a tall, skinny guy with black hair and a leather jacket. And they're looking around and he doesn't really even talk to me. I'm putting out food and we're in the middle of a slam and he's walking this guy around and showing him this, that, and the next thing. People are like, 'Who's that guy?'" Turns out it was another chef, to whom Waxman had offered the lead position at Jams. As a consolation prize, he offered Bromberg a demotion to sous chef. "I got all pissed off," says Bromberg. "I told him to go fuck himself, but I got over it. And then I decided maybe that was a good thing. And so this guy comes in and he knows Jonathan's food and I go from being the one in charge to being this odd castoff, except I did all the morning prep, worked lunch, and then set everything up for dinner and then he was going to be the dinner guy."

One night during dinner service, Bromberg was about to leave, when he heard the expeditor call out, "Refire three red snappers that were raw."

"The chef was trying to pick up the fish to put it back on the grill and cook them more. And he's sort of sweating and looking peculiar. And right in the middle of it, his eyes rolled back in his head and he frigging collapsed right at the grill. He was a junkie. Heroin issue. Passes out. Everyone thought he was dead. The dishwasher and I dragged him around the side. EMS came, they did what they did, took him out. I got on the grill, got everything back in order, cooked throughout the night, and then the next morning I came in and told Jonathan I was leaving, he and his junkie buddy could do whatever they wanted."

"ARE YOU DOING IT WITH MIRRORS?"

In 1984 and '85, a proliferation of restaurants in New York City with varying degrees of California in their DNA blurred the line between the coasts, making it difficult to quantify the influence California had on the rest of the country.

In 1984, Jerry Kretchmer and partners opened Gotham Bar and Grill. In 1985, a young restaurateur named Danny Meyer launched Union Square Café on 16th Street, with Ali Barker as chef, replacing him in time with Michael Romano. (Meyer made a fact-finding tour of Los Angeles and Bay Area restaurants, which influenced his ideas about hospitality and menu offerings.) And restaurant consultant Clark Wolf collaborated with chef Brendan Walsh, a native New Yorker who had left the East Coast to cook at Jeremiah Tower's Stars in San Francisco, to launch a Southwestern restaurant, Arizona 206. It was, easily, the most transformative period in New York City dining since 1979.

Kretchmer, who had been Mayor John Lindsay's sanitation commissioner and once ran for mayor, was a fan of "big restaurants" Café Seiyoken, Joanna, and Capsouto Frères. When plans to build a motion picture studio in Hoboken with partner Jeff Bliss fell through, Kretchmer told him he wanted to build a restaurant. Bliss thought he was nuts—neither of them knew the first thing about the business—but Kretchmer, an instinctual animal, pursued it, began sniffing around for a big space reminiscent of the culinary hangars to which he gravitated as a diner. The first space his broker showed him was a gargantuan loft on East 12th Street that had been a drug rehab center and was currently functioning as an antiques auction house. As much as anything, Kretchmer was drawn to the practical convenience of a garage right across the street. They brought in Richard and Robert Rathe, who ran a New York City–based exhibition production company, as partners.

"We didn't know anything about the restaurant business," says Kretchmer. "But I said, 'I grew up in the Catskills. I've been waiting on people for a long time.' I ran a dining room. I'm a politician. I know how to make people happy." They considered three restaurant consultants, eventually hiring Barbara Kafka.

Despite the dining public's growing fascination with chefs, Kretchmer had no interest in focusing on one. "I started out going the other way," he says. "That was not my interest at all. My idea about this restaurant was a great big cafe, cafeteria, whatever you want. It didn't have anything to do with fine dining; it had to do with being family comfortable. I had taken my kids to all these restaurants. They were comfortable, but they weren't *so* comfortable. And I wanted to get past that. And that's how come the first Gotham menu had chopped liver on it, had chicken soup on it, matzo balls, a tagine, Jerry's burger. It had all of that stuff that kids would eat. And the Gotham plates were these big, black, funky plates. And the dessert service was a very beautiful Villeroy & Boch, very modern-looking cup and saucer that contrasted with the dessert plates from the same set. And it was all intended to be sort of joyous and very playful. It wasn't intended to be serious cuisine because I didn't know anything about that."

In addition to creating the menu and hiring a chef, Kafka took Kretchmer to the "it" restaurants of the moment, and introduced him to the chefs and restaurateurs, including Waxman and Master at Jams. "This is what it'll look like," she said, waving her arms at the Jams dining room, pointing to menu items. Rasped New Yorker Kretchmer: "It's too California for me."

There were stylistic missteps, such as those black plates, which became notorious. Says Danny Abrams, a waiter at Gotham in its first year: "I remember the black plates. There was a really big, pretty room. Maybe it was a little overwrought for the time. I just think that from my experience, it could have been a little bit simpler: the plating of the food, the types of china they used, the style of service.

I think it was trying to be actually what it is now, but they didn't have the personnel to carry it off, certainly not from the front of the house."

And yet, the restaurant was instantly successful, earning an unheard-of $60,000 in its first month. The Kretchmers took a ten-day trip to France that June, returning to discover the restaurant had descended into slapstick. "It was all about drugs," says Kretchmer. "Everybody was stoned: front of the house, the chefs. Everybody. The customers. I mean, [my wife] Dorothy and I, we used to go down and chase them out of the bathroom. They'd be doing lines." He also had to ask people to snuff out their joints in the dining room's smoking section. Complained one customer: "How can you taste the food if you're not stoned?"

Things were also loosey-goosey on the dining floor. After dropping a check, Abrams would turn from a table, pirouette à la Michael Jackson, and say "Beat it!" then moonwalk away.

"The front of the house, God, we were just doing crazy stuff every day," says Abrams. "Everything from running out during service to go make out with the coat-check girl at the Dumpster around the corner, to—I had this gig where if I got along with a customer, I would say, 'Are you a gambling man?' and if the guy said yes, I'd say, 'Okay. This is the deal. I'm going to flip you double or nothing for the tip.' One night I did it to Jerry's friend—who loved it, by the way—and Jerry walked over and he was like, 'Jerry, this kid's great. He just beat me for thirty-two bucks.' I think that was my last night at Gotham.

"The ages were very drug fueled," says Abrams. "In a weird sense it was a very pure time of doing drugs. You know how today it's all pharmaceuticals and pills? Then, there were three: People were drinking, snorting coke, and smoking dope. And that was it."

Abrams also recalls pyrotechnics in the kitchen: "Everybody knew to stay away from the kitchen. I think it was a very typical 1980s kitchen with a lot of yelling. That chef was a yeller and a screamer. There was a lot of profanity. You know, '*Give me that fucking dish right now! What are you doing?*' It probably wasn't very different than a lot of kitchens at that time, but compared to kitchens today where everything is politically correct and they're kind of quiet and everybody's respectful, this was not a respectful kitchen."

On the other hand, says Abrams, the food *was* treated with respect: "There was extensive education about the food in the beginning. They were very serious about it. I think [the chef] was very serious and I think Barbara Kafka was very serious. Barbara would come in a lot. And I think there was a big disconnect between the chef making the food and the person who conceived of the food. It seemed to me there was a clash of cultures there. There was a whole chicken served in a bowl on a bed of noodles, and they wanted to serve it medium rare, and it was *chicken*. So every time our customers would cut into it and they saw it was bloody, they would send it back. And I used to get into huge fights with [the chef]. And I'd go back and say, 'I need more fire on this chicken.' And he would say, 'Nothing is wrong with that chicken. Take it back to the table.' I would say, 'But it's bloody.' He's like, 'That's the way we're going to serve it.' And I said, 'But they don't want it.' And we'd have huge blowouts about this one dish. That's the only dish that I remember."

"I used to hang out on the floor at the Gotham when we first opened a lot. I was there almost every night," says Kretchmer. "I worked a lot of tables. I had a huge fight with Arthur Schwartz[*] on the floor over whether the chicken was cooked properly or not. And so I went downstairs and talked to them in the kitchen and the chef said that's the way Barbara told him to cook it. It was a little raw at the joints. And he was bat shit. And I went back upstairs and said, 'Listen. I don't know anything about this, but that's what she told

---

[*]   Restaurant critic for the New York *Daily News* at the time.

me.' And he then wrote the most scathing review and he attacked me on the radio, said I didn't belong in the business."

In a New York minute, the restaurant was struggling. The *New York Times* awarded it no stars, deeming it "satisfactory." Kretchmer fired the man charged with executing Kafka's menu "because . . . the food wasn't coming up and it was really a mess." Sous chef Brendan Walsh, a Bronx-born Culinary Institute of America graduate serving as a Gotham sous chef, had already given his notice, but agreed to stay on for two months to train a crew that could keep the kitchen afloat. (He would leave to *stage* in Auch, France, then head out to San Francisco and Jeremiah Tower's kitchen at Stars.)

Kretchmer and company made a deal to sell the restaurant to Michael Weinstein, a restaurateur who had begun his career with the Museum Café on the Upper West Side and was becoming known for big-box restaurants. But Waxman asked Kretchmer if he had the stomach to stay in the business a little longer, told him that he knew just the right guy for the job, a saucier at French chef Jacques Maximin's Tucano restaurant in Midtown: Chardack's boyfriend, Alfred Portale.

Portale was a stoic former jewelry designer from Buffalo, New York, who had discovered cooking when Chardack began showing him cookbooks such as *Larousse Gastronomique* and the works of Henri-Paul Pellaprat. When some of his design proofs were stolen at a trade show, he took it as an omen, decided to give cooking a chance. The young couple matriculated at The Culinary Institute of America together. The CIA was a party school, and Portale was older and more driven than many of his fellow students, which earned him the nickname "Mr. Perfect." It was not, he knew, a compliment.

After graduating the CIA, Portale and Chardack took jobs at Michel Guérard's prepared-food shop at Bloomingdale's, staying there a little more than a year. Guérard was often there, as were Michel Troisgros and other French notables. The shop became a stop on the circuit for an emerging group of foodies, such as George

Faison and Ariane Daguin, who were starting up their foie gras business, D'Artagnan. Portale says, "James Beard came in. Julia Child. Gael Greene. We used to get visitors up on that eighth-floor kitchen. And one time, I don't know who he was with, it might have been Troisgros's son, I'm not sure. The guy came in and talked to the chef for a few minutes and walked out. And he said, 'That guy in a few months is going to become the new reviewer for the *New York Times*.' It was Bryan Miller. Now, that meant nothing to me. I didn't live in New York, I didn't read the *New York Times*, and I wasn't into restaurants."

Portale and Chardack parlayed the gig into *stages* in France, starting with Troisgros. Before starting work, they leased a car and toured the great restaurants, spending six weeks in Paris alone. They kept a map on their apartment wall, tracking their progress with pushpins. They then spent six months working for Troisgros, and six months at Guérard. One day, in a bit of foreshadowing, Portale experimented with a salad during prep time, leaning the leaves against one another to create height; walking past, Guérard took note, and asked him in French if his father was an architect.

When Kretchmer met Portale, the chef was decked out in a mauve sweater and mauve corduroy slacks. "If you cook as good as you look, we'll be all right," said Kretchmer. Portale wrote some audition menus for the group, and Jeff Bliss visited Tucano to get a bead on the level of the food. A few weeks later, they offered Portale the job. He asked for $75,000. "I told him to go fuck himself," says Kretchmer. "Well, probably not those words, but I was really harsh about it because I thought it was a big demand from a guy who hadn't done anything yet. Then three weeks later I called him back and I said, 'Listen, I'm losing that much a week. You want to come, I'll give you seventy-five." The deal made, Kretchmer and company decided to roll the dice with Portale. It all happened so quickly that the closing with Weinstein was still calendared—the Gotham owners no-showed.

Portale assembled a kitchen team, including a sous chef named Tom Valenti, a young cook from Ithaca, New York, whom he'd met on a flight home from France when, by coincidence, they were both wrapping up their *stages.*

"When I came here it took me, I think, four or five weeks to change the menu, to put my menu in place. For those five weeks I never touched the other menu. I just ignored it. And then I completely cleaned up. There was this dish called messy linguini with crayfish. And it came out in this horrible green bowl. And the way they used to do it, it was just this tomato sauce with maybe some shellfish flavor, and spaghetti or linguini. And they would take live crayfish, steam them, and arrange them along the top of the bowl. I guess you were supposed to shell them at the table and eat the pasta. But in this particular case the guy didn't leave them in long enough so when they put the plate in front of the guest, the crayfish started twitching. This was just before I got here."

"It was very slow," says Valenti of Portale's early days at Gotham. "We would perfectly roast a duck breast, perfectly render the fat, perfectly let it rest, slice it, and fan it out perfectly, all the while doing fourteen covers. He had an application and an aesthetic that was so defined then that I thought to myself, *If this place ever gets busy, we're fucked.*"

Portale, who had been not only a jewelry designer but also a member of the Japanese Bonsai Society of Greater Buffalo, brought a distinct visual style to his dishes. A seafood salad based on an Italian American staple of his youth was piled pyramid-high; baguette croutons rose out of his tuna tartare like the Twin Towers; fish fillets were halved and stacked. It seemed like a gimmick, but Portale has always maintained that it was employed strictly out of practicality: "I wanted control of the dishes and I had an inexperienced crew. The factors that led to the whole presentation were trying to build consistency. The fact that I was trying to do food that I had done in France for one hundred guests with forty cooks, I was trying to do that with about twelve cooks, doing two hundred guests. So I figured out a way to prep and to cook or precook and reheat and cut out a lot of the human error so that things could be done fast. Rather than trying to cook a big piece of fish, I'd cut it into two thin pieces and then stack them. It was all a really deliberate way to control the consistency and the speed coming out of the kitchen."

"It was an illustration on the plate," says Valenti. "It was like the endive went at two o'clock, the salmon went at six, and the other thing went at ten. The volume drove a decision. Because we went from fourteen to forty to four hundred, we had to come up with something to make it consistent." (There was slight friction between Portale and Kretchmer, who, though he professes not to be a food authority, has absolute confidence in his street smarts, and that he knows what people like. He wanted Portale to keep a handful of populist dishes from the original menu, but Portale only agreed to a hamburger at lunch.)

Gotham Bar and Grill bridged the gap between the au courant chef-forward restaurants and the big-box restaurants, which weren't known for their chefs. Portale remembers Joe Baum and other industry giants visiting the restaurant. "They were astonished at the presentation of the food and how intricate it seemed relative to the size of the restaurant," says Portale. "They didn't know how I could do it. They would say, 'Are you doing it with mirrors?' Then we went up to three hundred covers. People just didn't understand it."

"Bear in mind, Alfred and I were in France at the same time," says Valenti. "It was just the way Rick Moonen and Charlie Palmer and Frank Crispo were friends; Michel Rostang, Guy Savoy, and Jean Troisgros were all friends. So there was an exchange of information. It wasn't so much the cooking technique or the ingredients;

it was the *application on the plate*. We braised endive in Paris and we gratinéed it. Alfred braised endive at the Gotham, sliced it lengthwise, and turned it into a fan. That was the difference."

The reviews came fast and furious. "Gael reviewed us first," says Portale. "It was a dual review: Montrachet, with David Bouley as chef, and me here. And that kicked up the numbers substantially. It went up to like one hundred sixty after Gael's review and then the *New York Times* just blew the doors off of this place." Miller did note in his review that he had been spotted, and he was right: Portale had been making twice-nightly patrols of the dining room, trying to recall what that visitor to the Bloomingdale's kitchen had looked like. "One day I was walking up to the dining room, and I looked up and I saw a man coming, being sat, and he looked down and I went, '*That's him!*' And sure enough, it was. Everybody looked at him, and—what is now commonplace—we looked for the phone numbers he had used to make his reservation. He came in six times. And one time he brought in Pierre Franey and Craig Claiborne. That was the last one. They were in for lunch. They ordered all this stuff."

The night the review came out, Portale and his partners engaged in a ritual followed by the entire industry at the time: They went to Times Square to get the paper when it was, literally, hot off the presses. And there it was: three stars.

"The Bryan review was a humongous milestone because it was eight months or so into my employment here," says Portale. "It really shocked New York, shocked the industry, and pissed off a lot of people as well because prior to us getting three stars, three stars were strictly reserved for a white tablecloth, tuxedoed waiter, fine-dining, expensive, pretentious, silver-plated experience. And we were pretty casual back then. I inherited the restaurant's black plates with yellow bread-and-butter plates and green bowls. The flatware was crap. The waiters wore sneakers, khakis, and pink Oxford shirts, no tie. It was very casual. And the whole air of the place was casual, just didn't fit the prior mold or formula for a three-star restaurant."

Before long, journalists had dubbed Portale's style "tall food." It helped make him famous, but quickly became an albatross; he felt it overshadowed the classical nature and quality of his growing repertoire, especially when chefs around town and around the country began imitating him. "When it got coined *tall food*, that's when it went national. I got calls from all over the country, sometimes two or three a week: 'I'm writing an article on tall food and everybody says you're the pioneer.' Over and over and over again. When it reached that point, that's when I backed off and said, 'I don't want to do it.' Articles would come out with guys mounting up mashed potatoes and piling carrots on top of that and sticking herb sprigs on the top of that, and I'm like, 'I don't want to be associated with this.' I did not embrace it on any level because I was always quite proud of saying that Gotham was not a trend. It had a sort of a timeless quality about it. And I basically keep the food current. There were a lot of trends in cooking: the minimalist, the deconstructive, the this, the that. And a lot of derivative food. So suddenly I was being connected to this silly trend. There were a lot of chefs who kind of looked down on that notion of tall food. That really bothered me. That's why I tried to distance myself from that."

Danny Meyer, who had just opened his Union Square Café four blocks north of Gotham on West 16th Street, lived above the restaurant: "The first thing I would do every single morning before coming to work would be to study the cartons of empty wine bottles that had been poured the night before to see what they had sold. And inevitably their average wine sales were at least forty percent higher than ours." He took it as a symbol of the difference in character between his very California restaurant and the Gotham. "Union Square Café was like your favorite old sweater. Gotham was like your nicest dinner jacket."

Bill Telepan, a young cook from Sayreville, New Jersey, who came to work for Portale in 1987, hadn't heard of the restaurant when he took the job, but when Portale told him Charlie Palmer had forwarded his résumé, it was all Telepan needed to hear. Benchmark restaurants were so scarce that Telepan was working at a generic eatery at the South Street Seaport when he was tapped for Gotham: "It wasn't until I started working in Gotham that I saw what was going on," says Telepan. "The energy. Just talking to the cooks and where they worked and who they worked for and how important it was. Until I started working at Gotham I didn't feel the excitement, the energy. They became important, the top, top chefs. And there were only about ten of them when I was working at the time." Telepan was also struck that the media was beginning to cover not just the food, but the chefs as lifestyle icons: "They were being written about, not just for their cooking, but people gave a shit what shoes they wore."

Telepan was struck by the emerging American creativity represented at Gotham, especially a dish of rare tuna with pappardelle, tapenade, and summer savory. "Raw tuna," says Telepan. "It was probably well known at the time but I was a kid from Jersey, went to the CIA, and all of a sudden at this three-star restaurant in New York that's banging out three hundred covers and the tuna is *raw*. It wasn't even like cooking. You just seared it real quick. It's this hodgepodge: The sauce was French. The tapenade and the pasta were Italian. It was raw tuna, and I had never seen a fish. To myself, I was like, *What the fuck?* And then I'm eating it and saying, like, 'Oh, this is so delicious,' and saying, 'How the fuck did he think of this?'"

Telepan could also feel the excitement of the restaurant, which he says was "the heart of New York cooking at that time. It was busy and it was so intense. After a couple days I felt like everybody was watching what Alfred was doing because of the reviews. We could feel that in the kitchen. And just talking to the guys. Talking to the cooks. It was all Americans at the time, and these guys all worked at great places and they all wanted to be chefs, and it was amazing."

"I COULD FEEL IT LIFTING OFF."

In June 1985, the Stanford Court Gang reunited, with other chefs, for a blowout Citymeals on Wheels benefit at Rockefeller Center. The fund-raiser—which has been held annually for more than thirty years—featured tasting stations where each chef offered a scaled-down portion of food. For those who worked under the Gang, it was a chance to glimpse the larger world beyond their home city, sparking their own version of the epiphanies that had happened at the Stanford Court.

Stephanie Lyness, one of Jonathan Waxman's chefs at Jams and his second restaurant, Bud's, in New York City, saw the group as a sign of the larger sea change across the country: "The point at which I began to feel that something was going on was at that first Citymeals on Wheels thing in Rockefeller Center in 1985. There it was really clear. It may have been the first sort of big thing like that that I had done. A roaming tasting benefit. There we are, we're in Rockefeller Center, where you're in the center of this New York world that is really cool. We had done all our prep. We were probably making Jonathan's red pepper pancakes with caviar and crème fraîche. So we'd probably done all the prep and brought it over. But then backstage there were all these chefs doing prep work at their stove. It's like visiting the New York neighborhoods, you could just go from one person to the next. You'd pretty much met everybody by that point, and you'd say hi. [Chez Panisse chef] Paul Bertolli was there. Larry would have been there. Alice would have been there with Paul. Jeremiah was there. Probably all those guys were there. Wolfgang was there. You did have the sense of being in this group of people. I was Jonathan's chef. So I was in there by virtue of his relationships. So you had the sense of being included. It was like a family. It was this family you were being included into and it was a cool family. And the food was good. And people were excited. People were having fun. . . . I felt like I was in the middle of something that was big," says Lyness. "I didn't have the sense of where is this going. But this is *big*. It was happening *now*. And it was important. Not important like a treaty to end a world war or anything, but it was lifting off. It was lifting off. I could feel it lifting off."*

After the party, the Stanford Court Gang decided they needed a break.

"The first year, the day after the event we loaded up into a bus and I rented basically this country inn in the Hamptons and we all went out there," says Forgione. "This was Wolfgang and Barbara. Jeremiah, Jonathan, Alice, Jimmy, Bradley, Jonathan, Melvyn, myself, Mark Miller. Basically the crew from the AIWF."

"We were in the bus and we were trying to get out to the Hamptons," remembers Schmidt. "We were running late. And this garbage truck was blocking traffic in front of the bus. And they were like, nothing is going to happen quick. And Barbara goes, 'Open the door to the bus.' And she walked up there, gave them a couple little pointed fingers or something like that. I couldn't hear her. And everybody was going, 'Are they going to kill her first and throw her in the dump truck, or are they going to throw her in the dump truck, and then

---

* August 1985 also brought a seminal *Time* magazine article, written by Mimi Sheraton, who had recently departed the *New York Times*. The piece, titled "Eat American!," which Sheraton first delivered in 1984 and periodically revised over the ensuing year, describes the moment. It demonstrates how much oxygen the Stanford Court Gang took up, naming and quoting many of them. Perhaps most helpfully, Sheraton, a New Yorker, cut through the California cuisine/New American Cuisine dilemma, essentially erasing the line between them: "Also designated as Californian because so many of its highly visible practitioners are on the West Coast, this new cooking is an intellectualized, even esoteric style, characterized by the use of fresh, native products and seemingly disparate ethnic influences in a single dish. In addition to local produce, some of the trademark foods are goat cheese, blue cornmeal, wild mushrooms, and game." Problem solved! She also gave a nod to American wines and the strong Southwestern influence that was spreading across the country.

kill her?' And the garbage truck *moved*, went off into traffic. And we asked how she did it. And she goes, 'I'll never tell my secrets.'"

In a sign of their burgeoning celebrity, when the all-star crew made it to Long Island, says Schmidt, "The people at the inn said, 'You guys can have the kitchen. We're not cooking for you.' And everybody brought out things that were left over from the event. . . . Let's say including spouses and things, there were maybe twenty people going out for this day in the country, or two days in the country. I think we started with twenty cases of wine, and I would guess that we were out of wine by dinner."

As for the food: "Wolf brought foie gras that he had left over," remembers Forgione. "I brought out buffalo that I had left over. It was a great setup. There was a big wood-fired grill. And it was just drinking wine and putting slabs of foie gras that were two inches thick on a grill, and somebody else grilling bread and making little foie gras sandwiches. It just went on and on."

As ever, the stark contrast in personalities was evident, as in Forgione's enduring memory of Tower: "I thought of him as the so-phisticated English gentleman. Here's Jeremiah dressed to the tee, everything perfect. He's on a bicycle with one of those little bells that you have to pull with your thumb. And he's riding down the street going into town with one hand on the handlebar and the other hand up in the air holding a flute of Champagne, ringing his little bell as he goes through town."

(If there was a criticism that could be leveled at the group, it was that it was tight, and felt exclusive to other chefs. "I always felt that there was a small sort of powerful group that was hard to penetrate, hard to get asked in," says Portale, who was indoctrinated into the Citymeals event in its second year. Says Forgione, "I think it was a combination of the people we knew, the people we knew that could execute something like this, people that we knew that would have fun doing it. And yeah, we were all friends. So did it seem cliquey? Absolutely.")

Just like that, the chefs were participating in charity events around the country, which doubled as networking occasions. "As soon as I did the New York event and met all those guys, I was invited by Wolfgang first to go out and do something with the Cleveland Clinic, some big charity event that he started with the same cast of characters," says Portale. "Then the following year, I got asked to go to Los Angeles, where he does the wine and food festival."

"Somebody got the harebrained idea that 'Oh, we're going to get all these chefs together in a big room and make them raise money for something,'" says Valenti. "That helped accelerate the bonding because Larry and Jonathan and Alfred and Wolfgang would be together doing that and then Lee Hefter, who is for all intents and purposes Wolfgang's partner at Spago, would show up and he'd say, 'Well, make sure when you're in L.A., you look me up.'"

"It wasn't a competitive environment," remembers Steve Vranian, who cooked for Tower back in California and was a frequent aide-de-camp on the road. "I think now it might be a lot more competitive amongst chefs, but back then it was just a bunch of cowboys going out to get drunk."

The day after the first Citymeals event, as night descended on the Hamptons, Puck, Miller, and a few other chefs biked down to the beach to watch the sunset, forgetting for a moment that they weren't in California anymore, and that they were looking east, not west, over the wrong ocean. But darkness came all the same.

"THEY OPENED IT WITHOUT A FLOOR."

Waxman and Master evolved according to the Puck-Lazaroff model, branching off into new concepts. First up was a Southwestern follow-up to Jams. They landed a space on the far side of Central

Park, at Columbus Avenue and 77th Street, naming it Bud's, after their mutual term of endearment.

The Southwestern focus was a sign of the times, of the blurring of lines from coast to coast, and of the prominence attaching to Waxman and his peers. Freshly minted chefs in other regions were beginning to take their cue from the Stanford Court Gang and their contemporaries, none more so than a small cadre of chefs operating in the Southwestern mode. Two of the earliest pioneers, ironically, flowered in California: Mark Miller, still at Berkeley's Fourth Street Grill, and John Sedlar, who had worked for Bertranou and others in Los Angeles. In 1981, Sedlar, financed by loans from family and friends, had opened Saint Estèphe—a nouvelle cuisine restaurant in Manhattan Village, a shopping development in Manhattan Beach. (The loans barely got him to the finish line; with no money for a sign, he wrote one on cardboard, rested it on a chair outside the front door.) Sedlar, reared on a steady diet of Hispanic food in Santa Fe, New Mexico, had grown up ashamed of his ancestral cuisine; if walking down the street with, say, a burrito, his mom, a Latina, would caution him to conceal it. Saint Estèphe, which debuted with a French menu, was failing; as a Hail Mary, Sedlar began applying the technique and plating he'd learned from Bertranou to ingredients and recipes from his childhood: "I realized the food had a lot of value, so I started shipping chiles to Los Angeles and I started shipping blue cornmeal and blue corn tortillas and I started what was a fusion of Southwestern food and French haute cuisine. We'd serve caviar and lobster and smoked salmon on little small blue corn tortillas with crème fraîche and Bermuda onion, and we would do salmon mousse tamales with a little bit of masa."

Word of these developments reached Texas, driving some homegrown toques to mine their native cuisine after the fashion of Miller, Sedlar, and—closer to home—Prudhomme. Dean Fearing forged a fancified Southwestern style at Agnew's, then at The Verandah Club at the Loews Anatole Hotel in Dallas. When he became chef of the Mansion on Turtle Creek in 1985, he went all in. Stephan Pyles, a musician turned chef, had picked up his trade at his family's truck stop, and began evolving to a higher style at Dallas's Routh Street Café, shoring up his efforts with *stages* in France. Robert Del Grande, trained as a biochemist, followed a similar MO at Houston's Café Annie. This community followed a staggered, slightly altered version of the path forged by their predecessors in New York, California, and Louisiana: They revered food writers, only instead of the French explorations of Olney and David they obsessed over Diana Kennedy's Mexican cookbooks and the writings of Patricia Quintana. And in place of Michael McCarty, they had Anne Lindsay Greer, who was consulting to the Loews Anatole Hotel in the early 1980s, and named the emerging style "Southwestern." (She also arranged for guest chefs such as Forgione, Ogden, and Puck to visit the hotel to cook wine dinners, giving the Texas chefs a prized chance to meet them.) In August 1984, Greer organized a gathering to bring this emerging group together. Known today as the "Pot Luck," they gathered together, each showing off their own dishes, talking over ingredients, techniques, and inspirations. Greer understood the value of press and invited Michael Bauer, then editor of the gourmet section of the *Dallas Times Herald*, who was the first to write about the movement, comparing it to the California school. In 1984 and '85, the *Great Chefs* television series aired a twenty-six-part arc called *Great Chefs of the West*. In April 1986, many of the chefs began cooking for the Hill Country Festival in Austin, and were being welcomed into the national fold at Puck and Lazaroff's Meals on Wheels benefit in Los Angeles and the Citymeals on Wheels summer fund-raiser in New York City. Miller would open his own seminal Southwestern restaurant, Coyote Café, in Santa Fe, New Mexico, in 1987, following it, in 1991, with Red Sage in Washington, D.C.

Another sign of increased cross-pollination: Back in New York City, with Bud's slated for a September opening, Master and

Waxman—who'd brought California cuisine to town—struck a deal for Paul Prudhomme to make the space his home for the summer, importing his K-Paul road show and New Orleans food to New York, as he'd done two years prior in San Francisco. (*Pop-up* wasn't yet in the vernacular; the participants referred to the residency as an "instant restaurant.") Prudhomme kicked off the five-week stint with a party, then—because a city official who had attended the opening observed exposed wires, flies, improper meat storage and oven ventilation, and no operating permit—the health department ordered a shutdown. Waxman claimed to the *New York Times* that his team had reached out to the mayor's office. "We'll see who's more powerful," said an increasingly cocky Waxman. "The Mayor or his Health Commissioner." With notices posted on the door, two hundred fifty people queued up along Columbus Avenue—drinking beer and wine in anticipation of blackened redfish, Cajun jambalaya, shrimp remoulade, sweet potato–pecan pie, and bread pudding.

The city official who ratted out Waxman and Master also observed "unfinished floors" at Bud's. One former waiter remembers those floors, considered them a sign of burgeoning hubris: "They opened it without a floor, just cement. It was kind of an important time where I think they thought they could do anything, Melvyn and Jonathan; they thought their shit was just gold. Every day we'd go into work, we'd have to move the tiles that hadn't been set to a different area and then bring it back in so the tile setters could set it the next day."

Regardless, Bud's scored, earning a two-star review in the *New York Times*. Bryan Miller contrasted the "simplicity and freshness" with the Upper West Side's "quiche belt," commenting that "it's no wonder the locals are rushing to Bud's like surfers to 10-foot swells."

One of the cooks in the kitchen at Bud's was a young, carrot-topped Bobby Flay, a self-described "knockaround" kid and corner boy from the Upper East Side who had dropped out of high school, discovered the kitchen around 1981 when his father got him a job at the Theater District mainstay Joe Allen. Flay had always been attracted to cooking—early memories focus on the alchemy of the kitchen: making deviled eggs, or stirring My-T-Fine pudding mix until it thickened. Flay wasn't attuned to the uptick in American cuisine, didn't read the *Times* or *New York* magazine, wasn't privy to the revolution, hadn't heard of Forgione or Wine or the Waltucks, let alone anything happening out West. But six months into his time at Joe Allen, he woke up one morning, stared up at the ceiling, and thought to himself, *I cannot wait to go to work today.* "I'd never felt that before."

Flay's first inkling of the possibilities of the profession came when managers returned from Joe Allen's Los Angeles outpost, with menus from Spago in hand. "To me, Wolfgang had it all: He was a great chef, and he had the environment: He had Hollywood. What do they do in Hollywood? They make people stars. That was the first time I had heard of somebody being known for their cooking in this other way, in this *star* way. That might sound trivial at this point, but we really didn't know the name of the chefs in the restaurants. That was the first time I became aware of it."

In 1984, Joe Allen himself ponied up the $6,800 tuition for Flay to attend a new culinary school based in New York City, the French Culinary Institute (see footnote, page 216). Flay was one of nine inaugural students at the SoHo-based school, still under construction when he started. He was the youngest by five or six years, and one of the few people that wasn't on a second career or recovering from divorce. The AIDS epidemic was in full force and claimed about a third of his class within a few years, along with many of his coworkers from Joe Allen. "People would get a cough and be in the hospital, be dead in six weeks," he remembers.

After the six-month program, Flay took a job as sous chef at Brighton Grill, a new Upper East Side restaurant by a first-time restaurateur, socialite Stephanie Guest. The chef, says Flay, had a multitude of issues: "He would sleep on the dirty laundry in the restaurant all night. He liked tequila and a lot of it. That lasted a week. I was standing there [so was promoted to chef]. I just used my ability from hanging out in the streets to fucking get it done. But I was completely overwhelmed, insecure. I wouldn't hire people who were too good, or better than me, because I'd be exposed. I was insane. I'd go to the Fulton Fish Market every morning. I got the restaurant under control and we had good business, but after a year I could not stand up. I said, 'I cannot do this anymore.'"

The next job he landed was at Bud's. "I walked into this kitchen, I didn't know this world existed," says Flay. "If there were ten cooks there, everybody was Michael Jordan. One person after another was a fucking amazing cook. Jonathan wasn't in the kitchen a lot, so we all sort of learned from each other." Flay lacked expertise, but was faster than anybody, made himself invaluable by helping the kitchen keep pace with the never-ending rush of orders.

"*Fire up the grill* wasn't turning some buttons; we had mesquite wood. We made beurre blancs in every color of the rainbow—blood orange, chive. It was butter and cream sauces and vinaigrettes that were sauces as well. Lots of relishes and sauces, because it was a Southwestern restaurant. I remember watching this girl taking corn off the cob and thinking, *That's how it's done.*"

Flay was taken with the Southwestern palate of the restaurant, and on several levels: He found it shrewd because it dovetailed with the American love for "bastardized" Mexican food and the attendant tequila—a surefire revenue generator—at its apex in 1980s New York City. And he found the ingredients exotic: "Blue corn didn't come as a tortilla chip in a bag, we had blue *cornmeal.* We had all these fresh and dried chiles, all these different beans. These things had never come to the East Coast in this form before. *Never.*"

As Massachusetts native Mark Miller had before him, Flay—who would found his career on the style—gravitated to Southwestern flavors, even though he came from the East Coast: "When I think about it, those flavors meld very well with my personality.

My first cookbook was *Bold American Food*. It meant not only the ingredients but also an approach. Those ingredients at that point in my life made perfect sense for me. I needed ingredients with attitude. I was seduced by the idea, went from Brighton Grill, a neighborhood restaurant, just feeding people, to this other world I didn't know existed."

Like so many fellow cooks at the time, Flay was fully immersed in food. Waxman and Master opened a third restaurant, Hulot's, in summer 1986, and Flay and other cooks—many of whom bounced around among the growing empire's restaurants—would go in on Sunday, when it was closed, and work on slow-cooking preparations.

Most intoxicatingly, the burgeoning American chef society was literally paraded in front of Flay at Bud's: "Our kitchen was open, you'd go downstairs, off the dining room, like three or four steps—you had to go through there to get to the bathroom. So I'd be cooking and all of a sudden Mark Miller would be eating my *mise en place*, or Wolfgang Puck would come in. During the Citymeals on Wheels week they were all here. Dean Fearing and Stephan Pyles, and Alice Waters. I was like, *What the fuck is going on here? This is like Disney World*. Now I know who they are. I'm paying attention to food. I'm like, *These are the American gods of food and they're eating my corn relish off my* mise en place. And that's the power of Jonathan; he's part of this situation."

The Southwestern presence, and the California influx, in New York City deepened at the hands of Clark Wolf, who had found his way to Manhattan and was functioning as a consultant to Sign of the Dove owner Joseph Santo. Wolf recruited Brendan Walsh back from San Francisco. He also enlisted Judy Rodgers—a Chez Panisse alumna who would go on to take over the kitchen at San Francisco's Zuni Café and turn it into a classic—as consulting chef at Yellow Fingers in the same building. Walsh says he picked up "a little bit of that anti-structure, the change in the French model of the kitchen" from San Francisco. "When I come back to do Arizona 206, everybody's involved in the menu, collaborative. I had fifty percent women, fifty percent men. Because of that environment, I think that's why the food was so much fun."

New York City had become a magnet, and not just for Americans. Brother and sister Gilbert and Maguy Le Coze imported their fashionable, cutting-edge fish temple Le Bernardin from Paris, opening on West 51st Street in 1986. That same year, Jean-Georges Vongerichten, an alum of the kitchens of Paul Haeberlin, Bocuse, and Outhier, came to Lafayette in Swissôtel The Drake, bringing with him a distinct marriage of French finesse and Asian influence picked up in stints in Thailand, Singapore, and Hong Kong. Though French, these chefs were definitely of a new guard, both on the plate and in their attitude toward Americans; years later, Vongerichten would enshrine Barry Wine's pizza on his menu at Mercer Kitchen.

"THE GENERAL PUBLIC WAS BECOMING INTERESTED."

These years saw an uptick in media coverage and business opportunities for chefs in the United States. Profiles and lifestyle features proliferated in local and national newspapers and magazines, and more powerfully on television, where the ability to perform a cooking demonstration choreographed for studio cameras and timed to meet a producer's specs became a requirement for any self-respecting chef, many of whom began enlisting media trainers; an early and prestigious television series was PBS's *Great Chefs*, which debuted in 1982, and focused on the chefs of particular cities, countries, and regions.

"There was a confluence of two circumstances," says David Kratz, who launched a successful chef and restaurant public relations firm in New York City starting in the mid-1980s, when such a specialization was novel, and signed the Gotham Bar and Grill as a client immediately after Portale was hired to be the chef. "One was this American cuisine explosion; the other was a media explosion. It was right at the time when cable TV was just coming online. There weren't thousands of channels. That was a big wave. All of a sudden there became a need for people who were really professional at understanding media outlets and the difference between them and what they would be interested in and how to navigate them and how to talk to different ones. . . . Chefs started to become interesting in other ways because these guys were young and attractive and well spoken and standard bearers for a new type of style. New Yorkers had started generally to become proud of the fact that there were these good restaurants. They were New York restaurants and they were American. New York had always had famous old restaurants, but even then you probably wouldn't have known who the chefs were particularly. They were just famous as these fancy restaurants. Other types of media also started to become interested because culturally it was shifting and the general public was becoming interested."

In another shift, the industry began giving itself awards, staging events that combined the pomp and grandeur of the Stanford Court dinner and charity tasting events with the aggrandizement of the *Food & Wine* Honor Roll of American Chefs and the *Great Chefs* television series. In 1984, *Cook's Magazine* introduced its "Who's Who in American Cooking," which became an annual happening in New York City.

"Hollywood has its Oscars. The television profession gives Emmys. Now the food world in this country has begun to honor its producers, chefs, vintners, writers and restaurateurs," wrote Margaret Engel in the *Washington Post* in 1985.

"Last year everyone was talking about new American cooking," said *Cook's Magazine*'s Christopher Kimball on the occasion of the second annual awards, held at the cavernous Palladium nightclub in downtown Manhattan. "Now the awareness has grown that it's not just a trend and people simply refer to it as American cooking. . . . It's taken this country a long time to recognize its roots, but now that it has, the cuisine is flourishing."

The second annual Who's Who awards were held in October 1985. James Beard had died earlier that year and the James Beard Award for Special Achievement was introduced; it went to Alice Waters. The awards spoke to the still-relative paucity of noteworthy chefs around the country as the number of honorees was reduced from fifty in 1984 to twenty-five.

That same year, Harper & Row published Ellen Brown's book *Cooking with the New American Chefs*, the latest attempt to corral and chronicle the emerging chef community from across the country. Brown's book includes non-Americans like Wolfgang Puck and the legendary Jean-Louis Palladin, a native of Condom, in France's Gascony region, who had come from two-Michelin-star success in France to open Jean-Louis at the Watergate in Washington, D.C., in 1979, and became a heroic figure to many East Coast chefs for his larger-than-life personality, mad natural talent, willingness to hire Americans, and tireless efforts to help establish a network of sources by deepening the relationship between chefs and farmers and purveyors. He also embraced traditionally American ingredients like corn and crawfish and eschewed the term *nouvelle cuisine* in favor of the more approachable *free cooking*.

"For me, he was one of the most inspiring chefs that I felt played a role at the time that he worked here in America," says Thomas Keller, who made regular pilgrimages to Jean-Louis at the Watergate to see what the genius chef was up to. "He was super dynamic. Here was a guy who would change his menu every day. He'd have four different menus every day. So I look back on what I was doing, and he truly inspired what I was doing. There was repetition in the menu, but still, it was four different menus every day, four different prices. He would handwrite it. It was all about the product coming in. Where was the product coming from? That drove his menu. And they were changing it right up to the moment service started. It was extraordinarily presented in a refined atmosphere with great service, great wine. This was everything I wanted to do. And so for me he was truly inspiring. You look around and I think a lot of people would point back to Jean-Louis as one of those first individuals who really changed the way we cook, the way we think about cooking in a holistic way."

"He was like a rock star," says Traci Des Jardins, who cooked for Palladin. "He was like Mick Jagger. He was skinny, wiry—but so intense. I can remember him coming over and tasting stuff I was making and looking at my station and talking to me and talking to Joachim [Splichal] about me. He was like this curious force, like this animal in the kitchen. And you could just tell he was taking in all of it. He was looking at every cook. And he always remembered what each person was about and what they did well—that guy made sauces, and she was the fish cook. He never forgot. He was a force."

"He really to me should be considered an American chef," says Jasper White. "Jean-Louis was a magician. He was the chef of chefs in the U.S. Forget about the cerebral part of cooking. Let's just talk about skill. Jean-Louis, if he did a tasting menu for you, he could cook as long as you could stand it, he could just keep putting stuff out. But not only would he do a course, but if there were four of us at a table, and let's say the combination was shrimp and corn, he didn't do one dish with shrimp and corn and all four got it; he did four dishes so you'd have a tasting menu where every course had four different dishes on it. It was freaking mind-boggling but he could accomplish it. And I know it was a flow of creative genius because he didn't sit around and read books and stuff. He was out partying all the time, smoking and drinking. He was a lot of fun to be around. I think a lot of chefs would agree, anyone who really knew him would say that he was the chef of chefs in America. It was too much too fast for an ordinary human; I don't know how he did it. It was an endless flow of, like, every chef that ever lived funneled into this energy. He was brilliant."

The book was also noteworthy for its geographic breadth, including chefs such as Amy Ferguson from Houston, Texas; Robert Rosellini from Seattle, Washington; and Richard Perry from St. Louis, Michigan.

"THERE WERE TWO PEOPLE STANDING WHERE I USED TO WORK."

For all the focus on new American food, these were also productive years for American chefs operating in the French tradition. In 1985, Drew Nieporent, a 1977 graduate of Cornell University's School of Hotel Administration who had worked on cruise ships and at such New York hotspots as Maxwell's Plum and Tavern on the Green, opened Montrachet, installing chef David Bouley in the kitchen. Nieporent had discovered Bouley across the country, at lunch at Sutter 500, the gig to which Vergé had dispatched him from Le Cirque. Bouley cooked Nieporent a tasting menu, which the restaurateur still recalls as one of the best he'd ever eaten. He raised the money to open Montrachet—named for a Burgundy wine-growing region—on the edge of Tribeca, which wasn't much more developed than it was when Odeon opened years earlier. He hadn't realized it in San Francisco, but as he saw the chef's food up close on a daily basis, he realized that "Bouley was literally pinching, like, the lobster salad or there was a Girardet dish. Basically David took a dish from Troisgros, Girardet, Vergé. But I think in David's head he was elevating the dish because he's that skilled. So he didn't see it as *taking* the dish."

Nieporent dressed like a waiter on the service floor, wearing the standard-issue Montrachet uniform. Remembers Daniel Rothstein, who had previously worked with the Waltucks at Chanterelle and helped Nieporent manage the front of house at Montrachet: "We all dressed in a uniform. It was silly. It was all black with a silver tie. Drew dressed just like that. Because he worked. He was a waiter. I mean, he was the maître d', but he didn't want to distinguish himself. He liked that, and he also felt he could be sort of undercover, too, sometimes, so people didn't know him. He was on the floor. He would bring out dishes. He had no problems with that. He had no attitude. That guy was working. He was working the floor. He was dressed like everyone else."

Before long, Nieporent and Bouley were at odds, in part because Bouley—who brings an artistic temperament and manner to the kitchen—took his sweet time, keeping people waiting inordinate lengths of time for their courses, a bad fit with Nieporent's tendency to overbook.

"I don't know if they were ever friendly," says Rothstein. "I certainly didn't feel that from Bouley. He just looked down on Drew. And Drew has a big ego. . . . One of the things I was impressed by with Drew: Drew sucked up to the important people. He knew them by name, gave them the best table. All over them. But if you pushed him far enough, there were customers, if they pissed him off, I saw him throw people on the street twice. Drew overbooked. It was the hottest restaurant. He was going to take advantage of it. He was going to make money. So people were waiting at the bar for a long time. They'd made the reservation a month in advance or two months in advance. Sometimes people would get really angry. Someone got really angry at him and he just went off on him. He'd say, 'This is my restaurant. I'm the owner. You can't talk to me that way. I'm not serving you. Get out of here.'

"He was very ambitious," remembers Rothstein. "He would say, 'I'm going to be the next Joe Baum.' He knew everybody. I mean, just the way he remembered your name. I couldn't believe it. Some vice vice president of CBS would walk in the door. Maybe he'd met the guy, but he knew who it was. He must have studied the papers. He understood that with these important clientele and the rich, powerful people in New York, you know them by name and you greet them. He was amazing that way."

Nieporent also took no chances where critics were concerned. "The different owners would call each other and they would try to get descriptions," says Rothstein. "No one had a really good pic. If he thought there was a reviewer, he might call someone who had seen them to come over and take a look in the dining room. I think what Drew did, which Karen and David [Waltuck] wouldn't, if it was a reviewer, he would stop the kitchen. I mean, every restaurateur wants to make a perfect thing. But Karen and David would be sort of like, 'Whatever.' They wanted it to be good, but no one else was going to suffer for it. [At Montrachet,] other people would probably have to wait longer."

Kerry Heffernan, who had cooked with Bouley at Le Périgord Park, returned from a *stage* in Europe circa February 1986 and joined his old chef in the kitchen at Montrachet.

"I was garde-manger," says Heffernan. "And garde-manger there, it sucked, because it was a tiny little space. And you had to make an eggplant terrine every day, which meant slicing and frying a case of baby eggplant, making a pesto, making a red pepper coulis, baking off a custard in a terrine mold, you know, the bottom of the terrine mold with two half moons of goat cheese into it, and then layering this eggplant, pepper, pesto, probably fifteen layers, and then the pepper coulis had a little gelatin in it so it would hold together. And then you had to get it set and then slice it and then lay it on a plate and then warm it and serve it with a parsley sauce. It was still a wonderful dish. It was a beautiful dish.

"In those days I wasn't quite aware of what was happening in the dining room. It was a bit of a mystery. We went in early, we busted our ass, we got out late, we drank Pabst Blue Ribbon. It was intense, but it was fun. There was a camaraderie."

The restaurant earned three stars from the *New York Times*, but like more and more chefs in New York, Bouley had designs on opening his own restaurant and was making moves in his free time. The situation led to Nieporent making his own moves, worthy of Michael Corleone.

"Bouley was taking calls," says Rothstein. "The phone was on the bar. He would be in the dining room. He was on the phone all the time at the end. And Drew was pretty sure he was talking to this investor, which turned out to be true. He would invite him; the guy would come in for dinner. So Drew started to feel like Bouley was just flaunting it. And that he was going to leave. It was pretty bad. I mean, I understand Bouley, you know, Drew was extreme that way. But they just broke down. They just were not a good pair. And I think Drew felt [Bouley] was going to leave and he wanted to be preemptive. That was pretty bold of Drew. I was impressed that he was confident enough to [do that, with three stars on the line]. And he kept those three stars.

"This is the thing," says Rothstein. "He loved the restaurant but he was a businessman. And he is a businessman. He knows how to make money in a restaurant, which is not an easy thing to do. Basically that's the story of the conflict between him and David Bouley. David Bouley was an artist and didn't care at all about money, and Drew watched every penny."

With plans to fire Bouley, Nieporent began training a phantom crew, because he knew that the cooks would follow the chef out of loyalty.

"I didn't understand how to do it," says Nieporent. "So I basically trained an entire kitchen at a friend of mine's kitchen. I had a chef and four cooks. His name was Brian Whitmer. He had been sous chef to Bradley Ogden. I couldn't hire another chef to replace a chef. I had to hire a friend."

Recalls Heffernan: "Memorial Day rolls around and Drew says, 'You guys are going to get two days off. You're going to get Sunday off, you're going to get Monday, too. But take your knives and your shoes and all your stuff out of your lockers because we're going to exterminate and that stuff gets everywhere.'"

When Bouley showed up after the weekend, Nieporent had packed all of his belongings into a van. "Here are the keys to the van. All your stuff's in there," he said. Bouley, says Nieporent, was incredulous: "So he comes down to the restaurant and he walks in, he sees that whole crew was cooking . . . and what was interesting is I knew we'd make it because the next day, we always had one-hundred-plus covers on the book. And one of my very best customers, I see they're walking towards the kitchen because a lot of people would walk into the kitchen if they knew David. And I stopped them. 'Oh, we want to thank David. Tonight was the best meal we ever had here.' It was the first day of the new chef. I went, 'Oh, it's his birthday. I gave him the day off.' Which I didn't realize it but it had been his birthday the day prior."*

"So we come back on the Tuesday and the only person he had fired, to my knowledge, was David," remembers Heffernan. "Everyone else was still employed but there were two people standing where I used to work."

"And what he did with the next [chef]," says Rothstein. "It was basically Drew. Brian Whitmer was the next guy. . . . He was a nice guy. It was completely different. Drew was basically executive chef and was saying, 'This is what I want.' They worked on the menu together. Brian would do it. Brian had his own ideas, too, but Drew was very controlling. You know, he sort of wasn't going to let that happen. And amazingly, they were able to keep three stars there for a while."

A young Thomas Keller, who had worked at various Midtown French restaurants and at La Rive in the Catskills, took his first stab at opening his own place in December 1986, partnering with Serge Raoul, owner of the popular SoHo bistro Raoul's.

---

* Bouley has never discussed the breakup on the record, and declined to with me.

Rakel (the name was a mashup of Raoul and Keller) was a bit of a mutt, representing Keller's and Raoul's sensibilities: Keller, a dead-serious perfectionist, had a piano kitchen,* insisted on absolute cleanliness at all times. Meanwhile, the artistic Raoul positioned a camera on Varick Street, featured a closed-circuit television in the dining room, projecting the traffic outside. He enlisted Tom Colicchio as sous chef. (Heffernan, who had become friendly with Colicchio during a *stage* in Auch, used to meet up with him after service, to "talk about our crazy bosses.")

"WE FUCKED IT UP."

The devastating "Black Monday" stock market crash of October 19, 1987, rippled through the industry. Some restaurants closed. Others reconsidered their formality and pricing. The party line is that the economy claimed the Waxman-Master empire, but Master was already feeling it slip through their fingers months earlier. Tensions among him, Jonathan, and Janie—exacerbated by Melvyn and Janie separating—grew, and the three were quickly becoming overextended, including a Jams in London.

"It was an accident waiting to happen," says Master. "I don't know what we were thinking."

By July 1987, just three years after Jams launched in New York City, the party was breaking up: Master told Colman Andrews of the *Los Angeles Times* that "all our restaurants have really been more in Jonathan's character than mine" and that he longed to open a restaurant in the vein of Washington Square Bar and Grill and Stars in San Francisco. Sagebrush Canyon, with a Western theme, was still

---

* A configuration in which cooks work around a central stove rather than in a line.

going forward in SoHo, with the Jams team as investors only, while a plan for an L.A. branch of Hulot's was scuttled.

By 1988, Bud's had been closed, Jams London was sold off. Waxman renamed Jams J.W.'s.

Karen Rush, who waited tables at J.W.'s, remembers witnessing the decline of the restaurant: "Orders start coming in COD; there's your first clue. You know, the wine isn't really being restocked. There's some shrinkage going on. And then the announcement that we'll be closing for a week or two to do some renovations."

About a week into the renovation, Waxman called Rush: "I have some good news and some bad news."

"What's the bad news?"

"We're closed."

"All right, Jonathan. What's the good news?"

"You don't have to work for me anymore."

"We fucked it up," says Master. "I mean, Jams London was ridiculous, trying to do that. We had all these uniforms from Alexander Julian, the designer, that were shipped over. Jonathan wanted to have all those over there. They were all the wrong size when they arrived. It was a clusterfuck."

"It happened quickly and unraveled quickly," says Flay. "Part of the problem was that Jonathan didn't have any backup. You need backup. I think Melvyn was incredibly charismatic, a good front man. But underneath being the front man you also need a foundation. Jonathan was by himself. It didn't seem that way but he was by himself and he had these three properties and he was going to open others. All of a sudden they're doing photo shoots with Jonathan in his fucking robe laying on a bed. There are some things you just don't do. You get caught up in it all and all of a sudden you're at a photo shoot and some photographer says, 'You know what would be a good idea?' You have to say no because people don't forget that shit."

Says Master, still rueful after all these years: "It sort of was tragic, because what we had was, I think, so special. No one in New York had seen anything like it. It really, really was different. Everybody who was anybody was at Jams. It was incredible. It was an amazing high. But I think honestly that we forgot kind of who we were, where we were going, and what we were doing and what we had. And I was not a good administrator. I would say that right off the bat. Jonathan's strength was he was a fantastic teacher. He wasn't in the kitchen much. He was always off eating somewhere else or he was always off going to Paris. I mean, you've heard that, I'm sure, from everybody about Jonathan. And that was one of his biggest problems. He just didn't want to be there."

Rakel, which downscaled after the crash, was also assumed to be a casualty of the economy, but Keller is quick to expand: "There's never one reason that anything fails. It's an accumulation of a lot of different things, some of them small, some of them big. The big thing of course was the downturn in the economy. That was huge. That affected a lot of people. But a lot of restaurants thrived in that period in New York City. So what was it about Rakel? Well, we didn't have a sound business structure there. Accounting was void. There was really no accounting, so who knew what we were spending or how much we were making or where we needed to cut, where we needed to add? I mean, I had no clue.

"The managers that we hired weren't sufficiently skilled in accounting. They were really good dining room managers. They knew some procedures. I was a good chef but I wasn't a good businessman. I mean, I had a clear vision on what I wanted to do from a food point of view. Was I able to maintain food costs? Evidently not. Was I able to maintain labor costs? Evidently not. So was it the best location? Not really. You know, we thought it was a great location, but in actuality, I mean, Christ, you have the Holland Tunnel three blocks south and the traffic is just ridiculous. You can't get to the place at certain times of the day. So what we thought was great in proximity to Raoul's and SoHo, it just didn't work. So a lot of different things. Poor design, poor name. Rakel? Is that a really good name? Most people thought of Raquel Welch.

"It had a lot of good things about it but a lot of confusing things about it as well. Was it fine dining? Was it a bistro? Serge, his popularity and success at Raoul's was evident. And the struggles at Rakel were evident. It's like, why can't we be more like Raoul's? So he's struggling with me; his partner, you know, has a clear vision on food, and he has a clear vision on the success. It was a struggle. . . . Rakel was going to change, and Serge, we came to an agreement that, you know what? In order for him to have an opportunity to make his money back, you know what I mean? He's running the whole thing, right? And Serge is an extraordinary man who was an extraordinary supporter of me and did an extraordinary thing for me and several things after that that I'll be forever thankful for. . . . He wanted to change it. He needed to make the restaurant successful so that he could at least get his money back. And I appreciated that. He appreciated the fact that I wasn't the person that was going to make it successful. So we agreed to part ways and to modify the restaurant and bring it to casual and call it Cafe Rakel." (Keller went on to consult for David Liederman at Chez Louis and for John Clancy's, a Greenwich Village fish house.)

Meanwhile, in the face of the recession, Charlie Palmer—the former linebacker—pushed forward, realizing his longtime dream of opening his own restaurant at precisely the wrong time. But what was the threat of failure to a kid from Smyrna, New York? "Everybody's looking at me like, 'How stupid is this guy? He's opening a high-end restaurant in the worst economy in twenty-five years.' And I'm like, what am I going to do? I'm in the middle of this thing. I didn't give a shit, honestly. I didn't care. I was twenty-seven. I had no debts. I had no family. I always knew how to live poor."

He had considered following the action downtown, partnering with Steven Greenberg, publisher of *Fame* magazine, owner of the

Roxy roller disco, and scene maker, who envisioned the restaurant in a space on Greene Street in SoHo. But Palmer had his heart set on opening what he imagined as "an American Lutèce . . . and to me that meant I wanted a restaurant in a townhouse. I felt at the time, whether right or wrong, that to compete with the great restaurants in New York and be considered in that realm, I had to be between 59th and 72nd Streets and I had to be between Fifth and Lex. That was the criteria." And so he partnered with Steve Tsolis and Nicola Kotsoni, who had done well partnering with Tuscan Pino Luongo in Il Cantinori and had recently opened their own Greek restaurant, Periyali, and were willing to meet another of his criteria, that he wanted to own the real estate along with them.

Palmer brought along some key members of his crew from The River Café, including Gerry Hayden and Neil Murphy, put the guys to work on the space and also on the upper floors, creating rentable apartments. After the kitchen was installed, Palmer would walk out onto the street, invite random swells to come in and try the food he and his crew were developing.

"We called them Sheetrock dinners," says Palmer. "At the end of the day we'd sweep all the crap in the corner and we'd put a table down and we'd cook." For Palmer, everything about the scenario typified the times: "We didn't have anybody telling us this is the way it had to be. You weren't bound by tradition in any way. It was a no-brainer to be cooking and practicing what you do in an illegal situation and literally bringing people off the street saying, 'Hey, do you want to taste some food?' We did that every night. Total strangers. We were not dressed in chef's clothes but we were just in work clothes. People look at you like you've got fricking three heads. Like, 'What are you talking about?' And then you explain to them, 'We're opening a restaurant. We're just chefs. Tell us what you think about it.' They'd be like, 'Oh, yeah, okay.' They'd be, like, total strangers sitting down like, 'Hi, I'm Pam.' 'I'm George,' you know, kind of thing, and they would taste food. We always had some wine. We'd get every wine guy coming in there trying to sell me stuff, leave some bottles because we're going to cook tonight. Half of them were open already."

Aureole opened in 1988 and earned two stars from the *New York Times*.

Different American schools began to emerge in New York City, and with Waxman temporarily off the grid and Keller and Bouley associated more with France than America, Palmer and Portale were seen as being at the very point of the cutting edge.

"It got really vibrant," says Telepan. "And there was a lot being written about it. Restaurants got looser. Danny opened Union Square at the time. At Gotham you could go eat—you're in a suit and I'm in a pair of jeans and a T-shirt. We could eat there together. I guess it was somewhat radical to have a meal like Gotham or Jams, where it was totally casual but the food was really terrific and really well thought out. . . . I think that moment made everybody more comfortable about eating out. So you were getting the sophisticated French cuisines; even Alfred did beurre blancs at that time. All these guys went to work in France. Charlie worked in France. Alfred worked in France. All these guys went out there and they came back and brought their French techniques. And they, of course, were thinking about what was going on in California with Jeremiah. I mean, Alice, her whole thing was based upon France. Her whole cooking was based upon France using California ingredients.

"You would meet over the years certain people who worked for each guy and the truth is—nothing against Charlie, because obviously Charlie has done very well for himself—but there's two kinds of cooks, right?" says Telepan. "There's the kind that love talking about getting crushed and, 'Oh, my station was in the weeds' but they don't talk about food in terms of taste and layers and textures. And that was the great thing about Alfred. You learned. When I came to Alfred's kitchen as a cook . . . Alfred's about flavor, flavor, flavor. And the guys that I worked with, that was it. It was about flavors. When Alfred would talk about a dish, it wasn't like, 'Throw it on the grill and let's fucking sear the shit out of it.' It was all about seasoning correctly."

"It was Jean-Jacques Rachou at La Côte Basque, it was Daniel Boulud, and it was Alain Sailhac and three or four chefs who historically trained everybody," says Geoffrey Zakarian, who worked around New York City during these years. "Then it became Charlie Palmer, then it became Alfred Portale, then it became that school. So the tree grew very rapidly." These two groups were summed up in a 1993 piece by Trish Hall in the *New York Times*, remembered to this day by the cooks who worked for Palmer and Portale. (Though the piece focused on Gotham and The River Café, Hall's primary River Café reference point was Palmer.) "While there are exceptions to every generalization, two characteristics seem to stick," wrote Hall. "Gotham cooks all make tall food, and The River Café guys (and they are all guys) look like rugby players."

"I STARTED TO, WITH HUGE RESISTANCE, UNDERSTAND WHAT HE WAS ABOUT."

Despite a seeming burnout, Waxman made a comeback. He returned to California to open the short-lived Table 29 in the Napa Valley, most notable because it put Waxman in place to pass through Yountville, notice that The French Laundry was for sale, and tip off Thomas Keller, who had migrated to Los Angeles and would go on to open there. Waxman returned to New York, opened a succession of restaurants, then settled in at Barbuto in the West Village in 2004. Today, he's attached to several restaurants around the country, and has emerged as one of the industry's most beloved elder statesmen.

In addition to his own phoenix routine, Waxman grew in the estimation of many who worked for him, including several former kitchen skeptics.

"The funny thing is, I have a lot more perspective now," says Tom Carlin, who today owns the Gladstone Tavern in New Jersey. "At the time I thought he was a complete fake, phony, and he didn't really do anything. Of all the chefs I've worked with, my style is probably closest to his. So when he told me some things, it really stuck with me. I remember his philosophy well because I'm kind of doing it. I've been doing his half chicken since I was there. It's one of the best things that we do here."

"It's funny," says Ed Fertig. "Doing things simply, having the great ingredients, I've carried that through me, no matter where I've been. Even right now, the company I'm with, we have four Irish pubs, but we make everything in-house. We're known as much for food as our twenty-five beers on tap. And on the specials sheet, I'll kind of do whatever and it usually works really well. When I was chef at a place in Aspen for years, I did a foie gras dish that was awesome, and it was really simple. Had I not had the Jams experience, it probably would have been a lot more involved and it didn't need to be. I think you need both—you need that tough French cooking training and then you have something like Jonathan."

"That was me in my twenties. My naïveté and my overinflated ego," says Gerry Hayden. "I look back now and realize what Wolfgang was doing; he had done so much of that cooking, that French, European-style cooking, that he was sick of it. And he was expressing what Wolfgang wanted to cook. Now I get it. Wolfgang was creating his own style. And Jonathan, too, absolutely. He's a pioneer. If you asked me when I was twenty-one what I thought about Jams, I would have told you it's an overpriced place where they serve chicken and shoestring fries. Because I was young and stupid."

Perhaps most jaw-dropping is Eric Bromberg's revelation. Not

only did Waxman—who could have had a side career as a chef re-
cruiter during these years, an American Marc Sarrazin—set him
up with a job at the American Hotel in Sag Harbor, shocking his
former employee, but Bromberg—who today presides over the Blue
Ribbon restaurant group with his brother Bruce—also came to value
his experience at Jams more than he might have imagined possible.

"I started to, with huge resistance, understand what he was
about," says Bromberg. "Taking all the French knowledge and re-
moving the fluff and bullshit and just cooking well. And just, for
instance, the restaurant I worked at in Paris and all the food I learned
in cooking school: a pigeon, okay? Take the pigeon, the whole pigeon
with the head on. Sear off the skin, put in the mirepoix, put it in
the oven, deglaze it with sherry or whatever we did, and then make
a butter out of the drippings. Take the bird, present it to the guest,
bring it back to the kitchen, cut it off the bone, lay it out, put the
vegetables, do this whole composed thing. Six people are involved in
making this one dish, including the waiters. And at Jams the squab
was cut from the back and butterflied. Take the carcass, take all the
center bones out, lay it out, cook skin side down on a grill, season,
put it on a plate with a pile of shoestring fries and a little bit of, like,
a port glaze.

"That was it. And it couldn't be more opposite. So it took me a
while, I would say, to get over the resentment and the anger and the
restructuring of what my brain thought of as food. At first, I was
like, 'This guy's an asshole, and what a mess, and why not make this
cool presentation of the pigeon? Why do it this way?' But ultimately,
in the long run, that experience had more of an impact on my style
of cooking since then than anything. The simplicity of cooking each
thing properly and separating out the ingredients, even if they go
together on the same plate. You know, the leg and thigh don't cook
the same time as the breast, so why not break it down first and do it
separately and then put it back together? Why cook the vegetables
for twenty-five minutes or whatever it may be, and do white wine and

butter and this, that, and the next thing? Why not just blanch them for a minute and season them with sea salt and a little bit of olive oil or whatever?

"That kind of spirit of light and quick cooking struck me. And I'd never cooked on a grill to that extent. And keeping a fire on a wood grill going and consistent so you can grill stuff all throughout a night when you have six hours of service and you have to load charcoal, you're loading wood in while you're cooking and having enough cooking space to do it. That was a pretty intense learning curve.

"Had I not had that experience, I would be somewhere in the fancy-food high-end French world now. Experiencing that brought me back to America and brought me to understand what this movement really was and what the point of it was. And I'm not sure I really saw it while it was happening. It took me a while to really grasp it and understand."

7

SHE'S NOT THERE

We did the dinner that they served on the Titanic.
—Andy Pforzheimer

HOW JEREMIAH TOWER POURED HIS LIFE INTO STARS,
CREATING THE AMERICAN BRASSERIE, WHILE—FOR BETTER
AND WORSE—NEVER LETTING GO OF THE PAST

It was New Year's Eve 1985, and in the Stars kitchen things drew to a standstill just before midnight. The final minutes of 1984, the restaurant's maiden year, were at hand, and the team—at the behest of their leader—stopped to savor them before they ticked away into the past. Jeremiah Tower popped open a nebuchadnezzar of Dom Pérignon Champagne, strode among the stoves and grill, pouring flutefuls for his chefs and cooks from the fifteen-liter bottles which stood higher than the restaurant's tables. Stars was just six months old, but had sucked up most of the available oxygen in San Francisco's dining community. Fashioned after Paris's La Coupole and credited with birthing the American brasserie, Stars was an immense multilevel space with a piano player, an open kitchen and oyster station, its walls adorned with Art Nouveau posters and historic menus, its entrance set not on Polk Street, where there was a door, but in speakeasy style, on Redwood Alley alongside.

If the story of the American restaurant chef to this point was the exploration of self and country through food, Stars amped things up with restaurant as autobiography, a seamless, delirious, ostentatious marriage of food and design, service and style, all of it exploding from one man's life and times. Over the course of its fifteen years, in an industry bubbling over with larger-than-life figures, Tower emerged as the most operatic, scaling the greatest heights, taking the steepest falls, and—seemingly indestructible and indefatigable—capable of repeating the cycle ad infinitum. It was, and remains, quite a ride.

"HE WOULD SORT OF INFUSE IDEAS INTO US."

The facts of Tower's life are such that he'd be compelling even if he'd never become a chef, or accomplished anything of note. Born into a wealthy family—his father, an abusive man whom he detested, an international managing director of Western Electric, lived impossibly well on his family's oil fortune—Tower spent his childhood in far-flung locations around the world (London, Sydney, Hawaii), and on ships such as the *Queen Elizabeth*. He was, he claimed, first turned on to the wonders of food at age six, in Australia's Great Barrier Reef, by an Aborigine named Nick who taught him to drink coconut water from the shell and roast barracuda. The man, in an episode Tower has only ever referred to with abstractions and metaphors, taught him about the birds and the bees, schooling the young boy in what to do with his "lizard." Whatever happened on that beach, he would forever link food and sex.

Food became a comfort to Tower, a source of pleasure and nurture, what he called in his memoir *California Dish* "an escape into a private universe of glorious sensation." One of the many things that set him apart from his contemporaries was that he didn't have to discover the best food in the world as an adult; it had always been there for him, savored in the finest restaurants and at sea, as when, in 1950, his family took a trip around the world.

Following Tower tradition, Jeremiah became a Harvard man, entering the university's School of Design. An Atlantis obsessive, he drew up plans for "an underwater habitat project" and a bridge-tunnel passageway from England to France, but they were met with skepticism, the faculty directing him toward public housing. He famously created a presentation titled "Champagne While the World Crumbles," a film loop of a mushroom cloud set to rock and roll and best appreciated with marijuana cookies, which he served.

Tower hosted dinner parties in college, often extravagantly. He had become a collector and connoisseur of cookbooks and menus, and spent much of his leisure time deepening his connection to food, amassing enough information to rival his architectural education. In 1972, he moved to California and, early the next year—down to his last dollars and desperately in need of employment—had that fateful interview at Chez Panisse.

In the late 1970s, with Chez Panisse behind him, Tower—though he had no formal training himself—began teaching at the California Culinary Academy. Among his students was Mark Franz, a young cook born in San Francisco in 1952 to a German father and Yugoslavian mother. Franz recalls a tasting class Tower conducted. "It was a tasting class of anything," says Franz. "Olive oil, vinegar. He taught us how to make vinaigrettes, that kind of stuff. It was my sophomore class and there were twenty-five of us. It was fun because he really had no rules. It was more he said, 'Okay, you've got oil. You've got vinegar. You've got salt. You've got pepper. You've got this. You've got that.' And he would give you amounts but he would say, 'They don't necessarily mean much because it depends on the salad you're making, depends on the green that you're dressing. There's a million variations.' He empowered you. When you were done, you knew how to make the vinaigrette. And to this day a lot of people are clueless. So you learned step by step by step by step; he just kind of gave you the big picture."

Franz was dazzled by Tower: "He brought passion. Oh, amazing. He was extremely articulate. And in those days cooks weren't the sharpest pencil in the deck. So he brought arrogance. He was worldly. He traveled all over the world. The guy knew how to eat. He knew how to cook. He's a piece of work."

Franz remembers his classmates as "all older people reinventing themselves. . . . A lot of them were bikers, or ex-bikers. And they were ex-druggies and ex-this and they were trying to rearrange their lives. When we first started off in my freshman quarter, there were eighty-two people. When I graduated there were fifteen. They all just went by the wayside."

At the time, Tower was also heading up the kitchen of the Balboa Café, owned by notorious restaurateur Doyle Moon. At night, Franz and Tower would hit Vanessi's on Broadway, in San Francisco's North Beach neighborhood, and do what Franz reverentially refers to as "holding court." Inevitably, friends of Tower would come by, some flitting through town from Europe. They'd also put away unspeakable amounts of alcohol. "I learned how to drink from that man," says Franz, who considered Tower a genius, sensed that he was about to change the cooking game in America, and saw his meal ticket, becoming Tower's sous chef at the academy, running the production kitchen, fulfilling banquet obligations, then—crucially—honed his technical skills working under chef Jacky Robert at Ernie's.

Tower, again in conjunction with Doyle Moon, took over Santa Fe Bar and Grill after Mark Miller and Susie Nelson pushed off. The restaurant is remembered as a stopover, a paycheck, but the themes and approaches that would soon define Tower's career were in evidence. He assembled a group of cooks—headed by Franz, who was quickly solidifying his role as Little John to Tower's Robin Hood—and they would collaborate, brainstorm ideas over an after-service beer or Champagne (Tower's favorite) in the restaurant or at a bar. Nothing was off the table, from braising goat with cactus to devising new ways of cooking Dover sole.

"He would sit at the table and we'd be drinking Champagne and he would sort of infuse ideas into us," says Franz.

Steve Vranian, who would quickly become one of Tower's most trusted chefs and lieutenants, describes the vibe at Santa Fe as an academy unto itself: "During the day at Santa Fe Bar and Grill it was more like a history class; we were trying to go back in time and re-create things. We were always researching recipes so we had to go find old books and old magazines, and this was before the Internet, before you could just Google something. I think part of it, for me at least, was just this huge interest in history, and it didn't matter what the culture was. A lot of us took that stuff home and came back the next day or if we did go out to eat we would be picking it apart—not just the food; you would sit there and say, 'Ah, their vents are dirty. What's up with these guys?' Or 'Their bathroom's a mess,' or whatever; it went beyond the food."

"We got kinky and we had fun," says Franz.

Vranian describes the distinctly Bay Area sensibility of the cooking community: "I don't know how to talk about it. It was just family. It was an extended family and it's what you did. We didn't even call each other chefs. Anywhere that I worked but especially at Santa Fe Bar and Grill, if you were at a certain level, you went by initials J.T., S.V., M.F. Otherwise, it was just the first name. And if East Coast guys came in the kitchen for events and they were all saying 'Chef,' we would all go, 'Oh, *oui, Chef, oui, oui.*' Really sarcastic. And to this day, the only person it would be meaningful to have recognize me as a chef, and call me *chef*, would be Jeremiah, frankly."

"I don't recall any of us thinking that this was a career or thinking it was a job; it was more of a *lifestyle*," says Vranian. "I never thought I was going to have my own restaurant. I never thought anything like that. It was my lifestyle. I wanted to be in a place where the food and the wine and the people you were with reflected what you do outside of it. I wanted to eat the food there that I would eat at home and vice versa. And it had to be that. And so somehow you had to find a way, whoever that leader was, and to me I was specifically thinking Jeremiah, who could round up all these people that had like values, although I don't think it was intentional; I think it just sort of happened."

"WE WEREN'T GOING INTO KITCHENS OF ESTABLISHED RESTAURANTS; *WE* WERE THE PEOPLE THAT SET UP THE KITCHENS."

Another defining characteristic of the industry in the Bay Area at this transitional time was that it was, uniquely among Western culinary hubs, not just welcoming to women in the professional kitchen, but—with the significant exception of Tower—largely dominated by women chefs and restaurateurs.

Waters was, of course, the most powerful of them all, and many of the women who followed her worked for a time at Chez Panisse, either at the inception of their careers or midstream: Joyce Goldstein of the Mediterranean restaurant Square One, opened in May 1984, just weeks before Stars debuted; Deborah Madison of the vegetarian Greens, opened in 1979; and the late Judy Rodgers of the enduring local classic, Zuni Café, where she took over the kitchen in 1987, to name just three. (Chez Panisse also launched the careers of several male chefs, including Paul Bertolli, Christopher Lee, and David Tanis, among many others.) Beyond Chez Panisse alumni, there were: Nancy Oakes of L'Avenue, launched in 1988, and then Boulevard in 1993; Patricia Unterman of Hayes Street Grill, opened in

San Francisco's Performing Arts District in 1979 (and before that of Berkeley's Beggar's Banquet, which she purchased and took over with no real professional experience); and Napa Valley pioneer Cindy Pawlcyn of Mustards Grill, opened in 1983, and other restaurants, including San Francisco's Fog City Diner, opened in 1985.

"Females did dominate the Bay Area for many, many, many years," says Goldstein, who taught cooking classes for close to two decades, first in her home starting in 1966, and then in her own school, before discovering the professional kitchen at age forty-six at Chez Panisse. "They don't dominate anymore, not so much. It used to be way more. At that time, women ran the Bay Area."

Why were San Francisco area kitchens so open to women when in virtually all other cities they were centers for sanctioned sexism and harassment?

"Because San Francisco is the least traditional place in the country," says Unterman, who in addition to being a chef and restaurateur was the *San Francisco Chronicle*'s food critic for fifteen years. "The strictures of society are the loosest here. There was the whole self-discovery/gay movement. There are no barriers here. And we're at the end of the continent here, the Wild West. We've also been a boom-and-bust society up here, of the Gold Rush and whatnot. Anything is possible, and nothing holds you back."

Gayle Pirie, who with partner John Clark was co–chef de cuisine at Judy Rodgers's kitchen at Zuni Café, and today co-owns Foreign Cinema restaurant with him, echoes the sentiment: "We're new. We're like two hundred years old in 1970. New York is, like, four hundred years old . . . plus the size, the dynamics, the hierarchy of the city, the age of it. I do think it was old school in the seventies and eighties, New York. Trying to apprentice in a hotel, corporate, male-driven—I'm sure [women] all had a problem. Out here was the fucking Wild West. Chez Panisse, I mean, opened up *in a house*. . . . The West Coast is just not as old as New York and we had less constraints. It was just very free and hippy-ish here; it really was. . . .

We were a younger society, there was real estate and space, and less people. And in New York, it's older, there's more people, there's more structure, and we just didn't have it out here. The sky was the limit, the sky."

Unterman applies the same logic to why it was so easy for inexperienced American cooks—both men and women—to find their way into kitchens in San Francisco in the first place: "Because we *created* them. We weren't going into kitchens of established restaurants; *we* were the people that set up the kitchens. So, of course, there was no barrier. No one had even worked in a restaurant. For me it was just starting at such a basic level, and being fearless and jumping in and learning step by step how to do it."

A philosophical and practical distinction between chefs in New York City and Northern California, one which facilitated the introduction of so many untrained cooks into the Bay Area's culinary workforce, was the relative emphasis on sublime, local product (Northern California) over transformative ambition and technique (New York), or vice versa.

Unterman says that, for her, dining in New York City in the 1980s "seemed like it was in another age. Different. They were too far away from their ingredients. The food got its energy here *from* the ingredients. And there, the product was really far from what you ended up getting. Everything was manipulated, overly cooked. . . . Nobody did have technique out here, but we had the advantage of having really tasty raw materials and so you really didn't have to do so much to it to make it taste really good because the stuff itself was so delicious. You add a little good butter and a great just-picked vegetable—oh my God. I don't care what you do to the damn thing, it can't be surpassed with cooking. So that's the difference. We were the place where all the good stuff was. You went to New York and you just felt, like, *Well, it's very French.* But somehow in France you felt much closer to the ingredient."

Whether or not this speaks to an inherent difference between

men and women chefs is debatable, but many key players believe it
does: "When men get food they want to transform it into something
else," says Goldstein. "We don't want to transform it; we want to
bring it up, and the guys want to take it and change it. That's just
a different headset. Now, I also want to say that I never wanted to
have an all-female kitchen. The hormone level is insane. There's too
much *Are you all right?* It makes you crazy. And you don't want to
have an all-male kitchen either because there is all the competition:
chop, chop. So you want to have this balance of female energy in the
kitchen and male energy. It's a good thing to have. The men who
end up working for women chefs turn out to be better chefs later on
because they've had two different approaches in their learning career
and also because they've been nurtured by the woman chef, so that
maybe when they go to open their own restaurant they're not throwing pans at people and calling them motherfucker and screaming at
them and humiliating them in public."

Echoes Waters herself: "I think you need both points of view;
they complement each other. When the restaurant becomes too male-
oriented, I want more women in the restaurant. Front and back of
the house. I think there's a very important balance that needs to be
maintained. I just think that men think about food differently, and
women are—I mean, they have it in them. This is just part of their
genes. They're into the nurture play. . . . [Men need] to be creative, to
be career-oriented, to be recognized, to be all of that. But that comes
from the culture that pushes on that, demands that of men. I think
of myself as a more masculine woman, and I think of a lot of men
that I work with as feminine men, and I think it's a beautiful thing to
strive for, that we can meet in that place and understand each other."

Another by-product of the unique gender dynamics of San Francisco kitchens, which admittedly flirt with the stereotypical, was
that they were, on the whole, collaborative and communal.

"It was, *We're all in it together,*" says Goldstein. "*We all want to
make it, but we all want to help each other out.* Not, *Fuck you, this is*

mine. I think that made us democratic in every way, not just towards who dined in the restaurants, but also how we ran our businesses."

It sounds romanticized, but San Francisco had a sort of mystical pull on people in those days, and not just because of its politics. Native New Yorker Goldstein moved there after spending time in Italy for apolitical reasons: "We came back from living in Europe and traveling around the Mediterranean, and I looked at New York and I said, 'This city is so ugly, I can't live here. I've been living in the Mediterranean and I need to see light and water and the sky and trees.' My former husband had worked in San Francisco for a summer and he said, 'The only city in the country that looks like the Mediterranean is San Francisco.' We packed up everything we owned in our car and we drove across the country. I'd never been and we didn't know a soul."

(Dominique Crenn, who now presides over her own two-Michelin-star Atelier Crenn, first came to San Francisco years later in search of a less chauvinistic professional community than the one back home and ended up working for Tower at Stars. She experienced an epiphany the moment she arrived. "I was still in the airport, and I felt something," she says. "I don't know what it was. I just felt like I was home.")

"We all love it here," says Goldstein, more than half a century later. "That's why we're here."

Sue Conley and Peg Smith, partners in Cowgirl Creamery, were part of the Northern California cooking community at the time—Conley as a cook for Bambi McDonald at Hotel Obrero in Chinatown, and then Fourth Street Grill in Berkeley under Paul Bertolli, and Smith as a cook and then manager of the Chez Panisse Café kitchen—and they echo Goldstein's point: "It was very collaborative back then," says Smith, who describes how cooks from different restaurants freely compared notes on dishes and preparations. "You'd talk to cooks. Deborah Madison would come and cook with us, then somebody would go cook at Greens. And the idea was learning and perfecting. It wasn't holding secrets. It wasn't competitive. It was so collaborative. Well, maybe amongst a few people it was competitive. But the cooks were very collaborative."

"Zuni was a community of women," says Pirie. "When I got to Zuni it's fifty percent males, fifty percent females. A lot of the males didn't have any authority, but they were lead line cooks who were extremely helpful, so I have that. And then I have also the experience of just all these great women showing up to help Judy. You know when she went to Africa, she asked Amaryll Schwertner, of Boulettes Larder, to come and be chef. When she went to Italy, she asked Catherine Brandel to come and help. [Both Schwertner and Brandel were fellow Chez Panisse alums.] It was this great community of women who would come and dovetail—I mean, I don't know anybody that I could call and say, 'Can you be chef for a month while I go to Africa?' No way. *No way.* Anybody who is a chef is buried in their own shit, so deep they just are trying to figure out how to get through the day, really; that's what we're all trying to do. . . . There were women spilling out of places and Judy had deep roots with Chez Panisse. And within the Chez Panisse family, there's hundreds of wonderful people. And as bohemians, sometimes you have a month off, and then there's another person who needs a job for a month. So I would say, at Chez Panisse, it's still very bohemian because they still run it on this bohemian thing where chefs take sabbaticals and another chef from somewhere else comes in to fill in, or a local person comes in to fill in. I think it still goes on there, probably not as deep, but that's what it was. . . . You can't even find a cook today, a line cook, let alone to hire a sister visionary to come and run your place while you're gone. Who does that? But that happened; that's what it was."

"I think Chez Panisse might have set a tone in Berkeley that was contagious," says Conley. "That collaborative tone, and that people would leave there and that was okay because then they would take the ethics and the vision with them."

Smith feels that this sentiment was extended even to outsiders. "I remember Wolfgang [Puck] coming up, and it was before he opened Spago. I remember him sitting in the booths. He came and looked at how we did the pizzas and asked a lot of questions. It wasn't, 'Sorry, we can't tell you that; this is classified information.' It's just *pizza*. Everybody thought, *This is food. This is not a life-or-death situation that we're doing here. We're just trying to make things as good as they possibly can be.* It's like, *Carry the message out to the world.* I really think it was an offspring of the feelings of the protest, the Free Speech Movement."

Christopher Lee, who began working at Chez Panisse in 1986, eventually becoming co-chef with David Tanis, believes that Waters taught "a way to live, a way to treat people, a way to be in the kitchen. She was one of the people who also taught us not to shout and throw things in the kitchen." Much of this wasn't stated explicitly, says Lee, but rather "in a way that a dog pack might teach its young, where you're very specific, you get a correction, and that's it. But mainly it's sort of by your own observation. You see, first of all, it's a kitchen at that time run by women, a significant number of women on the staff, so that took some of the brutality out of it. Now I'm not saying that there are no brutal female chefs; there certainly are. But it was a different tone . . . and I think the Bay Area is sort of fifteen or twenty years ahead of New York in that respect. . . ."

Jesse Cool, chef and owner of Menlo Park's Flea Street Café since 1981 (and before that of Late for the Train) and a pioneer in organic practices, so associated the profession with abhorrent male behavior that "I didn't like the word *chef* because I thought chefs were assholes.

"We used to struggle with what to put on my card," says Cool. " 'Cooker person?' They said, 'You can't use cooker person.' 'How about head cooker person? Lead cooker person?' "

Continues Cool: "Chefs were arrogant and egotistical and they were rude to women. I cooked at the Ahwahnee Hotel twenty-six or

-seven years ago. They would stick me in the corner by the dumpster. I had to bring every ingredient. I had to bring my own tools. They didn't want anything to do with me because I was a woman, untrained, and had purple hair."

Cindy Pawlcyn, whose Mustards Grill helped establish a new era in Napa Valley dining, had had a particularly bruising experience as a cook back home in Minneapolis. A male chef for whom she worked would enter the kitchen and say, "Good morning, cunt," to her every day. If something broke, she might get an angry call from him on her day off, blaming her "woman juju."

"I just ignored it because I learned a lot," she says today. "And the minute I sucked everything out of him I could, I left.

"I wanted to become a chef," says Pawlcyn. "I tasted his food and I saw how he ran his kitchens and I knew I wanted to learn from him. So the fact that he was an asshole didn't bother me as much as the fact that he wasn't realizing that I was getting stuff out of him. And it built my confidence, in hindsight."

But the experience also influenced Pawlcyn more than she realized. She became a kitchen screamer the first time she became a chef herself, in Chicago: "I was really intense and pushed people a lot. Because I followed their example, until I realized what I was doing and I went, 'Wow, this isn't how I want to live.'"

In 1979, when her colleagues Bill Higgins and Bill Upson moved to California to open restaurants, they asked Pawlcyn if she'd relocate and chef for them at a rib restaurant at McArthur Park. The three went on to open Mustards Grill in the Napa Valley in 1983.

Much as Mary Sue Milliken had, Pawlcyn looked to a very few predecessors as her guiding lights: "I'll never forget: I came out here with my sister-in-law and my brother, and just before we came out, she sent me a *Sunset* magazine and there was a little picture of Sally [Schmitt, original chef and, with husband Don Schmitt, co-owner of The French Laundry in Yountville, California] and her herb garden, and I put that on my wall and said, 'See, there's a woman chef.' And there was one small book on woman chefs in France. That's kind of what kept me going."

"WE'RE OVER. THIS IS THE BEGINNING OF THE END."

In 1983, Tower and a few of his cooks traveled to the Astor mansion in Newport, Rhode Island, to cook lunch for one hundred journalists, invited there by Ocean Spray's ad agency. It was the kind of thing that was happening at the time, increasingly prominent American chefs being weaponized in service of a product or produce. But the French still ruled: Paris's Guy Savoy had been enlisted to cook dinner, Tower and his crew the lunch. When Savoy's French *brigade*, already prepping their meal, wouldn't surrender the stoves, Tower marched his crew outside, improvised a grilled feast—even the dessert—cooked by his team while he mingled about with a glass of Champagne, discussing the meal with the writers, who promptly wrote it up for their papers.

The lunch opens Tower's *California Dish* along with the claim that the term *California cuisine* might never have become known had it not gone down. It's as signature a Tower gesture as the glass of Champagne and red-rimmed sunglasses that would become his sartorial trademark. Just as vintage was the emotional roller coaster that ensued when he and his crew boarded their flight back to California: "When I got on the plane," he says, "I was sitting and my chefs and cooks were sitting in front of me, and Steven [Vranian] looked around to toast with Champagne and he saw me sitting with tears streaming down my face. And he leapt across the back of the chair: 'Oh my God, what's happening?' I said, 'We won. It's a success.' And he said, 'What's the problem?' I said, 'We're over. This is the beginning of the end. This is a very, very dangerous moment. Our lives will never be the same again.'"

Spend enough time considering Tower's life and it's clear that he probably meant what he said on the plane—because his saga is defined by a series of points high and low, which any capable screenwriter will tell you is the secret of good drama, plunging the hero into the depths of desperation, then hoisting him back to an optimistic place, before lowering the boom once again. The man's a human sine curve. And so . . . Jeremiah comes to California nearly penniless and becomes the chef of Chez Panisse; Jeremiah leaves Chez Panisse and wanders the land as a gun for hire, then opens Stars. Lather. Rinse. Repeat.

On that airplane, things couldn't have been further from over: They were just beginning, again. Balboa Café and Santa Fe Bar and Grill had been auditions for Tower's dream restaurant, which Moon had finally agreed to finance. Tower envisioned an audaciously gargantuan brasserie after the fashion of Paris's La Coupole, with influences drawn from a variety of personal heroes and touchstones, such as the life and writings of Lucius Beebe, the columnist credited with coining the term *cafe society*, and a Slim Aarons photograph of Clark Gable, Van Heflin, Gary Cooper, and Jimmy Stewart, in topcoats and tails, at the Hollywood restaurant Romanoff's on New Year's Eve in 1957.

Only a former architect or born restaurateur could love the space that Tower found, a rat-infested warhorse in a run-down section of town that horrified James Beard, Barbara Kafka, writer James Villas, Stanford Court's Jim Nassikas, and actor Danny Kaye (a plugged-in foodie during these years) when he brought them by for a look-see. But where they saw a ruin, he saw the glittering, magnificent brasserie of his dreams—a space he would not just resuscitate, but reanimate. And the location said it all about the democratic restaurant he envisioned: near both the Civic Center, so convenient for office workers, and the War Memorial Opera House, one of the gathering spots for San Francisco society.

He had first found the space in 1981, but there were delays and funding gaps and ongoing horn locking with Moon. But by 1983, construction was moving apace, and word spread of the project. Emily Luchetti, who had cooked in New York City, moved to San Francisco in the spring of 1984, had heard about the impending opening, went to the space. "We moved out around March of '84. And I remember it was completely under construction but you could see that it was going to be this big, big restaurant. Just physically a large space. Because you walk up the stairs and there was a bar that was about forty feet long and there's just this huge dining room and the kitchen on the right. And it was going to be an open kitchen, which, not to say it was the first open kitchen of its kind, but it was one of the first where you could see all the action going on.

"Jeremiah had a clear vision of what he wanted it to be," says Luchetti. "And that was the thing that was so amazing about him: He is extremely creative. You could see his vision of taking all that French traditional, classic, really good stuff, giving it a real twist, both culturally and with California ingredients, and creating something for everybody, but it's such a high level of quality that people will just be blown away by it.

"I remember being offered a line position there and I was offered a position at Vivande, Carlo Middione's place, and I didn't really have any idea how big Stars was going to be because you just had this vision of this guy and it was like, 'Oh, I guess I'll just take the Stars thing.'"

For the remainder of Stars's buildout, Luchetti was assigned to Santa Fe. "It was much simpler. It was real kind of bar-and-grill food but they were doing grilled raclette with french fries and steamed mussels and that kind of thing. And Jeremiah had obviously come from Chez Panisse so he was really focusing on American ingredients, and really taking advantage of what California had to offer in terms of seafood and produce. I started out at the oyster station opening oysters and making pizzas."

Stars opened on July 4, 1984. (In the small-world department, like Jams before it, Stars had committed to a preopening party before they were fully ready to go, and Franz ended up cooking on a charcoal grill indoors, throwing open the windows for cross-ventilation.)

There was no opening-night supernova for Stars. The restaurant, built for volume, was slow for its scale, and only open for dinner.

Late that summer, Andy Pforzheimer, a Harvard-educated cook, arrived in San Francisco, eager to work for Tower. He presented his résumé to Franz, who ran it back to the boss, who in turn emerged to confirm Pforzheimer had gone to Harvard and cooked in France. Five minutes later, Franz hired him, asked him to start two days later.

"Mark looked like what I expected chefs to look like," says Pforzheimer. "Jeremiah didn't. To this day, Jeremiah doesn't look like what you expect a chef to look like. He's what you expected the owner of the restaurant to look like. Except that he was in whites. But even when he's in whites, he's not really in whites. His pants are light colored and his shoes are spotless. It's not a kitchen look. Soltner had shit on his aprons. Puck was a mess. Jeremiah never looked like that."

Initially, Pforzheimer found himself working the oyster bar alongside Clark Frasier, who with partner Mark Gaier went on to open Arrows restaurant in Ogunquit, Maine. It was a transitional time for the restaurant, which was gathering steam, growing busier. "Nobody was sure what to expect," says Pforzheimer. "And it was so radically different. The dining room was so different than the Santa Fe dining room. It was bigger and fancier and next to the opera house. It was just a different thing. And I was very much an outsider in that group because they mostly knew each other."

Business picked up, says Franz, after Caroline Bates's review in *Gourmet* magazine. Customers began showing up with the article in hand.

"Jeremiah and Mark quickly weeded through the level of talent that started showing up at the door," says Pforzheimer. "And the volume they did meant that they started getting rid of the weaker Santa Fe Bar and Grill people very quickly. There was a lot of turnover when I got there. And within two months I was surrounded by people who were all rock stars. And I was very intimidated. They were one of the most talented kitchens—still the most talented kitchen I've ever worked in by far."

The dining room quickly attained Tower's vision, offering whatever one was in the mood for, from a casual bite to a multicourse meal. "We had a huge bar area there," says Luchetti, "and one of the amazing things about Stars is people would come in for oysters and a glass of Champagne, or they might come in for a hot dog because we had a hot dog on the bar menu as well as a pizza. So you could come in and spend thirty bucks or you could come in and spend three hundred bucks. It was really kind of all depending on what you wanted to spend. And you had people that would be going to the opera and you'd have people going to the ballpark or coming from the 49ers game or something like that. Before that, the dressed-up people, the fine-dining people, stayed away from the lower classes."

Says Michael Bauer, who moved to San Francisco in the mid-1980s to become restaurant critic of the *San Francisco Chronicle:* "I think it was Wolfgang who kind of started it, then you have people like Jeremiah, which I think was the other, to me, transformative restaurant, because you could have a hot dog in the bar. It catered to the opera set as well as the very casual, artisan set. And it was, to me, if you look at it, kind of the first American brasserie. He actually took Vanessi's, which had an open kitchen, and that was his inspiration. If you look at the open kitchen in that style restaurant, it started at Spago and Stars. Spago was a little different. Stars kind of upped it a little bit. And it was very much of a brasserie with the open kitchen. That really kind of fueled the open kitchen trend that you see. I mean, even ten years ago you went to the East Coast and you didn't see open kitchens. And now it's like everyone has it. . . . He is very handsome. And again, he was a brilliant cook. You can't leave that out of the equation. . . . His combinations. The way he used food . . . there were so many dishes that to me were a revelation. It was the first time I had watermelon and tomatoes and red onions together at that restaurant, which I still remember. It was just a party."

Even nonnatives viewed the Bay Area sensibilities as inherent to the restaurant. Says Luchetti, "I think the fact that it was in San Francisco made it so it could be successful. Because San Francisco is probably more democratic, at that time, than New York was, for instance. You look at the history of San Francisco in general, the whole Gold Rush thing; the people that made the money and discovered gold, they were a pauper one day and they had tons of money the next day. So I think there was always that more egalitarian tradition in San Francisco. The common denominator was just going to be the good food and it didn't matter who you were, everybody had access to this food."

"That was one of the greatest spots in San Francisco history," says Unterman. "Because it was just a crossroads. Everyone from every part of society was there—the upper ones, the lower ones, the artists, the poets, the socialites. It was just one of the greatest mixes. You could sit at the bar and have a hot dog. You could be in the little special place and have Champagne. Jeremiah was such a flamboyant character. He was completely democratic and completely outrageous and gay and it just epitomized the society, the freedom of San Francisco."

And everybody came: "We counted covers," says Pforzheimer. "We were doing one hundred eighty a night, then we were doing two hundred thirty, then—*whoa*—we did three hundred fifty, then it was back to two hundred thirty, then—*whoa*—four hundred ten. Then every weekend seemed to just pick up steam. And after a while we were hitting five hundred on the weekends and doing three hundred during the week."

Just as diners flocked to the dining room, aspiring cooks rushed the kitchen: "There were so few places to go in the United States if you were like me," says Pforzheimer. "If you were educated, hungry, dying to not only cook but cook something amazing, you could count on one hand the places that would just take you in partly because of the French training, partly because of the French identity, partly because of how much volume there was and the ability to hire. Stars was a magnet for that kind of thing, for I-just-want-to-cook, the way Dan Barber's place is now for—you know: You've got a farm-to-table bug up your ass? You go to Blue Hill: 'Can I have a job?' And so we had that going on. We had rock stars. It was all celebrities and there was press in and out. Every dish that went on the menu, you read about it. So people came from everywhere. They wanted to work there. He had the ability to hire."

Tower could also, says Pforzheimer, be "scary. I remember it was salads. It was true of everything. He would comb through your salads.* I mean, these salads were big. You'd make fifteen of them at a time. He would come through. And he had an eye and he would go like *that*. His whole head would turn and he'd go right for one of them and he would reach into the middle. He had very long, elegant fingers. He'd reach in and out would come this—you've seen what a bad leaf of lettuce in a bag of lettuce looks like? It would be rotten and kind of droopy. And he would walk up to you and he would take his fingers and he'd put it right in your mouth, pushing up against your lip, and say, 'This one's for you.' And the first time he did it I was—'Huh?' He goes, 'This one's for you.' And I was staring at him. He goes, 'Eat it.' And he goes, 'Well, you wanted someone else to eat it, right? Eat it.' He shoved it in my mouth. And it doesn't taste good. He was just dead quiet. I saw him do that to many people.

---

* Tower posted a single-spaced, two-page document on how to properly clean salad greens in the Stars kitchen.

And it wasn't just salads. Sometimes it was something else. You put a bad anything out and he would just pick it up. And after a while he didn't have to say anything. He'd just hold it up and you'd eat it. I'm not sure I could legally do it anymore, but I'm telling you, it sure made you pick through your salads carefully. You lived in fear of him coming over. And he would just stare. And if he didn't say anything, walked away, that was a good day.

"He would turn bright red and he would get very clipped," says Pforzheimer. "And it would be, you know, 'What is this? What are you thinking? *What are you thinking?*' That kind of thing. Just sort of a cross between 'I'm disappointed in you' and 'I'm controlling myself so I don't hit you.'"

On the flip side there was Tower's intimacy with the gods of food—Julia Child, Richard Olney, Elizabeth David—that heightened his aura among the crew.

"We busted our asses for a week just for the moment at nine-thirty when service was winding down and Tower would come in the kitchen and just kind of hang out," says Pforzheimer. "Kind of lean over by the grill and start talking about something that he did with Julia Child in France ten years ago. We'd all kind of slide over, kind of keep an eye on your pans. But he would just talk ten, fifteen minutes about it. That's why we were all there. Just to hear that story. Because he tells a great story. He tells an amazing story. And he lived bigger than any of us ever could."

Remembers another former cook: "One night there is a world heavyweight championship boxing thing going on, pay per view, somewhere in town. And Tower comes in with the mayor and the chief of police. They come into the restaurant, and they invite him out for dinner to go see the boxing. So he goes out with them to go see the show. And he comes back at like eleven-thirty at night, dinner is over, supper has started. I'm in the pizza station that night and I'm working late so I'm in there. And I see him walk in. And he walks into the restaurant and he has got—and he's an impeccable dresser—he's got the chief of police badge, the six-pointed badge, the San Francisco Police badge, on his jacket. And he walks into the kitchen and he's wasted. He walks into the kitchen and he just screams out, 'Who's the new sheriff in town?' And all the cooks turn around, and—I remember this guy now because he went far in the San Francisco restaurant scene. He became a general manager. At the time he was a busboy. Really handsome gay kid. 'Who's the new sheriff in town?' And he's standing there like this. And [the guy] is coming out of the kitchen—just happened to be coming out of the kitchen, toward the dining room. Jeremiah is right there and walks up and goes, 'You! You're under arrest!' And he starts walking up to him. And he is like *what the fuck?* And he starts backing up, backing up. Jeremiah goes, 'Freeze, you're under arrest!' He kept saying, 'Freeze, you're under arrest." And the busboy keeps backing up and he backs up to the hot line. And now meanwhile, the whole dining room is right here and they're all like looking at J.T. and he goes, 'You're under arrest!' And he backs him up against the hot line. And he goes, 'Now I'm going to frisk you!' It was fabulous."

"I remember once, it was a late night and I think people were going to do something," says Pforzheimer, and he said, 'Are you going?' And I said, 'No, I think I'm going home.' And he looked at me like, 'Why?' And I said, 'I'm tired. I want to go to sleep.' And he said, 'I'm going to sleep when I'm dead.' Just very matter of fact. I remember that stuff. I'm fifty-three. It sticks in my head. There's so much that I teach people now. I teach classes. I have a bazillion employees.* And a lot of it came right out of Tower. Not that it was an original statement, it was just the way he said it. He was actually living it."

---

* Pforzheimer owns a chain of Spanish wine bars.

"JEREMIAH'S JEREMIAH"

In 1986, Harper & Row published Tower's first cookbook, *Jeremiah Tower's New American Classics*, a rectangular tome—modest in heft next to some of today's doorstops—that was dedicated to Elizabeth David, Richard Olney, and the staff of his restaurants (Balboa Café and Santa Fe Bar and Grill were fresh enough that they are referenced alongside Stars). The book doesn't promote the restaurants so much as it does Tower himself through stories of grand meals and an aristocratic lifestyle. Photographs depict Tower and friends on a hunt in the countryside, or lunching in a vineyard.

The headnotes and chapter introductions shimmer with a depth of knowledge and detail only possible from an author who has spent a lifetime in adoration of food. Compared to McCarty's first cookbook, published three years *after* Tower's, *New American Classics* truly is *American*—with recipes for stuffed chiles with black bean sauce, grilled vegetable salad with Texas ham and aioli, and a black-and-white ice cream soda. It also neatly encapsulates the dichotomy of Stars with dishes as high-minded and Eurocentric as sea urchin soufflé and as everyday as a chicken club sandwich, both treated with equal seriousness.

Through it all Tower continued to live big. He made frequent trips to Europe, sometimes with Franz at his side. Before and after Stars opened, the two would often connect with Richard Olney in London, take in a four-hour wine-soaked lunch, then refresh and get back out to dinner, talk nothing but food the entire time. "Richard Olney was Jeremiah's Jeremiah," says Franz. Tower also often brought his crew to New York City, booked a limo for the night, toured restaurants with them. Sous chefs and above at Stars were required to have passports, in case he had a sudden urge to expose them to standard-setting experiences, such as breakfast at the Hôtel de Crillon in Paris. He called these reference points "benchmarks."

"YO, WE'RE GOING TO EAT SOME CLAMS."

Stars continued to draw young talent, even from across the country, like Bruce Hill, a young cook who had motorcycled cross-country to San Francisco, wanting in. He got a meeting with Franz but there was no opening, so he campaigned, returning with stalker regularity, until he happened by the day after Brendan Walsh left to return to New York City and was hired.

Hill was taken by the mix of high society and everyman at Stars: "One night that was incredibly memorable was the night that Run-DMC and the Beastie Boys came in for dinner," says Hill. "They were playing a concert together, so they were at the same table. And I'll never forget that Jeremiah was really cool; he was totally taking care of them. They didn't really understand the food. So he was cooking things that would be more understandable to them. And one of the guys from Run-DMC saw some clams on the oyster bar display—there was this oyster bar that had about six counter seats and that was right where the salad guy was. And this guy was like, 'Hey, man, can you make us some clams?' And Jeremiah says, 'Sure, I'll steam you some clams.' And so the guy's in the kitchen watching Jeremiah cooking these clams. And Jeremiah goes, 'Okay, they're ready, go back to your table. I'm going to serve them.' And this guy is walking out of the kitchen. He's like, 'Yo, we're going to eat some clams!' And right as he's walking out, some socialite woman is coming out of the bathroom going back to her seat up in this little area called the club area, which was where all the socialites sat, and that's where all the menus were as well. And I'll never forget the look on her face. It was like the clash of two worlds: the socialite and some rapper from New York. And it was so beautiful. It was incredible. And that's really what Stars was all about. It was a place that attracted all these different people."

"It was the Second Coming of Christ," says Mario Batali, who was installed as a sous chef at the Clift Hotel in the mid-1980s. "It was the most interesting thing I've ever seen. Jeremiah was a fascinating character and renowned. He was loved by society and cooks. He had created a place where—kind of like La Coupole, kind of like Balthazar later—a place where you could go in a tuxedo or you could go in golf shorts and feel comfortable. The food was serious. It was seriously priced but it was of the moment and remarkable for its variation. They changed the menu every day. The way they'd do it, they would come in and they'd have fifty pounds of scallops, they'd put it on the main course menu, and tomorrow if there were nine pounds of scallops left, they would make scallop ceviche. You just watched them, how they cycled the stuff through, and Mark Franz and David Robins and Steve Vranian and Loretta Keller, they would all have a little meeting at the end of the night to look over their stuff. 'How much do we have left of this?' In addition to being artistic, it was clearly a business that was being run smartly by the people. Not necessarily Jeremiah's business smarts because he wasn't that smart business-wise, but he was a genius in PR and the best possible front man. There wasn't a person who didn't love Jeremiah. I'll never forget a lot of things but one of the things I saw that most impressed me: Paul Bocuse is in there and they served him prime rib and cauliflower gratin. And I just thought, *Really? You didn't serve him the black bean cake or something crazy?* And at the end of the day what you realize then is when chefs really want to impress chefs it's never so much with technique, it's always with product. So he must have gotten the most amazing American beef and he knew that was going to blow Paul Bocuse away."

Batali was also drawn to Franz: "That's all that mattered to me was impressing particularly Mark," says Batali. "Mark was the godfather of all of my gastronomic ambition. He was just the smartest, goodest guy. He got it. He was fair. He was even. He was passionate. He was a great cook. He was the first guy that was curing his own salami and making his own prosciutto before everyone else started to take credit for it. He was the taciturn but sage leader and it was great to watch him operate. He was the operator of that restaurant. Undervalued historically like you can't possibly imagine, the single most important influence of my life."

Batali would park at the oyster bar. "I would sit there for six hours. Drink a single-malt Scotch and watch the whole situation night after night after night or I'd sit at the bar. Maybe I was annoying. I thought I was their friend.

"They would do seven hundred fifty covers a night. I mean it was insane how much volume they were doing. And I mean they were packed at four and they were packed at eleven-thirty. Babbo [Batali's New York City hit, opened in 1998] was modeled after Stars. I wanted it to feel comfortable and yet elegant enough that if you wanted to put on a tuxedo you'd feel comfortable. And a big menu, they had a big menu. They had a lot of stuff."

Some of that "stuff": Jeremiah's snapper ceviche with avocado-mango salsa, marinated red onions, and cilantro; grilled braised sweetbreads with potato gratin, swiss chard, roast shallots, and pesto; grilled lamb shank with roast eggplant, roast garlic, and a red bell pepper sauce.

The restaurant, also—as Tower had done at Chez Panisse—created themed meals, sometimes based on historic menus or events. "We did the dinner that they served on the *Titanic*," says Pforzheimer. "It was very over-the-top things."

It all kept Tower front and center in American chefdom, but Tower always felt that his homosexuality kept him from being fully accepted, both among his peers and his clientele.

"It has always been a barrier," says Tower. "Social San Francisco, which I had complete entree to because of [San Francisco socialite] Denise Hale, and they all came to Stars. I was so famous and they wanted to—they had to be at Stars. So they had to never comment on it. San Francisco society figures couldn't comment on it. But I knew there was still a kind of barrier there that if I had been straight wouldn't have existed.

"More generally, I think there was a lot of confusion how somebody could be so famous and successful and be gay. And that meant my fellow chefs. You know, I think there was—with some, with many, I don't know—a lot of resentment that because I was gay I shouldn't have been able to achieve. In their book, the rules were that I shouldn't have been able to do what I did."

None of this was ever explicitly stated to Tower. "This was all a vibe. I mean, I never made a point about it. I never said I was gay and I never denied it because it wasn't for me. It had just gotten really not much to do with it. For me your sexuality is not a political thing as it became with many, many people. So that was just boring. I mean, I'd rather talk about the politics of foie gras than that. But it was definitely a confusing thing for a lot of people, and I knew that but I just didn't feel—I mean, I didn't—there was nothing to deal with, really. But I knew that there were a fair number of chefs who felt resentful. It just wasn't fair somehow, you know?"

At various times, Tower has also claimed that he hated the demands of his fame and success but now says, "For the most part, I sort of enjoyed it. . . . I did all my public relations. I'd sit at Zuni's with a glass of Champagne in the afternoon and make notes. And every letter or phone call, anything I ever received or Stars received got a handwritten letter, so there were fifteen or twenty a day that I signed and sent off. So Jeremiah Tower was a construct, a business construct. And the Jeremiah Tower who said hello to three hundred fifty people a day out of the thousand that came through Stars, I mean, you can't do that. You can't do that if you actually think that's who you are. If you are, then you're a little bit crazy. And also, I never read the good reviews. I read only the bad ones. Because I knew I couldn't stand it. I knew I was in trouble if I believed my own press. Is there anyone who it wouldn't go to their head? So, the times that I made big mistakes was when I was starting to believe my own press. That I was this superstar who could do anything he wanted."

In 1989, a tuxedoed Tower appeared in a Dewar's ad campaign on which the Scotch giant spent $100 million. Tower also opened a smaller restaurant, Speedo 690, in San Francisco.

As was the case with other members of the Stanford Court Gang, Tower was in perpetual motion, not only around his various properties, but also at charity events, creating a circuit for the top echelon of chefs that found themselves thrust together around the country, serving morsels of signature dishes at tasting stations, then popping into each other's restaurants for the star treatment.

"Anytime when we went to New York, to Jams or Bud's or wherever, of course we'd be wined and dined there, and anytime Jonathan Waxman came to Stars, he'd be wined and dined," says Vranian. "And we were talking Cristal or whatever. I remember an evening where Jeremiah was sitting there and said, 'Jonathan, we've got to stop this. We're going to go broke.' There'd be no check, everything was free. It was just hilarious. But it wasn't just chefs coming through, of course. Richard Olney was there, Elizabeth David came through."

There's a general belief among many of his peers, including Waxman, that Tower spread himself too thin, that being in other restaurants meant there was no Tower at Stars, and Stars without Tower's immaculate presence, and omnipresent flute of Champagne, wasn't Stars. Among the places that siphoned his attention were a Stars cafe, Stars offshoots in Oakville, Palo Alto, Manila, Seattle, and Singapore, and a dream project, Peak Café, on the other side of the world in Hong Kong.

Franz traces the beginning of the end to the San Francisco earthquake of 1989: "The kiss of death was the earthquake. Stopped. Overnight. Thirty thousand office workers from the federal and state [buildings] which were all around us who came for lunch on a daily basis were gone. Life was never the same."

Franz was home when the quake hit: "I was pouring myself a beer, sitting down. As I was sitting down I heard this crash coming from behind me. It was a wave. It was just this wave. But of noise, you know? The world just going like this. And it was the beginning of the Oakland A's and the San Francisco Giants for the World Series. First game of the World Series. I remember standing out on my foyer looking out over San Francisco and seeing smoke, thinking, *Oh my God. The world is done.* That is what happened. The world just changed. San Francisco doesn't like earthquakes. And nobody comes. Once that happens, they don't come back for a couple years. It takes them a long time to forget. Really. And what happened was, you know, the Bay Bridge was closed. They all stopped coming. They realized that they had food in Berkeley. And it's never been the same. Ever. San Francisco's not ever been the same. Not that way."

Stars held on another decade, then shuttered in 1999. Tower moved to New York City. He wrote a memoir, *California Dish*, published in 2003. It doesn't hold back, especially about his feelings about Waters.

"A lot of people have complained about how he's been," says Franz. "That was a pretty wicked book. It got deep. He burnt many, many, many, many bridges. . . . A lot of people can't believe he actually comes back to San Francisco. That's how much they feel about it."

Sitting with Alice Waters during our Chez Panisse interview, I ask her about the split with Tower.

It was, she says, "a sad, unfortunate parting because we certainly had great, great times but it really fell apart, like a marriage. Very painful ending . . . but you know, when I really do think about it, we went our separate ways and it seems much more of a logical parting because I was much more political. I mean, I *was* political. He's *apolitical.* . . . I was an idealist and he was cynical. And the restaurant sort of had a life bigger than both of us at that point. It had a momentum."

"I've interviewed him a couple of times," I say. "It's hard for me to picture him here. It really is. Stars I get, not having ever been there but knowing all about it."

"But you *could* picture him if you [could] see him in his twenties," she says. "And somebody that had never been a professional chef and getting into his whites and thinking about, you know, those blinis that his aunt made or whatever it was. 'Oh, let's do them so that there's butter dripping down off your elbows. Let's serve it with *that*.' I mean, he was playful in that way and a little nervous that there was only one meal; you had to have it on or it didn't work."

"When Stars came along," I suggest to Waters, "it seems to me like it brought what each of you was fundamentally about into high relief."

"I would say that," agrees Waters. "I think that that's really accurate. . . . We both went on and made what we wanted."

This was my only sit-down with Alice Waters but that portion of our conversation is the one I can still hear, the one that rang the most true, the least guarded.

"WHAT'S THAT DOING THERE?"

Sometime during the writing of *this* book, I recognized that while it's of course desirable to relate history with the authority of one who was there, it can also be dishonest. These stories were told to me, and a thorny theme was the desire of many involved to shore up their respective legacies; one former River Café cook, a good friend of mine no less, even told me he dreamed up the chocolate Brooklyn Bridge. There were moments when I felt more like a beleaguered gumshoe than a guy who just wanted to relay the evolution of the American chef, and never more so than when trying to disentangle the Tower-Waters double helix.

The question is so front of mind that when I imagine Stars, there's one image that floats to mind above all others—it's not the groundbreaking low-high combination of a burger and glass of Lafite at the bar, or Tower mingling amongst the people, the chef-impresario, ruler of all that he surveyed. It's not the famous photo of him astride a motorcycle purchased the same day he defeated Doyle Moon in a lawsuit, or laughing uproariously with his bar patrons. It's not his Dewar's ad.

I've seen all those things, and yet the image that comes to me is of a handwritten letter, hung on the restaurant's wall, just below the VIP section. It was a letter written to Tower by Waters back in the mid-1970s, praising his talents, in very personal terms.

The letter lodges in the memory of many. One of the first interviews I conducted for this book was with Jonathan Waxman. I wasn't sure where I was going with it when I asked him if I could bend his ear. We met at the lounge of Batali's Chelsea restaurant Del Posto, which—as Stars once did—had a piano player when it first opened. Jonathan, whose lack of vanity I find lovable, arrived in checkered chef's pants, a purple Izod polo shirt, and sneakers. We began interviewing and this, literally, was the first unsolicited thing he said to me: "There is a famous incident from when Jeremiah Tower opened up Stars. There is a VIP section at Stars and he put letters from friends and fans up there and he put up a letter, a love letter, that Alice Waters had written to him. When he left Chez Panisse, Alice wrote how much she adored having him at Chez Panisse. It was a love poem. I am not going into the psychological analysis of what she means but it was a letter that was meant for his eyes only. It should never have been in the public. It should have been an intimate thing but Jeremiah put it on the wall. I kind of know why he did that. He wanted to flaunt his independence. It was kind of a crazy, wild thing to do. I would have never done it. But in a way it sort of showed what Jeremiah was all about. It also showed the emotion of what was going on those times. Because everybody knew that it was kind of like [Edward] Teller in Los Alamos. He was the genesis of making American food what it is about now. That is all because of Jeremiah and Alice."

Why did Jonathan mention that letter, I wondered. It wasn't a secret. It's been written about in the *San Francisco Chronicle*, and in Thomas McNamee's book *Alice Waters and Chez Panisse*. And those who saw it remember it. "There was a letter from her," says Pforzheimer. "It was like a love letter up on the wall. And at some point over the course of a year and a half working there I'd read everything on the walls but I never asked about it. I knew it was weird that that was there because I knew that they didn't get along, but I guess I was too chicken to ever pull someone aside and say, 'What's that doing there?' He stuck it there as kind of a 'fuck you' as I recall. Everything else on the wall was the 1983 Schramsberg tasting and menus of the *Lusitania*."

"Well, first of all, my comment on that action is . . . if you'd like to be in the hospitality business, you have to maintain good manners, and if you don't have good manners, you're an asshole. The end," says Clark Wolf. "Jeremiah Tower behaved badly in public. Shame on him. The end. . . . He stopped having a voice for me and a lot of other people when he went to the self-aggrandizing negative. He invited the press—mostly the *New York Times*—to Chez Panisse hoping for fame and glory. Turns out he is not what they found interesting and it's bitten his ass forever. Honey, get over it. When you light your hair on fire, what you get is a burnt scalp. . . . I'm not saying Alice is Mother Teresa, but then as I understand, neither was Mother Teresa."

During our Chez Panisse interview, I ask Waters about the letter. "What letter?" she asks, stunning me.

"The letter from you that he put up on the wall at Stars."

"You know, I can't even remember the letter. What did I say?"

"I've never seen it. But it was after a dinner here and you were singing his praises and he put it up on the wall at Stars near the VIP area."

"Oh, yes. I do remember it."

I tell her that a former waiter from Stars told me that Waters had come in for dinner a few times, and that I couldn't square that with their vituperative separation.

"I think the letter was describing a meal that maybe he made for Richard Olney, I think it might have been. And I think he was proud of the meal, and the fact that I really liked him sort of proved that I really liked his cooking. Yeah, it was a personal letter, but I can't remember the details of it. But I do know that it was a personal letter to him. And I probably wouldn't have put something like that on the wall . . . [but] it didn't keep me from going."

"THERE ARE THREE SIDES TO EVERY STORY . . ."

Jeremiah Tower had long fascinated me, enough so that I sought him out for an interview for my blog before I'd sold this book. Jeremiah had flitted in and out of the public eye since shuttering the Stars mothership in 1999, and his absence, as absences can, had inflated his character. He had skipped the work-for-hire stage to which so many chefs submit themselves. It was well known that he was in Mexico, falling back on his architecture degree, flipping houses.

Tower and I met at Michael White's Midtown restaurant Ai Fiori for drinks and to conduct an interview. He was everything the legend had led me to expect: handsome, dapper, with a pocket square tucked into his checkered sport coat, and commanding.

Tower was also in the early stages of a mission. He had recently launched a Twitter account, of which I was one of a handful of followers. He had also launched a website. He was puttering around with Facebook, establishing connections with old friends and colleagues.

The interview was a pleasure, because Tower is willing to play ball, answer just about anything. And we hit it off, making dinner plans at the Chinese restaurant RedFarm two days later, though I remember being surprised at his availability. We stayed in touch, but it wasn't until the following year that I learned the extent of his PR mission. In November 2013, Gayle Pirie and John Clark re-created Stars for one evening at their Mission Street restaurant Foreign Cinema in San Francisco. It was a happening: San Francisco restaurant critic Michael Bauer was there. In the kitchen were Stars alums: Bruce Hill, Dominique Crenn, Emily Luchetti, and Loretta Keller. Tower was in a chef's coat, toasted the diners with a flute of Champagne. (Franz, who says he wasn't consulted before the event was scheduled, was on holiday in Europe.)

The next day, Tower gathered a group of his old crew and some new friends, including a couple from Cozumel, for lunch upstairs at Zuni Café. Luchetti was there, as were Steve Vranian and his wife, Jules, who also cooked at Stars. Everybody was mic'd up and a small camera crew circled the table on tiptoe, filming the conversation; Zero Point Zero, the production company responsible for the television series *No Reservations* and *Mind of a Chef*, were considering making a documentary about Tower and gathering exploratory footage. (Zuni still holds a place in the hearts of many who once cooked in San Francisco: Word spread to the balcony that Jonathan Waxman was simultaneously dining downstairs.)

During the lunch, somebody referenced a dispute they'd had. "There are three sides to every story," Tower yelled to Luchetti. "Your side, the other side . . ."

"And the *truth!*" Luchetti yelled back, and everybody burst into laughter. I've since learned that the line is a favorite of Tower's, a go-to chestnut which, it seems to me, is meant to inoculate him against any claims that his side of any story isn't 100 percent accurate.

Since then, Tower's been making up for lost time, showing up at food festivals, including one devoted to honoring him—the second annual Roots of American Food conference, a small gathering in Chicago in 2014. (Full disclosure: I performed an onstage interview with Tower at the event.) And that documentary became a reality: *Jeremiah Tower: The Last Magnificent* made its theatrical debut in 2017.

A curious through line to all of this is that Tower seems almost as preoccupied with demanding his credit for Chez Panisse as he is with celebrating and memorializing Stars. At the Roots of American Food conference, Tower gives a talk. The first third to half are devoted to his telling of the Chez Panisse story. He runs down all the greatest hits: a story in which he nearly quit over the substandard quality of green beans delivered to the restaurant by a friend-of-the-house purveyor, his odd-couple relationship with Willy Bishop, the regional American dinner.

One name is left conspicuously unspoken, as it was from a virtually identical speech he gave at MAD, René Redzepi's Copenhagen think-conference earlier that year: Alice Waters.

It reminds me of the time I broached "the letter" with Jeremiah. "I think it was okay to do it," he tells me. "It's the only public evidence that she thought . . . up until that point . . . it was the only time she admitted to anybody that she thought I had done something valuable. . . . To this day, it doesn't horrify me that I did it. Not at all."

Tower traces the depth of his resentment to the moment in 1982 when Waters scarcely credited his contribution to her first cookbook, which featured many of his recipes and menus. "This is the woman who took my name out . . . when she did the first book." But it's swelled over the years, to monster proportions.

When I meet with Ruth Reichl for an interview on a rainy midweek afternoon at BackBar restaurant in Hudson, New York, she tells me the genesis of the documentary: Years prior, the Zero Point Zero people had asked Reichl whom they should profile in the second season of *Mind of a Chef*.

"And I said, 'Jeremiah,'" says Reichl. "And Lydia [Tenaglia, co-founder of Zero Point Zero productions] said, 'Who's he?' They'd never heard of him. . . . That is the Alice-Jeremiah problem right there. I mean, this is just, maybe, five years ago."

"Well, he's made a lot of headway," I say.

"Yup."

I share with Reichl that I've had a rough time sorting out the credit issue and ask if Tower is wrong to feel as he does.

"You know, no, he's not wrong," says Reichl. "I mean, yes, he is wrong. I mean, actually: He was an important piece of Chez Panisse at that time but Chez Panisse is Alice's creature. And you know, I mean, I think the thing that is so interesting about that dynamic is just you're looking at two sides. You're sort of looking at Berkeley and San Francisco, you know? And Alice is a revolutionary. And her goal has always been to change the world through food. And Jeremiah is all about glamour and power and position. . . . Alice, she drives a Prius. She lives in the same house she's [always] lived in."

(A similar sentiment was offered by Boulevard restaurant's Nancy Oakes: "Alice changed what we eat. Jeremiah changed in reality *how* we eat.")

In November 2014, Tower stunned the food world by taking the executive chef job at the embattled Tavern on the Green in New York City's Central Park, which had been taken over by two Philadelphia restaurateurs and had earned zero stars from both the *New York Times* and *New York* magazine. He actively pursued the job, even going through a fire drill at one point when the owners asked him to cook five dishes in seven minutes. "And I did it and it was fine," he says. "I ran around the stations. You know, I already knew what they were serving but, you know, I sort of went to one of the sous chefs and said, 'Okay. What's great? What's in-house that I don't know about?' And he said, 'We have some filet for one of the banquets. You can have one of those.' And I saw some chanterelles, and I quickly made some Robuchon mashed potatoes and put a dish together with that. And then there were some heirloom tomatoes so I chopped those up and made a wonderful sort of French-Mexican salsa out of that, put some tilefish in the pizza oven. There was some corn in there so I cooked that with basil and olive oil, did a bed of that with the fish and the salsa on top. And a few other dishes like that."

The familiar Tower pattern had been activated: He'd landed a shocking, attention-generating gig, but by April 2015, he was out of Tavern. Once again, he'd gone from low to high and back to low again.

It only took a year for the next recalibration: Before I knew it, it was April 2016, and I was sitting on a picture-perfect Saturday afternoon at the premiere of *The Last Magnificent*. In the audience are David Burke, Drew Nieporent, former cooks and front-of-house staff from Stars. (My world had also become bizarrely small; my publisher Dan Halpern, seated mere feet from me, was set to publish a revised edition of *California Dish*, newly titled *Start the Fire*.) On the screen, Tower's life plays out in reenactments, archival footage, and interviews. Mario Batali pronounces Stars more influential than Chez Panisse. We watch as seventy-two-year-old Tower goes through the Tavern folly. Notably absent from the film is Alice Waters, who didn't consent to an interview.

The afternoon is a triumph for Tower, who's brought up on stage after the screening for a conversation with Tenaglia and Bourdain, moderated by Charlie Rose, who wears sneakers with his dress pants. Tower is greeted by a standing ovation, peppered with people from throughout his life—it feels something like a Hollywood ending. In the ensuing months, the film shows at festivals around the United States, he travels to the events, teases them on Facebook. Oh, and in his spare time, he's written and released an etiquette book, *Table Manners*.

The day before the premiere, my friend chef Jimmy Bradley and I interview Tower, Bourdain, and Tenaglia for *The Front Burner*, a podcast we host on the web-based Heritage Radio Network. Afterwards, Jimmy and I rounded the corner to the elevators to find Tower standing there, trench coat draped over his arm.

"Can we buy you a drink?" we asked.

"Can't do it," he said. "Meeting people at Marea."

Tower was, once again, in demand.

And yet . . . just as Waters was missing from that speech in Chicago and the movie, she's also missing from the battle for Chez Panisse. As Tower travels around the world chasing his legacy, she relaxes in Berkeley, travels at her leisure, with—whether right or wrong—nothing to prove. Another moment that haunts me from our interview: Did she really not remember that letter from her former collaborator and lover, framed on the wall in San Francisco's hottest restaurant for all to see, or was she sending a sly signal that it doesn't matter? The letter may survive somewhere—for all I know it hangs in Tower's kitchen in Cozumel—but there's no public wall on which to flaunt it.

"Whether this was all Jeremiah or all Alice or some of each or neither or whatever is kind of beside the point," says Colman Andrews, when I interview him, before launching into a description of Chez Panisse's relevance. What's funny is that I never asked him who deserved the credit. He was clearly anticipating—perhaps dreading—the question, weary of it.

Professional cooking can be cruel. Not only does it demand that a chef prove his or her mettle every day, from scratch, but maintaining a place in the public consciousness demands a restaurant in which to do it. "I don't really see myself as a chef because I don't put on my whites," Tower said to me in our first interview. "I get to go out to dinner instead of cooking it. So, no, I don't see myself as a chef so much anymore. I would be again the moment there was a restaurant and I put my whites on. But that's not my identity now for myself."

This, it seems to me, is one of the key lessons of Tower's saga and explains his fixation, after all these years, on Chez Panisse, as well as his attempted comeback at Tavern on the Green. A chef without a restaurant is, almost by definition, incomplete, if not impossible.

Those who were there will tell you that even by the early 1980s, Waters had attained the messianic glimmer that she exudes to this day. Even then, Chez Panisse was hailed in many circles as the first link in the new American restaurant's evolutionary chain. Maybe Tower sensed all along that his ocean liner was fated to go the way of most restaurants, while Chez Panisse—with a prominence poised to sustain its modest scale in perpetuity—was built for longevity. Stars menus are tucked away in the drawers of former cooks, its laughter faded, the dishes surviving only in the pages of Tower's cookbooks. And so I imagine Tower, looking out over generations who know nothing of Stars but make pilgrimages to Chez Panisse, and can understand why he still wants to claim it after all these years, because while his masterpiece's legacy endures, the place where he—in every sense of the word—*left* his mark literally survives, as much a museum, or a shrine, as a restaurant. You could have dinner there tonight, if you planned far enough ahead to have secured a reservation. That way lies immortality.

8

A ROOM OF THEIR OWN

Bobby wasn't Bobby, Mario wasn't Mario. . . . We were all just cooks.

—Bruce Bromberg

HOW BLUE RIBBON CREATED THE LATE-NIGHT CHEF CULTURE OF THE 1990S, AND THE FOOD NETWORK CAME OUT OF NO-WHERE TO IRREVERSIBLY ALTER THE INDUSTRY

Of all the unknowable aspects of professional kitchen life, perhaps none is more misunderstood by the general population than the late-night post-service rituals of cooks and chefs. Outside observers are as fascinated by the drinking and mating habits of the culinary set as they are by what happens in the pan or winds up on the plate. Cooks party. Hard. But for all the literal and virtual ink that's been devoted to their nocturnal exploits—to what happens after the whites are in the bin and street clothes have been donned— what most outsiders fail to grasp is that cooking doesn't just happen to attract people who like to drink to excess and go to sleep when vampires do, that it's not a coincidence that cooks party but rather it's the work itself that necessitates it.

Consider: For the average cook working a dinner shift, the day begins in the late morning and continues almost unbroken until well past midnight. The early hours may be calm, a time for prep work and banter. But as sunset approaches, the screws begin to turn and pressure builds toward the dinner hour. Once the orders start flying, heads turn downward and don't turn back up for five hours or longer. During that time, each cook will ready, fire, and plate a handful of dishes probably dozens of times. They will lose themselves in the tumult of service, acting on intuition. There will be periods of soulful, Zen-like synchronicity. There will also be accidents, miscues, and recoveries. Tempers may flare along with the gas jets. Burns and bruises may accrue. Massive amounts of water and caffeine will be guzzled; trips to the bathroom will be rare.

After performing, cog-like, for hours, subordinating personality to the kitchen organism, the need for release is immense, and the easiest way to achieve it is, and always has been, through the consumption of alcohol. And so it's a phenomenon of the industry that those who cook develop a metabolic callus to massive alcohol intake, and to functioning on levels of sleep that would test a med student's stamina.

"We needed to decompress quickly because we had to come back the next day, so we would drink," says Paul Zweben, a veteran of David Burke's River Café kitchen in the 1980s. "The normal intake for a cook was anywhere from six to twelve beers a night. Twelve beers, you were wasted, but ten beers, you were fine, you were like, 'All right, guys. Good night. I'm going home.'"

"Even now, I drink more than the normal person," says Zweben, who co-owns a few Manhattan restaurants and has transitioned to a successful career in Manhattan real estate. "If I went to the doctor and he asked me how many drinks I had a week, he'd say, 'You have a drinking problem.' I remember there was one day I was bringing back recyclable bottles from my apartment and I had, like, fifteen cases of recyclable bottles and my neighbor said, 'Oh my God. Did you have a party?' I just looked at him and said, 'I have no idea what you're talking about. I'm just recycling my bottles.' It was like we were on two different planets."

"There was always the drinking culture," says Tom Colicchio, who followed up his gigs at The Quilted Giraffe and Gotham Bar and Grill by helming the kitchen at Mondrian in the late 1980s, where he became one of the few Americans of that decade to earn an elusive *New York Times* three-star rating. "But it's not surprising. It's a tough life in a way. It's always glorified but it's fucking hard work. You're working holidays, you're working weekends, so your friends are the people you work with. It's very, very difficult to maintain relationships even with your buddies because your friends are the friends who you're working with in the restaurant. And then the problem you have when you chef in that restaurant, is that you can't be friends with these people anymore. It's much more of a screwed-up culture than people understand it to be. You start drinking when service ends. Last ticket goes out, you start drinking; you're cleaning up the kitchen, you're drinking; and you'd go out and you'd drink some more; and you start doing drugs. It's nowhere near as glamorous as people think it is, the lifestyle."

Daniel Boulud recalls that when he was running the kitchen at The Polo restaurant at the Westbury Hotel in the early 1980s, a trio of young American cooks would often work so late for him, helping prepare banquets and such, that he would put them up in a guest room. "The problem was that I needed to deliver a case of beer to them. They were true American kids in this way. I never experienced that in France, the fact that they needed a case of beer before they could go to sleep."

Says Stephen Kalt, who cooked under Boulud at Le Cirque in the mid-1980s, "Daniel runs a pressure cooker. He ramps it up and cranks it up and gets it as tight as it possibly can be. And so what are you going to do afterwards, go home and read a book? You're not going to go to sleep, because you have adrenaline going and it doesn't stop. It winds down a little, but it's eleven p.m. and you just served two hundred forty very high-end meals to everyone from Woody Allen to Richard Nixon to Jack and Jane from Connecticut. And he's already working on specials for the next day and you're already thinking about when you've got to come in and what you have to do in the morning because you just used up all your stuff. It's not like today where people can't work more than eight hours."

This is a common lament among those who made their bones in the 1970s and '80s, that employment regulations and the specter of legal action create a climate where excessive working hours and the tough love of a chef, verbal or otherwise, can have devastating consequences. The exertions and pressures of life in a less evolved time created an even greater need for release than today's cooks feel. And in addition to the desire to decompress (read: drink) came a craving for human interaction, to commiserate with comrades after suppressing the stresses and frustrations of a shift.

In the early days of the movement, the nocturnal scene was scattershot, lacking a focal point. Chefs and cooks tended to hang with their own crews at whatever bar was most convenient. In New York City, Charlie Palmer and his Aureole gang hit strip clubs or the Old Town, a nineteenth-century tavern on East 18th Street. Others closed down the Subway Inn, a dive bar around the corner from Bloomingdale's in Midtown, or whatever Irish bar was convenient. Boulud says that sometimes, by coincidence, cooks from different restaurants might end up at the same watering hole: "Next to the subway station would be a bar and all the cooks from every restaurant within a ten-block radius would meet there after work." Zweben remembers that there was a bar on Montague Street in Brooklyn Heights that he and his fellow River Café cooks frequented, but he doesn't remember the name. "Honestly, it didn't matter," he says.

"IT WAS ALSO IN THE LIGHT OF DAY, WHICH IS JUST SOMETHING THAT NEVER HAPPENED."

Much would change in chefs' social landscape in the early 1990s, connecting them with each other and with their growing fan base in unprecedented ways. The proliferation of charity events from coast to coast throughout the mid-1980s helped foster a national network by introducing chefs from different cities to each other. But as the 1990s dawned, the daily life of American chefs transformed as well, especially in New York City, where a community of cooks coalesced as never before.*

An early agent of change was Gerry Dawes, who hailed from southern Illinois, fell in love with wine, especially Spanish wines and culture, and had become a restaurant sales rep for The Winebow Group. Because he sold to what he referred to as "all-star chefs" in New York City, Dawes began organizing industry parties to help promote his portfolio. Most of these were in New York City, but one memorable event was held in Spring Valley, New York, for which he hired a unicyclist as entertainment. There was just one problem: "He was stoned and couldn't stay on the unicycle," drawls Dawes, whose accent sounds more Southern than Illinois.

Rather than spawn larger and larger parties, these events led Dawes to create a more intimate, periodic gathering of chefs who met once a month at each other's restaurants, where the host chef would prepare a five-course lunch for the others. The inaugural group included future culinary deity Thomas Keller, still stuck in

---

* One reason for this was likely practical: Unlike in most American cities, chefs and cooks in New York City didn't have to drive, and in most cases didn't own cars, relying on the subway or taxis as their primary means of transportation, so they could drink as much as they wanted, as late as they wanted, without fear of an accident or DUI conviction.

consulting mode; La Côte Basque alum Rick Moonen, cheffing by then for Buzzy O'Keeffe at his waterside Manhattan restaurant The Water Club on the Manhattan side of the East River; Tom Valenti, chef for former Rakel manager Alison Price Becker at Alison on Dominick Street in Tribeca; Arizona 206's Brendan Walsh; original Union Square Café chef Ali Barker; chefs Phil McGrath and Matthew Tivy; Hudson River Club's Waldy Malouf; and Andy Pforzheimer, who had returned to the East Coast and was chef at Punsch. It also included New York Mets veteran Rusty Staub, who owned two Manhattan restaurants at the time.

The name of the group: Chefs from Hell.

Dawes announced his intentions with an invitation, dated December 1989, that read as follows:

CHEFS FROM HELL
ACROBATIC UNICYCLISTS & WINETASTERS CLUB
CHARTER *(Raison d'eat.....and drink)*

I am forming a winetasting club for chefs, because chefs are often neglected when it comes to getting enough wine to drink, that is, to taste. Since chefs ought to know what wines are good for their food, they should get more opportunities to taste wines in a relaxed atmosphere where they can trade impressions with their fellow chefs and shoot the breeze about wine with visiting winemakers, wine geeks, winery owners, etc. We will have special theme luncheons several times a year featuring guest winemakers, area specialists, and winery reps. We will not be conducting winner/loser blind tastings; our aim is to get a group of wines together and let the host chef create something to complement them, so we can enjoy the wine, the food, and the camaraderie, and learn more about using wines to enhance food.

Our wine luncheons will usually be held on the first or second Monday of each month. They will begin promptly at the appointed hour. (Once or twice a year we will have special tasting dinners.) If you call to attend

*a luncheon, we expect you to show up or give us ample warning, so that
we can get a replacement. Only invitees, and no substitutes or uninvited
guests, may attend. Except on special occasions, each luncheon will usually
be limited to about 15 chefs, the guest wine hosts, and yours truly, so it
is important that you reply early, if you wish to attend. If you know an
out-of-town chef who is visiting, please call and we will see if we can make
a place for him. No restaurant critics will be allowed to attend except
by prior approval of the group. We will, however, invite a prominent
restaurant critic to join us once a year for the chef's roast for critics. If they
don't show up, we will roast them anyway.* Our arrangement with all
restaurants hosting our monthly luncheons will be a $50.00 flat fee, tax
and tip included, and no corkage. If we have not been able to arrange for
the host winery to pay the tab for the group, and they usually will, please
be prepared to pay $50.00 in cash. Except for special occasion luncheons
or dinners, I really don't foresee the group having to pay for many of our
regular functions. (Please cough up an extra $10 apiece each time to
sweeten the tip pool.)*

The first lunch was held at Charlie Palmer's Aureole. The chefs
showed up in the light of day, in their street clothes. Moonen brought
his knife kit along, and was asked to check it at the door. (See Rule
#5, below.) Such a gathering is commonplace today, but at the time
was uncharted territory. "It was a little awkward at first," says Dawes.
"They really didn't know what to expect. But after a couple glasses of
wine, things started to loosen up and they were cool with it. There
was no problem getting them for the second one, and they started
recommending other guys to bring in." (Not all chefs were on board
from the get-go; Dawes says that Terrance Brennan, though he
eventually joined, commented that it was an unserious forum and
wasn't interested.)

---

* The roasts never happened.

With his tongue firmly in cheek, Dawes created a series of by-laws that was expanded periodically, eventually swelling to fifty-nine items. Among them were (asterisks indicate rules that were broken, with multiple asterisks indicating multiple infractions):

1. ABSOLUTELY no acrobatic unicyclists allowed.

5. Meat cleavers and other cutlery are to be checked at the door.*

6. If a chef cannot attend, it is not permissible to send dead monkfish, or any other fish or animal, alive or dead, to sit in his seat as a proxy.*

7. There will be no overt criticism of the host chef's food while he is in earshot, and, while we will allow spitting out of wines, we will not tolerate spitting out the host chef's food.* * * * * *

10. The word *slut*, regardless of which sex it refers to, is forbidden at our gatherings.* * * * *

11. Urinating on the shrubbery or fire hydrant outside the host restaurant in daylight is strictly forbidden.*

15. This rule should be obvious to anyone in this group with class: We really discourage moon shots during service. It draws attention away from the host chef's food, and it is just not the image we want to project.

22. We really want to discourage these chefs' war stories about sex in a walk-in. Some of our members haven't had any anywhere in so long that this kind of talk just makes them jealous.* * * * * * * * * *

23. We were successful in getting some women to attend Chefs From Hell functions. After Rusty Staub's Mardi Gras luncheon, we think it prudent to advise members that we will not tolerate shouts of "Show Your Tits" or any other such sexist remarks (by either sex), even at Mardi Gras luncheons.*

25. All meals will be limited to five courses, if courses are full portions, seven if they are tasting portions. Addendum to rule #25: Furthermore, combinations of caviar, truffles, and foie gras are limited to three maximum on any one plate. Any chef who breaks this rule should be advised that the penalty is severe. We will send a copy of the menu to the owner of your restaurant reminding him/her of the $50.00 per head rule and thanking him for his charitable donation to the Chefs From Hell.* * * * * * * * *

26. We would like to discourage the past Chefs From Hell trend towards wretched excess in the dessert category, therefore, the official position on desserts from here on will be as follows: We will frown on creations that move, smoke, or require batteries, and we will be especially critical of those configured to pick up radio broadcasts. We really don't want to eat something from FAO Schwartz [sic].* * * * * *

27. God, why do we even have to consider this one a rule. To any civilized person, it would seem obvious that one does not discuss surgical scars, let alone show them during the course of the meal. It also would seem to go without saying that detailed discussions of the fine art of circumcision would fall in this category.*

28. The Pittsburgh Pirates hat procurement rule has been deleted. They are no longer the official baseball team of CFH. They threatened to sue for defamation.

43. For future outings, where cars are required, we will appoint a designated driver for Colicchio, whether he has had anything to drink or not.

53. It should go without saying that the unwritten rule amongst gentleman chefs (an oxymoron, if there ever was one) about not breaking wind at these functions is still a rule, written or not. We have a good idea who has been

doing this, so just remember, if you are caught, you risk a one function suspension, enforced by the Sergeant-at-arms, if and when we ever find him again.*

56. We are tired of these feeble excuses for missing Chefs From Hell functions. Among some of the more notorious and overused ones are:

    1) I got married.

    2) I had to play in a charity golf tournament.

    3) I can't stand my husband's (the host chef's) food.

    4) I got locked in a walk-in.

    5) I am sunning my ass in Mexico.

And, worst of all,

    6) I had to work!

From now on the only valid excuses for not attending a CFH function are:

    a) I was hung over.

    b) I caught a social disease for which I was not the primary distributor.

    c) My restaurant went Chapter 11 and I was held at gunpoint by an irate supplier.

    d) The host chef is my former sous chef (sorry, chef de cuisine) and I taught him everything he knows.

57. It also goes without saying that rules #11 & #47 prohibiting urinating on fire hydrants, shrubs, etc. also includes the pig fountain at the James Beard House.* *

"And the unspoken first rule is 'We'll break every damn rule in this rule book,' which really appeals to chefs, because they're rule break-ers," says Dawes.

It doesn't sound like the kind of association with which the pathologically serious Thomas Keller would associate himself, but he says he believed in the cause: "It's camaraderie. It's the one thing that we don't really do enough at any time throughout our careers. I think one of the things that inspired me to become a chef or continues to inspire me to become a chef was the book *The Great Chefs of France*. You look at that book and you look at those guys and they were all comrades, they were colleagues, they were friends. They did things together outside the restaurant. And we didn't have that in this country. We were skeptical. We were apprehensive. We were threatened by other chefs. So the idea of bringing chefs together is an extraordinary thing. When Gerry did that, it was like, 'Wow, this is pretty cool. I get to meet these other guys. We get to spend time together. We get to do things together outside the restaurants.' I think that was a very important thing."

Prior to Chefs from Hell, says Keller, New York chefs were too busy to connect. "As a community of professionals, we are one of the few that actually doesn't spend time together. If you're an attorney, there are always these guilds, there are always these symposiums. And it's not about press. That's where we got off track. Today, we do things together only if there's a press angle to it, only if there's some value for somebody to write about it, because it gives us more recognition and feeds our ego. Doctors, attorneys, they don't do their meetings to be written about; they do it to exchange ideas, because they enjoy one another. Chefs from Hell was kind of like that. There was no media angle. Gerry brought it together just for the benefit of us, to have fun. We'd go out with—Rusty Staub, I mean, Christ, he'd take us to opening day at Shea Stadium.* Who gets to do that with Rusty Staub? Rusty is still a friend today."

Tom Colicchio remembers it less loftily than Keller, to whom he was a sous chef at Rakel in the late 1980s: "We would literally sit around and drink and laugh our asses off. A lot of these guys have their 'chef personality.' When you get together in a room with them,

---

* The New York Mets' home stadium prior to Citi Field.

they're funny as hell. I remember sitting next to Tom Valenti and just fucking laughing so much that wine's pouring out of our noses. We had a good time. And some of it was poking fun. If someone bombed a dish, we'd all fucking get on him. You never gave the person the business but you'd comment to each other. Like Tom Valenti would say, 'You'd eat this? This sucks.' It was also in the light of day, which is just something that never happened. We'd always get together in bars.

"The organization wasn't an organization. It was literally, 'Who's cooking this month and where are we going?' And that was it. But if you were the chef cooking, you were showing off because these were all your peers. So to me, it was a great time because when do you get to hang out with guys who you work with? I worked with Tom Valenti at Gotham, and so he's cooking at Alison on Dominick, and I'm doing what I'm doing, you don't see him. So all of a sudden you have this luncheon and you're with all these guys that you know and you like and you all came up at the same time. It was a blast."

Charter member Rick Moonen says that prior to Chefs from Hell, there was scant cross-pollination among cooks from different kitchens, although as more and more young Americans entered the profession and advanced from job to job, a network was being established. "But Chefs from Hell accelerated that process by a large margin," he says.

Dawes freely admits that he had several motivations for starting Chefs from Hell. One was to sell his wines to the chefs. Another was that he was tired of hanging out with cork dorks, preferring the company of cooks: "I saw chefs as kind of blue-collar guys in those days that knew how to have fun. They got off late, they went out and raised hell."

It was quickly established that the host chef was going to show off for his peers. At The River Café, David Burke, in accordance with his signature River Café chocolate bridge, made the centerpiece of his dessert presentation a chocolate stove that actually smoked, and Rick Moonen fashioned a ship sailing across a coconut-raspberry sea to a cookie island (see Rule #26, above). Burke also served a tuna tartare covered with crème fraîche and smothered with osetra caviar (see Rule #25, above). "If Buzzy had caught him, he'd have probably kicked his ass," laughs Dawes.

Rick Moonen says that getting to know his peers "excited me, inspired me to do better." The lunches, he says, became an outlet for healthy competition, such as the one served by Tom Valenti at Alison on Dominick Street. "I remember having a cylinder—[like] a filet mignon—of swordfish. It was served medium rare and wrapped in bacon, or some sort of a pork product. I remember it as if it was yesterday."

As in any boys' club, there were the inevitable pranks: Dawes created a Chefs from Hell barf bag by having his daughter draw a design on an airline bag. At an Alison on Dominick Street lunch, the chefs summoned Tom Valenti from the kitchen to inform him that his food had made Rick Moonen sick. When Valenti emerged, they pointed to an ashen Moonen, holding the bag. (It helped that Moonen was actually queasy that day, so he looked the part.) Dawes, who had surreptitiously loaded the bag with vegetable soup, asked for it.

"He gives it to me and I opened it up and said, 'Hey, man. This looks better than the shit coming out of the kitchen.' I get in with a spoon and take a bite. I thought Valenti was going to have a hemorrhage."

Another gag occurred at The Water Club. Recounts Dawes: "Buzzy O'Keeffe always did things right. He had this tuxedoed waiter running the show. He has an upstairs dining room. Moonen had the whole place full downstairs for lunch. And he was feeding us and we had Bob Haas's Burgundies. They had these beautiful floral arrangements on the table. That's where I got the rule about you can't eat the floral arrangements because they cost more than the entrees. Andy shows me that he's brought this big plastic beetle. So there's a salad course and I pick a little bit of the salad and I stick the bug in it and I call the guy over. I said, 'Would you please take this down to the chef and tell him that he really should take more care in washing and cleaning his greens?' So Moonen's down there getting slammed and apparently the guy brings it to him. He says, 'What the fuck? Who sent this down here?' The waiter says, 'The guy who's running the luncheon.' Nothing was said. Guy didn't come back and say, 'Moonen tells you go fuck yourself,' or anything like that. But come dessert time, on my plate, one of the chocolates is this plastic beetle covered in chocolate."

On the more serious side, after a few lunches, Dawes instituted "show-and-tell," asking each chef to stand up and "update us on what they were doing, if they'd changed restaurants. Tell us how things were going for them, all this kind of stuff. So they all basically got up and did that."

In the 1990s, the group would expand and contract, counting among its members such chefs and industry figures as Odeon chef Stephen Lyle; D'Artagnan co-founder George Faison; Union Square Café's Michael Romano; Tribeca Grill's Don Pintabona; '21' Club's Michael Lomonaco; Tom Colicchio; Mario Batali, who moved to New York from San Francisco; Bobby Flay, who had found his Southwestern voice first at Miracle Grill and then at Mesa Grill, in partnership with Gotham impresario Jerry Kretchmer and partners; and James Beard Foundation president Len Pickell. (Notably absent were Jonathan Waxman and Larry Forgione, which Dawes says was due to the fact that they were traveling in their own rarefied air, part of the more nationally known clique of celebrity chefs of the day.)

Though largely a boys' club, women did join the pack, including Arcadia's Anne Rosenzweig, Rose Levy Beranbaum, Teresa

Barrenechea, Pamela Morgan, and honorary member Julia Child. Dawes invited Martha Stewart to join a lunch at Gramercy Tavern when Tom Colicchio was at the helm. Remembers Dawes of that day's show-and-tell: "When Martha's turn comes, she gets up and tells a story that has *fuck* in it because she wanted to show that she's one of the guys. It was about some guy who had gotten pissed off and quit and had sent out a Christmas card with 'And I hope you have a fucking good Christmas,' or something like that, printed on it. And they had to call all these people who'd received these cards and tell them it was some disgruntled employee who had sent it. So she got to work her *fuck* in to show that she's one of the boys. Later on, she had us all up to her place in Connecticut."

Chefs from Hell charter member Rick Moonen also belonged to an intimate, less well remembered group, the Red Meat Club, that started up around the same time. (Never mind that at both The Water Club and then at Oceana he was known as one of New York's premier fish chefs.) The club, also centered around lunches, included sommeliers Traci Dutton and John Fisher, legendary bartender Dale DeGroff, and chef David Page.

"Red Meat Club met the second Tuesday of every month, different steakhouse," says Moonen. "You were only allowed to order two types of cocktails: a Beefeater martini or a Bloody Mary. Why? *Because those are the rules!* Because we're a fucking red meat society and we eat red meat and we mean it. If you ordered it rare, you had to follow it with 'And I mean rare!' Those are the rules. 'I'll have the ribeye steak rare. And I mean rare.' And everybody would go, 'And I mean rare.' We'd sit around and we'd get drunk on the second Tuesday of every month. At Palm, Palm Too, Ben Benson's.

"This was real," says Moonen. "This wasn't some phantom twelve-month thing. This was the Red Meat Club, man. There was the Chefs from Hell and the Red Meat Club. Not to be taken lightly."

"YOU CAN ONLY DO THAT SO LONG."

In 1990, Moonen partnered with two fellow La Côte Basque alums, Charlie Palmer and Frank Crispo, then the chef at Andiamo, to take the emerging society of New York City chefs to the next level, to combine the desire for community with their universal late-night habits at a restaurant called Chefs Cuisiniers Club.

The idea was hatched, remembers Crispo, on Super Bowl Sunday that January: "We were all looking to go out and there was really nothing to do. We found ourselves at Rusty Staub's eating frozen Weaver drumsticks, or whatever they used to serve there. And we started saying, 'Hey, let's open up a place just for cooks, for where *we* can hang out.' I had a friend that knew this Mexican restaurant on 22nd Street that wanted to get out of business. We put the finances together and I did the plumbing and all the stoves and Charlie's sister, who had worked for Adam Tihany, did the design."*

The ability to jump in underscored the differences between chefs who owned their own restaurants, even in partnership with others, and those who didn't. Palmer didn't need to ask anybody's permission, but for Moonen, working for Buzzy O'Keeffe at The Water Club, things were more complicated: "I had to ask permission from Buzzy to be a partner in it. He wasn't too keen on it."

The concept was greeted enthusiastically by the media, a logical next step in the growing fascination with the American chef community. "The only potential problem," mused the *New York Times's* Bryan Miller, "is when hip New York night owls sniff it out, will there be any room for chefs?"

Situated in a narrow, rectangular space on East 22nd Street, with a long bar that gave way to an intimate dining room, the Chefs Cuisiniers Club (or "the Triple C" as the owners came to refer to it)

---

* Palmer's recollection is that the idea was hatched at the Old Town.

opened in early fall 1990. On the walls were framed menus from the owners' heroes such as Georges Blanc, Paul Bocuse, and Alain Chapel and a bulletin board advertising kitchen employment opportunities. There was also a library of cookbooks and food magazines, and in 1992 Palmer commissioned a nine-by-four-and-a-half-foot mural, a Last Supper–ish representation of legends such as Bocuse, Blanc, Chapel, Marie-Antoine Carême, Auguste Escoffier, Alain Ducasse, and contemporaries Wolfgang Puck and Le Cirque impresario Sirio Maccioni.

Early menu items, turned out by chef Peter Assue, a Palmer protégé, included warm goat cheese over warm potato salad and a tomato-shallot vinaigrette, eggplant and lentil terrine, and braised cod in a broth with oven-dried tomatoes. But the menu changed often, and not always based on Assue's inspiration. "He's got three guys telling him what to do," says Palmer. "And then we'd all go down there and do shit on our own. It was kind of like, 'What do you feel like eating late at night *this* week?' I mean, literally, we'd change the menu that Monday night at the bar, at two in the morning."

The trio of chef-owners leveraged their industry clientele to secure great deals and giveaways from vendors. For example, the food was served on a hodgepodge of plates from luxury producers like Wedgwood and Villeroy & Boch who gifted them to the restaurant for exposure: "The idea was we'd get plates from every manufacturer, so there would be a mix and match on the tables. So if you like the plate, you'd turn it over, and say, 'Who is this by?' So we'd haggle a little bit and get it for free. Because of all the cigar smoking, we got Partagas to do a party," says Crispo.

There were Halloween parties (Crispo dressed as Aunt Jemima), Oktoberfest bashes, Christmas and New Year's Eve bacchanals. "We never made any money because every time we made some money, we'd throw a party," says Palmer.* "These were epic parties, I mean,

---

* Crispo doesn't agree with that characterization.

epic. Spilled into the street. People complained about the noise. Police came every time."

There were also gag events, like a lamprey eel–eating contest to be judged by Montrachet owner Drew Nieporent (who opened Tribeca Grill in partnership with Robert De Niro the same year Chefs Cuisiniers Club launched) that was promoted with a flyer circulated to restaurants by fetching young females from the Triple C's front-of-house team. The flyer was real; the event was pure fiction.

The emerging community of star chefs flocked to the restaurant: David Burke, Larry Forgione, Tom Colicchio, Jean-Georges Vongerichten, Daniel Boulud, and chef-couple Bobby Flay and Debra Ponzek, who would go on to marry, and divorce. Like Chefs from Hell, early on Chefs Cuisiniers Club seemed like a boys' club, all the more so for the cigar smoke that filled the air late in the evening from, among others, Palmer himself, although as Palmer says, "We got the chefs but also got the chicks that like chefs. It was exactly what we hoped it would be."

There was one downside to an industry clientele: "We had a ton of house accounts because nobody ever paid for shit," says Palmer. "Chefs would be like, 'What are you going to say, No?' That's what we did the place for. There's a lot of deadbeat chefs, you know?"

The critical reception was mixed. *New York* magazine's Gael Greene was swept up in the scene, on the whole enjoyed the food. The *New York Times*'s Marian Burros, in a one-star takedown, complained that "providing moderately priced food is not a license to hire an untrained staff and inflict them on paying customers." She also hypothesized that "perhaps when Mr. Palmer and his chef friends arrive after midnight, they are too tired to notice the lapses. Perhaps they get better treatment and more carefully prepared food than the average customer."

The *Times* review still rankles at least one partner: "It was weird," says Crispo. "She was digging at him for no reason. They singled out Charlie because he had Aureole."

Beyond the job listings, Hervé Riou, a Frenchman who moved to New York City in 1988 and ran the kitchen at the Plaza Hotel's Edwardian Room, remembers another function of the Chefs Cuisiniers Club: to find new hires on the spot. "If you needed a job, you could go there, speak to a chef, do a line of coke, order a burger, and if you were lucky, you would stay until closing and go to work with him that very morning," says Riou.

Chefs Cuisiniers Club also began publishing a newsletter, something the Red Meat Club, Boulud, and Danny Meyer were also doing, deepening a connection with customers even as chefs were forging improved relationships with each other. In addition to its newsletter, the Triple C also hosted tastings of everything from Spanish olive oil to Chablis and oysters to a roster of twenty-seven chocolates one summer afternoon. There were also wine dinners at which menus were built around a particular vineyard's offerings.

What started well faded quickly. Chefs Cuisiniers Club lost its mojo, and its chef clientele. "It started out just being a hangout," says Crispo. "But the egos of the chefs involved possibly made the place more of a restaurant." As the best chefs in town made it their after-hours destination, the owners felt they had to step up the food. "Next thing you know, instead of just doing funky stuff like tripe, we found ourselves having a traditional menu: appetizers, main course, and Richie Leach, Charlie's pastry chef, would do pastries."

Palmer cites another reason for the Triple C slowing to a halt: "I had to stop the party. I was dying. Frank and Rick and I, we were there till, like, two, three in the morning every fricking night, practically. You can only do that so long."

The chefs decided to go their separate ways, divvying up what little profit remained, with Palmer holding on to the lease. In the fall of 1994, Palmer partnered with Fernando Saralegui, a veteran of Café Luxembourg and Raoul's, to recast the space as Alva (after Thomas Alva Edison), a cigar bar and restaurant. When the *New York Times* asked Saralegui where the chefs would congregate after the Triple C served its last supper, he replied, "Blue Ribbon, where they already have been hanging out for the past two years."

"YOU KNOW, I HATE THIS WALL."

The desire for community, a place to eat and drink and connect after hours, was finally fulfilled, once and for all and against all odds, by a Sullivan Street restaurant that was a debacle in its first incarnation. F. Scott Fitzgerald wrote that "great art is the contempt of a great man for small art." Well, Blue Ribbon largely grew from two brothers' contempt for their own small art, a failed restaurant launched in June 1992, with a name made for calamity: The Crystal Room.

The Crystal Room was launched by siblings Bruce and Eric Bromberg and partner Philip Hoffman. The Bromberg brothers had been raised across the Hudson River in New Jersey in a food-crazed Jewish American family. Their father, an attorney, bon vivant, and adventurous home cook, exposed them to every imaginable food, and their grandmother was, by the brothers' estimation, one of the best cooks in her tight-knit conservative Jewish community. The brothers grew up loving food, with a special fascination for the theatrical, like the Japanese steakhouse chain Benihana, where the cooks performed miraculous knife work in harrowingly close proximity to diners. They were also raised to be Francophiles; dad had a house in Venasque, near Avignon in Provence, where a local chef would let the boys visit the kitchen, pour Cognac over his shrimp Provençal to flame it. "We thought it was the coolest shit," remembers Bruce.

Born five years apart, both brothers attended Le Cordon Bleu cooking school in Paris. On his return to the States, after working for Jonathan Waxman at Jams, Eric honchoed other kitchens before opening, in 1989, Nick and Eddie, a popular SoHo restaurant fashioned after the timeless aesthetic of New York watering holes—all dark wood and mirrors, with a bar in the front room—that served stripped-down food such as a spinach and bacon salad, roast chicken, and an uncommonly sophisticated burger, counterprogramming to the increasingly complicated plates being turned out by other young Americans around town. Nick and Eddie was an early bastion of what Eric considers "New York food" and would come to be known as "comfort food." The restaurant also broke with another given in hotspots of the day with a no-reservation policy designed to keep the place accessible to neighborhood diners. When an appealing space opened nearby on Sullivan Street, Nick and Eddie partner Philip Hoffman nabbed it and put together a partnership with Eric, who summoned Bruce to return from France and collaborate with him.

The brothers' enthusiasm waned as The Crystal Room evolved, under Hoffman's direction, into the very antithesis of Nick and Eddie. "As brilliant as Nick and Eddie was, The Crystal Room was as nonbrilliant," says Bruce. "It was like an exclusive social club. It was just all wrong."

Because of its connection to white-hot Nick and Eddie, reservations at The Crystal Room were hard to come by early on, although first-time visitors were aghast at the restaurant's design. "It was horrible," says Bruce. "There was a Grecian scene painted on the walls and Byzantine columns." The room was dimly lit, but "not dim enough."

According to Bruce, within four weeks, Hoffman stopped showing up. "He saw the writing on the wall. He knew this was a major disaster."

Eric had sunk everything he had into the restaurant, plus money from their father and family friends. Within ten weeks, The Crystal Room had been left for dead by the citizenry. "All of a sudden it was me and my brother and our core team sitting there, and we basically realized we were going out of business," says Bruce.

One midnight after service, Eric emerged from the kitchen.

"Guys, we're done," he said. "We're not going to open tomorrow. I've pretty much lost my shirt. I can't continue to lose any more of my family's money. I can't take purveyors' food and not pay them for it, which is what we're doing."

The crew, including runner Sean Sant Amour, cook Chris Pollack, and waiter David Brown, some of whom came with Eric from Nick and Eddie and others of whom were new to the team, soaked up the news, then Sant Amour stood up, sauntered over to the wall that separated the lounge from the dining room, and said, "You know, I hate this wall," and put his foot right through it.

"About an hour and a half later, that wall was completely gone," remembers Bruce. "Eric was just sitting there with his bottle of Scotch in the corner, drowning his sorrows, and we were like, 'Dude, we can rebuild this. We can make good food. It's a good location. Let's do it.' The next day we called my dad and asked him for $25,000."

With no real plan, the team began remaking the dining room. "People would come by and ask, 'What kind of food are you making?' We'd say, 'Good food.' We didn't have an idea. Up until a couple days before we opened, we hadn't written a menu. We didn't know what it was."

Before the menu came the name, for which they were desperate. Their father, based on the Sullivan Street location, suggested Gilbert's on Sullivan, even though there was no Gilbert involved. Thankfully, the brothers resisted. Late one night, hanging out in the space, drinking beers with Nick and Eddie bartender George Gilmore, the brothers began bandying about names.

"What's this place mean to you?" asked Gilmore. "What do you want it to be?"

"I want it to not be French but somehow I want everything we've learned and everything we're about to come through," said Bruce.

"What's the name of that school you guys went to?" asked Gilmore.

"Le Cordon Bleu."

"What's that translated into English?"

"Blue Ribbon," said Bruce.

And he said, "Well, then you're done."

Recalls Bruce, "And Eric and I looked at him and said, 'You are right. We are done.'"

A few nights later, with the space still months from completion, the brothers hosted a party.

"We were playing roller hockey in the dining room; we all had Rollerblades and we had a goal set up on either side of the restaurant. And we were all drunk, skating around, having a ball," says Bruce. "And I sketched out *Blue Ribbon* on the wall. I think I had a couple markers, Sharpies or something like that. Sean, who's now my partner and manager of all our restaurants, went to college for graphics. He sat down with a piece of paper. He took what I drew on the wall and we were all pretty lit, but he drew this thing. And, literally, what he drew is the logo that's been there for twenty-five years now."

By mid-October, Blue Ribbon was close to opening, but there was still no menu. One day, Eric's wife, Ellen, became exasperated. "This is ridiculous," she said to the brothers. "We need to order food. We need to print menus. Will you guys go sit down and write a friggin' menu?"

The brothers walked around the corner to Souen, a macrobiotic restaurant at Prince Street and Sixth Avenue, and over bowls of steamed vegetables in miso, with Eric scribbling on a yellow legal pad, improvised the Blue Ribbon menu.

"What is your favorite thing to eat?" asked Eric.

"Lobster."

"What else?"

"Fondue. I love fondue."

"How about stuff Grandma made? Matzo ball soup's really cool."

"All right. Let's do matzo ball soup."

"What else? What's festive?"

"I like paella. Paella's really cool."

It all went on the list, and ultimately on the menu. One element of the menu had already been discussed: *Les frères* Bromberg, based on their memories of Parisian *fruits de mer* platters, were dead set on having a raw bar and had incorporated it into their design, with a station built right in the window.

"Everyone told us it was a terrible idea, that nobody was going to accept it," says Bruce.

"Sure, there's an oyster bar in Grand Central but it's not really a New York thing," said the naysayers.

"But it used to be the heart and soul of New York a hundred years ago or whenever it was," Bruce protested. "I was like, 'We should bring it back.' It's so cool in Paris. Why wouldn't it be cool here? One of our wine salesmen who was a very high-end salesman for Château and Estate was like, 'You're making a mistake. It's going to turn people off.' And we were like, 'Seems friggin' cool to us. It's my favorite shit to watch when I'm in Paris walking on the streets at night.'"

The eclecticism of the menu reminded the brothers of a diner menu, a long document offering a mix of ethnicities and styles. "There's seventeen soups, there's these kinds of sandwiches. And kind of anything goes in a diner, right? Kind of anything can be on the menu."

Blue Ribbon would have other things in common with a diner: While they wouldn't be open twenty-four hours, it was part and parcel of the brothers' vision that they would seat customers until 4 a.m., with the kitchen welcoming orders until then (desserts even later), and that after the democratic example of Nick and Eddie, they would not take reservations.

"It's changed a little bit but it hasn't changed in about twenty-five years," says Bruce.

"JUST SEND US ONE OF EVERYTHING."

Blue Ribbon opened on November 3, 1992. "We had forty-five seats. We still have forty-five seats. We'd do a turn and a half to two turns. It was really exciting and good. But nobody would come in after midnight. We would sit there for four and a half, five hours, and we'd do sometimes zero, mostly zero, but every once in a while somebody would show up. And it slowly started to happen, but very slowly."

"It" was that Blue Ribbon slowly became a draw for cooks and chefs. One of the first was a young, unknown Mario Batali, recently arrived from cooking in San Francisco, honchoing the kitchen around the corner at Rocco on Thompson Street (the current home of Carbone at the time of this writing), and living above Rocco in the same building. "I was there the day it opened," says Batali, nicknamed Molto in those days. "They had a sign in the window that said *oysters* and then the neon sign for Sierra Nevada Pale Ale on draft. I'm like, 'Of course I'm coming in here.'"

"He was our buddy who stumbled by one day and was like, 'Holy shit. I'll have some oysters,'" says Bruce. "He was in New York six months or something. And I'll never forget. We were closed on Mondays. We took the whole team to Rocco's. And fifteen of us sat upstairs and Mario made us dinner. We did friggin' everything together."

One tipping point in the restaurant's success occurred just a few months in, the night Montrachet owner Drew Nieporent stuck his head in. Bruce remembers that the bearded, excitable impresario opened the door and exclaimed, "Holy shit! I heard about this. Are you really doing this?" Nieporent, says Bruce, studied the menu for a few minutes and said, "I'll be back. I'll be back." (Nieporent especially remembers the first impression made by the oysters: "They had this guy opening oysters. It was perfection. In terms of food, oysters happen to be one of the gifts, and they put the guy in the *window*.")

And come back he did, always with an important chef or industry figure in tow.

"I don't want to say Drew single-handedly made us, but he did an amazing thing for us, started coming back with Roger Vergé, [original Tribeca Grill chef] Don Pintabona and the team. Then he called Bobby Flay and told Bobby to come." (Pintabona remembers seeing Batali and future partners Joe and Lidia Bastianich sitting at a round table in the front of Blue Ribbon having one of their first-ever meetings.)

Nieporent pretty much loved everything about Blue Ribbon. "You go in there and it's this menu of favorites. Nobody back then had the cojones to put matzo ball soup with fried chicken with a pu pu platter. And it was *good*. And they were so humble, the brothers and Eric's wife. I would get on the phone with Gael Greene and say, 'Have you been to this place?' Because in those days, word of mouth was key." ("Can the childhood comfort foods of the fifties nurture us through the traumas of the nineties?" posed Greene in her April 1993 *New York* magazine review. "Yes, says the crowd at Blue Ribbon, where the flames of the once nearly extinct pu pu platter cast a soothing glow and the menu flits from suburban rec room to Cordon Bleu . . . a jumble of every adolescent and yuppish craving.")

There was one slight bump, when Nieporent's enthusiasm butted up against the restaurant's utopian mind-set: Because he was partners in the San Francisco restaurant Rubicon with Robin Williams, then at the height of his Hollywood success, the actor-comedian used to phone Nieporent when he hit Manhattan, asking where he should dine, and for Nieporent to make the requisite reservations.

"This one time [he] called me at the last minute on a Saturday night," remembers Nieporent. "It was impossible, then I thought,

Blue Ribbon! They don't take reservations!" He called and spoke to a manager who told him, in accordance with the restaurant's democratic policy, "He might have to wait a little bit."

"I said, 'Listen to me, you either want to take Robin Williams or you don't.'"

After some cogitating the restaurant team came to a solution: They would sit a fake party at Williams's table, then swap Williams and friends in when they arrived.

"He might have to wait a *little* bit," said the manager. "We'll put him at the bar."

"No!" shouted Nieporent. "He's a recovering alcoholic. You can't put him at the bar."

"Anyway," says Nieporent today, "I don't know how that all got worked out, but I know that Robin Williams went to Blue Ribbon that night."

Nieporent also figured in an early, formative night when another of the brothers' idealist policies, the 4 a.m. mandate, was put to the test. It was the weekend prior to Martin Luther King Day, 1993. There was a blizzard that Sunday and with the restaurant closed on Monday anyway, Bruce didn't see the point in keeping the doors open and the staff around.

"It was three in the morning. Nobody had been in the restaurant since 10:45 p.m.," says Bruce. "It was miserable."

"Should we just close?" he suggested to Eric and Ellen.

"No," said Eric. "We've got to stay open. We've never closed. It's part of what we do."

But Bruce coaxed consent from his partners. Downstairs, he fashioned a handwritten sign to let visitors know they'd be back after the holiday. As he was about to affix it to the door, a fleet of taxis pulled up in the slush outside.

"Twenty people get out of the taxis and they walk up to the door," remembers Bruce. "It's Charlie Trotter and his whole team, who had just done some James Beard event. He had a huge crew in the city. I'm literally there with tape to put this sign up, and I'm like, 'No, we're open. Come right in.'"

"I don't need to see a menu," Trotter told him. "We've heard from Drew that we've got to come here. Just send us one of everything."

Batali, who himself showed up later that night, remembers it well. It was the first time he'd ever been in the same room with the already legendary chef from Chicago. "He had one of everything on the menu and I thought that was so extravagant."

"THERE WAS SOMETHING ANIMALISTIC ABOUT IT."

That's how Blue Ribbon began to take its place as *the* late-night New York City chef hangout through the 1990s.

Frank Castronovo, a native New Yorker who today co-owns Prime Meats and Frankies 457 Spuntino, was cooking at Jean Claude just up Sullivan Street from Blue Ribbon at the time and would occasionally join Batali there after service. "At one in the morning I'd roll down the street and walk in," says Castronovo. "I was there when they first, first, first opened. And you know, Mario started coming with me in the beginning. Scott Bryan would meet up over there. I think that I was definitely there for the birth of the late-night dining scene for chefs at Blue Ribbon. That happened on that block at that time. It would go all night, man. Two, three, four a.m. As late as you wanted it to. And in those days you had Eric, Bruce, and Ellen in the room, so you had all the principals. And the energy.

"It was weird because I was there in the very, very beginning when the first couple of hangs happened, and then I didn't partake. Three weeks later, four weeks later, a month or two later, you realized there was already a thing starting to happen. It's growing. You go back for another hang three or four weeks later, it's like, wow,

there's like twenty chefs hanging out now. Then you go there five
months later and it's like, *everybody's* onto it now."

"It was assumed that everybody would be there," says Alan Harding, who was the chef of Nosmo King, a nonsmoking restaurant in
Tribeca, at the time. "If you had just gotten paid and you wanted to
drop some scrilla, you would go there. Otherwise, it was Chinatown,
but Chinatown was you and your sous chef or a cook. It wasn't like,
'Let's all meet up and go to Wo Hop.' That was hardly ever done. It
would have required too much organization."

According to Batali, by about two in the morning the place was
wall to wall with industry: "It was amazing how we all knew each
other and we all hung out, and that was at least twice a week we
would all be there, maybe at different tables, maybe all at one table.
I'd take my whole staff down there every now and then."

Daniel Boulud remembers it the same way, saying that when he
entered the restaurant, he would high-five his way to the back of
the room—slapping hands with David Burke, Charlie Palmer, Jean-
Georges Vongerichten, and any other luminaries between the front
door and his table.

Says Tom Colicchio, who preferred Tribeca's Odeon to Blue
Ribbon but observed the success story from a slight remove: "I think
also chefs got tired of going out and just drinking. We wanted something to eat so we started going down there."

In addition to the universal craving for food and drink at un-
godly hours, the restaurant fulfilled the need for commiseration
with people who understood the rigors of the job. "It was Mario and
Bobby and I, two nights a week, three nights a week up until two or
three in the morning, eating and drinking," remembers Tom Valenti. "We talked about food. We talked about technique. We would
bitch and moan and talk about the stove that broke down and the
walk-in that didn't work."

Says Boulud, who would go on to host the Hulu show *After*

Hours with Daniel, inspired in part by late-night grub and gabfests with fellow chefs: "The importance was that we were sharing the same passion. We were sharing the same sacrifice. We were sharing the same problems. We were sharing the same ambition. I think we are a breed apart and we believed that we could sit down around the table and have conversations with each other."

"There was something about Blue Ribbon that resonated with everyone. They could come to Blue Ribbon and revel, totally blow off steam," recalls Bruce. "There are some really funny nights that stand out: Daniel Boulud had a pretty entertaining party one night with a bunch of his staff and they all got completely lit. I'll never forget him coming out of the bathroom with [wine director] Daniel Johnnes, wrapped from head to toe in toilet paper, hysterically friggin' laughing and running around the restaurant."

Another unique aspect of Blue Ribbon was the elimination of the barrier between front of house and kitchen: "Some chefs would bring me this and that and cook it," says Bruce. "They'd come down in the kitchen with a bottle of Jäger and shots and fiddlehead ferns and put them on the cutting board. Mario would bring a lot of shit, like live eels. We'd just have fun. 'Hey, look what I have in the restaurant tonight.'"

Recalls Batali: "I hung out in the kitchen sometimes because they were my buds and they were busy so I'd just go down there and bring something with me and we'd just hang out for an hour and a half down in the kitchen drinking beer. I remember once it was *cotechino,* which is a pork sausage. We glazed it and we all sat down in the kitchen and we ate it. It was a different time."

"Every single night there was not a table in the restaurant that wasn't the Daniel Boulud crew, the Gotham crew, the Mesa crew, the David Burke crew, Mario and all his buddies," remembers Bruce.

If no such place exists today, blame the advent of cellular and smartphones, enabling friends and cliques to text each other and customize their plans and rendezvous points to suit their own tastes and shifting moods. In the early 1990s, when one's only hope of connecting with a colleague was to catch him or her on a kitchen phone, it was a far easier enterprise to simply head down to Blue Ribbon, knowing that was where you'd encounter anybody who was looking to extend their evening.

As for why Blue Ribbon connected in a way that no other restaurant did, "It was the simplicity," says Batali. "The cooky-ness of it without it being cheffy. These were chefs but they were making fried chicken and they were making paella and they were making a hot dog. It was just the most magnificent place because you could go in on any mood, you could have gourmet, you could have bone marrow—that was the revolutionary bone marrow, the bone marrow with oxtail marmalade that *made* bone marrow. It was fucking awesome. And it was so cheffy that you could bring your chef friends from out of town and go to a restaurant at one in the morning and they were like, '*Fuck! This is New York.*'

"And everyone in that room was aware that something was happening in New York and they were part of it," adds Batali. "It was exciting. And I don't think anybody thought they had to beat anybody or outduel anybody. They all knew that if the rising tide came, all of our boats would go up."

Frank Crispo, one of the triumvirate behind Chefs Cuisiniers Club, pays the Brombergs the ultimate compliment: "You know who did a better job than us—and I say this wholeheartedly—the guys from Blue Ribbon. They just slowly let it build and build. They had that grassroots foundation. Ours, although it came in honest, seemed more deliberate."

"Chefs Cuisiniers almost accomplished this," says Nieporent. "For a while it was a great idea, but Blue Ribbon caught us off guard. We didn't necessarily know these people but the day we went in there we knew these people. Their brand of hospitality made you feel welcome."

"That's part of why I think Blue Ribbon resonated whereas Chefs and Cuisiniers kind of didn't," says Bruce. "Chefs and Cuisiniers was formal. It was trying to be a cool restaurant for chefs. And ultimately, not that the food wasn't great, but it wasn't that 'Let's just let it all loose' environment. It was a little too precious, ultimately. We weren't trying to be cool. It was like, leave it all behind you. I would say to my brother, 'There must be some little space-dust dispenser at the front door of Blue Ribbon because everyone's in this euphoric mood.' Everyone is totally comfortable in that environment. We weren't pretentious. Nobody really knew who we were. Yeah, Eric had a very successful good restaurant, but we all just connected. We were all going through the same stuff. We were all working our asses off. And trust me, we didn't partake in the party, but we were part of it, too. There was something animalistic about it. Mario would be shucking oysters and pouring himself beers. It was our friggin' hang. And it was un-friggin-believably fun.

"Little did we all know where it would all lead."

"IT TOOK ME BY SURPRISE."

Where it would all lead was to the next era in the evolution of the American chef, to an age of unprecedented celebrity.

Says Bruce: "I've got to say, what was really great about it—and don't take this in the wrong way—but Bobby wasn't Bobby, Mario wasn't Mario. . . . We were all just cooks."

There had, of course, already been an uptick in celebrity. A then-anonymous Anthony Bourdain occasionally dropped into Blue Ribbon with buddy and fellow chef Scott Bryan, but wasn't part of the scene, didn't get asked to join any of the power tables. Years earlier, thanks largely to newspaper coverage, he had discerned an unmistakable sea change in how chefs were perceived. "The civilians started wanting to fuck the chef," says Bourdain. "That was a first.

That was new. Just by virtue of the fact that you cooked. Just the way people talked about chefs was different. Suddenly they were sexy. No one ever said that before. We were dirty, smelled bad, and *were* bad, generally the last person in the world you wanted to be in a relationship with."

The solidifying of the chef's place in the culture meant more opportunities, and recognition. In 1988, *Food & Wine* magazine introduced its *Best New Chefs* program, identifying ten rising-star toques from around the country. The inaugural class demonstrated the expanding geography of American chefs and the erasure of the line between American and European. Among the inductees were Daniel Boulud and Thomas Keller from New York City; Rick Bayless, who had introduced his take on Mexican cuisine at Frontera Grill in Chicago, Illinois; Gordon Hamersley of Boston, a Ma Maison alum who had cooked under Lydia Shire and launched his own Hamersley's Bistro; and Johanne Killeen of Al Forno in Providence, Rhode Island.

Writing a cookbook became an appealing and attainable rite of passage for many American chefs, some of whom—having completed their traditional education before switching gears to enter the kitchen—were able to pen their own text rather than enlisting collaborators. Norman Van Aken, the Florida chef and one of the acknowledged fathers of New World Cuisine, marrying French technique with the ingredients he discovered in his adopted home of Key West, Florida, says of his debut book, *Feast of Sunlight*, published in 1988: "I would never have thought about writing a book had I not been asked to write it. I would never have had that gumption. A person came from New York, had my food, loved the food, and asked me if I'd write a book."

There were also the first baby steps toward the intellectualization of the craft and the new creativity being attached to it. Though few and far between, early precursors to the rampant conferences that are a defining component of the current era were staged. Recalls

Van Aken: "There was this new group called the Society for [American Cuisine] that I think was coming out of Louisville, and they created events around the country. The first one that I went to was in '86 in Charleston and that was the first time with my own eyes I began to see. . . . Oh, God, there were just some people that really rocked me. Seeing [Commander's Palace owner] Ella Brennan and going, 'My God, that's Ella Brennan.'"

The following year, Van Aken was invited to speak at the organization's conference in New Orleans, where he delivered a speech credited with putting the word *fusion,* borrowed from music, to cuisines that mingled myriad cultural influences.

"We were on the plane," says Van Aken. "I think we must have flown from Key West to Miami, Miami to Dallas, and then Dallas to Santa Fe. When we stopped in Dallas, we were on a smaller commuter plane and I remember just pushing myself back in my chair because I realized the person who was sitting in front of me was Dean Fearing and he was talking to Robert Del Grande. And I was next to [my wife], and I was like, 'Jesus, that's Dean Fearing.' And he had a book out. I knew about him from the press. And I must have known that he had a book out, the Mansion on Turtle Creek book. And I knew we were going to go see a lot of people in Santa Fe."

Back in his Chicago days, Van Aken was the first chef to employ a shy young aspiring cook named Charlie Trotter. The two became close friends and stayed in touch as Trotter crisscrossed the country, working in kitchens on a self-guided educational tour, and then, in 1987, opening Charlie Trotter's, his ambitious European-style restaurant in Chicago. Trotter had become friends with another young chef, Emeril Lagasse, who had taken over the kitchen at Commander's Palace.

"I hadn't met Emeril yet," says Van Aken. "Charlie was going to be there. I knew a lot of the people that were going to be there. We got off that plane and we get to Santa Fe and we got to our hotel and all of a sudden it was like, 'Holy shit, there's that person, there's that person, there's that person, there's that person.' I mean, Mark Miller and Lydia Shire and Jasper [White]. And then Charlie's like, 'You're going to meet Emeril tonight. You're going to love him. You're going to love this guy.'

"And funny story, too. I met him but it was that Woodstock moment of *Holy shit*, you know, a meteor hits the roof of this place, American cuisine is going to be seriously jeopardized.

"And we were just walking down the street and having this extraordinary awareness of all of these people being there at the same time and it was joyous, and it was a little nerve-racking, butterflies in your stomach and *Holy cow*. And I was invited. I was part of it, you know? I was like, 'They're having me here, too.' I felt really excited and proud to be called on to be recognized in this way. It was powerful. . . . There were some people that I just was in awe of. Even though I was wowed when I saw Dean, quickly we got to talking, we realized we were, you know, interested in the same kind of thing. . . .

"But it was always fun, too. It was not competitive. It was just like, we're on the same tour, we're doing the same music, just in different sort of emanations of it. And it was very parallel to I think the music world that we saw in the late sixties and the seventies but it was with food and we were part of this madcap rolling party. 'You did that? What ingredient was that? And how did you make that happen?'

"This was the party. This was the ballroom right now. People would be getting up and saying hello to each other and introducing themselves to one another. There were certain people that didn't have that social comfort maybe to do it, but by and large it was good. And comparing it to today, I think there's a lot more seriousness to it and a lot more kind of grouping that goes on. You know, like if we're part of this group or that group or this subset or that genre. I think that there are exceptions to it, but I think that it has become a different thing."

424 CHEFS, DRUGS AND ROCK & ROLL

Of his speech, Van Aken confesses: "It was just five minutes. Two and a half pages. I just wanted to get through it. I didn't think of it being an important moment. I had no idea. I had no idea that this word *fusion* was going to become something that people ever spoke about again.'"*

It was also a moment for chef empowerment. Shep Gordon, a music industry manager and devout foodie, struck up a friendship with many of the top chefs in the country, prompting them to approach him en masse one morning at Spago and ask him to represent them and get them properly paid for their participation in special events, festivals, and the like.

"I walk in and basically they say, 'Help,'" remembers Gordon. "'We all get fucked over. We get paid nothing. We get treated like shit. We're always the last one on the totem pole.' So I said, 'Okay, guys, I will do an agency. I'll do it pro bono. I will get you all famous and then I'm getting out of town because this is way beyond

---

* Van Aken, Trotter, and Lagasse would go on to become close friends, nicknaming themselves The Triangle because of their geographic locations. Lagasse would become a top television star, but public speaking did not come naturally to him. Remembers Van Aken: "The night before we were in some bar in a hotel in Santa Fe and Charlie's like, 'Come on, we're going to go meet Emeril.' And we go over and meet Emeril. And Emeril is kind of hunched over. He's got a sport coat on. And I was dressed more like I was in a country and western band, I think. I don't even know if I had a sport coat. But he was kind of hunched over. He was cradling, like, bourbon or Scotch or something like that. And as soon as he introduced me to him, Charlie had to go away, so it was just me and Emeril. And he goes, 'How you doing?' I'm like, 'I'm all right.' He goes, 'What about this speech thing tomorrow? What do you think about that?' I said, 'Yeah, I wrote something.' (It was me, Charlie, Emeril, Lydia Shire, and [Seattle chef] Tom Douglas, all asked to speak on why we cook the way we cook.) He goes, 'I ain't got a fucking thing and I'm fucking scared.' And his ice cubes were rattling in his glass. Right away I felt really protective of him, like, 'It's going to be all right.' Me not being so sure really in my mind that it's going to be all right. I was coming out of the islands. He said, 'I'm not used to speaking in front of people.' And, man, I just think back to that day and think, *Wow. You overcame it, buddy. You overcame it just fine.*"

me. This is too much work.'" Gordon formed Alive Culinary Resources and began negotiating on behalf of the crowd that included Wolfgang Puck, Larry Forgione, Lydia Shire, Paul Prudhomme, Mark Miller, Jonathan Waxman, Jean-Louis Palladin, and Alice Waters.

Awards, too, ramped up to the next level, as the James Beard Foundation Awards were founded in 1991, subsuming Who's Who. The biggest prize, Outstanding Chef, that first year went not to an American-born chef, but to the one who had set the tone for much of what happened in the States over the past decade and a half, Wolfgang Puck. Ironically, the man who redefined the Oscar party didn't put much stock in awards himself: After the ceremony, he went to Forgione's American Place, in its second home on East 32nd Street. "I said, 'What am I going to do with this medal?'" remembers Puck. "'Just hang it here in your restaurant.' And it goes there. I don't know where it is now. I didn't care. So what."

And there was another force trembling on the horizon in those idyllic Blue Ribbon days: the first tremors of the Food Network.

"It was the infancy," remembers Bruce. "There were no chefs on TV. There was the Galloping Gourmet, Julia reruns, and Jacques Pépin. There were a couple of cool shows, but there wasn't a lot of stuff going on. I remember when Mario told me, 'Hey, I've got this opportunity. I think I might do this thing. What do you think about it?' I was like, 'Sounds fun. I don't know. Are you into it? Do you think it's cool?' He was like, 'I don't know. I think it may be cool.' I remember Bobby [Flay], the same thing. I remember us all talking about these things."

In the case of Batali, Blue Ribbon figured prominently in the beginnings of his television career: After reading an article in the pink-tinged weekly newspaper the New York Observer about the scene there and Batali's place at the center of it, Jonathan Lynne, a Television Food Network executive, got in touch with Batali to begin exploring a show, setting in motion a chain of events that would lead to the debut of his first cooking show, *Molto Mario*, in January 1996.

"It took me by surprise," says Alan Harding. "I never thought of myself as a brand. I never thought of what we were doing as a brand. I never thought of television as more than something that you would just do for fun. I didn't think you could become rich doing it. Mario was very exciting and very entrepreneurial and very focused on what he was doing. I remember being on MTV a couple times. And I remember being on the *Today* show or whatever. And then, the next thing I knew, being on the Food Network every once in a while on [their nightly news program] *In Food Today*. I did a pilot for the Food Network, *What's in Your Fridge Right Now?*, that never got picked up. I never really did anything else with them. And then the next thing I knew, Molto had a show. And I was like, *Wow, motherfucker*."

"THERE'S A LITTLE BIT OF SADNESS IN IT."

Bruce Bromberg doesn't tell me his story from New York City, but from Las Vegas, where he lived at the time of our interview. There are eighteen Blue Ribbon outposts in the United States and the UK, including a bakery, sushi bars, and collaborations with Brooklyn Bowl, for which Blue Ribbon provides the food service. We meet at the bar of restaurant Echo & Rig in Tivoli Village, a ritzy Vegas suburb.

"There's a little bit of sadness in it." says Bromberg. "Not from a Blue Ribbon perspective, but there's two things happening now: There is a resurgence of cooking for the pure love of cooking. At the same time, what's been around for a while is this very calculated kind of 'I want to be a star.'

"I find myself meeting people, having interviews with people, fielding phone calls from friends and family who want me to talk to their son who wants to be a chef. And I was just kind of disheartened and shocked. Not to sound like the old guy going, 'Hey, I remember back in the day . . .' but that basic love and desire to cook and the passion for the art of cooking—not to be pretentious like it's an art, but that guttural desire to cook and make people happy is somehow slightly tainted with 'What's the real friggin' motivation?' There are some great, awesome people out there doing great, awesome things. But there is a huge friggin' amount of people out there for all the wrong reasons. I get résumés: *Objective: To be on* [The Next Food Network Star]. *To be on* Top Chef. That's your fucking objective? Wow. I'm like, *That's an interesting starting point.*"

Bromberg speaks for many of his generation, and those who preceded them. And while I understand and commiserate, I've also come to realize that it's simply the nature of things to change. The purity that drew so many to the cooking profession may be forever lost, but it's not all bad: Embarking on my first research trip for this book, I turned on the in-flight television and found myself confronted by *Master Chef Junior*, on which preteens compete, demonstrating impressive kitchen chops, all of which once would have been the stuff of sci-fi. Is that spectacle cartoonish and craven, or is it a tribute to the new reality that children can grow up wanting to be chefs with their parents' blessing, that cooks earn more respect and income than they once did, and have more options available to them? The answer, of course, is both. Sure, I was a little depressed when the man who media-trained Emeril Lagasse decades ago told me that culinary students come to him today for on-camera coaching while still matriculating at their institute of choice, but so it goes.

The original Blue Ribbon still operates on Sullivan Street, at least it did at the time of this writing. There will come a day when it and most—eventually *all*—of the other surviving restaurants recounted here will reopen under new ownership and new names or disappear completely, their spaces converted to something else entirely. The chefs, as chefs do, will fade away. Their food will be rediscovered in cookbooks, where even the most cutting-edge contributions have already settled into antiquity. But there are moments that abide as more than memories, and none more vividly than those nights— each scarcely distinct from the last—when the creators of a new world licked their wounds, drowned their thirst, came down from the rush of their work, behind the glass facade of an unassuming SoHo restaurant. They stayed until first light, or close to it, staggered out into the open air, and went their separate ways. Then they caught a few hours of shut-eye, rose up, and did it all over again.

ACKNOWLEDGMENTS

I don't know whether to be moved or embarrassed (probably both) by the number of people it took to help me write this book. My eternal thanks to the following, and a profound apology to anybody I might have inadvertently left out:

Caitlin Friedman, who endured more hardships, on more levels, than any spouse should have to in service of a book—the next one will be quicker, and easier!

David Black, my agent, advocate, sensei, and friend, in every sense of the word.

Mike Friedman, my brother, for constant support and encouragement, and for navigating life's sometimes rough seas with me.

Gabriella Doob, my wonderful editor, for your collaborative spirit and good heart, for sharing my geek love for the serial comma, and for understanding what I meant by "It's a chef book, not a food book!"

Dan Halpern, publisher at Ecco, for first believing in the book, for sharing my fascination for the subject matter, for the meals and drinks on the town, and for your patience, which wasn't endless, but was extraordinary.

The rest of Ecco's crack team: associate publisher Miriam Parker, production editor Rachel Meyers, copyeditor Suzanne Fass (whom I specially requested based on past experience, and am I ever glad I did), jacket designer Sara Wood, marketing director Meghan Deans, and publicist Ashley Garland.

Karen Rinaldi, who brought the book to Dan, and helped me sharpen its focus early in its development. We'll probably never conquer the waves, or the court, but it's sure fun trying, ain't it?

Declan and Taylor Friedman, my kids, for being your awesome selves and letting me work when I need to.

Sharon Saalfield, the best transcriber in the business, and a great sister in-law to boot. Couldn't have done it without you.

Rachel Balin, ace research assistant and a crucial reality check when the question of "would somebody your age find this interesting?" came up.

Erin Larson, the only intern I've ever had, for some early research help. I will travel to the ends of the earth, if necessary, to patronize your first bakery.

Sarah Crary Cohen, a true sage; this book might not have been finished without your wisdom and insights.

Jonathan Waxman, for being my first interview for this book, for the encouragement and occasional chats, and for connecting me with a certain Austrian-born chef I otherwise might never have interviewed.

Bob Grimes, for making many introductions and for being a real pal. Sorry I wouldn't let you read the book early.

Joel Buchman, who sadly passed away as I was proofreading these pages, for your friendship and that stack of old DB newsletters you sent along, but mainly for your friendship.

Bob Berensen, for making some crucial introductions.

Joyce Goldstein, for not caring that my book was possible competition with your own, and for generously sharing your Judy Rodgers interview with a stranger—I'm still blown away by that and think I always will be.

Gael Greene, for your flattering belief and for making some essential introductions, and for still cranking out those reviews every week.

Mimi Sheraton, for your insights and for connecting me with André Soltner.

Charlie Palmer, for trying to make that lunch (you know the one) happen, even if it never did.

Mark Miller, my Doctor Lecter and Jiminy Cricket all rolled into one. Thanks for the invaluable early direction and perspective.

Jeremiah Tower, for the many connections and perspectives.

Mark Franz and Pat Kuleto in San Francisco, and Joachim Splichal in Los Angeles, for generously hosting group dinners in support of this project.

Michael McCarty, for permission to use my favorite chef photo on the cover.

Gerry Dawes, for all your help in connecting me with the Chefs from Hell.

Jeff Levine at The Culinary Institute of America, for arranging a day of helpful interviews in Hyde Park.

Susan Chumsky, for giving this book a staggeringly close early read and showing up for lunch with pages of brilliant notes.

Sydny Miner, for reading and opining on two early chapters.

Cecilia Chiang, for your help arranging an interview with Alice Waters.

Sean and Renee Baker, Mike and Jessica Friedman, Ralph and Donna Seligman, and Lyle and Limor Zimskind, for your guest rooms, and your hospitality.

The Huntington Hotel and Hotel Vitale in San Francisco, for your media rate and hospitality.

Norman Van Aken, for one of the nicest emails I've ever received.

Skip Schwarzman and Lynn Buono, for suggesting an important subtitle adjustment.

Mike Colameco, Arnold Rossman, and Patrick Terrail, for your special help and enthusiasm.

For friendship and support over the last few years: Jimmy Bradley, Stefanie Cohen, Harold Dieterle, John Capanelli, Danit Lidor, Evan Sung, and David Waltuck.

And most of all, to the more than two hundred chefs and industry figures who sat for interviews with me, all of whom—even those not quoted—provided invaluable context and insights: Thank you for your time, your enthusiasm, and your trust. I tried to do the right thing with all of it.

NOTES

INTRODUCTION

5 *"You're not happily"*   Ruth Reichl, "How to Build an Empire."

11 *"the Henry Ford"*   Nathan Myhrvold, "The Art in Gastronomy."

14 *"The time has come"*   John Rockwell, *The Times of the Sixties*, page 22.

28 *Just as each commandment*   Heather A. Mallory, "The Nouvelle Cuisine Revolution."

31 *"Pot Luck was doing"*   Joyce Goldstein, *Inside the California Food Revolution.*

41 *"looked as if"*   Ned Smyth, "Gordon Matta-Clark."

42 *"What do I have"*   Ibid.

43 *"Please don't write"*   Milton Glaser and Jerome Snyder, "Food, Glorious Food."

44 *"still [didn't] know much"*   Bethsheba Goldstein, "Under the Brooklyn Bridge."

44 *"oddly ... kind of had"*   Ibid.

50 *"There are two camps"*   David Kamp, "Cooking Up a Storm." Brackets in the original.

1. NEW WORLD ORDER

55 *"It's not like today"*   Paul Freedman, *Ten Restaurants That Changed America.*

60 *"You'll never amount"*   Michael Barrier, "The Chef as Famous as His Customers."

61 *"He was my mentor"*   Wolfgang Puck, as told to Liz Welch, "How I Did It."

61 *"robust and poetic"*   Wolfgang Puck, *Modern French Cooking*, page xiv.

74 *"She wanted to put"*   Ruth Reichl, "How to Build an Empire."

81 *"He bragged about"* Ruth Reichl, "A Tip of the Toque."

84 *worried that the restaurant* Ibid.

87 *Referring to his kitchen team* Ruth Reichl, "Is This the Best French Restaurant in California?"

88 *"McCarty claims"* Bruce David Colen, "Michael, Throw the Gloat Ashore."

89 *"Given the egos of both men"* Ibid.

99 *"an area more"* Jeremiah Tower, *California Dish*, page 137.

106 *"The first special"* Lesley Balla, "Susan Feniger and Mary Sue Milliken Are Cooking."

113 *"I had $10,000"* Michael Barrier, "The Chef as Famous as His Customers."

114 *"I was so nervous"* Ruth Reichl, "The '80s: A Special Report."

118 *"It was so crazy"* Michael Barrier, "The Chef as Famous as His Customers."

120 *"I didn't set out"* Aljean Harmetz, "Hollywood: This Way In."

121 *"I paint my face"* Mary Rourke, "Extreme Taste."

123 *"They couldn't cook"* Susan Heller Anderson, "Coast's Latest: 'Francasian' Cuisine."

123 *"There are a lot"* John Soeder, "Dances with Wolf & Barbara."

124 *"I'm the bride"* Ruth Reichl, "Puck's Progress."

124 *"Yeah, this is cute"* Ibid.

124 *"Introductory material written"* Wolfgang Puck, *Modern French Cooking*, copyright page.

125 *"I know that everybody"* Ruth Reichl, "Puck's Progess," *Los Angeles Times*, June 12, 1988.

125 *"Lazaroff's most ambitious"* John Soeder, "Dances with Wolf & Barbara."

125 *"my animals"* Ibid.

126 *"Now the Astroturf"* Marian Burros, "In Los Angeles, High-Style Restaurant Fare."

2. THE OTTO SYNDROME

129 *"There is no way"* John McPhee, "Brigade de Cuisine."

129 *"the center of attention"* Ibid., page 44.

130 *"more than five miles"* Ibid.

130 *"His range is fabulous"* Ibid.

131 *"in the restaurant business"*   Ibid.

131 *"Why should we accept"*   Ibid.

133 *"pale yellow"*   Mimi Sheraton, "Dinner at the Elusive 'Otto's.'"

133 *"I have a little roadhouse"*   Bob Greene, "Business, Privacy Down the Drain."

134 *"I guess the press can't stand"*   Ibid.

138 *"another victim of"*   Gael Greene, "La Tulipe in Bloom."

153 *"Most of my practice"*   Ellen Brown, *Cooking with the New American Chefs*, page 113.

155 *"celebration of amateurs"*   Gael Greene, "A Celebration of Amateurs."

171 *"our idiosyncratic take"*   David Waltuck and Andrew Friedman, *Chanterelle: The Story and Recipes of a Restaurant Classic.*

172 *"David Waltuck is not"*   Gael Greene, "The Daring Young Man."

4. FRENCH RESISTANCE

214 *"The relative indifference"*   Anthony Blake and Quentin Crewe, *Great Chefs of France.*

215 *"Bocuse and his friends"*   Linda Bird Francke, "Food: The New Wave."

218 *"There is one person"*   Craig Claiborne, "Elegance of Cuisine Is on Wane."

219 *"It was also"*   Alfred Portale, *Gotham Bar and Grill Cookbook*, page 10.

222 *"One problem"*   David Shenk, *The Genius in All of Us: New Insights into Genetics, Talent, and IQ.*

223 *"those who work with their hands"*   Craig Claiborne, "Food News: From Court to Kitchen."

227 *"This was nothing short of"*   Pierre Franey, "Innocence Abroad: Memories of '39 Fair."

228 *"I think it gave people"*   Amy Zuber, "Henri Soulé."

228 *"Le Pavillon was"*   Ibid.

247 *"You can learn"*   Bryan Miller, "His Stock in Trade Is Cooks and Clout."

5. THE STANFORD COURT GANG

262 *"It seemed like an awesome amount"*   William Grimes, "Paul Prudhomme, Chef Who Put Cajun Cooking on National Stage, Dies at 75."

262 *"I remembered that the first thing"*   Bret Thorn, "Paul Prud-homme: A Remembrance."

263 *"The gumbo I did at Commander's"*   Brett Anderson, "Paul Prud-homme: An Oral History Chronicles His Role in Revolutionizing New Orleans Cuisine."

264 *K was a character*   Ibid.

264 *"Chef was the cook"*   Ibid.

264 *"People hadn't considered"*   Ibid.

6. CALIFORNIA DREAMING?

291 *"their own restaurants"*   Marian Burros, "Food Accent for the 80's."

296 *"California relaxed elegance"*   Gael Greene, "What's Hot, What's Not."

299 *"What's California food"*   Susan Heller Anderson and Maurice Carroll, "New York Day by Day."

304 *"He smiled and said"*   Ruth Reichl, "Goodbye to the Era of the Celebrity Chefs."

305 *"Californians are so enthusiastic"*   "Letters Home."

325 *"unfinished floors"*   Marian Burros, "New Orleans Chef."

330 *"Hollywood has its Oscars"*   Margaret Engel, "Cook's Magazine Makes Annual Awards."

330 *"Now the awareness has grown"*   Ibid.

344 *"While there are exceptions"*   Trish Hall, "Family Tree Nurtures a New Generation."

8. A ROOM OF THEIR OWN

408 *"Blue Ribbon, where"*   Florence Fabricant, "Off the Menu."

414 *"Can the childhood"*   Gael Greene, "The Tao of Pu Pu."

AUTHOR INTERVIEWS

Abrams, Danny (March 11, 2013)

Adams, Jody (July 23, 2014)

Andrews, Colman (July 7, 2014)

Avilez, Michael (November 7, 2013)

Barber, George (February 2, 2012)

Barker, Ali and Marcie (October 16, 2015)

Batali, Mario (June 5, 2014, and June 10, 2014)

Bauer, Michael (February 5, 2014)

Bill, Tony (March 11, 2014)

Birnbaum, Jan (November 7, 2013, and May 15, 2014)

Birsh, Andy (April 12, 2010)

Blau, Elizabeth (September 30, 2013)

Bouley, David (April 18, 2014)

Boulud, Daniel (July 7, 2014, and July 14, 2014)

Bourdain, Anthony (April 29, 2014)

Brennan, Terrance (October 17, 2013)

Bromberg, Bruce (September 30, 2013)

Bromberg, Eric (October 16, 2013)

Bryan, Scott (June 29, 2014)

Burke, David (September 12, 2015, and July 11, 2017)

Calhoun, Jay (December 5, 2013)

Carlin, Tom (April 2, 2014)

Carlson, Phil (March 4, 2015)

Castronovo, Frank (April 3, 2013)

Cerrone, Dominick (November 7, 2016)

Chardack, Helen (January 15, 2015)

Chiang, Cecilia (November 6, 2013)

Chiang, Philip (December 4, 2013)

Citrin, Josiah (March 12, 2014)

Clark, John (February 4, 2013)

Colameco, Michael (November 11, 2014)

Colicchio, Tom (March 31, 2014)

Conley, Sue, and Peggy Smith (February 3, 2014)

Cool, Jesse Ziff (November 7, 2013)

Crenn, Dominique (February 3, 2014)

Crispo, Frank (April 9, 2014, and April 24, 2014)

Cushman, Tim (March 8, 2016)

David, Narsai (November 7, 2013)

Dawes, Gerry (April 13, 2013)

De Mori, Silvio (March 14, 2014)

Des Jardins, Traci (October 9, 2013)

Dodge, Jim (February 5, 2014, and June 9, 2014)

Doherty, John (June 13, 2014, and July 15, 2014)

Ekus, Lou (April 13, 2010)

Feniger, Susan (July 1, 2010)

Fertig, Ed (February 21, 2014)

Flay, Bobby (November 16, 2016)

Forgione, Larry (October 10, 2013)

Forley, Diane (May 22, 2017)

Foy, Dennis (March 27, 2014)

Frank, Ken (August 23, 2010, and October 10, 2013)

Franz, Mark (October 7, 2013, and October 9, 2013)

Frederick, Hal (March 22, 2014)

Gesualdi, Chris (April 1, 2013)

Goin, Suzanne (October 3, 2013)

Gold, Rozanne, and Michael Whiteman (August 21, 2010, and March 5, 2014)

Goldstein, Joyce (May 12, 2014)

Gonzalez, Carmen (March 7, 2013)

Gordon, Seth (November 12, 2013)

Gordon, Shep (November 12, 2013)

Goutal, Jean (July 1, 2014)

Guilfoyle, Bill (November 7, 2016)

Harding, Alan (March 27, 2013)

Harris, L. John (May 15, 2014)

Hayden, Gerry (July 10, 2014)

Hazen, Sam (May 9, 2013)

Healy, Patrick (December 5, 2013)

Heffernan, Kerry (April 2, 2013, and October 29, 2013)

Higgins, Bill (May 12, 2014)

Hill, Bruce (February 4, 2014)

Hoffman, Peter (September 8, 2016)

Jones, Lee (January 16, 2014)

Kalt, Stephen (October 2, 2013)

Katz, Bill (March 20, 2014)

Keller, Loretta (February 3, 2014)

Keller, Thomas (December 3, 2013)

Kinch, David (November 6, 2013, and May 15, 2014)

Klausner, Manny and Willette (March 14, 2014)

Kleiman, Evan (October 4, 2013)

Kline, Miles, and Pamela Tozer (May 15, 2014)

Klugman, Roberta (October 7, 2013)

Kowalski, John (November 7, 2016)

Kratz, David (October 29, 2013)

Kretchmer, Jerry (June 3, 2010)

Kuleto, Pat (October 11, 2013)

Lazaroff, Barbara (March 13, 2014)

Lee, Christopher (June 21, 2014)

Liederman, David (November 6, 2014)

Lo, Anita (March 4, 2014)

Lomonaco, Michael (March 9, 2010, and March 31, 2013)

Puck, Wolfgang (June 6, 2016)

Puro, Karen (March 21, 2014)

Raoul, Serge and Guy
(January 12, 2015)

Reichl, Ruth (October 21, 2016)

Riou, Hervé (August 19, 2013)

Rodgers, Judy (interview
conducted by, and courtesy of,
Joyce Goldstein, May 20, 2010)

Romano, Michael (May 7, 2014)

Rosenthal, Mitch (February 5, 2014)

Rossman, Arnold (March 4, 2014)

Rothstein, Daniel (June 22, 2010)

Rush, Karen (March 7, 2013)

Ryan, Tim (March 14, 2013)

Sacco, Amy (April 16, 2014)

Sailhac, Alain (October 22, 2013)

Sailhac, Arlene Feltman
(October 28, 2013)

Salk, Donald (December 5, 2013)

Schenk, John (November 1, 2013)

Schmidt, Jimmy (March 15, 2014)

Schoenfeld, Ed (June 19, 2010)

Sedlar, John (October 5, 2013)

Selvaggio, Piero (December 4,
2013, and December 6, 2013)

Sheraton, Mimi (October 24,
2016)

Shire, Lydia (July 23, 2014)

Sibley, Barbara (November 16,
2016)

Silverton, Nancy (October 2,
2013, and March 13, 2014)

Soltner, André (December 5,
2016)

Somerville, Annie (May 14, 2014)

Sparks, Katy (October 24, 2016)

Splichal, Joachim (October 4,
2013)

Stoicheff, Jennifer Wren
(January 29, 2014)

Stone, Larry (May 16, 2014)

Swerman, Jannis (October 3, 2013)

Telepan, Bill (March 24, 2010)

Terrail, Patrick (April 20, 2014)

Tesar, John (April 7, 2014)

Thompson, Charles (October 3,
2013)

Tingle, Ralph (January 9, 2015)

Tivy, Matthew (December 1, 2014)

Tower, Jeremiah (March 5, 2012;
November 5, 2013; and March 6,
2014)

Traunfeld, Jerry (January 28,
2014)

Tusk, Michael (May 13, 2014)

Unterman, Patricia (May 13,
2014)

Valenti, Tom (March 24, 2010)

Van Aken, Norman (February 21,
2013)

Vranian, Steve (February 21, 2014)

Walsh, Brendan (November 7,
2016)

Waltuck, David (March 15, 2010,
and August 24, 2010)

Waltuck, David and Karen
(January 21, 2014, and
February 18, 2014)

Waters, Alice (August 19, 2014)

Waxman, Jonathan (March 15,
2010; September 16, 2014;
January 24, 2014; and
September 24, 2015)

Weinstein, Michael (March 21, 2014)

Weir, Joanne (October 7, 2013)

Wells, Barbara (December 9, 2014)

Wesson, Josh (October 5, 2016)

White, Jasper (July 24, 2014)

Williams, Jody (October 21, 2013)

Williams, Patricia (July 2, 2014)

Wilson, Herb (September 29, 2013)

Wine, Barry (March 8, 2010, and July 26, 2014)

Wine, Susan (July 15, 2017)

Wise, Victoria (September 2, 2016)

Wolf, Clark (March 22, 2014)

Yosses, Bill (April 17, 2015)

Zakarian, Geoffrey (March 15, 2010)

Zeidler, Marvin (October 1, 2013)

Zweben, Paul (September 18, 2013)

SOURCES

INTRODUCTION: PREP WORK

Batterberry, Michael and Ariane. *On the Town in New York: The Landmark History of Eating, Drinking, and American Entertainment from the American Revolution to the Food Revolution.* Routledge, 1999.

Brown, Ellen. *Cooking with the New American Chefs.* Harper & Row, 1985.

Burros, Marian. "American Chef's Long Road to Success." *The New York Times,* October 1, 1986.

Clark, Robert. *James Beard: A Biography.* HarperCollins, 1993.

Fabricant, Florence. "Celebrating the Ringmaster of the Restaurant Circus." *The New York Times,* February 14, 2007.

Francke, Linda Bird, with Scott Sullivan and Seth Goldschlager. "Food: The New Wave." *Newsweek,* August 11, 1975.

Friedman, Andrew. *Knives at Dawn: America's Quest for Culinary Glory at the Legendary Bocuse d'Or Competition.* Free Press, 2009.

Glaser, Milton, and Jerome Snyder. "Food, Glorious Food." *New York,* January 3, 1972.

Goldstein, Bethsheba. "Under the Brooklyn Bridge: The Origins of the Restaurant FOOD." Soho Memory Project (sohomemory.com), undated.

Goldstein, Joyce, with Dore Brown. *Inside the California Food Revolution: Thirty Years That Changed Our Culinary Consciousness.* University of California Press, 2013.

Haberman, Clyde, ed. *The Times of the Seventies.* Black Dog & Leventhal, 2013.

Kahn, Howie. "When Eating and Art Became One." *T,* May 10, 2013.

Kamp, David. "Cooking Up a Storm." *Vanity Fair,* October 2006.

Kennedy, Randy. "When Meals Played the Muse." *The New York Times,* February 21, 2007.

Kuh, Patric. *The Last Days of Haute Cuisine: America's Culinary Revolution*. Penguin Books, 2001.

Lam, Francis. "Edna Lewis and the Black Roots of American Cooking." *The New York Times*, October 28, 2015.

Mallory, Heather A. "The Nouvelle Cuisine Revolution: Expressions of National Anxieties and Aspirations in French Culinary Discourse 1969–1996." Dissertation, Duke University, 2011.

McNamee, Thomas. *Alice Waters and Chez Panisse: The Romantic, Impractical, Often Eccentric, Ultimately Brilliant Making of a Food Revolution*. Penguin, 2007.

Myhrvold, Nathan. "The Art in Gastronomy: A Modernist Perspective." *Gastronomica* 11:1 (Spring 2011): 13–22.

Pace, Eric. "Mario Savio, 53, Campus Protestor, Dies." *The New York Times*, November 7, 1996.

Reichl, Ruth. "How to Build an Empire: L.A.'s Bruce Marder, Who Gave Us West Beach Cafe and Rebecca's, Hopes DC 3 Will Also Take Off." *Los Angeles Times*, December 4, 1988.

Rockwell, John, ed. *The Times of the Sixties*. Black Dog & Leventhal, 2014.

Rodgers, Judy. *The Zuni Cafe Cookbook: A Compendium of Recipes and Cooking Lessons from San Francisco's Beloved Restaurant*. W. W. Norton & Company, 2002.

Smyth, Ned. "Gordon Matta-Clark." Artnet.com, undated.

Sokolov, Raymond A. "Anyone for Cooking Lessons in the Long, Cold Winter Ahead?" *The New York Times*, September 7, 1971.

Tower, Jeremiah. *California Dish: What I Saw (and Cooked) at the American Culinary Revolution*. Free Press, 2003.

Urvater, Michèle, and David Liederman. *Cooking the Nouvelle Cuisine in America: A Glorious Collection of Original Recipes*. Workman Publishing, 1979.

Waters, Alice, and friends. *40 Years of Chez Panisse: The Power of Gathering*. Clarkson Potter, 2011.

1. NEW WORLD ORDER

Anderson, Susan Heller. "Coast's Latest: 'Francasian' Cuisine." *The New York Times*, November 9, 1983.

Andrews, Colman. *My Usual Table: A Life in Restaurants*. Ecco, 2014.

———. "Views and Reviews of a Los Angeles Chef." *The New York Times,* January 28, 1981.

Balla, Lesley. "Susan Feniger and Mary Sue Milliken Are Cooking Like It's 1981." *Los Angeles,* February 16, 2016.

Barrier, Michael. "The Chef as Famous as His Customers." *Nation's Business,* July 1991.

Baum, Gary. "The Brilliant, Bitter History of L.A.'s Fabled Ma Maison, Where Welles and Nicholson Were Regulars." *The Hollywood Reporter,* July 24, 2015.

Burros, Marian. "In Los Angeles, High-Style Restaurant Fare." *The New York Times,* July 4, 1984.

Colen, Bruce David. "The Daring Young Chef Finds Another Maison." *Los Angeles,* September 1978.

———. "Michael, Throw the Gloat Ashore." *Los Angeles,* July 1979.

Eisner, Michael D., with Aaron Cohen. *Working Together: Why Great Partnerships Succeed.* Harper Business, 2010.

Freedman, Paul. *Ten Restaurants That Changed America.* W. W. Norton & Company, 2016.

Harmetz, Aljean. "Hollywood: This Way In." *The New York Times,* March 13, 1983.

Kuh, Patric. *The Last Days of Haute Cuisine: The Coming of Age of American Restaurants.* Penguin, 2001.

McCarty, Michael, with Judith Choate. *Welcome to Michael's: 85 Stellar Recipes from the Celebrated Michael's Restaurants.* Little, Brown and Company, 2007.

McCarty, Michael, with Norman Kolpas. *Michael's Cookbook: The Art of New American Food and Entertaining.* Macmillan, 1989.

Ochoa, Laurie. "Are You Ready for the New Ma Maison?" *Los Angeles Times,* November 27, 1988.

Puck, Wolfgang. *Wolfgang Puck's Modern French Cooking for the American Kitchen: Recipes from the Cuisine of Ma Maison.* Houghton Mifflin, 1981.

Puck, Wolfgang, as told to Liz Welch. "How I Did It: Wolfgang Puck." *Inc.,* October 1, 2009.

Reichl, Ruth. "The '80s: A Special Report." *Los Angeles Times,* December 24, 1989.

———. *Comfort Me with Apples: More Adventures at the Table.* Random House, 2001.

———. "How to Build an Empire: L.A.'s Bruce Marder, Who Gave Us West Beach Cafe and Rebecca's, Hopes DC 3 Will Also Take Off." *Los Angeles Times*, December 4, 1988.

———. "Is This the Best French Restaurant in California?" *New West*, June 18, 1979.

———. "Puck's Progress: On the Run with Super Chef Wolfgang Puck, Who Built a Food Empire from Designer Pizzas." *Los Angeles Times*, June 12, 1988.

———. "A Tip of the Toque: After Suffering Early Acclaim, Bankruptcy, and Illness, Ken Frank Is Still Cooking." *Los Angeles Times*, March 15, 1992.

Rossant, Juliette. *Super Chef: The Making of the Great Modern Restaurant Empires*. Free Press, 2004.

Rourke, Mary. "Extreme Taste: Spago Co-Owner Has Eclectic Style." *Los Angeles Times*, July 22, 1988.

Soeder, John. "Dances with Wolf & Barbara." *Restaurant Hospitality*, September 1992.

Spector, Amy. "Ken Frank: L'Enfant Terrible Grows Up, Plants Roots in the Napa Valley." *Nation's Restaurant News*, January 8, 2001.

Terrail, Patrick. *A Taste of Hollywood: The Story of Ma Maison*. Lebhar-Friedman Books, 1999.

Tower, Jeremiah. *California Dish: What I Saw (and Cooked) at the American Culinary Revolution*. Free Press, 2003.

Urvater, Michèle, and David Liederman. *Cooking the Nouvelle Cuisine in America: A Glorious Collection of Original Recipes*. Workman Publishing, 1979.

2. THE OTTO SYNDROME

Akst, Daniel. "New Owners Plan More Cookie Stores, Products: Less-Famous Rivals Passed Amos." *Los Angeles Times*. August 27, 1985.

Allison, Karen Hubert. *How I Gave My Heart to the Restaurant Business*. Ecco, 1997.

Asimov, Eric. "Karen Allison, 49, Restaurateur with Vision." *The New York Times*, December 21, 1997.

———. "Patrick Clark, 42, Is Dead; Innovator in American Cuisine." *The New York Times*, February 13, 1998.

Brown, Ellen. *Cooking with the New American Chefs*. Harper & Row, 1985.

Dean, Sam. "Inside the Beggar's Purse." *Lucky Peach.*

DiGiacomo, Frank. "The Odeon: A Retro Haven That Defined New York 1980s Nightlife." *Vanity Fair,* November 2005.

Greene, Bob. "Business, Privacy Down the Drain." *The Free Lance–Star* (Fredericksburg, VA), March 12, 1979.

Greene, Gael. "A Celebration of Amateurs." *New York,* July 18, 1977.

———. "Cuisine from a Marriage." *New York,* September 10, 1979.

———. "The Daring Young Man on Grand Street." *New York,* December 31, 1979.

———. "Eight Wonderful Dinners: The Sensualist at Table." *New York,* March 19, 1980.

———. "Huberts: Brain Food." *New York,* October 17, 1988.

———. *Insatiable: Tales from a Life of Delicious Excess.* Warner Books, 2006.

———. "La Tulipe in Bloom." *New York,* May 19, 1980.

Haitch, Richard. "Follow-Up on the News; High Rolling." *The New York Times,* July 8, 1979.

Hodgson, Moira. "New French Guide to New York City Stirs Controversy." *The New York Times,* May 17, 1981.

"Honor Roll of American Chefs." *Food & Wine,* May 1983.

"Life: Devouring a Small Country Inn." *Time,* March 12, 1979.

Magida, Phyllis. "David's First Cookie Led to Another and Another and . . ." *Chicago Tribune,* September 29/30, 1982.

McPhee, John. "Brigade de Cuisine." *The New Yorker,* February 19, 1979.

Miller, Bryan. "Peter Hoffman." *Food Arts,* June 2011.

———. "Restaurants." *The New York Times,* February 27, 1987.

Rice, William, and Tom Zito. "Hidden Entree." *The Washington Post,* February 23, 1979.

Robert L. Pritsker & others vs. David Brudnoy & another. 389 Mass. 776 (May 5, 1983–July 27, 1983).

Schwartz, Arthur. "Roman à Chef." *Saveur,* March 18, 2002.

Sheraton, Mimi. "Child Protégés Down from Boston." *The New York Times,* March 16, 1979.

———. "Dinner at the Elusive 'Otto's': The Disappointing Details." *The New York Times,* February 26, 1979.

———. *Eating My Words: An Appetite for Life.* Harper Perennial, 2004.

———. "A Good Kitchen That Travels Well." *The New York Times,* November 13, 1981.

———. "Restaurants." *The New York Times*, November 23, 1979.

———. "With Delicacy and Grace in SoHo." *The New York Times*, April 11, 1980.

"Tempers Boil in 'Otto' Affair." *New York*, March 19, 1979.

Waltuck, David, and Andrew Friedman. *Chanterelle: The Story and Recipes of a Restaurant Classic.* Taunton Press, 2008.

3. ON THE WATERFRONT

Burke, David, and Carmel Berman Reingold. *Cooking with David Burke.* Alfred A. Knopf, 2006.

Forgione, Larry. *An American Place: Celebrating the Flavors of America.* William Morrow and Company, 1996.

Grigoriadis, Vanessa. "Regine's Last Stand." *New York*, April 12, 1999.

Schrambling, Regina. "The Restaurant That Launched a Thousand Chefs." *The New York Times*, August 29, 2001.

4. FRENCH RESISTANCE

Blake, Anthony, and Quentin Crewe. *Great Chefs of France.* Abrams, 1978.

Claiborne, Craig. "Elegance of Cuisine Is on Wane in U.S." *The New York Times*, April 13, 1959.

———. "Food News: From Court to Kitchen." *The New York Times*, January 25, 1960.

———. "School Where Chefs are Made." *The New York Times*, January 28, 1971.

Culinary Institute of America website, accessed November 2014.

Fabricant, Florence. "Culinary Institute's Restaurant." *The New York Times*, August 11, 1982.

Francke, Linda Bird, with Scott Sullivan and Seth Goldschlager. "Food: The New Wave." *Newsweek*, August 11, 1975.

Franey, Pierre. "Innocence Abroad: Memories of '39 Fair." *The New York Times*, October 18, 1989.

McKenna, Kristine. "Eno: Voyages in Time & Perception." *Musician*, October 1982.

Miller, Bryan. "His Stock in Trade Is Cooks and Clout." *The New York Times*, February 25, 1987.

———. "Marc Sarrazin, 69, Meat Seller and Chefs' Mentor." *The New York Times*, November 2, 1995.

"Our Story." Culinary Institute of America website. Accessed November 2014.

Portale, Alfred, *Alfred Portale's Gotham Bar and Grill Cookbook*. Doubleday, 1997.

Saulnier, Louis. *Le Répertoire de La Cuisine*. Barron's Educational Series, 1976.

Schiff, Judith. "Angell of the CIA." *Yale Alumni Magazine*, January/February 2008.

Shenk, David. *The Genius in All of Us: New Insights into Genetics, Talent, and IQ*. Doubleday, 2010.

Sheraton, Mimi. "Leading School for Chefs Ousts Its Second Chief in Two Unsettled Years." *The New York Times*, November 9, 1979.

Wells, Patricia. "A First Course for Chefs." *The New York Times*, March 5, 1978.

Zuber, Amy. "Henri Soulé." *Nation's Restaurant News*, February 1996.

5. THE STANFORD COURT GANG

Anderson, Brett. "Paul Prudhomme: An Introduction to an American Culinary Legend." *The Times-Picayune*, June 12, 2005.

———. "Paul Prudhomme: An Oral History Chronicles His Role in Revolutionizing New Orleans Cuisine." *The Times-Picayune*, June 12, 2005.

Brown, Ellen. *Cooking with the New American Chefs*. Harper & Row, 1985.

Burros, Marian. "New Orleans Chef Takes On New York." *The New York Times*, July 24, 1985.

Grimes, William. "Paul Prudhomme, Chef Who Put Cajun Cooking on National Stage, Dies at 75." *The New York Times*, October 8, 2015.

"Honor Roll of American Chefs." *Food & Wine*, May 1983.

Thorn, Bret. "Paul Prudhomme: A Remembrance." *Nation's Restaurant News*, October 8, 2015.

6. CALIFORNIA DREAMING?

Anderson, Susan Heller, and Maurice Carroll. "New York Day by Day." *The New York Times*, December 29, 1983.

Brown, Ellen. *Cooking with the New American Chefs*. Harper & Row, 1985.

Burros, Marian. "Food Accent for the 80's Is Decidedly American." *The New York Times*, January 11, 1984.

———. "New Orleans Chef Takes On New York." *The New York Times*, July 24, 1985.

———. "Restaurants." *The New York Times*, March 16, 1984.

Chasanow-Richman, Phyllis. "*Cook's Magazine* Picks Its Who's Who." *The Washington Post*, November 4, 1984.

Engel, Margaret. "Cook's Magazine Makes Annual Awards." *The Washington Post*. October 27, 1985.

Fearing, Dean. *The Mansion on Turtle Creek Cookbook*. Grove Press, 1987.

Greene, Gael. "A Celebration of Amateurs." *New York*, July 18, 1977.

———. "Nouvelle Notions and Naïveté: Quilted Giraffe." *New York*, February 25, 1980.

———. "What's Hot, What's Not: The Young and the Listless." *New York*, September 24, 1984.

Hall, Trish. "Family Tree Nurtures a New Generation of Chefs." *The New York Times*, April 14, 1993.

"Letters Home." *Los Angeles Times*, December 29, 1985.

Meehan, Peter. "Life, and How It Happens to a Cook." *Lucky Peach*, Issue 9.

Miller, Bryan. "Restaurants." *The New York Times*, June 7, 1985.

———. "Restaurants." *The New York Times*, October 4, 1985.

———. "Restaurants." *The New York Times*, November 1, 1985.

———. "Restaurants." *The New York Times*, January 6, 1989.

Miller, Mark. *Coyote Cafe*. Ten Speed Press, 1989.

———. *Red Sage: Contemporary American Cuisine*. Ten Speed Press, 1999.

Portale, Alfred. *Gotham Bar and Grill Cookbook*. Doubleday, 1997.

Pyles, Stephan, with John Harrisson. *The New Texas Cuisine*. Doubleday, 1993.

Reichl, Ruth. "Goodbye to the Era of the Celebrity Chefs." *Los Angeles Times*, July 16, 1989.

Sharpe, Patricia. "And They Said, 'Let There Be Cilantro.'" *Texas Monthly*, August 2014.

Sheraton, Mimi. "Eat American!" *Time*, August 26, 1985.

7. SHE'S NOT THERE

Rodgers, Judy. *The Zuni Cafe Cookbook: A Compendium of Recipes & Cooking Lessons from San Francisco's Beloved Restaurant*. W. W. Norton & Company, 2002.

Tower, Jeremiah. *California Dish: What I Saw (and Cooked) at the American Culinary Revolution*. Free Press, 2003.

———. *Jeremiah Tower's New American Classics*. Harper & Row, 1986.

8. A ROOM OF THEIR OWN

Asimov, Eric. "25 and Under." *The New York Times*, December 18, 1992.

Burros, Marian. "Restaurants." *The New York Times*, November 23, 1990.

Fabricant, Florence. "Food Notes." *The New York Times*, December 9, 1992.

———. "Off the Menu." *The New York Times*, August 31, 1994.

———. "So Many Chocolates, So Little Time." *The New York Times*, August 26, 1992.

Freiman, Jane. "Dining Out." *Newsday*, April 29, 1992.

———. "Dining Out." *Newsday*, June 10, 1992.

———. "Dining Out." *Newsday*, July 2, 1993.

"Good Eating: Twentysomething: Flatiron Environs." *The New York Times*, February 27, 1994.

Greene, Gael. "Ay, There's the Club." *New York*, October 29, 1990.

———. "The Tao of Pu Pu." *New York*, April 26, 1993.

MacVean, Mary. "The CC Club: Chefs Set Up Their Own New York Hang Out." *Variety*, April 12, 1991.

Miller, Bryan. "Diner's Journal." *The New York Times*, October 5, 1990.

———. "Eating Outdoors." *The New York Times*. July 20, 1990.

Okun, Stacey. "Restaurants Offer New Appetizers: Hot Lines and Newsletters." *The New York Times*, May 29, 1991.

Salkin, Allen. *From Scratch: Inside the Food Network*. G. P. Putnam's Sons, 2013.

"Sunday Dinner; Bistro Fare, the Cuisiniers Club, Jazz and Italian Classics." *The New York Times*, February 17, 1991.

"The Youth of All of Us, with Sean Sant Amour at Blue Ribbon." http://tedwardwines.com/news/2015/05/21/the-youth-of-all-of-us-with-sean-sant-amour-at-blue-ribbon.

INDEX

Restaurant L'Oasis, 57–58
Reuge, Maria, 106
Revsin, Leslie, 221, 231, 233, 269
Reynolds, Burt, 120
Richard, Michel, 205
Riedi, Gus, 103
Riou, Hervé, 407
Risley, Mary, 289
Ritz-Carlton, 250
River Café, The, 158, 179–81,
    187–202, 204–9, 212, 255,
    267, 273, 291, 298, 342, 344,
    390, 400
Robert, Jacky, 352
Roberts, Michael, 98, 113, 270
Robins, David, 373
Rodgers, Judy, 30, 328, 354, 355,
    359
Romano, Michael, 234n, 308,
    402
Romanoff's, 363
Roots of American Food, 383
Rose, Charlie, 385
Rose et LeFavour, 33
Rosellini, Robert, 333
Rosenthal, Jacob, 131
Rosenzweig, Anne, 106, 402
Rossman, Arnold, 159, 166, 240–41
Rostang, Michel, 315
Roth, Frances, 217, 218, 223
Rothstein, Daniel, 333–37
Rourke, Mary, 88
Rozmarja, Anna, 132
Rubicon, 414
Rubin, Hank, 31
Rush, Karen, 339
Ryan, Tim, 26, 255, 269

Sailhac, Alain, 10–11, 165, 228,
    230, 236, 240–43, 245, 291, 344
Salk, Donald, 113, 115, 117
San Francisco earthquake (1989),
    376–77
Santa Fe Bar and Grill, 99, 267,
    274, 352–53, 363, 365–66, 371
Sant Amour, Sean, 410–11
Santo, Joseph, 328
Saralegui, Fernando, 407
Sarrazin, Marc, 194, 233, 245–47,
    255, 346
Saulnier, Louis, 238
Savenor, Jack, 139
Savio, Mario, 14, 38
Savoy, 135
Savoy, Guy, 315, 362
Sawyer, Diane, 306
Scandia, 57, 62
Scharff, Werner, 74
Scheer, Bob, 36
Schenk, John, 248
Schmidt, Jimmy, 14, 259–61, 266,
    267–68, 271–72, 273, 275,
    276, 278–79, 280, 281, 320–21
Schmitt, Sally and Don, 361–62
Schneller, Robert, 32
Schrafft's, 178
Schwartz, Arthur, 311
Schwartz, Leonard, 75
Schwertner, Amaryll, 359
Scott, Ridley, 7
Sedlar, John, 72, 76, 87, 323
Senderens, Alain, 245n
72 Market Street, 75
Shapiro, Bobby, 151
Shawn, William, 130